Alfred Orage and the Leeds Arts Club

1893–1923

Alfred Orage and the Leeds Arts Club 1893 -1923

Tom Steele

The **Orage** Press
2009

Originally published in hardback in 1990 by Scolar Press.
Published in paperback in 2009 by the Orage Press.

The Orage Press
16A Heaton Road
Mitcham
Surrey
CR4 2BU
England.

ISBN: 978-09544523-8-4

Printed by Lightningsource

For Lynne and Joe and to the dear memory of Mickey (1984–1988)

Contents

Acknowledgements ix
Introduction: A Provincial Avant-Garde 1

PART ONE Orage Before the *New Age*

1. 1893–1900: Socialism and Mysticism 25
2. Holbrook Jackson and Nietzsche: Egoistic Relations 45

PART TWO 1903–1911: Reducing Leeds to Nietzscheism

3. Foundations 1903–1904; the Superman, the Civic and the Guilds 65
4. 1905: What is the Use of an Arts Club? 88
5. The Discovery of the Future 106
6. 1906: The Celtic Revival and 'National' Socialism 117
7. 1907–1909: Expansion, Diversity and Division 136
8. Waiting for a Dancing Star 157

PART THREE 1912–1923: Metropolitan Intellectuals and Modernity

9. Sadler, Rutter and Post-Impressionism 177
10. Interventionist Patronage: the Sadlers, Kandinsky and Kramer 196
11. The Sorcerer's Apprentice 218
12. Epilogue: Experimental Drama 240
13. Conclusion: From Leeds Permanent to National Provincial 256

Appendix: A. R. Orage – 'What Is the Future of Socialism?' 269
Bibliography 271
Index 281

Acknowledgements

Books are collective productions and though I take responsibility for the finished work I should like to thank my very many friends and colleagues without whose research, conversation, criticism and active support this book would not have been written.

Griselda Pollock supervised the final drafts and did what she could to sharpen up its theoretical perspectives; Denis Warwick supervised and gave critical help on the earlier drafts. John Tagg urged me to get on with it and provided more than occasional inspiration and Janet Douglas introduced me to the history of Leeds. Much valuable research was done by Tim White and Malcolm Giles. Those who have listened patiently over the last five years and made valuable comments include Harold Best, Ray Brown, John Charlton, Delia Davin, David Goodway, Trevor Griffiths, Christine Hankinson, Julian Harber, Philip Hoy, Jill Liddington, Jim McGuigan, Colin Nicholson, Simon Poe, John Quail, Jerry Ravetz, Jonathan Ree, Chris Shaw, John Schwartzmantel, Kevin Stenson, Gabrielle Syme, Dick Taylor and Tom Woodhouse.

I am extremely grateful to the British Academy for their invaluable assistance to consult the Orage Collection in the Harry Ransome Center for Humanities Research, the University of Texas; thanks also to Cathy Henderson and the staff of that institution for making it so readily available. Particular thanks to Christopher Sheppard and Oliver Pickering of the Brotherton Collection, Mrs Heap of Leeds City Reference Library, Mr Harrison of the West Yorkshire Archives, the Brotherton Library, Adam White and Corrinne Miller of Leeds City Art Gallery, Mrs Forster of the Thoresby Society, Mike McGrath of the British Library, Bradford, Keighley and Sheffield Public Libraries, Wakefield Public Records Office.

Richard Orage generously allowed me the run of his collection of his father's letters and notebooks and I am very grateful to him for permission to quote from them. I am indebted to Geoffrey Woledge, who, until this year the last remaining member of the Club told me of its twilight days, Denis Mason Jones for his father's scrapbook and permission to publish his father's sketches and photographs, Sheila Colville for her Eyebrow Club scrapbook, Agnes Patrick for the wonderful find of Millie Price's autobiography, and Catherine Thackeray for Marjorie Ingle's, Bill Oliver, Yvonne Fearnley, Harrogate and Leeds Lodges of the Theosophical Society.

I should like to thank Sara and John Roberts for permission to quote from Jacob Kramer's letters and to reproduce his photograph, David Thistlewood, to quote from his valuable *Herbert Read, From Formlessness to Form*, John Carswell to quote from *Lives and Letters*, Leeds City Art Gallery for the photograph of Epstein's bust of Kramer, The University of Leeds for Mark Gertler's portrait of Sir Michael Sadler, the Courtauld Institute for Bruce Turner's portrait of Tom Heron and West Yorkshire Archives for the portrait of Isabella Ford.

INTRODUCTION

A Provincial Avant-Garde

Since Alfred Orage's interest in what he might become always took precedence over what he was, he systematically destroyed the evidence of his passing. Like its founder the Leeds Arts Club after a brilliant career vanished, a stone in the pond of collective memory leaving only its ripples to remind one it was there. In 1903 Orage, then a primary school teacher, his friend Holbrook Jackson, a lace merchant and free-lance journalist, and a few theosophists, socialists and businessmen founded an arts club in Leeds with the object of 'reducing Leeds to Nietzscheism'. It became one of the most interesting sites of radical thought and experimental art outside of London. It popularized the introduction of Nietzschean thought, cradled the early formation of Guild Socialism, exhibited impressionist and post-impressionist painting, translated and debated Kandinsky's aesthetic theory and fostered the nascent talents of young artists and writers like Jacob Kramer and Herbert Read. Its contributors included G. K. Chesterton, Hilaire Belloc, George Bernard Shaw, W. B. Yeats, Florence Farr and other pioneers of the modern theatre movement like Ashley Dukes and William Poel. In 1906 it hosted W. B. Yeats, J. M. Synge and the newly formed Abbey Theatre company, who performed six one-act plays in the space of two evenings and in 1914 a 'cubist and futurist' exhibition organized and presented by Percy Wyndham Lewis. The socialist 'New Life' philosopher, Edward Carpenter, was a regular contributor and founding influence.

Nine years later, after Orage and Jackson had left Leeds to edit the *New Age* in London, Herbert Read, then an undergraduate at Leeds University, joined the Club, founded he recalled, by

> . . . a man who was at this time, the most lively mind in England – A. R. Orage, a man 'interested in everything except vulgarity', as Bernard Shaw said of him. He had left Leeds three or four years before I arrived, and was then in London editing the *New Age*, a weekly periodical to which all the avant-garde in art and literature was then contributing. Not only newcomers like T. E. Hulme and Ezra Pound but also established writers like Arnold Bennett and G. K. Chesterton, and even on occasions, Bernard Shaw.[1]

The Club he had discovered was then nurturing what a recent biographer of Read, David Thistlewood, described as 'a surprisingly advanced aesthetic: abstract drawing and painting were accepted practices and there were links with Wassily Kandinsky and the *Blaue Reiter* group in Munich'.[2] Furthermore, Thistlewood suggested that 'Leeds, as a centre of the English avant-garde of art was second merely to London'.[3]

This 'remarkable institution', as Read called it, was the culmination of a number of attempts by Orage and his friends to make a cultural intervention into what they saw as the sordidly materialist life of the great manufacturing town. Orage had been appointed by the Leeds School Board in 1893 on leaving Culham College, had joined the newly founded ILP in the following year and, soon lionized, began writing a literary causerie for its newspaper the *Labour Leader*. But in 1896 already impatient with the ILP's worthy but plodding collectivism, he joined the Theosophical Society, inspired by Annie Besant's transcendentalism and Edward Carpenter's mysticism. Here he lectured provocatively on philosophical, psychological and political matters to the great concern of orthodox theosophists who thought him rather dangerous.

In 1900 he met Holbrook Jackson, then a Fabian, who introduced him to a rare translation of *Thus Spake Zarathustra*, which transformed his intellectual universe and, bonded by this experience, they decided to find a way of putting Nietzsche's ideas into practice. The Arts Club was the outcome of this. While the central aim of introducing the concept of the superman, or 'Beyondman' as they called it, was promoted by them and a theosophical architect called Albert Waddington, a variety of related cultural and political concerns was left to extremely able local and, frequently, national figures like Shaw and Chesterton. Other members like Tom Heron, the father of Patrick Heron the painter, made practical experiments in enlightened cooperative enterprises and he later set up Cresta Silks along Guild Socialist principles. Under Orage's guidance the rationale of the Club's activities was a kind of existentialist experimenting where nothing was outlawed on moral grounds and the only permitted guide to action was the aesthetic. Jackson, it has to be said, tempered this with a thoughtful political philosophy of 'citizenship' and acted as a counterbalance to Orage's more fanciful flights. Nevertheless, for two decades the Club was Leeds's key cultural meeting place, the encampment of the aesthetic opposition, the Nietzschean underground.

Orage is an enigmatic figure, whose persistence in burning his boats down to the last laundry list has left little in the way of documentary record. Memoir and anecdote have more than filled the vacuum with a likeable, almost saintly, figure. This is the case with the architect and social theorist Arthur Penty, whose *The Restoration of the Gild System* (1906) was the founding text of what came to be called Guild Socialism (though it was never a title that Penty used, preferring to call himself a National Guildsman). Orage had a great effect on him as he noted in the *New English Weekly*'s 'A. R. Orage Memorial Number':

> I first met Mr. Orage in the autumn of the year 1900 at Chapel Allerton. In those days he was an elementary school teacher, and ex-Socialist who had been one of the original members of the Leeds ILP and a Theosophist. He talked of Nietzsche, Heine, Ibsen and Bernard Shaw (who was then unknown outside a very limited circle) and as a result of our many long talks I began to feel that I knew where I was in the world.[4]

G. K. Chesterton in the same edition added a kind of superman dimension: 'everyone who knows anything knows that Orage was the most vigorous and lucid exponent of economic philosophy in our time'.[5] He also suggested his provenance:

> Like W. B. Yeats to whom he bore some resemblance, he originally stemmed out of the more intelligent and independent growths of a sort of theosophical thought: and though their gods were not my gods, they had saved both men from the godforsaken cheap materialism of most revolutionists in their day. It was this that helped him to substitute Guild Socialism for State Socialism; and even in this gave him sympathies that could stretch from Mr Penty's religion of craftsmanship to Mr Cole's bureaucracy of trades unions.[6]

On the occasion of his first talk to the Arts Club in 1904 Chesterton vigorously attacked the superman ideology then being advocated by Orage and on a later visit with equal relish savaged 'the Puritan' Shaw, but he too saw Orage as in some way its embodiment. He was enthusiastically received by the club members on both occasions and one of them, the Rev. John O'Connor, who became the model for 'Father Brown', in 1922 received him into the Roman Catholic church.

These, and many other, descriptions of Orage have constructed an exotic figure for cultural history and if the process of revealing the provincial schoolteacher in the metropolitan editor is to leave more than just a spectral shape, caution has to be exercized. Orage's own account of his development is both illuminating and unsatisfying, for while he wryly describes the eclecticism of the socialist movement of the 1890s, he somehow forgets to include Nietzsche.

> (Socialism was) a cult, with affiliations now quite disowned – with theosophy, arts and crafts, vegetarianism, the 'simple life', and almost, one might say, with the musical glasses. Morris had shed a medieval glamour over it with his stained glass *News From Nowhere*. Edward Carpenter had put it into sandals, Cunninghame Graham had mounted it upon an Arab steed to which he was always saying a romantic farewell. Keir Hardie had clothed it in a cloth cap and red tie. And Bernard Shaw, on behalf of the Fabian Society, had hung it with innumerable jingling epigrammatic bells – and cap. My brand

> of socialism was, therefore, a blend or, let us say, an anthology of all these, to which from my personal predilections and experience I added a good practical knowledge of the working classes, a professional interest in economics which led me to master Marx's *Das Kapital* and an idealism fed at the source – namely Plato.[7]

He was indeed an 'anthologist' of remarkable if mystifying proportions and Nietzsche, as we have seen, should have been included about the autumn of 1900. It is suggested that Orage made both an occultist and culturist reading of him. He linked Nietzsche's ideas of *ubermensch* to both Eastern spiritual transcendence and reincarnation on the one hand, and on the other to Carlyle's charismatic hero. Despite an enthusiastic article by Havelock Ellis and Hubert Bland's encouragement to the Fabian Society to read him in the mid–1890s, Orage had taken little notice of Nietzsche's work until he met Holbrook Jackson, who had himself first come across Nietzsche in 'a little egoistic journal' called *The Eagle and the Serpent*. So Orage in a sense anthologized himself in what Herbert Read thought were some of the finest paragraphs in journalism and was anthologized by others, who remembered the marvellous epigrams but searched in vain for the definitive *oeuvre* which he never wrote.

According to his friend George Bernard Shaw Holbrook Jackson was the more solid of the pair.[8] Thus when they founded the Arts Club in 1903, Jackson organized while Orage provided the inspiration. They recruited their acquaintances and comrades as founding members. Orage drew in some of his fellow theosophists and ILP comrades like the suffragist Isabella Ford. Jackson on the other hand got some of his more 'artistically minded' business acquaintances to join and, moreover, back the venture with hard cash. Amongst the occupations of the members teachers were probably the largest group including a large proportion of women, but there were also journalists, architects, artists, photographers, typesetters, printers, clergymen and a few university lecturers. To an extent this recruitment can be seen to reveal the social base for the modernist politics and cultural practices of the following years. It was a conjunction of Tory businessmen with Socialist professional workers, the line of unity surfacing often as an intense antipathy to nineteenth-century Liberalism, with what they believed was its moral hypocrisy, its smug belief in perpetual progress but mostly its philistinism. Initially this membership was only forty-five but by the end of the second year it had doubled and in 1907 Jackson wrote to Orage:

> We shall never forget how our little band of members worked, and how the Club flourished; nor how respectable Leeds at first held back fearing our revolutionary ideas, and then gradually came forward

> reassured by the excellence of our exhibitions; and how in turn many of these people joined the Club and actually became revolutionaries themselves.[9]

Membership was open to men and women upon election, at 10s 6d (52.5p.) per annum (almost exactly 30 per cent of Orage's weekly wage as a teacher). Initially the club rooms were rented in the centre of town on the first floor of the headquarters of Leeds Permanent Building Society, who occupied the ground floor (another unimpeachable example of base and superstructure?) The building stood on the corner of Park Lane and Calverley Street, immediately in front of the library and next to the town hall. It was also close to the art gallery and the bookshop of W. H. Bean, a theosophist and leading freemason friend of Orage's and one of the Club's founders. But in 1908 the Club moved up hill to much larger premises in 8 Blenheim Crescent, about two hundred yards from the university, reflecting its greater popularity and perhaps a more vigorous involvement in it by the new Leeds University staff.

It operated on termly basis offering regular Saturday afternoon lectures, Friday night discussion groups, occasional weekly meetings with speakers like G. B. Shaw, G. K. Chesterton, W. B. Yeats, Cobden-Sanderson, Hilaire Belloc, Edward Carpenter and Percy Wyndham-Lewis; exhibitions of architecture, painting, sculpture, craft work and photography, musical recitals and demonstrations. In addition there were literary, sketching and musical groups, a book club and library. Club premises were shared with the Theosophical Society and the Fabian Society, membership of all three societies being common. Four years after its formation it spawned a Playgoers Society for the promotion of drama and opera in response to public demand. This rapidly outstripped the parent body in membership and towards the end engulfed it. While the Arts Club never had more than a hundred members, the Playgoers Society at its height had nearly a thousand.

In classical style, it is tempting to divide the Club's history into gold, silver and bronze ages but this would only intensify the mythology. More likely, two main periods can be discerned (though the period from about 1920–1923 when it was merged with the Playgoers Society is legitimately a third). In its original phase, 1903–1911, the Club's intellectual programme centred on discussing and 'materializing' ideas taken from Nietzsche's later works, centring on *Zarathustra*. This 'Dionysian' project has to be seen as primarily an attempt to modernize the local culture with Europeanism. This included Ibsen and Strindberg's drama, the music of Wagner and Hugo Wolf, the stories of Maeterlinck and Turgenev and the poetry of Heinrich Heine. European languages and Esperanto were similarly encouraged. French Impressionist art was introduced by the Bradford-born painter and subsequently Principal of the Royal College of Art, William Rothenstein, his brother Charles frequently lending paintings from his large collection for exhibition. The sculptor Rodin was widely admired and his work exhibited. To this was added what they saw as 'advanced' English taste such as English Impressionism of which another local patron, the worsted coating manufacturer, Sam Wilson, possessed a remarkably comprehensive collection (Wilson Steer, Frank Brangwyn and Whistler for example) which was also occasionally loaned to the Club.

Orage and Jackson assiduously nursed their creation into independence for nearly three exhausting years, when the Club sometimes met five times in one week, but inevitably, in 1906, first Orage and then Jackson left for Town. Here with H. G. Wells, Eric Gill and William Rothenstein, the Club was used as a model for their next venture, the Fabian Arts Group, the scourge of the Fabian old guard. But they kept a paternal interest in the Club and returned regularly over the next decade. With George Bernard Shaw's help they then bought an ailing Christian Socialist journal, the *New Age*, the following year and under Orage's editorship it became the most influential weekly in London. As a contemporary wrote:

> There are in London two or three men, not known to the general public, whose influence on modern thought is most profound and most disturbing. Of these men A. R. Orage the editor of the *New Age* is quite the most distinguished. What circulation his paper enjoys, I do not know; it cannot be large; probably it is not more than two or three thousand; perhaps it is not even so much as that. But the men and the women who read it are the men and the women who count – people who welcome daring and original thought, who hold important positions in the civic, social political and artistic worlds, and who eagerly disseminate the seeds of thought they pick up from the study of the *New Age*. Tens of thousands of people have been influenced by this paper who have never even heard its name. It does not educate the masses directly: it reaches them through the medium of its few but exceedingly able readers.[10]

In fact at its peak in 1908 the *New Age*'s circulation was over 20,000 and never less than 4,000.

The Club, meanwhile, under the guidance of Albert Waddington lost little of its original energy and was still capable of creating considerable controversy in the pages of the *Yorkshire Post* in 1911 its year of transition. Though in these years Orage's Nietzscheanism was the dynamic ideology, there were a wide range of other influences. We have already noted those of Fabianism, theosophy and the Independent Labour Party. Feminism and suffragism were militantly championed by Isabella Ford and Edward Carpenter, not to mention Mary Gawthorpe and Ethel Annakin.[11] Some of the businessmen were freemasons and others were also members of the Society for Psychical Research. Others, like Waddington, actively promoted the garden city ideal and the arts and crafts movement was perhaps common origin to all.

In the case of another founder member, Rev. A. H. Lee, Anglican chaplain of Emmanuel church, theosophical spiritualism was allied with high church mysticism. He later became a contributor to the *New Age* and in 1918 co-edited the *Oxford Book of Mystical Verse*. The Christian Socialist aspect of Anglo-Catholicism was contributed by the members of the nearby Community of the Resurrection at Mirfield especially by Father Walter Frere, its first superior who lectured several times to the Club on mediaeval music. Significantly, another Community member, the Oxford philosopher J. N. Figgis, was instrumental in shaping the Guild Socialist view of the state and with Orage was a formative political influence on G. D. H. Cole.[12]

In 1911, for reasons that are not entirely clear, there was an abrupt change of leadership in the Club. The new phase was dominated by (later Sir) Michael Sadler, Frank Rutter and subsequently the artist Jacob Kramer. With Nietzsche's star somewhat in decline because of the proximity of war with Germany, Post-Impressionist painting now became the Club's focus. Like Orage and Jackson, though at a more exalted level, Sadler and Rutter had moved to Leeds for professional reasons. Sadler, a leading educationalist, was appointed Vice Chancellor of Leeds University in 1911, while Rutter, a London art critic and founder of the Allied Artists Association was appointed curator of Leeds Art Gallery. Unlike Orage and Jackson they were already well-formed metropolitan intellectuals bringing with them other avant-gardist practices and ideas. Sadler had one of the largest collections of Post-Impressionist paintings in Britain, much of which he had on permanent show in his house in Headingley Lane, Leeds, and was also in close touch with Wassily Kandinsky and the *Blaue Reiter* group. On their own accounts, both Herbert Read and Henry Moore saw Sadler's art collection in Leeds as their first actual contact with modern art.

It was partly because of the hope Sadler's appointment offered that Frank Rutter, who knew most of the leading London painters, took up the post of curator of Leeds Art Gallery. Charles Ginner and Harold Gilman of the Camden Town Group visited him regularly and did a good deal of painting and sketching of Leeds industrial subjects and it has been argued that Ginner's theory of neo-realism, first published in the *New Age* in 1914, originated in the Club's discussions.[13] A number of talented painters such as Jacob Kramer and Bruce Turner, were attracted to the Club and experimented quite boldly with new techniques which made a powerful impact on the young Patrick Heron, who saw Bruce Turner's work as 'utterly avant-garde'.

Swept up in the exuberant atmosphere of experimentation, it was precisely at this time, 1912, that Herbert Read joined at the age of nineteen. Within five years he had become part of Orage's *New Age* circle where he first met T. S. Eliot who regarded him as Britain's finest war poet. His reputation as an art critic steadily advanced and he was instrumental in promoting the acceptance of the sculpture of his fellow Yorkshireman Henry Moore who, while never a member of the Club, shared its discourses. In a curious analogy with the craft-guilds politics he espoused Read played the apprentice to Orage's craft-master. While the Club nursed his early aesthetic development, the *New Age* formed his political and literary ideas. Finally Orage assiduously taught him the secrets of the craft of writing and intended handing over the *New Age* editorship to him. But though he took over Orage's coveted 'Readers and Writers' column Read could not bring himself to occupy the editor's chair and opted for a safe post in the V & A. Between 1914 and 1918 Read was in many respects the 'journeyman' travelling between the Club and the Cafe Royale, where Orage held court, on his leave from the front. His direct connection with the London avant-garde – T. E. Hulme, Wyndham Lewis, Ezra Pound, T. S. Eliot and of course Orage himself – reinforced the Leeds club's involvement in modernist developments. Even as Read moved in these circles, however, the club had hosted an exhibition of 'Cubist and Futurist' paintings organized and presented by Wyndham Lewis in 1914 (a little over a month before he launched the Vorticist manifesto), probably through the mediation of Rutter, Heron or Kramer. Read began regular contributions to the *New Age* under Orage's tutelage and on T. E. Hulme's death in action was asked by Orage to edit and publish his essays, which he eventually did as *Speculations*. The journal was avidly read by Club members and formed the basis of a continuing dialogue with the metropolis.

In its final phase the Club was overwhelmed in true Sophoclean fashion by its own thespian offspring when the stage which it had promoted as a means to cultural renewal became an end in itself. Michael Sadler gave away some of his collection and left to become Master of University College, Oxford; Frank Rutter was sacked by the municipality for buying a modern picture without consultation and Herbert Read joined him in London to edit *Art and Letters*. Henry Moore and Barbara Hepworth left to join William Rothenstein at the Royal College of Art. Jacob Kramer remained but the cultural moment seemed to have evaporated along with the alcohol he now so desperately consumed. In 1922 the year that saw the publication of two seminal achievements of 'English' modernism, *Ulysses* and *The Waste Land*, Orage, who was not in tune with either of them, retired to Gurdjieff's *prieurie* in Fontainebleau. Guild Socialism exploded in bitter antagonism, some joining the newly formed Communist Party and others like Penty drifting off into the preservation of rural England and eventually fascism. The following year the Club held an American auction of its books, gave up the lease to its premises and though a number of other arts formations sprang from its ashes, rapidly became an object of Leed's collective amnesia.

What then did the Arts Club mean? What role, if any, did it play in the national culture? While it is a familiar metropolitan assumption that new ideas and avant-garde practices distil at the centre and then percolate to the 'provinces', this is clearly not the whole story here. Elements of the cultural labours in Leeds bore fruit not only in Yorkshire but later in London, when Orage and Jackson initially founded the Fabian Arts group, modelled on the Leeds club and then based many of the themes and concerns of the *New Age* on debates already initiated in the north. It is only one example that shows not only has metropolitan culture been continually rejuvenated by the energy of regional and colonial immigration, news from nowhere, it may depend on it for its vitality.

But beyond this there is also the suggestion that the national culture is somehow intrinsically provincial, if not parochial, compared with that of continental Europe. Was there not a certain insularity about native intellectuals and artists, a timidity about experiment and commitment to radical thought and practices that made them appear a shade reserved in relation to their contemporaries over the channel, as suggested by Terry Eagleton:

> While the European avant-garde was flourishing in the early decade of the twentieth century, England had E. M. Forster. While Vsevolod Meyerhold and Erwin Piscator were transforming the face of Russian and German theatre, the English drama continued to be dominated by that granddaddy of all naturalists, George Bernard Shaw. Dadaism, futurism, expressionism, surrealism: there are no substantial English equivalents of these cultural trends . . . The oldest capitalist nation in the world, traditionally provincial and deeply empiricist, ruled by a strongly hegemonic bourgeois class, was peculiarly unable to effect the modernist 'break', as opposed to providing such tides with a temporary or borrowed home.[14]

In the 1960s a persuasively argued theory which has come to be known as the 'Anderson-Nairn thesis' suggested that the failure of the British state to modernize itself was dependent on an 'historic compromise' made between the fledgling capitalist middle class and the landowning aristocracy in the English Revolution.[15] As a result of this the British middle class failed to realize a mature political and cultural dominance of its own and was perpetually subordinated to a landed governing class, whom it imitated and indulged. Perry Anderson and Tom Nairn revealed a consequent 'absent centre' of British culture: leaders and innovators who were habitually exiles and emigres from other cultures and a morbid adherence to feudal and undemocratic institutions. Martin Wiener subsequently produced a study of British society since 1850 showing that the entrepreneurial spirit of the early industrial revolution had because of this compromise been supplanted by anti-industrial and 'aristocratic' ideology that militated against economic modernization.[16] An insular imperialism guided by shopkeeper economics, and the rustic vision of the country squire was the dominant tone of these accounts, though Anderson has recently revised the significance of the material determinants of the national culture, the larger perspective remains.[17] Wiener became required reading in Tory policy groups. But persuasive as these accounts are, there seems a wilful almost masochistic denial of domestic potential, as compared with the Titanic ideological struggles of a putatively heroic bourgeois in Europe against the old regime, Britain's middle class barely made the Vauxhall League. Instead of a militant enlightenment philosophy of freedom, equality and fraternity the British had utilitarianism, self-help and the Saxe-Coburgs.

The Anderson-Nairn thesis can be seen as belonging to a significant genealogy of cultural criticism reaching back through George Orwell's 'England their England' to G. K. Chesterton and Hilaire Belloc's *The Servile State* in the twentieth century and ultimately perhaps to Carlyle. Many Victorian commentators, like T. H. S. Escott, took the historic compromise for granted and celebrated it not as a flaw in the national polity but as the sure ground of domestic stability:

> The antagonism between the aristocracy of wealth and birth has long been disappearing. The son of the newly-enriched father is identified in education, social training, habits, prejudices, feelings, with the scions of the houses of Norman descent. At all times there has been a tendency on the part of birth to ally itself with wealth, and it would be found upon examination, that for the greater part of their princely rentals many a noble English stock is indebted to purely commercial sources . . . Our territorial nobles, our squires, our rural landlords great and small have become commercial potentates; *our merchant princes have become country gentlemen*. The possession of the land is the guarantee of respectability, and the love of respectability and land is inveterate in our race. (My emphasis)[18]

While the nobility benefited from the new wealth generated by the mercantile and industrial capital, the Bradford millionaires learned style, manners and the Burkean ideology of landed stability from their social superiors. The two classes it appeared, had begun to fuse. What could be better? Observations like this leant weight to the thesis. In Leeds the well-documented account of the Marshall family's extensive estates and gentry life in Westmoreland and Benjamin Gott's Armley Park estate with its landscapes, vistas and Palladian residence are significant. Gott and Marshall were Leeds's largest manufacturers. In 1912 however, Michael Sadler was not convinced the balance was right. From a railway carriage in Germany he wrote:

> It is interesting to see in this Rhineland, with the succession of big towns coming quickly one after another, the German counterpart of our Lancashire and Yorkshire industrial region. One feels that *this* is much the older civilisation – with a stronger tradition of the amenities & discipline of city life. The country side of things is much less socially attractive than with us. The merchant is a merchant in these great German cities, with a city patriotism. In England he becomes a country gentleman.[19]

Recently historians of urban social history have criticized the Anderson-Nairn thesis. The northern industrial middle-classes, they argue, were neither excessively supine in relation to the nobility nor as philistine as metropolitan commentators averred.[20] Indeed the great northern industrial towns were a testament to a vigorous bourgeois class consciousness. Here a non-conformist and independent manufacturing class took advantage of the Municipal Corporation Acts to effect local government free of aristocratic and metropolitan interference with a large measure of civic pride. Testaments to this new spirit were evident in the massive town halls in gothic and renaissance style that heaved out of the ground all over the north between 1850 and 1870. There were also substantial art markets, art patronage and art collections. Some of the major British paintings of the century were commissioned by industrialists and collections such as Leathhart's were both extensive and tasteful. John Seed has shown the existence of a flourishing art network in Manchester and in the creation of the Royal Manchester Institute a significant relocation of cultural activities into the heart of the city and the industrial middle class. For the Manchester industrialists art was to have a social function of great importance. 'Art in other words, was to become one of the means by which the youth of the town's middle class were educated for the role of cultured gentleman and prepared for the morally and intellectually improving use of their wealth and leisure' which was 'not merely a crude emulation of aristocratic social behaviour and leisure activities'.[21] This is a useful correction to the thesis though it is still doubtful that the concept of 'gentleman' ever escaped its class connection with the aristocratic. Moreover it was an emulation of one kind of upper-class behaviour even if not 'crude'.

In Manchester, Liverpool and Newcastle there can be no doubt that a more confident industrial middle class prepared to spend its surplus capital on art and culture for the education of their sons and the improvement of the citizenry did exist by the mid-century. But one can be less certain that this was equally the case in the relatively less-prosperous Leeds. The manufacturing élite of the early nineteenth century had made great strides in civic consciousness with the founding of the Philosophical and Literary Society and Mechanics Institute. Architecturally, Broderick's Town Hall, Mechanic's Institute and Corn Exchange are the lasting testaments to this moment. However, Leeds is notable for its lack of grand buildings other than these and a kind of architectural incoherence which appears to have left it uncompleted. As Maurice Beresford points out, Colonel Harding's attempt to create City Square as a greeting for passengers from Leeds City Station in 1896 was only half finished and left the south side of the square 'distinctly shabby'.[22]

The Industrial Revolution, R. J. Morris reservedly noted, had provided 'the wealth and contacts that built a cultural life of rich and incoherent profusion' but 'there was always a danger that the citizens would become merely the purchasers of cultural products, most of them from London, and would gain a passive rather than an active and creative culture'.[23] The Liberal dissenting culture of the Leeds élite severely favoured science and technology. By 1870 the membership of the Phil. and Lit. was already in decline and by the 1890s in crisis, the outcome of which was selling its museum to the town and its library to the new University of Leeds. The solution to the decline of Leeds middle-class culture of the nineteenth century was, says Morris, increasingly in the hands of these two institutions. The municipality's contribution had gradually grown through the latter half of the century from the building of the Town Hall in 1858, the Reference and Central Lending Library in 1871–2, the Art Gallery in 1888, the City Square in 1896 and finally the purchase of the Phil. and Lit.'s museum, modest but important steps in making art and culture public. With the integration of the Yorkshire College into the Victoria University in 1887 (along with Owen's College, Manchester and University College, Liverpool) Leeds took another faltering step forward. It shortly proved somewhat embarrassing however as when both Manchester and Liverpool demanded independent university status Leeds was ill-prepared to go it alone, possessing neither the quality of arts and social science faculties necessary nor adequate funding. These were rapidly cobbled together in 1904 but as Maurice Beresford recently remarked it took Michael Sadler to drag out of its Yorkshire parochialism and transform into a university what was basically 'a jacked-up technical college'.[24]

By the late nineteenth century Leeds would not therefore be the most outstanding example of the triumph of bourgeois culture. But it may well exemplify the post–1850 structural conflict between middle-class strata suggested by Simon Gunn, 'with small and big business commonly contesting political space on a variety of important local issues: rates, docks and transport, municipal expenditure, civic improvement'.[25] With the enormous growth of the municipality, finance and commerce in Leeds during this period, the white-collar professional, technocratic and creative, supervisory and educational, emerged as a distinct stratum with its own cultural needs. In the relative vacuum left by the decay of the academicized semi-official institutions sponsored by the old Liberal élite, evident in the demise of the Phil. and Lit. and Mechanics Institute, many small societies rushed in to fill the gap. These reflected more specific cultural interests, like the Leeds Fine Art Club and the bohemian Savage Club, the Dickens Fellowship, The Priestley Club and Thoresby Society. Similarly the sudden blossoming of political societies in the 1880s and 90s, in local branches of the Social Democratic Federation, the Socialist League, the Fabian Society (three branches in Leeds in the early 1890s[26]) and ultimately the Independent Labour Party reflected a heightened political consciousness. The leadership of these groups, like Albert Marles, Tom Maguire, Alf Mattinson, and D. B. Foster, was frequently drawn from white-collar workers and professionals. Mary Gawthorpe, a schoolteacher, attended the Labour Church and the Tolstoyan Brotherhood Church was newly active. Thus a young, articulate and vocal professional class, many new to the city, without ties of loyalty and often politically committed, by the turn of the century had arguably created a cultural underground which interfused art, politics and religion. It was unquestionably this professional group with a sprinkling of older established figures for whom the Arts Club functioned.

When Orage and Jackson founded the Leeds Arts Club in 1903 it was in just such an oppositional vein. Jackson, for example, wrote of the club's 'contempt of pedantic philosophy and academic art' and of 'the necessity of applying ideas to life'. The last thing the club attempted, however, was a celebration of Leeds or West Riding regionalism. Indeed what they summoned up was the America of Walt Whitman, the Celtic fringe of Yeats and Synge and the Europe of Nietzsche, Ibsen and Wagner. As incomers to Leeds bearing the imported ideas and practices into what they perceived as a cultural wasteland, they appear a microcosmic confirmation of the later analyses.

Could this be considered an avant-garde movement? In terms of its style of *épater le bourgeois*, its quixotic intellectualism, existential experimentalism and a commitment to an illuminated elect derived from theosophy, the early Club fostered an attitude of avant-gardism even though its artistic products were quite modest. But subsequently with Sadler's and Heron's patronage and Rutter's organization this was converted into an artistic experimentalism which produced results.

The concept of the avant-garde first gained currency in the Paris of the mid-nineteenth century, embracing the painters of the early Impressionist movement and the *vers libre* poets including Baudelaire, Verlaine and Rimbaud. It was represented as the cutting edge of art and literature and has been applied to modernist metropolitan experimentalist groups ever since. But Tim Clark has argued that the category of the avant-garde is fundamentally illusory, a profoundly ideological concept which constructed a false identity for an only apparently oppositional group within what was actually a unitary artistic world in Paris.[27] The avant-garde, he argued only gestured at opposition and innovation and membership of it was no more than an initiation rite after which its members would return to privileged status. The real history of avant-garde innovation is precisely of those who bypassed, ignored or rejected it. Thus though Millet, Daumier, Courbet and Baudelaire, for example, had truck with the avant-garde it was problematical and their *achieved distance* from it was crucial. Clark concludes that the real avant-garde can only be uncovered by critical interrogation of the concept.

Griselda Pollock and Fred Orton extended Clark's argument into consideration of the American avant-garde of the 1930s and '40s and particularly the reflections of Clement Greenberg on the subject.[28] The avant-garde, they argued 'must also signify . . . a range of social postures and strategies for artists by which they could differentiate themselves from current social and cultural structures while also intervening in them'.[29] This implied only a transitory period of engagement with metropolitan social and economic life. Though he saw it as inevitably tied to the bourgeois, in his luminous phrase, by an 'umbilical cord of gold', Greenberg's specific contribution was to see the avant-garde as functionally located as a special instrument of society for cultural advancement but in a place apart, a disengagement from both hegemonic and oppositional politics.[30] The effect of Greenberg's contribution was to create a space for a reconstructed avant-garde consciousness and a specified form of painting.[31]

Increasingly, then, the concept of the avant-garde has been eased away from a simple identity with the metropolitan art establishment and is argued to be at its most effective when operating at a distance, socially and politically from it. While it has the function of cultural advancement, Thomas Crow has suggested another refinement which sees the avant-garde as involved in the special function of brokerage between high and low culture for an elite self-conscious audience.[32] Here Crow conceptualizes a system where, by means of the avant-garde, the élite demand for novelty is satisfied by importing specific marginal styles to the centre. The passage however evacuates from the marginal style its vitality and creates even more extreme fringe practices, hence 'the cycle of exchange which modernism sets in motion moves only in one direction appropriation of oppositional practices upwards, the return of evacuated cultural goods downward'.[33]

Although the actual circumstances of any cultural grouping will only offer further complexity to any theory of the avant-garde, it is clear that the Leeds Club can be seen to participate in this functional cycle. Its cultural distance from the metropolitan centre was intensified by geographical distance but it maintained a permanent linkage with it at first through the mediation of Shaw and Chesterton and then through Orage's circle and the *New Age*. Orage himself is a good example of a theoretical innovator whose Nietzschean style was swiftly sought by a new cultural élite frustrated by Victorian academicism but unable to mobilize against it effectively. As an unknown provincial with no allegiances (except to a heretical Fabianism of his own devising) he was able to move freely through the caste divisions of the metropolitan élites seeking he said 'the New Samurai'. His catholic editorship of the *New Age* provided the precise vehicle and point of expression for such diverse emergent currents that it was almost impossible to label politically. The Club, in its turn, moved on from the realist aesthetic of Orage's early days towards a total abstractionism which it adapted from Kandinsky, but 'knew' already from an earlier common source in theosophy.[34] From this more extreme aesthetic moment emerged the figure of Herbert Read who, taking time out only to become a war-hero, replicated Orage's cultural trek to London.

The apparent paradox of Read's position may stem from this moment; a soldier/pacifist, conservative/anarchist, classical/romantic, spiritual/-atheist, he was offered the editorial chair of the *New Age* when the modernist moment and the hope of revolution had died. His sustained argument for abstractionism secured a privileged place for the work of his friend Henry Moore who became the most celebrated public artist of the twentieth century. Ironically, abstract sculpture with exquisite attention to truth to media, became the public institutional form par excellence – though perhaps the 'public' is mostly visitors to elite cultural and social institutions. Thus what we see in Leeds is a cycle of the regeneration of an artistic élite and style over a period of twenty years at first in ideas and then in abstract art whose effect was intrinsic to the renewal of the national culture. This, it could be argued, is one function of an avant-garde.

Which returns us to the problem of the modernizing project. What was it exactly that this new grouping was demanding that an older, now listless, bourgeois culture, ironically at the pinnacle of its imperial power, was denying? The re-emergence of a vigorous socialist movement in the northern industrial towns combining not only with 'old dissent' but with utopian spiritualist movements imported from America[35] was eagerly heralded by the emergent professional stratum. A decade or so later D. H. Lawrence, another provincial schoolteacher indebted to Edward Carpenter's ideas, saw his work as preparatory for a new world when the War to End All Wars had swept away the old.[36] But the paradox, which continues to validate Eagleton's view, was that the ground plans suggested for the New Order bore a strong resemblance to a much older one, namely, feudalism. Thus it seemed almost inevitable that youthful guerilla culturists who, from their bases in the little magazines like *Blast*, the *New Age*, and *The Egoist*, attempted to dynamite the establishment with art would find themselves like T. S. Eliot, in his seniority, and D. H. Lawrence, posthumously, its high priesthood. Curiously, some argued, the doors they had attempted to blow apart were not apparently locked. In 1927 one who was never admitted, the perpetual enemy, Percy Wyndham Lewis, celebrated the ironic success of the blasting years:

> *Blast* was as its name implied destructive in intention. What it aimed at destroying in England – the 'academic of the Royal Academy tradition' – is now completely defunct. The freedom of expression, principally in the graphic and plastic arts, desired by it, is now attained and can be indulged in by anybody who has the considerable private means to be an 'artist'. So its object has been achieved. Though it is only ten or twelve years since that mass of propaganda was launched, in turning over the pages of *Blast* today it is hard to realize the bulk of the traditional resistance that its bulk was invented to overpower. How cowed those forces are today, or how transformed![37]

Was it something of Pyrrhic victory then that demolished the old guard of the Academy only to confirm the hegemony of the artist of 'considerable private means'?

In his masterly analysis of 'The Bloomsbury Fraction', Raymond Williams has outlined a method of understanding the function of English avant-garde groupings which goes some distance to illuminate this paradox and offers a comparison to the Leeds Club.[38] Bloomsbury represented a new style characterized by a 'cool frankness' as a dominant intellectual tone, sexual tolerance and an active 'social conscience'. It was the product of an older, metropolitan, professional group already part of the upper class, conscious of its intellectual responsibility, intolerant of ruling class stupidity and concerned for its working-class victims, to whom it related as a *matter of conscience*. It was more than just a group of friends but a true fraction of an upper class which had broken from its dominant values and ideas and yet was still a part of it.

Williams identified four key sociological elements contributing to the specificity of the Bloomsbury group's formation. Its provenance in the professional and highly educated sector of the upper class; the contradiction of this 'intellectual aristocracy' with ruling institutions; the marked contribution of intellectual women excluded from the conventional male formations and the internal needs of the upper class as a whole in a period of socio-cultural crisis.

Whatever the aims and ambitions of the individuals (who refused the name group and never issued a manifesto) Williams sees their collective function as essentially internal to the needs of the ruling class. They were a forerunner of a more general mutation in the professional sector in two key areas. Firstly, the liberalization of personal relationships of which aesthetic enjoyment and intellectual openness were signal elements. Secondly, in modernizing semi-public manners through increasing mobility among other cultures and generating more adequate intellectual systems. They did not so much cause these changes as prominently represent what were anyway not so much basic changes as adaptions to the new social needs. In short their avant-gardism functioned as a new model of style, taste and thought for the dominant order, which was subsequently widely absorbed. But their pivotal social construction was of the 'civilized individual' rather than the collective and so they remained wedded to the classical values of bourgeois enlightenment and liberal thought. Their opposition to social evils was not so much for a whole society as for 'the pluralization of civilized individuals'.

In a shorter comparative analysis Williams saw the Pre-Raphaelite Brotherhood as having a similar function. It formed a break from the commercial bourgeoisie, but essentially as a means for the next necessary stage of that class. Its easy formality and bohemian tolerance were a revolt against the class of their fathers but in the long run its interest and its emphases of style became the popular bourgeois art of the next historical period. Not so William Godwin's circle of the late eighteenth century which was composed of relatively poor working professionals, an emergent small bourgeois intelligentsia with no other means of social or political influence. Unlike Bloomsbury or the Pre-Raphaelite Brotherhood Godwin's circle was not a fraction or break from an upper class but an emergent sector of the then relatively small independent commercial bourgeois.

Williams's sociological analysis of these cultural groups suggests further ways of understanding the Leeds Club and to an extent the *New Age* circle in London. In Leeds the professionals and small businessmen who made up the Arts Club were, like Godwin's circle, not a break from the ruling class, except for Isabella Ford, even the local ruling class, but in the majority, 'poor working professionals'. Significantly the intervening century had seen the severe reduction of the small bourgeois traditional independence, based on their fee- or profit-making ability, and their absorption into wage-earning employment. The growth of the municipality, school boards and monopoly corporations had increasingly mutated the lower professionals into bureaucratic functionaries whose conditions of service resembled those of skilled workers. It was a kind of proletarianization of the lower middle-class and like the working-classes, whom they had to supervise or educate or generally have much closer relations with, these professional groups found it necessary to form trade unions or 'professional associations' to protect their conditions. They were moreover generally in sympathy with the emergent working-class movements though also rather anxious about them.

As with the Bloomsbury Group, though a little before, the Club adopted the intellectual style of disarming frankness, shading however into the impudence of *épater le bourgeois*. As Williams notes this was also common with Shaw and the Fabians. They were not so much sexually tolerant as experimental, particularly outside marriage, in an open, almost detached, way and intellectual women were prominent in organization and discussion.

The most profound difference from Bloomsbury, and by inference Cambridge philosophy, was their acceptance of social organicism, raised by Orage in particular to a mystical level. The 'civilized individual' was if anything their object of scorn; what was wanted was the mystical union of individual and society in a transcendent totality. In this respect they clearly reflected the working-class ideologies of collectivism and cooperative action on the one hand but grafted onto them a kind of romantic humanism more affected by the creative artist. They believed in an ordered corporate hierarchy with a meritocractic élite intuitionally responsive to the mass. Hence the Club's twin concerns for the doctrine of the superman and Guild Socialism. Their relationship to the dominant order was therefore rather ambiguous. Though they were fundamentally against the 'commercial system' or capitalism because of its waste and inhumanity they had no enthusiasm for democratic socialism which they saw as the cult of mediocrity and the graveyard of heroism. In trying to follow a middle way, therefore, this might be characterized as merely petit-bourgeois radicalism, but that rather loses the flavour of it.

It really appears to represent an attempt by professional workers of the newly emergent technological, creative, educational and supervisory stratum to make common cause with the working class but under the terms of their own dominance. The ultimately tragic or perhaps more correctly tragicomic fate of this ideology was its rejection by both the working-class leadership who opted for incorporation into a modified capitalist corporatism under Labour and by the professional classes who opted for Bloomsbury's 'civilized individual' Social Democrat. Ironically, perhaps, its residual influence remains strongest among that intellectual proletariat, the liberal and fine arts staff in higher education.

But this was a new culture of the cities in which the Club exemplified the new site for cultural experimentation and modernization. Here lower-middle class professionals collectively renounced 'materialist' and determinist models inherited from Spencer and Victorian conventions and instead made the free choice of style, ideas and political commitment central to their lives. Their literate and numerate skills and positions of supervisory and educational authority, the new technology of communication and representation gave them access to a hitherto unparalleled range of cultural models. The Club ransacked European and especially German and Scandinavian culture, Eastern mysticism, Celtic myths and American democracy. Even a provincial city such as Leeds could become a recipient of gregariously eclectic global influences, through its imperial trade and commercial links. The Club's 'solution' to modernity, if such there was, was the creation of revolutionary myths. The bourgeois gentleman of the high Victorian era (Nietzsche's 'camel') was to be replaced by the petit-bourgeois superman (through Nietzsche's 'laughing lion'). Ironically it heralded the emergence of the wholly integrated personality at the moment of its fragmentation and the superman, though a genuinely galvanizing myth, was destined to remain an atavistic attachment to a decadent German romanticism and not a model for the future. In its embryonic Guild Socialism the Club also demonstrated an heroic but inappropriate attraction to pre-capitalist craft technologies.

The aim of this study is to demonstrate that something of significance to the national culture was happening in Leeds during these years and it is not out of the question to talk about a provincial avant-garde. From the Nietzschean interventions of Orage and the founders of the Club to the promotion of abstract expressionism by the Sadlers, Rutter and Read, new theories and practices were produced rather than simply consumed. While the Club's first phase could be seen as transitional from late Victorian naturalist and symbolist forms, the second phases's development of abstract aesthetics prepared a larger public for 'modern art'.

But what is highlighted in this study is the conservative and aristocratic stance inherent in this radical impulse, even when it is called socialism. It helps to explain not so much the emergence of fascism but, paradoxically, its rejection by the intellectual and aestheticizing élite who opted instead for something closer to the neo-feudalistic corporatism of T. S. Eliot's thirties Christian clerisy. This corporatism owed much to Christian Socialism and the debates of the Guild Socialists in the pages of the *New Age* and may say something about why democracy in Britain ossified under a medieval constitution and successfully resisted the modernization of European or American republican states.[39] In a more positive vein though it intends to reveal the roots of English modernism, not as 'mere provincialism', though some of those limitations are clearly visible, but in the great potential strengths of a regional cultural group.

A mere shadow of itself, the Leeds Arts Club was laid to rest in 1923.[40] In its twenty years of life it had been an oasis for many young people who were going to change the world. One of these was Mary Gawthorpe, an early member of the Club, school-teacher and militant suffragette, who became the national secretary of the Woman's Social and Political Union and was also a founder editor of the feminist journal *The Freewoman* which under Harriet Shaw Weaver became *The Egoist* and published some of the best writing of the new age. She wrote:

> It was stimulating and refreshing to be a member of the Leeds Arts Club circa 1904 . . . Here I laid aside the active role of labour worker, giving out all I could, mainly speech to fructify a cause. I was glad to receive, cooperating when possible, but receiving mostly. It was a draught of remembrance to carry carefully in days to come when it seemed that in its own sphere the Leeds Arts Club could not have been bettered. Those were living cultural amenities for first-hand enjoyment as opposed to the second-hand approach of scholarly inheritors and custodians. I have sometimes pondered the thought that the Club, founded by Orage and Jackson, had the germ of a new future, not necessarily to be matured in London, but capable of the completest enrichment of a community right on the spot.[41]

Notes

1. Quoted in *A Tribute to Herbert Read*, Bradford Art Galleries and Museums, 1975, p. 7.
2. David Thistlewood, *Herbert Read, Formlessness and Form, An Introduction to his Aesthetics*, Routledge, Kegan Paul, London, 1984, pp. 24–25.

3. Ibid.
4. *New English Weekly*, vol. VI, no. 5, 15 November 1934, p. 113.
5. Ibid., p. 98.
6. Ibid.
7. Quoted in Philip Mairet, *A. R. Orage a Memoir*, Dent, London, 1936, p. 40.
8. *New English Weekly*, p. 99.
9. 'An Open Letter to A. R. Orage' in Holbrook Jackson, *George Bernard Shaw*, Grant Richards, London, 1907, p. 13.
10. Gerald Cumberland, *Set Down in Malice*, Grant Richards, London, 1918, p. 130.
11. Who appears to have met her future husband Philip Snowden at a Fabian meeting in the Club rooms.
12. Margaret Cole, *The Life of G. D. H. Cole*, Macmillan, London, 1971, pp. 50–58.
13. Thistlewood, p. 27.
14. Terry Eagleton, 'Recent Poetry reviewed by Terry Eagleton', *Stand*, vol. 22, no. 2, p. 73.
15. Perry Anderson, 'Origins of the Present Crisis in *New Left Review*, 23, 1964 and 'Components of the National Culture', *New Left Review*, 50; Tom Nairn, 'The British Political Elite', *New Left Review*, 23, 1964, 'The English Literary Intelligentsia' in *Bananas*, Emma Tennant, (ed.) Blond and Briggs, London, 1977 and *The Break-up of Britain*, Verso, 1977; Terry Eagleton, *Exiles and Emigres*, Chatto and Windus, London, 1970.
16. Martin Wiener, *English Culture and the Decline of the Industrial Spirit 1850–1980*, Cambridge University Press, 1981.
17. Perry Anderson, 'The Figures of Descent', *New Left Review*, no. 161, January/February 1987, pp. 20–77.
18. T. H. S. Escott, *England: Her People, Polity and Pursuits*, Oxford University Press, London, 1885, pp. 22–25, reprinted in J. M. Golby (ed.) *Culture and Society in Britain 1850–1890*, Oxford, 1986, p. 27.
19. Michael Sadleir, *Michael Ernest Sadler*, Constable, London, 1949, p. 235.
20. Janet Wolff and John Seed (eds) *The Culture of Capital: art power and the nineteenth-century middle class*, Manchester University Press, Manchester, 1988.
21. John Seed, 'Commerce and the liberal arts', in Seed and Wolff, *The Culture of Capital*, Manchester University Press, pp. 67–8.
22. Maurice Beresford, 'The Face of Leeds 1780–1914' in D. Fraser (ed.) *A History of Modern Leeds*, Manchester University Press, Manchester, 1980, p. 110.
23. R. J. Morris, 'Middle-class culture' in Fraser, *Modern Leeds*, Manchester University Press, p. 218.
24. In a lecture on Michael Sadler at Leeds University, 28 April 1989.
25. Simon Gunn, 'The Failure of the Victorian middle class: a critique', Wolff and Seed, *Culture of Capital*, p. 31. Despite his critique of Wiener, Gunn is prepared to concede it might be possible 'to speak of a decline of entrepreneurial dynamism before 1914' (p. 30).
26. See the Fabian Archives, F85/1, Nuffield College, University of Oxford.
27. Tim Clark's seminal essay 'On the Social History of Art' appears in Francis Frascina and Charles Harrison (eds) *Modern Art and Modernism: A Critical Anthology*, Harper and Row, London, 1982.

2 Fred Orton and Griselda Pollock, '*Avant-Gardes* and Partisans Reviewed', *Art History*, vol. 4, no. 3, September 1981, pp. 305–327.
29. Ibid., p. 306.
30. Quoted ibid., p. 318.
31. Significantly, abstract art, echoing Sadler's emphases two decades earlier and Patrick Heron in the 1950s, though not for the same reasons. Greenberg saw abstract art as truest to the materials of painting, whereas the Arts Club wanted to achieve musical form and a symbolic code. Greenberg however parallels Sadleir's critique of cubism as never having achieved abstraction noting that abstract art had now emigrated to London.
32. Thomas Crow, 'Modernism and Mass Culture in the Visual Arts' in Francis Frascina (ed.) *Pollock and After*, Harper and Row, London, 1985.
33. Ibid., p. 258.
34. A Finnish Kandinsky scholar writes: 'One of the most important of Kandinsky's theosophical sources is Besant and Leadbeater's book *Thought Forms* which appeared in a German translation in 1908. A copy of this translation, *Gedankenformen*, is in Kandinsky's library in Neuilly-sur-Seine, and in the early 'twenties Kandinsky still referred to it', Sixten Ringbom, *The Sounding Cosmos, A Study in the Spritualism of Kandinsky and the Genesis of Abstract Painting*, Abo Akademi, Finland, 1970, p. 60.
35. See Logie Barrow, *Independent Spirits, Spiritualism and English Plebeians 1850–1910*, Routledge, Kegan Paul, London, 1986.
36. See Edward Delavenay, *D. H. Lawrence and Edward Carpenter: A Study in Edwardian Transition*, Heinemann, London, 1969.
37. Percy Wyndham Lewis, 'The Revolutionary Simpleton' in *The Enemy*, vol. 1, January 1927, pp. 61–62.
38. Raymond Williams, 'The Bloomsbury Fraction', in *Problems in Materialism and Culture*, Verso, London, 1980, pp. 148–169.
39. Orage's political correspondent on the *New Age*, Ramiro de Maeztu, however, went on to influence Franco's political philosophy and subsequently Peronism.
40. Interview with Geoffrey Woledge, ex-librarian of the LSE and last remaining member of the Club, January 1984, He died in December 1988.
41. Mary Gawthorpe, *Up Hill to Holloway*, Penobscot, Maine, 1947, p. 197.

PART ONE
Orage Before the *New Age*

CHAPTER ONE

1893–1900: Socialism and Mysticism

Alfred Orage was twenty when he returned to Yorkshire, the county of his birth, in the autumn of 1893. It was the first time since earliest childhood, when on the death of his father his near-penniless mother had returned with him and his sister to the family village of Fenstanton in Huntingdonshire. He had come to Leeds to take up the profession at which his father had so notably failed, schoolteaching. Orage was born in the village of Dacre about fifteen miles north of Leeds on the southern escarpment of Nidderdale. A hundred years later, the birth would have been in the shadow of the dishes of the USAF Menwith Hill listening station, where the etheric communications of all Europe could be overheard. Less than fifty years later Henry Moore would have passed through it on the way to sketch the weird wind-blown rock formations at Brimham just to the north.

Orage's father William died, having drunk his patrimony, when his son was little more than a year old, leaving his wife Sarah Anne to bring the children up as best she could.[1] Back in Fenstanton, Orage was sent to the local school where he excelled in all his subjects and at the non-conformist sunday school he impressed his teacher, Howard Coote the local squire's son, by his quickness and intelligence. Before long Coote was giving him the run of his library where he was initiated into the high moral discourses of Ruskin, Carlyle, Matthew Arnold and William Morris. At length, through Coote's intervention, he was rescued from his class destiny as plough-boy and sent to Culham training college in Oxfordshire, where, while training to be a teacher, he taught himself the craft of editor.

Through squire Coote's patronage Orage also obtained his teaching post in Leeds. Orage was appointed by Leeds School Board on 26 October 1893, as a trained certificated assistant.[2] This was possibly to Chapel Allerton School, as John Carswell thinks, but more likely to Ellerby Lane Boys, because in May 1894, just six months later, Orage was reported as having resigned from Ellerby Lane Boys to join the staff of Leylands Mixed School.[3] Orage, however, did choose to live in the comfortable suburb of Chapel Allerton whose contrast with the stinking slums of Ellerby Lane and the Leylands could only have been shocking to the country boy.

Earlier in the century Chapel Allerton had been a semi-rural village on the north of Leeds with a reputation for good clean air. Despite the quadrupling of the village population from 1,000 in 1800 to 4,000 in the early 1870s its atmosphere was still almost bucolic, though now it was becoming a respectable suburb. Ellerby Lane, however, was on the edge of the Bank, a densely populated slum on the northern side of the river Aire in the centre of town. It housed an enormous immigrant Irish population, possibly 20,000 strong, described by an inspector some years before as 'from the wildest parts of Connaught' and in urgent need of civilizing.[4] The crowded courts and alleys where disease and pollution were widespread, were the breeding ground for socialists like Tom Maguire. As he waited for the tram to take him into town, the young schoolteacher may well have contemplated the view from Chapel Allerton into Leeds with some trepidation, for the following year, he wrote:

> The view of the town from some outlying hill is like a peep from Abraham's bosom into the abode of Dives. Here on the height the air is fresh to the lungs . . . But yonder, down there, the infernal pot is boiling, and the steam hangs like a nightmare over the city. Dantes need no Virgil to show them Hell; and Miltons need not be blind. There, night and day, thousands of chimneys are allowed to belch out their poisonous breaths to be inhaled by human lungs below.[5]

and as for the river below the Bank

> The Aire is simply a huge sewer: it has the filth of Leeds in suspension. Unlike the Jordan seven dips therein would cause, not cure leprosy . . . it has been transformed into the oily-flowing mud stream, into whose waters no fish dare venture, on whose banks no leaves can breathe, no trees may grow.

Although it was in the suburb he settled, Orage chose what he called in the same article 'a knight errantry' in the boiling pot of the slums. Both Mairet and Carswell think that he lived in the end of a stone terrace called Ingle Row, which is opposite perhaps the prettiest police station cum public library in Leeds, though this cannot be confirmed from the Ward Roles. By 1896 he had moved down into Harehills a mile or so into town, but by 1900 had moved back again to Chapel Allerton.

Like Ellerby Lane Boys, the Leylands School no longer stands. It too was in a densely populated area of Leeds close to the centre of town across the York Road from the Bank. It was just starting to receive the first wave of Eastern European Jews fleeing from the pogroms, later swelling to a population of 15,000. Jews and Irish regarded each other uneasily across the York Road, occasionally skirmishing. Orage taught there for only a year and a half. In January 1896 he joined his third school, Harehills Board School, where he taught older children, probably eleven or twelve years old in Standard VI.

In September 1896, Orage received his first annual pay rise of £5, something he apparently forgot to tell Philip Mairet who was under the impression he never earned more than his initial salary of £80 a year. He remained here for three and a half years now living with his wife Jean in a small terraced house at 86 Elford Place, little more than a hundred yards away. The school log book noted that he was absent through illness for a day and a half – only marginally more disruptive than the arrival of Barnum and Bailey's Circus in 1899, for which the school closed the entire day.[6] Here he was befriended by Cyril Arthington Pease, a fellow teacher who possessed the rare distinction of a Bachelor of Arts degree from Oxford, but, not certificated, was paid even less than Orage. From a substantial middle-class family, Pease was also an active member of the ILP. He was one of those who had joined because he could not tolerate the idea that his privileges had been acquired at the expense of the impoverishment of the many and had posed the question for himself 'How can I live without robbing someone else?'

Like Orage, he had chosen to teach in a poor working-class area. He left Leeds ten years later to found a school run on progressive lines in Letchworth Garden City, in its pioneering days, and in 1905 invited Orage to join him. But by this time Orage had his eyes on higher things and passed the opportunity over to his colleague Millie Browne (later Price). In September 1897 Orage's pay was increased by another £5 but, the record shows, he declined to join the board's annuity scheme, preferring to put his trust for the future in his own wit rather than municipal thrift.

Harehills Board School was purpose built and founded in 1891. It was designed by William Landless in the Queen Anne style with 'scroll gables, broken rooflines and tall windows'[7] deemed appropriately uplifting by the board, but still overcrowded and underequipped judging from the HMI's reports summarized in the log: 'The population of the area is increasing so rapidly that the accommodation provided in this large school only opened three years ago is already inadequate and in spite of the use of large central halls for classes some of the class rooms are constantly overcrowded.'[8] Nevertheless the inspectors praised the school's tone, discipline and instruction. But, in another unexplained move in October 1899, now on a wage of £95, Orage returned to Ellerby Lane Boys where he remained until August 1902.

His last teaching post in Leeds was at Roundhay Road Boys which he joined on 25 August 1902. Like Harehills School, a little over a quarter of a mile away beyond some of the densest back-to-back housing in Europe, the school was new and imposing. The log records him as being absent once because of his sister's illness in December 1902, once due to matters of importance detaining him in early November 1903 and for nearly two weeks in early December of that year apparently without cause.[9] In June 1903 he had also been to Amsterdam for 'Miss Shaw's funeral' for three and a half days. The following year at the same time he was also in Amsterdam for seven days for a conference, almost certainly an international theosophy conference, to which Orage was one of the English delegates. He was away on only five other occasions in the three years at the school, the only cause given being, 'neuralgia', meant he was almost certainly exhausted. On 13 March 1905 he took a morning off because of his wife's illness. The doctor apparently suspected an infectious disease but sent a certificate with Orage in the afternoon saying it was safe for him to return. He finally left the school and Leeds School Board's employ not, as is usually given, in the summer but on 22 December 1905. It was supposed to be a temporary six months' leave of absence 'in order to write a book' but he never returned.

The Leeds School Board was the second largest in the country and one of the most progressive. Compared with the voluntary schools which they replaced the 45 new schools which the Board had built since the Education Act of 1870 seemed 'veritable people's palaces . . . lighter, loftier, better ventilated, more convenient in every way'. The board had set out to transform the condition of the children of Leeds and, according to a later educationalist, 'had in truth proved themselves to be great civilising and humanising agencies' who had turned out 'children who were disciplined and drilled in the rudiments of the three Rs'.[10] The Education Act's author, W. E. Forster, who was the brother-in-law of Matthew Arnold, was the Member of Parliament for Leeds neighbouring town, Bradford, where Margaret MacMillan had recently done so much pioneering work. Orage had come to Leeds during the great educational revolution, when it was fervently hoped by liberals and progressives that education would save the nation from anarchy. How far he was ever convinced by this is difficult to know but after only a year at the chalkface, he gave eloquent voice to his disillusion:

> Education has deluded the human race: it is bringing us to the wrong millenium. It promised us liberty; it oathed us equality; it hinted at fraternity. It pointed with prophetic finger to the perfection of man: Utopia was to be reached by easy stages and short cuts. Thus it piped and we have danced ever since: and the dancing is nigh killing us . . . Men are no longer their own, they have been bought with the results of the 'self-denials' of capitalists.[11]

He may at some stage have chosen to teach standard I, the very youngest of the schoolchildren, to free himself for extra-mural intellectual, political and other pursuits. Mary Gawthorpe was of the opinion that 'Standard I certainly gave more time for reading' but she also felt that 'Orage liked to teach little children because of an innate modesty. Washing the feet of little children was the idea which persisted',[12] a sentiment echoed by Mairet, who thought that he was a highly gifted teacher and a great success with children 'following all their sayings and doings with rapt interest'.[13] Millie Browne, on the other hand, remembered his advice to her on becoming a teacher was to 'Use the cane steadily for the first month, then put it away and never take it out again'.[14] His late time-keeping put him in bad odour with the authorities who occasionally suspended his annual increments and denied him advancement. Despite this, he was popular with both children and colleagues and active in the local branch of the National Union of Teachers.

In 1894, Orage had joined the newly formed Leeds branch of the Independent Labour Party. He became a socialist, says Mairet, by hearing Tom Mann, whom he regarded as the greatest orator he had ever heard, address a rally in Sheffield. But it is likely that local socialist leaders such as Tom Maguire, who died the following year at the age of 27, were just as important. Like Mann, Maguire was also a charismatic figure who was remembered by his friend Edward Carpenter as 'daring yet cautious, a dreamer and yet a man of action'.[15] A small consumptive figure, he was a photographer's assistant who preferred poetry to party politics and died tragically of tuberculosis when his political powers were at their height.

Though small, the socialist movement in Leeds had been intensely active in the previous decade, culminating in the gas workers' strike of 1890 and Maguire was, in Carpenter's words, the 'mainspring and inspirer of the movement in Leeds'.[16] This famous victory for the socialists succeeded in breaking the hold over the local labour movement of the Liberal Party and laid the foundations for independent labour representation. E. P. Thompson went so far as to claim 'if we must have one man who played an outstanding role in opening the way for the ILP, that man was a semi-employed Leeds-Irish photographer in his late twenties – Tom Maguire'.[17] Maguire and Orage collaborated on ILP propaganda. The Fabian Society branches, which had blossomed in the early nineties, decamped wholesale, according to Alf Mattinson, into the ILP upon its formation in 1893.[18]

The significance of the strength of northern provincial radicalism inherent in the formation of the ILP cannot be underestimated. As the historian of the Christian Socialist Movement, Peter d'A Jones has suggested the London Fabians misunderstood this while the Manchester factory owner Frederick Engels saw it very clearly. He told his friend

Sorge: 'The Fabians here in London are a band of careerists who have understanding enough to realise the inevitability of the social revolution, but who could not possibly entrust this tremendous task to the crude proletariat alone, and are therefore kind enough to set themselves at the head.'[19] True dynamism would come from 'the rush towards socialism in the provinces,' not from London, 'the home of cliques'. If only 'the petty private ambitions and intrigues of the London would-be great men are now held in check somewhat, and the tactics do not turn out too wrong-headed, the Independent Labour Party may succeed in detaching the masses from the Social Democratic Federation, and in the provinces, from the Fabians too, and then force unity.' A few weeks later Engels added:

> Lancashire and Yorkshire are again taking the lead in this movement too, as in the chartist movement. People like Sidney Webb, Bernard Shaw and the like, who wanted to permeate the Liberals with socialism, must now allow themselves to be permeated by the spirit of the working-men members of their own society . . . Either they remain alone, officers without soldiers, or they must go along.

By the time he came to Leeds this great wave of activism was subduing and a long-term realignment of politics was emerging in which organizational problems took precedence. Asked later to contribute to a pamphlet on why he joined the ILP, Orage was characteristically flippant, using the opportunity for a lesson in intuitionist philosophy.

> Well you see, I joined first and found out afterwards. Most people flatter themselves that they look before they leap: as a matter of fact, very few people indeed look until they have leapt; and the few who do never leap at all, and go down to the vile dust from whence they sprung, unloved, unmarried and unhung. The truth is Nature is too wise to make men too wise, and it is only in life's unimportant details, such as choosing a cigar or electing an M.P., that she allows us the chance of bungling . . . Do you suppose a young man weighs the probable results of his falling in love, or even thinks anything about its results before he falls? . . . As touch is the primary material sense, whence all the others spring, so the primary mental sense, of which thought, imagination, reason are mere modifications is Feeling. After all, you cannot be an optimist with a sluggish liver, nor a philosopher with the toothache. I joined the I.L.P. because I felt it the right thing for me to do: I continue in the I.L.P. because I know it is. The feeling, however, came first, and the reasons, in plenty, came afterwards.[20]

The ILP quickly recognized Orage's literary talents and immediately commissioned articles for a propaganda leaflet with the title of *Hypnotic Leeds*, in 1895. It was edited by the founder of the Fabian Society in Leeds in 1891, Albert Marles, and other contributors included Tom Maguire and Joseph Clayton, (from whom Orage later purchased the

New Age). Orage's articles were heavily coded literary pieces which discoursed the matter of Leeds's slumdom and poverty through biblical and classical references in the manner of Ruskin or Arnold (as can be seen from the extracts quoted earlier). The first, 'A Study in Mud' on the evils of Leeds slums advocated a secular mission or 'true Aristocracy', who would 'build their houses and live their lives in the slums'. In the second article, 'Quixotic Energy' (very quixotically for a teacher in his first year in post) he tilted at the 'payment by results' system in schools for its mechanical suppression of the child's innate creativity in favour of discipline and instruction (what D. H. Lawrence later called 'the din-din-dinning of Board Schools').[21] Orage sounded a clarion call of libertarianism in the traditionally conservative profession of teachers, which, as John Carswell perceptively notes, subsequently became a willing constituency for his writing,

> The new battalions of teachers required by the Education Act had to be sought in the schools of villages and slums for the possessing classes were neither numerous enough nor willing to see their children take up teaching on weekdays. The process was at work all over England, with immense social consequences for it had created, in three decades, a large and unprecedented social category, more than half of which consisted of women . . . here was the rank and file for womens rights, and a public for progressive journalism on a scale never known before. The teacher training programme not only gave Orage his first career: it gave him the audience for his second.[22]

His masters on the Leeds School Board, who prided themselves on their humane approach, may well have responded to Orage's challenge for the payments by results system was indeed abolished in 1897. However the dominant purpose in the board was still that of sanitizing the new generation rather than releasing creative energies.

Orage's involvement with the socialist movement was as much because of his passion for argument as conviction by its ideas. Mairet talks of him laying down his books on a summer's evening and strolling over to the newly laid-out Hyde Park on Woodhouse Moor, where socialist orators would be arguing the point with hecklers in the crowd. Orage would quietly intervene by picking holes in the heckler's argument, lead him into self-contradiction and then in a triumph of Socratism, 'deliver judgement with clarity, wit and humour'. The socialists, of course, welcomed him with open arms and for about four years he became one of the ILP's most energetic, though not wholly reliable, activists.

He flexed his own oratorical muscles on many occasions, once to a rally of eight thousand on Hunslet Moor on May Day 1896.[23] Soon a popular lecturer and debater, he lectured a number of times to the

Central ILP Club in Leeds and was entrusted with leading off for the ILP in debates against other organizations. The *Labour Leader* reported on 1 February 1896, a lecture to Halton (Leeds) ILP club was filled to utmost capacity, noting 'Socialism is making itself felt in Halton'. On 4 November he lectured at Yeadon and on 22 November chaired a meeting at which the Fabian leader and early advocate of Nietzsche, Hubert Bland, lectured on German socialism. In addition he regularly chaired the Sunday meetings of the Central ILP club.

He lectured to other ILP branches also and it seems that he often used these opportunities to develop cultural themes. At a meeting attended by Millie Browne, who thought the ILP members 'a drab uncultured lot', Orage addressed the York ILP branch on Shelley's 'Prometheus Unbound'. She appears to have been as much impressed by the speaker as the subject:

> . . . one meeting I went to was epoch making for me. A speaker was announced named A. R. Orage, and he was billed to speak on Shelley's Prometheus unbound. I listened spellbound as he read the rhythmical visionary verses, and attempted to interpret the mythological characters of the lovely but abstruse and metaphysical drama. I did not understand it at all, but I was fascinated by the lecturer. He was about twenty six at the time, nine years older than I was; tall and slender with a head noble as an Arab horse, which with his thick dark lock of hair falling in moments of eloquence over his forehead, he rather resembled. One of his dark eyes was spotted with gold, and that side of his face showed a dark golden stain where in his youth acid had been flung at him. His mouth was full and mobile, his manner of speech was golden also.[24]

Millie Price's attraction to Orage seems to have typified that of many young women teachers.

In July 1895 Orage began his career as political columnist with the first of his regular contributions to the ILP weekly paper, the *Labour Leader*, edited by Keir Hardie. In November these became his famous column, 'A Bookish Causerie', indicating that it was not merely conventional book reviewing but an attempt to change and reform the readers' tastes and appetites. To call his contribution a 'column' is somewhat misleading since it often occupied one-third to three-quarters of a page. It represented many hours of books devoured and thousands of words written, for which he received 5 shillings a piece to add to his meagre teacher's stipend. The journalistic company he kept was uplifting as, occasionally, the same page sees an article by William Morris at his head and another by Tom Mann at his feet. He kept the words flowing for about two years but in July 1897 the last contribution made its appearance. It cannot have been anything but an enormous taxing of his energies, Quixotic or otherwise.

A second venture into political journalism was offered to Orage by an ILP shopkeeper in Holbeck, who started 'a freely distributed propaganda sheet' called *Forward* from his own resources in October 1896. Under Orage's editorship the sheet was soon enlarged and expanded to a print run of 50,000 per month and distributed citywide. The shopkeeper, D. B. Foster, who became the founding secretary of the Leeds Labour Party, later wrote:

> . . . this effort to provide Socialist propaganda for the whole city brought around me quite a number of very helpful comrades amongst whom I well remember the name of . . . Mr A R Orage, who for some years now has been the editor of the 'New Age' as he really was of 'Forward' though my name was nominally associated with that position.[25]

Another contributor to *Forward* was the pioneer socialist and feminist, Isabella Ford, who wrote a regular women's political page called 'Up and Down the World'. From a well-established Liberal Quaker family, Miss Ford became an enthusiastic leader of the ILP and later one of the first supporters of the Leeds Arts Club, serving for a while as a committee member. Older and wiser, it is unlikely that she was affected by Orage in the same way as Millie Browne but Orage probably benefited from her company and that of her sisters Emily and Bessie at the Central ILP Club sessions in Briggate. The sisters were amongst the first members of the ILP in 1893 and brought many influential contacts into the club. Both William Morris and Peter Kropotkin had stayed at the sisters' house in Adel, as had a whole galaxy of agitators, political refugees and labour leaders. Edward Carpenter was also a regular visitor. Alf Mattinson recorded in his obituary of Bessie that during the 1890s, when the impoverished young socialists had sought the generosity of the Ford sisters,

> . . . the movement in Leeds entered on its palmiest days. Never before nor since those few years when the club radiated such activities has the Labour or Socialist cause shown the same enthusiasm, the same fighting spirit, or possessed such a galaxy of diversified talent.[26]

Isabella Ford also wrote a number of novels of industrial class struggle and the fight for women's independence during the 1890s, one of which *On the Threshold*, Orage reviewed as essentially 'a book of women for men and women' adding, 'Simple and even absent as the plot may seem, and weak in places as the style may be, there are scenes of real life among real people, touches of homely unaffected pathos, which make "On the Threshold" not only readable but re-readable'.[27]

In 1896 Orage was married to Jean Watson whom he had met when he was a student at Culham College and she an art student at the Royal

College.[28] Already a theosophist, it was probably she who introduced him to the Theosophical Society. The flourishing Northern Federation headquarters was then in Harrogate where many of its national illuminati were regular visitors. Here Orage first met Annie Besant, Cyril Leadbeater and G. R. S. Mead. Though still committed to the ILP Orage was depressed by its 'materialism' and lack of vision. His own strong mystical bent could not find expression even in his causeries and so he turned to theosophy to cultivate his esoteric interests. He once again ran into Millie Browne, who recalled:

> The Theosophical Society . . . opened out an avenue of interest and friendship. Harrogate was the hub of the Northern Federation of the T. S. There quarterly meetings were held attended by such famous theosophists as Annie Besant, C. W. Leadbeater, A. P. Sinnett, G. R. S. Mead, Jinaragadasa . . . I was elated at coming into contact with so many big names – sometimes I wonder whether I am an instinctive lion hunter who knows perhaps Carlyle's Hero and Hero Worship had bred this in me. I had not much time for theosophic study, but turned to Edward for instruction. He and Orage were friends so I met ARO again and he found my mind interesting.[29]

The idealist and occultist, to say nothing of other, leanings in Orage were well fed by these meetings. Theosophy, under Besant's leadership, was also a progressive social movement and one that did not discriminate between race, creed or sex in its membership. It was one of the few societies women might happily join and contribute to more or less equally with men. Orage, however, was not content simply to listen to Millie Browne's 'lions' and soon became one. Before long he was a regular lecturer at theosophical meetings, though what he had to say often disturbed the more orthodox, particularly when it took a Nietzschean turn after 1900. Nevertheless he published a number of articles in the *Theosophical Review* and a series of his lectures given to the Theosophical Lodges of Manchester and Leeds was published by the society under the title *Consciousness, Animal, Human, and Superman* in 1907. He also wrote a number of children's stories for the young people's magazine *The Lotus Journal*.[30]

Almost certainly Orage was studying the classical works of eastern mysticism by the mid-nineties. Many had only recently appeared in translation, though the second edition of Annie Besant's translation of the *Bhagavad Gita*, his favoured text, had come out in 1896. Mairet's suggestion that his growing powers of oratory were now exercised less on socialist platforms than in philosophic exposition is confirmed by Stanley Pierson, who sees Orage's shift of direction as part of a cultural trend:

> During the late 90s as the Socialist movement declined, Orage became

> a prominent speaker on the theosophical platforms of the North . . . like Carpenter and others in the socialist movement he was blending the mysticism of the east with the evolutionary optimism of late Victorian culture to provide a new foundation for personal and social hopes.[31]

Orage's mystical temperament was in fact directly encouraged by Edward Carpenter who was, as an Oxford University Extension lecturer and socialist activist, a regular visitor to Leeds. During the 1890s he lived in a cottage in the village of Millthorpe near Sheffield where he welcomed Annie Besant, Olive Schreiner and many more figures in the New Life movement. His own writing and poetry were especially influential. *Civilisation: its Cause and Cure* (1889) inspired Arthur Penty to write his *Restoration of the Gild System* (1906), and *Love's Coming of Age* (1896), it has been argued, deeply influenced D. H. Lawrence and formed the ideological structure of *The Rainbow* and *Women in Love*.[32] But it was his long poem *Towards Democracy* (1883) which had the greatest impact on Alfred Orage.

Orage's relationship to Carpenter began much as had Carpenter's to Walt Whitman to whom he had written in 1874, 'There are many in England to whom your writings have been as the waking up to a new day . . . (you) are the centre of a new influence'[33] and he believed the force of the new will to change was feminine, 'Yet the women will save us . . .' This feminized element in the new socialism should not be underestimated and there is no doubt that however cynically Orage's relationships with women might be viewed, he was influenced by it. For a while Carpenter was Orage's mentor. Something of this is revealed in a letter to Carpenter in February 1896.[34] The letter, addressed from 86 Elford Place, Rounday Road, Leeds, humbly hopes that Carpenter has noticed his Bookish Causerie column in the *Labour Leader* and feels that although he is unknown to Carpenter, 'I may write to you as a friend'.

> . . . you will see that I have been attempting though with much less success than I had hoped to read modern literature in the light of the new old conception you and Whitman have done so much to spread. And I want if it be in my power to go still further and more persistently into what inwardly I feel the deepest need for thousands like myself.

He goes on to say that this need is for a sure foundation for the more or less transitory intellectual, physical and ethical beliefs, and regrets the lack of unity of purpose in his *Labour Leader* pieces:

> But now with your help I would do better. Some comrades have written me asking for some notes on 'Towards Democracy' as my lover comrade and 'hers' have long felt even since we read you out

> in the mystic air of Perth pine woods that 'Towards Democracy' is just the book for comrades.

Orage wanted to write a series of articles which may help 'those who read to understand and those who do not understand to read' and he asked Carpenter to read his articles before they went to print. Carpenter's reply is unrecorded, though it was almost certainly affirmative and two articles on 'Towards Democracy' duly appeared in the *Labour Leader* in June 1896. Though initially it was a relationship of devout discipleship, Orage's affiliations soon shifted and the tone of reverence notable in the letter changed. By February 1897 he remarks in his Bookish Causerie, 'Carpenter without Karl Marx is useless'. Later during the early Arts Club period, 1904 or 1905, in a discussion with Holbrook Jackson on the relationship of Carpenter and Whitman, Jackson reports him as saying that Carpenter was in truth 'Mrs Whitman'.[35] Nevertheless, Carpenter was an extremely popular lecturer at the Arts Club and was made an honorary member, along with Chesterton and Shaw, in 1905. Orage also named him in a note at the end of *Friedrich Nietzsche, the Dionysian Spirit of the Age* (1906) as one of an elite band of living authors who might be considered 'Dionysian'.

But Carpenter's influence may well, with Jean's, have turned him to the Theosophical Society in 1896, in one of his recurrent moods of despair with socialist materialism. His brand of socialism, as we have seen, was anyway strongly idealist and was now embellished with Carpenter's visionary utopianism. Carpenter was also close to Annie Besant, not only a theosophist but a pioneering socialist and feminist whose activities frequently brought her to Leeds and the West Riding. Alf Mattinson, for example, records having heard her speak a number of times on the steps of Leeds Town Hall in the late 1880s, on freethought and socialism. On one occasion he and other Socialist Leaguers had had to rescue her from a hostile crowd who were after her 'atheist' blood.[36] More pertinent perhaps, was that Annie Besant had, on 13 May 1895, given a lecture in Leeds which could not have failed to grip the young schoolteacher's imagination: 'Man the Master of his Destiny'.

The theosophical movement had arrived in Leeds at almost the same time as Orage. The inaugural meeting of the Northern Federation of the TS was held in Leeds on 5 August 1893 with 30 members present, including G. R. S. Mead.[37] Although a regular Leeds TS lodge seems to have existed from 1895, Orage does not seem to have been a member of it. Instead he and Jean appear to have set up a mysteriously named 'Alpha Centre' and applied for admission to the Federation in May 1898.

Jean Orage represented the Alpha Centre at Northern Federation meetings until 1900, often in the company of future Arts Club founders,

Arthur Hugh Lee and A. W. Waddington. The Leeds TS lodge then seems to have been refounded in 1900. A certificate on the wall of the lodge's meeting rooms (still those opened by Annie Besant in 1911) in Queens Square, Leeds, reads that it was founded on 19 September 1900. The names of the founders include Alfred and Jean Orage, W. H. Bean and Miss A. K. Kennedy (Jean's cousin), who also became founder members of the Leeds Arts Club three years later. The Federation minute books still list a 'Leeds Centre' as well as a Leeds Lodge in 1907 but it has only one member. For the moment this remains an anomaly, though the explanation may owe as much to the internal politics of TS as to Orage's unorthodox approach. His temperament was also such that he was only happy in a group he led or founded.

As his commitment to the ILP declined, so his energy for theosophy increased and by 1900 he had become a regular lecturer at Northern Federation conferences. The record shows the following list of his lectures: 3 November 1900, 'Can we afford to neglect Metaphysics?'; 11 May 1901, 'The Neglect of beauty' (to which Arthur Penty contributes); 2 November 1901, 'Thought Power its control and culture'; 10 May 1902, 'Problems of Karma'; 29 November 1902, Orage leads discussion on 'What is the Personality?'; 20/21 February 1904, 'Methods of Lodge Work'. At the next federation meeting he was minuted to give a paper on 'Animal Consciousness' (also Jean Orage to give paper on 'Metempsychosis'); 30 July 1904, 'Animal Consciousness' (Annie Besant in Chair); 11 January 1906, 'Theosophy and Modern Physical Science'; and 24 February 1906, 'Theosophical Ideas in Commercial and Professional Life'.

As a regular Leeds lodge delegate he also contributed to organizational work: 2 February 1901, when he suggested that the next meeting's discussion topic should be 'Is Happiness Brotherhood?' '(On the Neglect of beauty)' and was noted as joining in the discussion on 'Our attitude towards Christian Enquirers'. Between this date and July 1904, he was the Leeds delegate on fourteen more occasions. At the council meeting of 21 February 1903, he and Jean contributed to a discussion on 'Policy and Methods of Propaganda'. He also offered to give a range of talks to local branches on theosophical and cultural matters, including 'What is Mysticism?' 'Theory of Reincarnation', 'Man and His Bodies', 'Some Hindu Short Stories', 'Theosophy and Literature', 'Nietzsche and Ibsen', 'The Republic of Plato', 'Theosophy and Modern Psychology', 'The Future of Humanity', 'What Theosophists are aiming at', 'Animal Evolution' and 'The Power of Thought',[38] an altogether ambitious programme of grass-roots education in popular philosophy.

Two other founders of the Arts Club also joined the programme. Rev. A. H. Lee offered 'Religious Ideas of the Celtic Races', 'Psychology and

Religion', 'Browning and His Message', 'Objects of the Society for Psychical Research' and 'Myers' Human Personality', while A. W. Waddington suggested 'Conventionality' and 'Mediaeval Guilds'. Waddington may also have come to theosophy along the same route as Orage. In 1896 he had been the secretary of Carpenter's Sheffield Socialist Society and had subsequently taken up New Life living with fellow architect, Arthur Penty. As Millie Price later recalled: 'A. J. Penty brought his Ruskinian ethics to cooperate with "Waddy" in producing furniture of simple, undecorated and unpolished woods, and the two furnished themselves a cottage as an example of what craftsmanship could do, and there in the country lived for a while an austere Thoreauesque kind of a life.'[39]

Orage was also elected to the English Committee of the International Congress and spoke on the international correspondence scheme. In July he was elected to the subcommittee to discuss the next international congress and at the same meeting proposed that his paper, on 'Animal Consciousness', which he presented to the conference on that day, with Annie Besant in the chair, be published as 'Transactions'. ('Animal Consciousness' in fact became the first part of *Consciousness, Animal, Human and Superman*, published by the Theosophical Publishing Society, in 1907). He proposed for the next conference, papers on 'Art and the Arts' in order to define the value of the arts in education and to discover the relative importance and place of the arts in human life. His paper on F. H. Myers's theory of human personality which he had been lecturing on to the Leeds lodge in 1904 was published in 'Transactions' as 'Man and Death'.[40] Though present at the council meeting of 13 May 1905, when his friend Waddington was elected secretary of the discussions committee, he resigned suddenly from it in August. Not surprisingly, the reason given was 'strain of overwork'.[41]

However, Millie Price revealed that it was not all metaphysics and astral bodies at the Harrogate meetings as occasionally Orage attended to more corporeal ones: hers.

> When at a Theosophical conference at Harrogate Orage suggested we should play truant for one session and take a stroll on Harlow Moor. I was thrilled with delight at contacting his exciting mind in an intimate way. For he had an exciting mind. He excited himself with brilliant speculations on the structure of the soul and the universe. The doctrines of what was then called 'Esoteric Buddhism' were the most fruitful in this respect and he devoted himself to lectures on these being daringly imaginative and convincing. His mind too was crammed with poetical literature so that I owe to him my early knowledge of Yeats, for he had seized upon my copy of the Wanderings of Oisin, purloined from Dr. O'Leary's collection, and read to my entranced ears:

> Autumn is over the long leaves that love us,
> And over the mice in the barley fields
> Yellow the leaves of rowan above us
> And yellow the wet, wild strawberry leaves.
>
> stressing its colour values in the words used. Craftily he read also To An Isle In The Water:- 'Shy one, shy one shy one of my heart' . . .

and the rest can be guessed at, presumably in the absence of Jean Orage for whom Millie had an awed respect. She tells of many more trysts and holidays by the seaside together which, though romantic, appear to have been unconsummated. Orage, she said, called her the 'Ice Maiden'.[42]

Theosophy carried Orage through his remaining ten years in Leeds including his discovery of Nietzsche and the formation of the Arts Club, as we shall see in the next chapter, and provided him with a circle of friends and an audience for his experimental humanism more congenial than the ILP. He carried many of these like Lee and Waddington into the Arts Club with him and through it he reached a far wider social spectrum than was otherwise available to a schoolteacher of modest means. It was probably his rites of passage into a wealthy social group which included academics, businessmen and bankers, one of whom subsequently put up half the cash for the *New Age*. How convinced he was by theosophy, as opposed to finding it a congenial vehicle for his own ideas, is another matter.

He may have belonged to theosophy's inner esoteric section. Like W. B. Yeats and Florence Farr, both of whom later visited the Arts Club on more than one occasion, though Ellic Howe does not mention him, he might have become a magician of the Hermetic Order of the Golden Dawn, an esoteric offshoot of theosophy, formed in 1888 by Macgregor Mathers.[43] Orage was later taken up with Aleister Crowley, the beast himself, who was briefly leader of the order, and according to Beatrice Hastings, would have filled the *New Age*'s pages with his 'turgid out-pourings' had she not prevented him.[44] Ms. Hastings, a brilliant though erratic talent had herself met Orage at a theosophical meeting in London in 1906, when he had jumped up on the stage in the absence of the advertised speaker, to give an impromptu lecture, and shortly after became his lover. She wrote that after about a year,

> when Aphrodite had amused herself at our expense, I found a collection of works on sorcery. Up to this time, Orage's intimate friend was not Mr. Holbrook Jackson, who thought he was, but Mr. Aleister Crowley. . . . Well, I consigned all the books and 'Equinoxes' and sorcery designs to the dustbin.[45]

She lived with Orage for some years in London, at one time sharing their apartment, and possibly Orage himself, with Katherine Mansfield, becoming virtually co-editor of the *New Age*. When she parted company with him (later to live with Modigliani) she accused him, with her customary acrimony, of 'paranoic mystagoguery'!

Though Beatrice's account has been contested by others of the *New Age* circle, Orage told C. S. Nott some years later, that he had met Crowley when he, Orage, was acting secretary of the Society for Psychical Research in 1906. The poet, Edwin Muir, remembers Orage as having been 'a member of a magic circle which included Yeats' which James Webb, the historian of the modern occult movement, thought must have been the Golden Dawn, which had split up into quarrelling factions in 1900, with Yeats and Crowley on opposite sides of the fence. Webb also refers to a Golden Dawn temple in Bradford – there is no record of one in Leeds – but it seems unlikely that the leading theosophical lecturer of the North could have avoided coming into contact with some of its members. The temple in Bradford has recently been rediscovered and there is a short account of it in a local occultist journal. The anonymous writer notes 'There was a particularly active occult scene around this time in Yorkshire. A number of mysterious groups existed such as the Rosicrucian Fathers of Keighley . . . and the less mysterious August and Oriental Order of Light Garuda which was based in Bradford.'[46] In a more serious and sustained study Logie Barrow has shown that the West Riding had been one of the most important centres of spiritualist activity in Britain since its arrival from the USA in the mid-nineteenth century.[47] Subsequently many spiritualists joined the re-invigorated socialist movement and the ILP, imparting to it some of their own utopianism. Support for Orage's dabbling in magic might come from the fact that his diary of engagements was so full that astral-planing was the only possible way of getting from one to the next.

Back in the real world, in 1897 he and Jean moved to an apartment at 3 Exmouth Grove, Harehills, owned appropriately enough by a Mrs Tempest. Whether Orage was still pronouncing his name as it had been spelt in Cambridgeshire or whether his new landlady had put ideas into his head would be interesting to know. After all, as Carswell remarks, a hint of *stormy* Huguenot ancestory in one's surname has to be more impressive than something that rhymes, as Shaw used to say, with 'porridge'. Nameplaying may well have been a passing diversion for a man still attempting to construct his persona. On the Ward Role of 1898, for example, he even enters himself as *Alfred O'Rage*! Another move, in 1898, took him to 11 Rossington Place, Harehills, and then in 1899 up the hill to 36 Hawthorne Mount, Chapel Allerton, where he stayed until 1905. His final Leeds address was 33 Potternewton

Road, which was where Mary Gawthorpe remembered receiving a certain corporeal communication.

As for his intellectual movements between 1898 and 1900, he was certainly not merely sinking into spiritualism. But he had given up his Bookish Causerie in 1897 and his editorship of *Forward* in 1898, when it passed into more orthodox hands, and appears not to have published any more journalism until 1902. His school work at Harehills, teaching the older children of standard VI, with classes of 50 and more was undeniably demanding, but a notebook dating from this time suggests that he was still devouring books at a great rate. He appears to have read most of George Gissing, some Henry James, Kipling, Mark Twain, R. L. Stevenson, Alexander Dumas, a range of oriental and biblical texts, romantic poets and cultural criticism. The biggest single entry is from the *Philosophical Dialogues* of the French essayist, Ernest Renan, critical of what he called 'the acid of reasoning'. One quotation Orage has copied, points forward to the Arts Club and Nietzsche: 'Endeavour to be beautiful and then do act every moment as your heart inspires you'.[48]

In the meantime he had to earn a living and became an active though not especially successful member of the National Union of Teachers. In 1898 he stood for election to the Leeds and District executive but succeeded in coming only twenty-second in the poll. The following year he did even worse, getting fewer votes and coming twenty-seventh. But in 1901 he was successful, collecting 157 votes and coming eighth in the poll. Despite this his victory was short-lived. In the following year's election although he picked up nearly 90 votes more, he and most of the other sitting members were swept off the executive in a wave of revolt.[49] A slate of candidates organized by the Direct Representation Association opposing the 1902 Education Bill carried the day. They objected to non-certified teachers being transferred to board schools as cheap labour with the merging of the voluntary sector, but Orage does not appear to have sympathized.

His involvement in the NUT may have been more motivated by its potential as a platform for his own ideas, for, in a letter to the *Leeds Teacher's Journal*, he complains about the misuse of something called the NUT 'Literary Branch' which sounds like an institution Orage himself may have thought up:

> Referring to the announcement made by the Literary branch of a series of lectures (September 1902 p3) may I enquire whether the original intention of the branch has been deliberately or only thoughtlessly lost sight of. From what I can remember it was the object of the branch to provide primarily opportunities for the discussion of ideas, mainly of course such ideas as are expressed in literature'.[50]

His complaint was that 'the literary feature seems to have been more or less retained but the teachers and the discussion are apparently omitted'. Clearly Orage was seeking another forum for debate but unfortunately the NUT 'Literary Branch' was not destined to be it. Was it seen as a forerunner of the Arts Club? Significantly, C. W. Whitmell an unusually popular school's inspector, in 1903 gave the same lecture to the Literary Branch as he gave a couple of years later to the Arts Club: 'The Dypsichus of Clough'.

As the century drew to its close the 26-year old Orage had promoted a libertarian pedagogy more or less successfully for six years (an inspiration to A. S. Neil of Summerhill). He had held mass audiences on both socialist and theosophical platforms, had distinguished himself as a cultural critic in the *Labour Leader* and had edited a successful local socialist journal, *Forward*. A quotation copied into his notebook from Kipling revealed his feelings about that: 'Any fool can write but it takes a god-given genius to be an editor'.[51] Though he made it plain to his female colleagues he believed in free-love, he was probably married to Jean Watson and had settled in to an end-terrace house in Chapel Allerton, 36 Hawthorn Mount. His life was full of immensely promising fragments but no achievable synthesis. The means to this lay in his next chance encounter.

Notes

1. Most information on Orage's early life is from Philip Mairet, *A. R. Orage A Memoir*, Dent, London, 1936. Mairet heard it all from Orage himself, but it is not as accurate as could be desired. This is supplemented by John Carswell, *Lives and Letters*, Faber, London, 1978, which, while generally excellent, has also borrowed some of Mairet's inaccuracies.
2. Leeds School Board, Education Committee Minutes, October 1893, West Yorkshire Archives, Sheepscar, Leeds.
3. Leeds School Board, School Staff Ledgers, 1894, West Yorkshire Archives, Sheepscar, Leeds.
4. Quoted in M. A. Travis, 'The Work of the Leeds School Board' in *Researches and Studies*, The School of Education, University of Leeds, no. 8, May 1953.
5. A. R. Orage, 'A Study in Mud' in Albert T. Marles (ed.) *Hypnotic Leeds*, Leeds, 1894, p. 17.
6. Harehills Board School Log Book, Harehills Primary School, Newton Garth, Leeds, pp. 127, 145, 162.
7. Derek Linstrum, *West Yorkshire Architects and Architecture*, Lund Humphries, London, 1978, p. 260.
8. HMI's report, September 1894, Harehills Mixed Log Book, Harehills Primary School, p. 58.
9. Roundhay Road Board School Log Book, West Yorkshire Archives, Sheepscar, Leeds, pp. 447, 450, 452, 453, 455.

10. M. A. Travis, op. cit., pp. 92–93.
11. A. R. Orage, 'Quixotic Energy' in *Hypnotic Leeds*, p. 43.
12. Mary Gawthorpe, *Up Hill to Holloway*, Penobscot, Maine, 1962, p. 192.
13. Mairet, op. cit., p. 10.
14. Millie Price (née Browne), *This World's Festival*, unpublished autobiography in typescript, property of Agnes Patrick, 16 Bainbrigge Road, Leeds 6, p. 5.
15. Edward Carpenter, 'A Memoir' in Bessie Ford (ed.) *Tom Maguire: A Remembrance*, Labour Press Society, Manchester, 1895, p. x.
16. Ibid.
17. Edward Thompson, 'Homage to Tom Maguire' in A. Briggs and J. Saville (eds) *Essays in Labour History*, London, 1960, p. 279; and Tom Woodhouse, 'The Working Class' in Derek Fraser (ed.) *A History of Modern Leeds*, Manchester, 1980.
18. Alf Mattinson, *Journals*, vol. 1, p. 270, Leeds City Reference Library.
19. Peter d'A Jones, *'The Christian Socialist Revival' 1877–1914*, Princeton University Press, 1968, pp. 141–2. The letters are Engels to Sorge, 18 January 1893; Engels to Sorge, 18 March 1893 (K. Marx and F. Engels, *'Letters to Americans, 1848–1895'*, New York, 1953, pp. 246–247, 249.
20. Alfred Orage in J. Clayton (ed.) *Why I Joined the Independent Labour Party Some Plain Statements*, Leeds, no date, p. 11.
21. D. H. Lawrence, 'Nottingham and the Mining Country' in *Selected Essays*, Penguin, London, 1950, p. 119. Lawrence could only have been eight years old when Orage, some seventy miles to the north, and twelve years his senior, started in post. But like Orage, he was part of that generation and social class swept into school teaching by the demands of the 1870 Education Act. Later he became an avid reader of the *New Age* and many of its opinions became his own.
22. Carswell, op. cit., p. 16.
23. *Labour Leader*, vol. VIII, no. 110, 4 May 1896, p. 155.
24. Millie Price, op. cit., pp. 83–84.
25. D. B. Foster, *Socialism and the Christ*, published by the author, Leeds, 1921, p. 31.
26. *Leeds Citizen*, 1.8.1919.
27. *Labour Leader*, 16 November 1895.
28. In a letter to Edward Carpenter, he refers to her as his 'lover-comrade' but John Carswell could find no trace of a marriage certificate in Somerset House. Nevertheless Orage was convinced he was married since he demanded a divorce from Jean in 1915, which as Roman Catholic she refused him. (Letter from Jean Orage to Holbrook Jackson dated 24 April 1915, Harry Ransome Center, University of Texas.)
29. Millie Price, op. cit., p. 86.
30. His story 'The First Men', a creation of myth, appeared in *The Lotus Journal*, August 1907, pp. 108–11 and 'The Princesses and the Gardener' in another issue.
31. Stanley Pierson, *British Socialists: the journey from fantasy to politics*, Harvard University Press, 1979, p. 193.
32. Emile Delavennay, *Edward Carpenter and D. H. Lawrence: A Study in Edwardian Transition*, Heinemann, London, 1969.
33. Edward Carpenter, letter to Walt Whitman, 12 July 1874, copy in Alf Mattinson Collection, Brotherton Library, University of Leeds.

34. Alfred Orage, letter to Edward Carpenter, 3 February 1896, Carpenter Collection, Sheffield City Library.
35. Holbrook Jackson, 'A. R. Orage: Personal Recollections', *The Windmill* (Heinemann house journal), London, 1948, p. 44.
36. Alf Mattinson, 'Journals' 1925–28, vol 1, p. 293. Leeds City Reference Library.
37. Northern Federation of the Theosophical Society Minute Book 1893–1900, held at Harrogate TS Lodge, 6 Alexandra Road, Harrogate.
38. A list of lectures offered to federation lodges recorded in the minutes of September 1903.
39. Millie Price, op. cit., p. 113.
40. *Leeds Mercury* Weekly Supplement, 13 February and 5 March 1904, reports Orage lecturing on Myers's *Human Personality* and 'Telepathy and Clairvoyance', based on Myers, calling the theory of evolution 'panaesthetic'.
41. Northern Federation TS Minute Book, 12–13 August 1905.
42. Millie Price, op. cit., p. 98.
43. Ellic Howe, *The Magicians of the Golden Dawn*, Routledge, Kegan Paul, London, 1972.
44. Beatrice Hastings, *The Old 'New Age': Orage – and others*, Blue Moon Press, London, 1936.
45. Quoted in James Webb, *The Harmonious Circle*, Thames and Hudson, London, 1980, p. 210.
46. 'The Lamp of Thoth', vol. III, no. 4 (undated), Leeds, pp. 33–35. Available from 'The Sorcerer's Apprentice', Hyde Park Corner, Leeds 6.
47. Logie Barrow, *Independent Spirits, Spiritualism and English Plebeians 1850–1910*, Routledge, Kegan Paul, London, 1986.
48. Leeds School Board, 'Daily Notes', notebook, 'VI A' handwritten on cover, no page numbers, in possession of Richard Orage.
49. *Leeds Teacher's Journal*, monthly journal of Leeds and District National Union of Teachers, January 1899, January 1900, January 1902 and January 1903, Brotherton Library, Leeds.
50. Letter dated 18 September 1902, in The *Leeds Teacher's Journal*, Oct/Nov 1902, p. 5, signed 'A. R. Orage'.
51. Notebook entitled 'Leeds School Board, Daily Notes, VI A', undated but from internal evidence not before October 1896, p. 27, in the possession of Richard Orage.

CHAPTER TWO

Holbrook Jackson and Nietzsche: Egoistic Relations

Orage was introduced to Nietzsche's work in 1900, the year of his death. Still a shadowy figure in England, with only three volumes of his works in translation, Nietzsche was, for many who had only heard the name, a dangerous anarchist, the model for Conan Doyle's Moriarty, arch-enemy of Victorian society's gentlemanly protector, Sherlock Holmes. But some of the Fabian camp's bolder spirits like Bernard Shaw and Hubert Bland had already recommended him as a purgative for Victorian moralism. Their opinion of him was not shared by all but for Orage the shock of the meeting was galvanic.

Holbrook Jackson introduced Orage to Nietzsche's *Thus Spake Zarathustra* in the autumn of 1900. Jackson was a lace merchant, Fabian and freelance journalist who had but recently arrived in Leeds, a town which compared most unfavourably to his 'beloved' Liverpool. Leeds he had decided was an 'intellectual desert . . . ugly and dirty and no one seemed to care'.[1] He knew no one, but one afternoon wandering round a bookshop in search of the intellectual nourishment missing from his everyday commerce with the actual inhabitants, he bumped into Orage, doing much the same. Recalling the meeting seven years later in the prefatory letter to him in his book on George Bernard Shaw, he wrote:

> My Dear Orage, – You will remember now, some years ago, we were thrown together by the fates in that smoky chaos which is known to geographers and others as Leeds. I have a clear recollection of the exact circumstances. It was in a bookshop, into which we had both turned, probably to find in books that community of ideas which we unable to find locally among men. We were pottering around some shelves of the genus Second-hand, which were set far back in the partial gloom and comparative quietness of the remote end of the shop. We stalked our quarry in that absorbed and dilatory way peculiar to the book hunter. After a while I heard you throw the intelligence department of the emporium out of gear by enquiring for a volume by a modern writer, well enough known among thoughtful people, but evidently a dark continent to Leeds . . . I was amazed for a moment. I felt as one who had stumbled accidentally upon a new planet. I made an involuntary movement towards you; my instinct, I remember, was that of one bent upon catching hold of a thing too good to be missed.[2]

It was the beginning of a 'joyous association' which was to last for many years. Orage had been looking for Fiona Macleod's (William Sharp) romance of the Celtic Revival *The Watcher at the Ford.* Though not possessed by Walker's Bookshop in Briggate Street, Jackson did and hauled Orage off to a nearby coffee-shop to get the full flavour of him.

> We walked out of the shop into Briggate where the tramcars clattered, and, over coffee in a restaurant where we took refuge we talked about Fiona Macleod, Yeats and the 'Celtic fringe' from which Orage seemed to expect some revelation of great human value. Thus began a conversation which continued for nearly ten years, and friendship which lasted until Orage died thirty-four years later.[3]

It turned out that they shared a common bibliographic interest, though Jackson's reading was wider where Orage's was deeper and one author almost unknown to Orage was Nietzsche. Though he may have read a little in magazines and possibly in French, for the last few years he had been deeply into the newly translated classics of Eastern mysticism and in particular the *Bhagavad Gita.* They remet shortly at Jackson's home in Buckingham Mount, Headingley, and after an earnest night of discussion, Orage went home with Jackson's copy of *Thus Spake Zarathustra*, leaving him with the *Bhagavad Gita.* What Jackson thought of his end of the swap is not known but Orage was transformed. Jackson recalled:

> The moment was opportune for he had just got all he could out of Plato (or was it Poltinus [sic] or Blavatsky? one or the other but no matter) and he wolfed the Dionysian philosophy as if he had not had a feed of ideas for months.[4]

Orage, who had undergone one of his regular bouts of restlessness when Jackson met him, was once again teaching at Ellerby Lane Boys School, now earning exactly £100 per annum,[5] allowing him perhaps a few shillings a month extra to spend on books. He was not however entirely bereft of intellectual companionship since he was at this time leading a philosophical discussion circle called the Plato Group, or by some, the 'Plato Lodge'[6] but it hinged on Orage's own brilliance rather than Socratic equality. Nourishment was provided by guest speakers and Jackson remembers the name of John Kenworthy as a bait to get him to attend. Kenworthy was a Tolstoyan who in 1893 had published a very popular attack on the evils of capitalism called *The Anatomy of Misery.*[7] This particular meeting was in the house of a Presbyterian priest, the Rev. James Rogerson MA, at 49 Reginald Terrace, Chapeltown. Other meeting places of Orage's 'Plato friends' included the house of wealthy and influential architect Thomas Butler Wilson

(1859–1942), later Clerk of Works at the House of Commons, whom Philip Mairet believes was a friend of Orage's wife Jean. The circle also apparently included some professors from the Yorkshire College.

Jackson's description of Orage at this time reveals a magnetic personality which may well have attracted the wealthy lay seeker after knowledge as well as academics.

> In appearance Orage was at that time, slim and dark haired. He dressed conventionally, except for a soft felt hat, then unusual, and probably an indication of aesthetic revolt. It was usually perched on the back of his head. Another unusual item was a hand-woven silk tie, sometimes blue but oftener orange or flame colour. His hair was straight, and worn short except for an unruly tuft which liked to stray over his forehead. His eyes were hazel, lively and challenging, and in moments of excitement they seemed to emit a red glint. It was a feline face and there was something cat-like about his movements. He walked as if he were going to pounce on something, just as his mind pounced on an idea or an opponent. His self-possession was feline, and he had a cat's love of appreciation and under restraint he sulked like a cat. His expression was earnest, without being solemn. There was wit in his poise and manner, and he was good to look at without being good looking. But he did not impress by features so much as by something outside and beyond features. He had an *aura*, and impressed so much by his presence that you forgot details, even the vague birthmark which broke into his complexion like an irregular sunburn, and seemed to become deeper when he was bored or out of humour.[8]

Jackson was also of the opinion that, though he was a born teacher, his employment under the Leeds School Board was as incongruous as 'Swinburne at Eton or Shelley at Oxford'.[9] He had an ability to put the diffident at ease while having a quite extraordinary effect on women. Generally in good health, a fact confirmed by school log books which show his absence through illness as little more than a few days in the whole time he was a teacher, he had 'a sense of superiority tempered with humour and a genius for non-possessive friendships'. He also had a gaiety of spirit which spread to those around him and it was in this way he spent his evenings and weekends teaching 'strange doctrines to his older contemporaries which included esoteric matter from Blavatsky to F. W. Myers'.

Despite his increasing reputation as a guru he nevertheless inclined to rational criticism of the occult, for what drove him on was more the mystery of human psychology than meaningless profundity. Although in Vienna Freud and his colleagues were establishing the foundations of psychoanalysis, in Britain the study of mind was almost inseparable from spiritualist experimentation. But when a decade later Orage did hear of Freud's work he immediately encouraged one of the pioneers in Britain, M. D. Eder, to translate it and write commentaries in the *New Age*. Eder did in fact publish the first translations of Freud and Jung outside of the specialist journals in it, dating from 1913. Though he could not, however, entirely rid himself of his spiritualist aura, rationality was always dominant. Eder later pondered: 'Was he a mystic? Only in the sense that we are all mystics. At the bottom we know so little and the philosophies are all so futile; A. R. Orage never deluded himself with knowledge when sense existed, never pretended that things were what they were not.'[10]

During 1902 his theosophical group undertook a detailed study of F. W. Myers' influential book, *Human Personality and its Survival of Bodily Death*. He lectured on it to theosophical groups and under his direction the TS published a critical account of it called *Man and Death* in 1904. Described by Mairet as a 'dull very cautious and sensible pronouncement',[11] Millie Price recalled that his mind was not entirely on it: 'At this juncture he was pledged to give a series of lectures on (it) but his absorption in Nietzsche left him little time to study that epoch making book so I made a precis of its contents for him'.[12]

Orage still saw theosophy as his primary commitment. Annie Besant was an active presence and she had lectured to the Leeds lodge on 14 November 1898 and to Orage's Alpha Centre on 22 January 1900, the day before his birthday.[13] He even reprimanded Holbrook Jackson for being 'deficient in reverence for her' to which Jackson responded genially that they were all 'yoga-stricken mugwumps'. Although Orage founded deep friendships in theosophy and attracted strong loyalty, few seemed to offer him the intellectual partnership of Jackson whom he met on the ground of equality. Jackson offered him a Fabian alternative to theosophy and together they started to plan assaults on 'the supreme evil of the age, Plutocracy'. Jackson recalled that though like Orage he had been an early member of the ILP he had later turned to Fabianism, while Orage was struggling at that time to discover a new synthesis of theosophy and Neo-Platonism: 'Orage I was to learn, was always *neo*'.[14] Their first plan was for an anthology called *Path of Action*, of which nothing came, and then collaboration on a book on Bernard Shaw.

The Shaw book, the first biography of him, was published under Jackson's name alone in 1907 though Orage had a large hand in it. Although Orage had written a draft chapter on Shaw's philosophy, Shaw and, more particularly, Mrs Shaw strongly disapproved of it and asked Orage to withdraw it, which he did. In return however Shaw agreed to help him with his first book on Nietzsche, *Nietzsche the Dionysian Spirit of the Age*. He made lengthy marginal notes on the galley proofs Orage sent him, especially on Nietzsche's relationship with Wagner, the published work only slightly benefiting.[15] This debt to Shaw has not previously attracted attention, but it marks the beginning of a long and not always harmonious association which included Shaw's gift of £500 to Orage and Jackson for the purchase of the *New Age* which he intended to use anonymously as his own mouthpiece.

Work on Nietzsche, including a forty-five-page essay entitled 'Nietzsche contra Socialism' and two notebooks of translations of Nietzsche's aphorisms, increasingly absorbed Orage.[16] While Orage was modernizing himself in this way, Jackson felt the need to apply their ideas practically and 'their first and most joyous venture' became the Leeds Arts Club. Jackson recalls that what hastened their decision to form a club was the discovery of like-minded men and women hidden away in various parts of the city 'dreaming similar dreams to ours and thinking like thoughts'. They began to meet more frequently,

> . . . and turned quiet corners of local cafes into temporary forums, often extending the lunch-hour in a way quite heretical in Yorkshire. At these talks the name of Bernard Shaw was often heard. We were all more or less familiar with his point of view, for in many ways he had been the touchstone of our aquaintanceship; but this does not mean . . . that we accepted G.B.S. without demur. On the contrary, we did nothing of the sort, but we at least recognised in him the most acute and suggestive mind in contemporary English literature. We knew he was a force to be taken into account; we were unanimous in our belief that only in the vitalised action advocated by him was there any hope for the redemption of a social system which had become a chaos and a social desolation, as our urban surroundings constantly reminded us. Out of these meetings was born the Leeds Arts Club.[17]

Though they were agreed on Shaw and Nietzsche they diverged on others. Jackson could not interest Orage in the Dickensian Fellowship, whose president was G. K. Chesterton, and on the one occasion when Orage did agree to lecture to the local group on *Pickwick*, the Dickensians howled with rage. Millie Price thought their personalities were complementary in that while Orage was brilliantly inventive, Jackson imparted order and thoroughness to their activities 'preferring the savour of orderly civilised living to Bohemianism'.[18] Jackson found Orage a cultured, intelligent and civilized friend, as willing to be led along intellectual paths as to lead and keen to share his enthusiasms. He was impressed by his physical and intellectual stamina which allowed him to 'teach urchins all day' and talk, read or write all night, claiming he never suffered from ill health unless he ate mutton. They enjoyed country walks together and holidays on the moors and the coast, occasionally visiting Edward Carpenter in Sheffield and the

Rothensteins at Bradford where they saw Charles Rothenstein's (later Rutherston) extensive collection of modern paintings.

Books, according to Jackson, became 'archipelagoes of ideas' which they would discuss exhaustively and then move on. Thus *Zarathustra, Bhagavad Gita*, and Hudson's the *Purple Land that England Lost*, which Orage discovered in the local library all became temporary encampments. Myers's *Human Personality* became for a while 'like Nietzsche a King Charles's head in all his talk'. They also discovered Arnold Bennett's books and through their friend, Charles Smythe, the man himself. Algernon Clough's *Dypsichus* became a favourite and Clough became for them, like William Blake, an English anticipant of Nietzsche in what they constructed as a growing tradition of domestic Dionysians. Curiously the books themselves, so lovingly collected and written about by Jackson were of no interest to Orage once he had gutted them and he regularly purged his library down to a promising dozen or so. This appalled the hoarder and bookman in Jackson for whom it suggested a powerful image of his friend:

> He was always reconditioning his heroes and always sloughing off his intellectual skins – his career is strewn with the cast-off skins of Blavatsky, Plato, Shaw, Nietzsche, Penty, Douglas and Gourgieff [sic] . . . Orage's life was a process of getting tired of persons, ideas and movements. At the same time the process in his case had integrity, for capricious as it was, it represented a constant desire for spiritual control over material affairs. His life had a more or less regular rhythm which swung him backwards and forwards from the material to the mystical.[19]

Jackson, on the contrary, was a perceptive observer and meticulous detailer who destroyed nothing. His loyalty as 'a man of letters' was to 'Culture' beyond party politics and philosophical dogma. On his death, his friend Francis Meynell said of him that 'He made himself a writer out of the ordered abundance of his reading, and became a teacher because he was so great a student . . . Never have I known a man to carry erudition more happily, or to converse more generously, wisely or humbly'.[20] He compared him to Horace Walpole and his hero William Morris. Unlike Orage, Jackson claimed never to have been hooked on Nietzsche and wrote about the great German with an engaging and distanced humour. As well as Morris, his heroes were nineteenth-century idealists such as Whitman, Emerson, Thoreau and Ruskin but he was as much enamoured of their style as their message and his judgements were historically grounded and humane.

But, in common with other men of culture, he retained the élitist and defensive category of 'the Herd' for those who were not. Like Ruskin and Matthew Arnold the Herd was the stubborn object of his reforming zeal, outside Culture and wilfully refusing to enter. But even the Herd was no less distasteful to him than the philistinism of 'the plutocrats' whose attraction to Art was directly proportional to its marketable potential. His comments on Whitman reveal both antipathies:

> Whitman has never received the acceptance which he desired. The Laureate of the average man has been ignored by those for whom he sang and acclaimed by the intellectually exclusive and the emotionally peculiar, much as the productions of William Morris have been accepted by connoisseur and collector. He believed he was making a new folk poetry, but nothing could be further removed from the common taste than the irregularities of the Leaves of Grass. His tolerance would have been as intolerable to the instincts of the herd as his homosexuality would have been repugnant.[21]

Jackson's careful judgements balanced Orage's mercurial bohemianism and his progressive cultural reformism became the organizational foundation of the partnership on which the Arts Club was built. For him the Club was to become an oasis in the deserts of philistinia and even when Orage wanted to take flight to the metropolis, he still planned a network of arts clubs across the provinces, not convinced that London had anything more to offer. It was he rather than Orage who proselytized in York, Hull, Bradford and Halifax and insisted on the idea of 'the revival of local as distinct from centralised living with the Arts Club as the refuge and laboratory of the new life'.[22]

Jackson thus provided both the source and the firm base from which Orage's new found Nietzschean zeal might take off. Though he still remained close to theosophy Jackson's urbanity and mild amusement probably rescued him from too deep an immersion. Time and again, it later appeared in the Arts Club, it would be Jackson who reaffirmed the concreteness of their project of provincial renewal when Orage soared off on more fanciful, if more exciting, intellectual flights. As his seminal study, *The Eighteen Nineties* reveals, it was also Jackson who had the deeper understanding of the period's cultural formation. Central to the ideas of the nineties was the publication of translations of what Jackson called 'modern masterpieces from many European idea-centres'[23] which included Tolstoy, Ibsen, Zola, Turgenev, and D'Annunzio. Jackson argued that hitherto, because of the language barrier, these artists had been the property of the 'cultured classes'. Now cheap translations were available to nearly all, especially of course the new literate, creative and educational stratum (Orage's 'professional proletariat') which was to provide the base membership of the Arts Club and the readership for the *New Age*. Introducing these writers was, he says, in an unintentionally appropriate imperialist metaphor 'like opening up a new country to be immediately settled by ardent colonists'.[24] Their ideas were immediately absorbed and used in a vigorous criticism of life. First among these new 'egoistic' influences was Henrik Ibsen who had used the stage to devastating effect and had created a pattern for Shaw to follow. He also noted the effect of a small egoistic journal called *The Eagle and the Serpent*, 'a journal for free spirits and for those struggling to be free' first published in Edinburgh in 1898, whose masthead linked Nietzsche, Stirner, Thoreau and Goethe in one single 'Philosophy of Life'. The first mention of Nietzsche he could find in English was in George Egerton's *Keynotes* (1892), followed by John Davidson's *Sentences and Paragraphs* (1893). Thus it was abundantly clear that when Common's translations of Nietzsche's work became available at the end of the 1890s they were already inscribed into an 'English' tradition of European Romantic humanism.

Orage's reading of Nietzsche could therefore be seen as determined by a number of factors not the least of which were theosophic mysticism and Romantic humanism. At the end of 1905, five years after his first contact with Jackson and Nietzsche and countless hours of argument and debate he applied for study leave from the Leeds School Board to write the first introduction to Nietzsche in English. It may be appropriate now to consider what he made of it.

His 'study leave' in fact produced three short books. Two of them were introductions to Nietzsche's thought, *Friedrich Nietzsche the Dionysian Spirit of the Age* (1906) and *Nietzsche in Outline and Aphorism* (1907), which were the first attempts at a systematic introduction of his ideas to British readers – the latter, according to David Thatcher, as good as any written since.[25] The third book, *Consciousness, Animal, Human and Superman* (1907), the outcome of his lectures to theosophical groups in Manchester and Leeds, was an application of Nietzschean ideas to theosophical doctrine. In these works Orage developed ideas which he had experimented with in talks to the Leeds Arts Club and Theosophical Society. These elaborated the idea of the superman or beyondman as a practical programme of becoming, or transcendence over quotidian reality (something like Sartre's *depassement*). But Orage's view was that nothing less than the emergence or evolution of a new race was capable of steering the new society into the socialist millenium. Existing was nothing, becoming was everything, man was merely the bridge from animal to the superman. His programme simply put was for accelerating the process. If modern approaches to Nietzsche treat him as a French philosopher of the 1970s, it is tempting to have Orage cast him as a 1950s existentialist crossed with the occultist hero of a Victorian Romantic novel.

The most extensive treatment of Orage's interpretation of Nietzsche is still David Thatcher's chapter in his *Nietzsche in England, the Growth of a Reputation*, (1970), while Tom Gibbons' excellent *Rooms in the Darwin Hotel* (1973) includes a brief but illuminating section. Both agree that Orage's reading of Nietzsche is a mystical one which situates Nietzsche as a continuation of the occultist tradition. As Gibbons put it, 'he adapted Nietzsche's view to a predominantly Theosophical view of things, presenting him as a mystic who was no longer conscious of his own mysticism. No one who really understands Nietzsche', he tells us, 'will doubt that behind all his apparent materialism there was a thoroughly mystical view of the world'.[26] David Thatcher sees the central feature of Orage's reading as his emphasis on the role of human transcendence, which relates to mystical beliefs in the evolution of a higher type through achieved states of consciousness. Through mystically enhanced states man was capable of evolving the superman consciousness which would be as superior to man's as man's was to animals. But whereas the mystic's model was quietist, Nietzsche's was militant; his superman had a duty and a destiny to remodel the world.

To this mystical reading of Nietzsche Orage added a cultural critique which advanced Nietzsche as an antidote to the moral decadence of middle-class democracy. Like Ruskin and Morris, Orage was appalled by the absolute dominance of the marketplace over all areas of life and in particular the trivialization of art by commercial values. But, as we have seen, he was also dismayed by the suppression of individuality evidenced by socialist collectivism; for him, since it suppressed innate potential, equally a symptom of decadence as bourgeois philistinism.

The value of art and the aesthetic was thus another touchstone of his reading. Accordingly Orage, says Thatcher, saw the *Birth of Tragedy* as the key to Nietzsche's philosophy for here the essential value of art to social life and the tragic inevitability of authentic life was fully revealed. Art could save humanity and advance the evolution of superman. He endorsed Nietzsche's view of a romantically noble life in which the only authentic response was to struggle heroically, if necessarily, to the death for an unattainable ideal. Orage made creative use of the concepts of Dionysian and Appollonian found in the *Birth of Tragedy*, by attempting to prove through them that Nietzsche had a systematic philosophy. He related the Appollonian to the 'feminine principle' and the Schopenhauerian 'Will to Life' and the Dionysian with masculinity and the 'Will to Power'. Orage believed that the the decadence of bourgeois democracy was a direct result of the epochal predominance of the Appollonian. It was time historically to redress the balance through the Dionysian principle, in which the criticism and destruction of the old order could be achieved, and would be justified by the emergence of a new race of supermen – out of chaos would shine a dancing star.

Thatcher's description is extended by Tom Gibbons who locates Orage contradictorily in the post-Darwinian scientistic tradition of social evolution. The superman was to be an evolved development from man of a higher species who would possess new faculties but who was also the product of conscious intervention. Gibbons suggests that Orage's political purpose was the encouragement of Great Individuals as a new social élite ('I have Plato's guardians in my eye, Horatio'[27]), though as we shall see it contains its own discordances, namely, that an aristocratic élite is incompatible with a universal individualism, which of course would not tolerate subordination to such a hierarchy.

Gibbons also notes the evolutionary function of art to Orage's interpretation, which he calls 'art for evolution's sake'.[28] Its key element is the production of *ecstasis*, literally a standing outside of oneself, which, as 'a continuous state of visionary ecstasy' would be the characteristic mode of superman consciousness. The test of all art was whether it could produce this state in the beholder. 'Ecstasy as both cause and effect of all great Art' was central to all Orage's affirmative criticism, argued Gibbons. Art was in this sense the 'Enchantress' which was capable of stimulating visions and releasing *desire*. The artist would be coupled with the philosopher/critic whose role was to interpret these visions and desires to the process of becoming. Artists and philosophers were therefore to be uniquely important to the evolutionary process since they alone were capable of creating the new inspirational values. This might be seen as a familiar Romantic view, but Orage's reading of Nietzsche was to reverse the conventional roles. Now the philosopher rather than the artist was to become the standard bearer. The philosopher would create the ends and meanings while the artist's role would be to 'glorify and enamour them'.[29]

Some consideration of the texts themselves is necessary to qualify these general observations. In *Consciousness*, as the title implies, the key to the superman was indeed expanded consciousness, not just in degree but in kind. But Orage seems to waver about whether or not this is a humanist exercise: for while he begins by asserting that the superman is not just man made perfect but qualitatively different, later the superman becomes the fulfilment of man. Moreover, his assertion that in order to achieve superman consciousness, men must become more not less human seems to reveal some of the ontological uncertainty of his project.

The routes to this consciousness are similarly both recognizable – 'the great ways of Religion, Art and Love'[30] – and mysterious, the product of psychological exercises of transcendental meditation. He believed that the attainment of superman consciousness would be like awakening from sleep (as exemplified in Ibsen's play *When We Dead Awaken*) when ordinary consciousness would awaken to the permanently achieved condition of ecstasy. Superman consciousness would be to human consciousness what human consciousness was to animal, it would stand outside consciousness and observe it. The interiority of mind would thus be perceived phenomenally, by its own consciousness.[31] Superman consciousness was human consciousness folded upon itself. Thus by illuminating the notion of the superman through mystical practices, Orage's point was to suggest Nietzsche's own indebtedness to traditions of transcendentalism. As he says, 'The main problem of mystics of all ages has been the problem of how to develop superconsciousness, of how to become superman'[32] and Nietzsche was merely the most modern adept.

But the further aspect of Orage's reading was locating it in the context of post-Darwinian or Spencerian social evolution:

> As I have said already, the aim of the mystic was to develop in himself the powers and consciousness of superman. Only whereas in the outer world such development is by the slow means of natural evolution, in these (mystical) schools attempts are made to hasten the process by means of disciplines and trainings and methods.[33]

Associated with this was a downplaying of rationalism. Orage believed that the characteristic mode of the superman's powers would be intuitional rather than rational. Rationalism was merely a hiccup of the divided sensibility formed when human consciousness evolved from the animal. Superman consciousness would be manifested in 'swift winged judgement' and augmented imagination or 'swift winged process of deduction and induction'. This would be a renewed unity of instinctual life characteristic of animals but resolved at a higher stage, where the labouring powers of reason which characterize ordinary human activity would be liberated by the free passage or 'winged progression' of instinct through the mind. This would be, nostalgically, a return to a state of pre-lapsarian animal grace from which 'knowing' man had fallen, but including the benefits of rational thought.

The possessors of these extraordinary powers would perforce have a social role, which following Annie Besant[34] and orthodox theosophical teaching, rather than Nietzsche, Orage saw as the pastoral one of 'Shepherd of Men':

> In other words superman shepherds the minds of men. Thinking of the tradition of what are called Culture Heroes, those great beneficent heroic figures that have stood apparently around the cradles of every infant people, the suggestion irresistibly occurs that they were supermen. Certainly the altitude at which they must have stood above the

> contemporary humans, the influence they exerted apparently with so little effort, and the genius of their inventions, all point to a difference of kind between such beings and men.[35]

This emphasis on the pastoral role of the superman and of the apparently literal belief in the mysterious 'Culture Heroes' may have been designed to comfort his theosophical reader, who may well have been disconcerted by the leonine destroyers of his other texts. Thus while in *Consciousness* Orage had stressed the pastoral and human side of superman, *Nietzsche in Outline and Aphorism* stresses the destructive and the inhuman.

Here the tone is militant and catastrophist. No single race or nation of men, he claims, has found itself adequate for the necessary global tasks of regeneration; the division of men into creeds and castes has led only to petty squabbling over cosmically insignificant differences. Therefore it was urgent that some community stirred itself for 'the remote conquest of the globe'. Nietzsche's intention had been to stir up some nation for this historic task, to breed a new race for the future life of the planet. Even then such a race would not themselves be the supermen but only their necessary pre-condition.

Orage outlined Nietzsche's three phases of human existence as the camel, the lion and the child. The European ideal at the moment was that of the camel, the preserver the bearer of responsibility and the duty of service. Slow, bureaucratic, reliable but ultimately a block on imagination and creativity the camel was ripe for metamorphosis. The urgent social task was to destroy this ideal through the generation of the lion. The lion would destroy the camel. As the destroyer of the preserver, it repudiated responsibilities in ecstatic egoism. It was now necessary, said Orage, to 'trample on duties, refuse services, dismiss responsibility and aspire to a new mastery'. While the watchword of the camel was 'others', for the lion it was to be 'ourselves'. Nietzsche, he said, saw himself as one of the 'laughing lions', who were 'adventurous iconoclasts, mockers, destroyers; and round them will fall the ideals of duty and service'.[36] Out of this holocaust would come the era of the child who now in Orage's text appears recognizably the superman of his book *Consciousness*: 'the child in whom wisdom is instinctive', the resolution of instinctual life at a higher level. Orage comments that only students of mystical psychology could even conceive of this final metamorphosis and in this portrait of Zarathustra even Nietzsche had failed.[37]

Orage treats superman as the great achievement of Nietzsche's philosophy, the end to which it all led, and the rest of Nietzsche's writing as providing the grounding (Nietzsche's *grund*) for the concept. *Nietzsche in Outline and Aphorism* is divided into sections headed Philosophy, Life, Man and Woman, Art, Morality, Good and Evil, Willing Valuing and Creating, Superman and New Commandments where all the preconditions for superman are discussed. Nietzsche's first book, *The Birth of Tragedy*, he notes, contained his tragic conception of the world, while his last, *Thus Spake Zarathustra*, contained his positive antidote. Orage considered that their philosophical underpinning was of a wholly relativistic nature. It opposed absolutist ideas in all areas, saying that the world was perpetual flux and that the process of becoming alone was real. Nietzsche's philosophical precurser was Schopenhauer, whose foregrounding of the Will as the primary agency of authentic life was Nietzsche's starting point. But Nietzsche felt that the 'Will to Life' only partially described human life and that merely existing could never be authentic; only the 'Will to Power' could satisfy this criterion. Thus Nietzsche constructed in Orage's view a dualistic system in which Schopenhauer's Will to Life was posed as the ground from which the Will to Power sprung. As we have already noted, Orage related the Will to Life to the Appollonian or feminine principle which was both ground and other to the Dionysian or masculine principle of Will to Power.

In the section on 'Men and Women' Orage elaborates this duality further. The truly male is characterized not by violent power over others but power over himself and a self respect manifested in the use of that power. Men were the warrior type who would be the 'experimenting fringe and advance guard of the world-will'.[38] Women, on the other hand, were the ground and condition of men, embodying idealism and the principle of conservation. Her meaning and purpose was man. There was no question of subordination, he protested, perhaps too much, since the whole woman would quite naturally assume a place of means to his means and would willingly sacrifice to him who sacrifices himself (apparently a principle of which he had been unable to convince Jean, since by the time of the book's publication they were separated). Marriage had to be revalued as an institution since its only authentic function now was the production of the superior type. But what complicated the issue was that sexuality was itself still unresolved since the differentiation of the sexes was far from complete and nobody was wholly male or female. Yet, not much equivocation is shown in his choice of aphorisms to accompany the chapter: 'Thou goest to women?' he quotes Nietzsche, 'Remember thy whip!'[39]

If the relationship of the sexes was to be relatively functional then true romance was found only in art. Art was the great seductress of the life-will in which becoming could only be maintained by desire but, equally, art could as easily be the seducer to death. 'Casting the magic glamour of attraction over things, the artist may as easily endow with the power of evoking desire things which lie in the past stages of becoming as things which lie in the future stages of becoming'.[40] So art could be both ascendant and decadent and could present oases or only mirages to humanity. It was the nature of the artist which determined which quality his art should have. If his nature was superabundant and his spirit was active rather than reactive then all was well. Otherwise, only decadence would result. The central test of art as we have seen was 'ecstasy' which had to be both the cause and effect of Great Art. Orage quoted Nietzsche's aphorism 'Aesthetics is nothing but applied Physiology'.[41]

While art had a morality, morality itself was only something for the poor in spirit. The characteristic of the richly endowed man was, alternatively, the classical quality of virtue. The problem of right behaviour was bedevilled by an idealistic moral code which did not conform to practice. Right behaviour should be the opposite, ideals should conform to practice. True morality was inherent in man's nature:

> For if Nietzsche proposed to abolish Morality in the sense of an external formulated code, he never dreamed that by so doing he would not enable real morality, the laws whereby an individual lives, as truly as an acorn grows by the laws of oaks, to show itself, and take the place of the pretender and tyrant. To transcend Morality was, for Nietzsche, to substitute Virtue and a man's own inherent nature for conformity and hypocrisy.[42]

From this relativist standpoint good and evil were necessarily redundant and to be transcended. Since all moral judgements were only statements of approval or disapproval, there could be no question of passing absolute judgement on another's actions. Only those favoured individuals who could go beyond good and evil were of use to society, which was indeed saved by its rebels who were responsible to nothing but their own uniqueness. The superabundant vitality of this 'Aristocracy' was its own morality as had been manifest in many of the great men of the past. Jesus was a paramount example, but the triumph of Christianity, in which his laws were codified, had been the defeat of Jesus. Through it the superior virtue of life-giving had been subordinated to life-saving and the image of the suffering Christ had triumphed over the joyful Christ. This effect of the successful slave revolt had become the essence of slave morality where the morality of the many had succeeded in imposing itself on the virtue of the few:

> So successful had been the slave revolt that even now slave values dominate; even now the rich in spirit feel bound to pretend that they too are poor in spirit; even now individuals are ashamed of their individuality and of all that makes them different, unique. Upon that precious surplus of will, upon which depends the everlasting renewal of life, has been placed the ban of sin and shame.[43]

In 'Willing, Valuing and Creating' Orage returns to the role of artists, since they were among the few to constitute the true aristocracy. Since the world is only the raw material or 'ground' of existence and only humans value the world, its values can only be human values. The source of value is the promise of power, because things are only valued by men in proportion as they promise power. The role of the artist had been to give new significance to things and create new values where none existed before. But as we have seen, in Nietzsche's universe as in Plato's, the artist alone can no longer be trusted with this task. Since the artist had himself frequently become too delighted by society's decadence, his work had to be tested by the philosopher who was to hear the artist's cries and distinguish the sighting of new continents from the merely siren's songs. Art was too dangerous to be left to artists and had to be policed by philosophers, so tightly shackled are the libertarian and the totalitarian.

But in the brave new world, the roles were to be reversed: the philosophers were to assume the leadership in the creation of value. Now it would be they who advanced new meanings and values and the artists who would have to discriminate between philosophical ideas which were truly great, which they would glorify, and the merely popular ones which they would ignore. 'Whoever inspires humanity with a new need' says Orage 'lengthens the duration of the life of the race'.[44]

The key to creating new needs, or new objects of desire, was understanding the economy of human instincts. Instinctual life had to be released from civilization's enfeebling quarantine: 'The "civilized" man is either feeble or unhappy, either, that is, so poorly vitalised as to have no other needs than a civic corporation can satisfy, or so richly endowed as to be dimly aware of frustrated and thwarted longings in himself'.[45] Since will was derived from instincts, only when all instincts moved in the same direction, could there be a strong will. Thus the philosopher's task was to create needs which, made glamorous by the artist, would unleash instinctual desire. These desires would, of course, be refused by civilization and in the ensuing struggle the will would be tested and strengthened or the hero would be tragically destroyed. The triumph, or the tragedy, of the strongest would itself create new standards for the rest to emulate and humanity would find itself another evolutionary step along its path to the superman.

This was Orage's conclusion, when in 1907, he found himself seated behind a roll-top desk in a stuffy room in Cursitor Street, without a wife, a home or any visible means of support, just an ailing Christian Socialist journal he and Jackson had purchased with £1,000 of other people's money. He certainly was playing the part. He had sloughed off his Leeds skin and abandoned the Arts Club to its place in the heavens, but we must now see what kind of dancing star it was.

Notes

1. Holbrook Jackson, A. R. Orage; Personal Recollections, in *The Windmill*, Heinemann house magazine, London, 1948, p.41.
2. Holbrook Jackson, *George Bernard Shaw*, Grant Richards, London, 1907, pp. 9–10.
3. Holbrook Jackson, 'Personal Recollections', p. 42.
4. Holbrook Jackson, 'The Truth About Nietzsche', *T.P.'s Weekly*, 31 October 1914, p. 475.
5. Leeds School Board Education Committee, Minute Book 16, p. 344, West Yorkshire Archives, Sheepscar, Leeds.
6. Possibly his 'Alpha Centre'.
7. J. C. Kenworthy, *The Anatomy of Misery*, 2nd ed., with an Introduction by Count Leo Tolstoy, J. C. Kenworthy, London, 1900. Tolstoy himself was most impressed with it and had written in the introduction, 'Any one who reads this book with unprejudiced mind and sincere desire to find answers to the problems which confront people of our times, will find those answers and will arrive at a clear understanding of those things which most people imagine to be difficult and abstruse.' A review notice pasted inside the pamphlet claimed that it was the first time Ruskin had been reduced to a system.
8. Holbrook Jackson, 'Personal Recollections', p.43.
9. Holbrook Jackson, obituary letter to *New English Weekly*, 15 November 1934, p.114.
10. M.D. Eder, letter to *New English Weekly*, 15 November 1934, p.110.
11. Mairet, p.18. Holbrook Jackson says that Orage and Jean reviewed *Human Personality* for the *Theosophical Review* under the intitials A.J.C. and that the pamphlet was in fact their own work.
12. Millie Price, p 120. Millie recalled to that 'Unquenchable love still floundered in my own psychology, but how to make it "faithful in service" I did not know. I offered Orage the service of my mind but was too often aware the service of my body would have given him greater satisfaction' (p.120).
13. Northern Federation Theosophical Society Minute Books 1893–1900, Harrogate TS, Alexandra Road, Harrogate, entries for those months.
14. Holbrook Jackson, 'Personal Recollections', p.43.
15. 'The Holbrook Jackson Library', A Memorial Catalogue with an appreciation by Sir Frances Meynell, Catalogue 119, Elkin Matthews Ltd, Bishops Stortford, 1951, p.66. Jackson possessed both this proof and Orage's draft chapter, which were sold off at auction to private buyers as well as a long essay called 'The Future of Humanity' and three long poems called 'Love's Rainbow' inspired by George Meredith's *Love in a Valley*.
16. Ibid., p.60, of twenty-four and nineteen pages each dated 1902.
17. Holbrook Jackson, *Bernard Shaw*, pp.12–13.
18. Millie Price, p.111.
19. Holbrook Jackson, 'Personal Recollections', p.46.

20. Francis Meynell, 'An Appreciation' in 'The Holbrook Jackson Library', A Memorial Catalogue, No. 119, Elkin Matthews, Bishop Stortford, 1951.
21. Holbrook Jackson, *The Rise and Fall of Nineteenth Century Idealism*, Citadel, New York, 1969, p. 280. First published as *Dreamers of Dreams.*
22. Holbrook Jackson, 'Personal Recollections', p.48.
23. Holbrook Jackson, *The Eighteen Nineties*, Pelican, London, 1939, p.127. First published in 1913 this book is still the standard work on the 1890s and was republished by Harvester in 1976.
24. Ibid.
25. David Thatcher, *Nietzsche in England, the Growth of Reputation*, University of Toronto Press, 1970, p.232: 'it is no skeleton exposition which reduces ideas to the level of superficiality but a reliable handbook of masterly compression'.
26. Tom Gibbons, *Rooms in the Darwin Hotel*, Nedlands, 1973, p.106.
27. Ibid., p.109.
28. Ibid., p.110.
29. Ibid., p.112.
30. Alfred Orage, *Consciousness, Animal, Human and Superman*, Theosophical Publishing Society, London, 1907, p.85.
31. This also appears incoherent. Significantly, a similar incoherence in the Edmund Husserl's concept of the transcendent ego was later addressed in Sartre's *Transcedence of the Ego.*
32. Alfred Orage, *Consciousness, Animal, Human and Superman*, Theosophical Publishing Society, London and Benares, 1907, p.72.
33. Orage, *Consciousness*, p.84.
34. In her exposition of theosophical doctrine she had written of the *chela* who attains permanent nirvanic consciousness 'But has earth lost her child, is humanity bereft of her triumphant son? Nay! He has come forth from the bosom of light . . . But now his face is turned to earth, His eyes beam with divinest compassion on the wandering sons of men, His bretheren after the flesh; He cannot leave them comfortless, scattered as sheep without a shepherd. Clothed in the majesty of a mighty renunciation, glorious with the strength of perfect wisdom and "the power of an endless life", he returns to earth to bless and guide humanity.' *The Ancient Wisdom*, Theosophical Publishing Society, London, 1897, pp. 309–310.
35. Orage, *Consciousness*, p.79.
36. Alfred Orage, *Nietzsche in Outline and Aphorism*, Foulis, London and Edinburgh, 1907, p.157.
37. Ibid., p.146–158.
38. Ibid., p.49.
39. Ibid., p.54.
40. Ibid., p.60.
41. Ibid., p.69.
42. Ibid., p.90.
43. Ibid., p.111.
44. Ibid., p.130.
45. Ibid., p.131.

PART TWO
1903–1911: Reducing Leeds to Nietzscheism

CHAPTER THREE

Foundations 1903–1904; the Superman, the Civic and the Guilds

They found rooms on the first floor of the Leeds Permanent Building Society's headquarters in the centre of town. It stood on the corner of Park Lane, now the Headrow, and Calverley Street, obscuring the front entrance of the public library. It was separated from the town hall by Calverley Street and Queen Victoria Square, a popular public meeting place. A statue of the seated Queen Victoria, who had opened Broderick's Town Hall in 1859, sternly dominated the open space flanked by idealized statues of half-clothed muscular proletarians representing Industry, but modestly out of her eyeline. Close by was Bean's bookshop.

Buried in an inside page (above and separated by a thin black line from a macabre story headed 'Could Have Taken Poison – Leeds Woman's Strange Story') under the title 'New Arts Club for Leeds – Opening of Head-Quarters' the *Leeds and Yorkshire Mercury* of 10 October 1903 quietly announced the club's emergence in a tongue-in-cheek report:

> A new institution which should strongly appeal to those for whom it is intended has been established in Leeds under the title of the Leeds Arts Club. The object of the club is to provide a suitable meeting ground for the numerous groups and individuals interested in literature art and philosophy in its various forms, who are to be found scattered about the city. Club chambers have been secured in Victoria Buildings 18 Park Lane; and the premises which are centrally situated and in close proximity to the Public Library have been tastefully decorated and furnished by competent artists. Excellent accommodation is provided and while one room has been reserved as a reading and smoke room, open to the members of the club daily from 10am. to 10pm., another has been provided for the meetings of small societies, committees, &c., many of which have hitherto wandered from place to place unable to find suitable head-quarters of a permanent character.
>
> The club, which was formally inaugurated on Saturday evening last, (10 October 1903) starts with a membership numbering about forty of both sexes: and it is expected that the number will be considerably

> increased as the establishment of this common meeting ground for people of similar tastes becomes more generally known.

The reporter's joke, here, that the club's rooms were over the offices of the Leeds *Permanent* Building Society, no doubt tickled the membership as would his reference to the tasteful decoration by competent artists. They were in fact Jean Orage and Albert Waddington who had distempered the rooms and stencilled dadoes on the walls, in one room of a rose pattern and in the other of black and white chequer pattern. According to Millie Price these gave 'a lightness and gaiety to rooms sadly under the aegis of late Victorian decorative design.'[1] She and several others were roped in also to paint the cheap secondhand furniture they had bought. It was comfortable and relaxed, a refuge for those who simply wanted to escape grimy Leeds for a quiet read and a Camelot for Orage who would sit smoking his pipe leading discussions on philosophy and psychology amongst his knight errantry.

An account of the early days of the Club comes from Mary Gawthorpe who joined in the following year, 1904. She too was a schoolteacher, a voluble and ebullient suffragette who because she was attractive and small was inevitably described in newspaper reports of her activities as 'petite'. She became national secretary of the Womans Social and Political Union in 1907, the year after she was arrested and imprisoned in Holloway along with Mrs Pethwick-Lawrence and others for invading the House of Commons. She was also a founder and co-editor with Dora Marsden, 1911–1912, of the journal *The Freewoman*. (*The Freewoman* evolved into *The New Freewoman* and then, under Harriet Shaw Weaver, *The Egoist* a metamorphosis which reveals important links between feminism, Nietzscheism and Anglo-American modernism.) Mary Gawthorpe was a New Woman for whom the Club, as we have seen, offered the model for a free and creative way of life. A chapter in her autobiography[2] graphically revealed its atmosphere in the early years.

She and her fiancee, T. B. Garrs, a compositor on the *Yorkshire Post*, whom she always refers to as FL ('First Love') joined the Club in 1904. The entrance fee of 10s.6d would have represented something like one-third of her weekly wage (since women teachers were paid less than men and perhaps equivalent of £50 at today's prices). Membership was strictly by election and in their case their sponsor was a *Yorkshire Post* sub-editor. The club rooms, she mentions, also housed two of Orage and Jackson's other concerns, the Fabian Society and the Leeds Theosophical Lodge and membership of all three groups was not uncommon. Most nights there were meetings and the combined membership paid the rent. The books in the library reflected all three groups, while one wall housed only theosophical literature and another held philosophical, psychological and economic reading including the work of Wells and Shaw. All were available to any member who simply wanted to drop by and read. Mary Gawthorpe remembers being particularly gripped by Annie Besant's work on 'Karma' which seems to have been her road to Damascus, giving her the strange experience of having been read herself while in the act of reading.

It was at the Club that she first had the courage to speak in public, gently urged on by Orage. While formal debating was not the Club's style, making an art of the interplay of opinion and conversation was strongly encouraged. She also came into contact with contemporary art and artists for the first time in the intimacy of the Club rooms, an experience that was altogether different from the gloomy trudge round the chocolate box monsters hung on the walls of the art gallery across the road. It brought, she said, 'a new art reality into consciousness'. She was struck by the brilliance of the group, not only by Orage, though he was plainly charismatic, but for example by Jean who could pursue him with relentless logic in discussion while yet capable in the calm of her home of exquisite embroidery. The group she said 'had the unmistakable quality of being mature mentally'.

While for Mary Gawthorpe, the Club was a relief from political activism and an opportunity for cultural education not otherwise available, it was equally clear that what Orage, Jackson and their colleagues had in mind was an active engagement with the life of the town rather than simply the passive cultivation or contemplation of the arts. This was signalled in the Club's manifesto which appeared on the inside of its printed programmes:

> The Object of the Leeds Arts Club is to affirm the mutual dependence of Art and Ideas. The separation of beauty from use or use from beauty is in the long run disastrous to both; and only their union in a single clear purpose can restore to us the value of either. To this end it is necessary that real and enduring standards should be created anew, as well in the public as in the individual mind, by means of which art and ideas may be judged each in their intimate bearing on life.

The emphasis here is on the reform of taste in private and public life but from 1910 the statement was toughened up and emphasized the political imperative to reform.

> The Leeds Arts Club affirms that everyone in every place owes it to himself to make that place better and more beautiful. The divorce of Beauty from Life is disastrous; the existence of anything that does not add to beauty and truth is a stumbling block to the community. The Club values no enthusiasm for either Art or Philosophy which does not consciously react upon the ugliness, stupidity and chaos of modern civilisation.

Holbrook Jackson later confessed that the ostensible but not admitted aim of the Club was 'to reduce Leeds to Nietzscheism!'. The idea of a vitalized urban industrial culture was at the heart of the club's project and for this reason seems to have attracted people to its cause who might have been repelled by a straightforward party political platform. The programme itself was an example of good taste. Designed by Jean Orage, it featured on its cover a stylized aesthetic movement peacock trailing its tail with its head framed by the loop of a Tau cross. A grapevine motif, signifying Dionysius, borders the peacock's body in a rectangular design. An elegantly scripted typeface announced a syllabus of lectures, meetings and groups, the object of the Club and the committee of management.

Published twice yearly in January and September, the programme operated on a termly basis offering regular Saturday afternoon lectures, Friday night discussion groups and occasional weekly meetings with speakers like G. B. Shaw, G. K. Chesterton, W. B. Yeats, Cobden-Sanderson, Hilaire Belloc, Edward Carpenter and other nationally known figures. There were to be exhibitions of architecture, painting, sculpture, craft work and photography, musical recitals and demonstrations. In addition there were literary, sketching and musical groups for members and a book club and library.

The foremost of the Club's activities were the Saturday afternoon meetings, where there would be a speaker and discussion of the issues raised by his or her talk. Critical responses were encouraged and the talks were intended to be controversial. The first of these sessions was given by Orage on the subject of 'Friedrich Nietzsche' on the evening of Saturday 7 November 1903. The audience was apparently scandalized but this in part seems to have been the intention. The Club's style was distinctly *épater le bourgeois* and it was in Mairet's words 'a sensational success . . . The local bourgeoisie were flabbergasted when the shocking views of such as Nietzsche, Ibsen and Shaw were acclaimed in their midst by this heterodox seminary, and advocated with a mixture of aestheticism, moral earnestness and egoistic flippancy.'[3]

So began the Club's twenty-year career and though it went through a number of incarnations it was never less than an invigorating hub of intellectual and artistic speculation. Central to this initial phase was the pursuit of Nietzschean theory of the superman or beyondman of which Orage was the key interpreter. Both Jackson and Waddington also contributed to this strand but their key roles were to elaborate related themes. For Jackson this was the role of Shaw's drama and political philosophy, while Waddington lectured on medieval guilds and 'aristocratic socialism'. So while each followed their own interests they articulated the cultural/political interrelationships between them. Within three years it crystallized into a distinct programme of cultural politics which Orage articulated in his 'Politics for Craftsmen' in 1907 and subsequently in his 'Towards Socialism' articles in the *New Age*.

When the opening session of talks began Orage and Jackson assiduously wrote reports of the lectures and sent them to the *Yorkshire Post* and *Leeds Mercury* who published them often in their entirety. Surprisingly, Orage's first contribution was not reported, so what he said is a matter of speculation. It will have been a celebration of potential individual creativity freed from the straightjacket of Victorian 'Christian' moralism; the need for evolving a higher order of man through expanded consciousness and the guide given by Nietzsche's *Thus Spake Zarathustra* to the new life. The only other speakers were Jackson and Waddington who both talked on their major themes.

The first of these, Albert Waddington, lectured on 'Medieval Craft Guilds' the following Saturday, 14 November. Unlike Orage's talk, this was reported in the *Leeds and Yorkshire Mercury*. It introduced a second key platform: the relevance of the medieval guild system to current social problems. Waddington's argument was that in the modern age industry suffered from an absolute divorce from beauty. Historically there were dark ages when philosophy, art and religion had become separated from industry and craftsmanship, but the last period of unity had been the fourteenth century. There was an element in this culture necessary to our mental evolution and crucial for a renaissance of beautiful industry. Beauty, he believed, betrayed the existence of laws of nature which the sense organs perceived before the intellect. The function of work therefore was to train the senses to perceive and to stimulate the intellect to grasp these deeper laws. The greatest evidence that an artist had found the deeper laws of his craft was in the beauty of his work. Likewise, the greatest evidence that commercialism was unnatural was in its ugliness. By comparison with the intelligent and pleasing work of the fourteenth century most nineteenth-century work was ugly and vulgar because the medieval artist began with *use* whereas the modern man begins with *money*. In the symbolism of eternal ideas represented in medieval churches, the craftsmen had reached their zenith, for the true craftsman was an artist and the true artist a philosopher.

Waddington then developed his political point. After the fall of Rome the tradition of classic art had been kept alive by the early church, the schools of architectural craftsmen and the semi-mystic societies. Eventually in England after a long struggle with the feudal lords and the merchant monopolists the crafts had federated themselves and produced regulations for training both master and prentice. Thus no man could be a master until he knew his craft and could not employ more workers than he could train and supervise. Competition, bad work and under selling were penalized with the result that there were fewer middlemen, more regular employment and less of either poverty or riches.

The present demise of the crafts was due to monopolies in land, machinery and capital and only when these had run their course could industry shake off its money-masters and gain instead craft-masters. He then expressed the radically divergent view that 'the teachings of the guilds ancient and modern agree with Ruskin and William Morris that the Socialism which brings beautiful industry will not be that of collectivism, but a *Socialism of aristocracy in the Platonic sense* – the government of master of their craft. Collectivism can only prepare the way for this deeper Socialism.'[4] This was a new note and one which was to be central to the tone and tenor of the Club's beliefs, representing a significant attempt to reconcile the aristocratic politics of Nietzsche with the socialism of the arts and crafts movement through a semi-mystical Platonism.

This anti-democratic stress in Waddington's talk was continued three weeks later, on Saturday 5 December, by Holbrook Jackson who delivered his first talk on George Bernard Shaw. He argued that while believing in collectivism Shaw was by no means a democrat and that he saw the proper function of collectivism as being able to organize society for 'the fuller development of individuality and a broader and more joyous social life'.[5] Democracy was 'the last refuge of cheap misgovernment'.

Shaw was the 'artist-philosopher' of modern ideas whose plays were antagonistic criticisms of modern life in the form of philosophic parables. This attitude lay behind his criticism of Shakespeare whom he regarded as now old-fashioned, though superb critic of his own age, and it would be pointless to imitate him. Unlike Shakespeare's epoch which he regarded as the high point of medievalism, modern capitalism is 'little but a haphazard and wasteful scramble for wealth'. In advocating an aristocratic individualism in opposition to modern trends the individual might recognize they had a mighty purpose to fulfil namely 'that of being a force of Nature instead of feverish little clod of ailments and grievances, complaining that the world will not devote itself to making you happy'.[6]

The combined effect of these introductory talks was to introduce a radically new cultural politics which must have been not a little bewildering to many in the audience. To advocate socialism yet scorn collectivism, to talk about a natural aristocracy and belittle democracy while fulminating over modern capitalism was profoundly disorientating. Waddington's talk on the medieval guilds may also have raised eyebrows, for although the ideas of John Ruskin were widely appreciated in the West Riding (through, for example, the widely published *Fors Clavigera*) what was new was the idea that guilds could be adapted to modern industrial organization. Jackson's talk also foregrounded the importance of the modern drama as a vehicle of social reform and this was to have one of the most long-term effects on the Club. It was through this idea that play-writing and production became important activities, leading to the Club's sponsoring a Playgoers Society in 1907 for the promotion of drama and opera and eventually in 1925 Leeds Civic Playhouse. But what was most significant was that inscribed in the self-consciously modernizing aspect of the Club's activities was medievalism.

As if to heighten this contradiction the first of the Club's celebrated exhibitions was of modern hand-printed books. This was a product of Jackson's passion for books and represented a considerable coup. The exhibition opened on 27 November in the Club rooms in Park Lane and comprised books from most of the modern hand presses including Morris's Kelmscott Press, Cobden-Sanderson's Dove Press, the Vale Press, the Pissaro's Eragny Press, the Caradoc Press and Yeats's Dundrum Press. The report mentions that from the Kelmscott Press came an edition of Morris's *The Well at the World's End* with illustrations by Burne-Jones and decorations by Morris himself.[7] Jackson had also written to Elizabeth Yeats's Dun Emer Press but received the reply that she could not send their second book, *Nuts of Knowledge*, because it had not yet been bound.[8] The exhibition was a great success and was extended at the wish of the Lady Mayoress herself, Mrs Currer-Briggs. The most appreciated books were from the Kelmscott Press which displayed the 'purity and strength of Morris's virile style' and in particular the Doves's Bible in the typographic style Cobden-Sanderson had developed from Morris.

By Christmas 1903 the Club had already established itself as a significant cultural intervention, claiming the attention of all who were concerned about the social consequences of the neglect of art and displaying the finer products of the new craft movement.

Spring 1904

For the Spring session the Club offered a series of three lectures by Orage on Nietzsche's 'Beyond Man' or superman, thus extending the theoretical study of Nietzsche, while Jackson gave two talks on citizenship and democracy. Waddington appears once, in a talk in relation to an exhibition held in the Club rooms on domestic architecture. Lectures on Heine, Browning, Pater and Victorian drama were given by other club members establishing a literary and European dimension. The first guest speaker was Orage's early mentor, Edward Carpenter.

The first of Orage's talks on the superman took place on Saturday 6 February to a full-house. Interestingly, he denied that Nietzsche had originated the idea since it could be found in all utopian thinkers or, as he put it, 'every thinker in the past who had projected human virtues upon the magic screen of futurity.'[9] However, Nietzsche had popularized the notion for the time in a way no one had before. Orage then claimed that humanity would, in its superhuman condition, consist of three types: philosophers, artists and saints, quoting a passage from Nietzsche in support. He then read from Plato a description of the perfect philosopher, from the Japanese artist Hokusai on the perfect artist, but for the saint, he simply referred his audience to the world's scriptures.

He returned to the theme on Saturday 12 March with a lecture on Zarathustra, who, he said, would be difficult to cast as any of the types already described. Nietzsche had regarded himself as a forerunner of the Beyondman and therefore was not concerned so much with the types as *the* type. Also he regarded most of his work as the necessary destructive preparations for the new humanity rather than its positive outcome. Orage, however, advanced a portrait of the new man 'radiantly healthy, of proportions like the Appollo Belvedere, with a purified and perfected mind, with a conscious will, and a definite goal in life set for himself.'[10] He would appear as a god to ordinary mortals and live in a state of transcendent joy beyond pleasure and pain and beyond good and evil. Indeed such a man would not be slave to pleasure or pain but would need to experience all equally. But there were obstacles to attaining this state of grace, the first of which was overcoming those traditional and conventional modes of thought slave morality (pleasure and pain) and herd morality (social utility). His master proposition was that 'freedom is the will to be responsible for oneself'. Orage concluded that despite his melodramatic emphasis and staginess, Nietzsche was nevertheless not far in spirit from the great religious teachers of the world.

While Orage orbited the outer reaches of German romanticism, Holbrook Jackson concentrated on the material tasks of modern democracy in two talks, the first of which was on 27 February, the 'Possibilities of Citizenship'. This talk launched the opening shots of a campaign to socialize municipal government and reform Leeds itself. Jackson argued that the great need of modern cities was a fuller and more vital social life. Cities he said are the symbols of the collective ideas of those who live in them and until the ideas of citizens become more enlightened 'our cities will be no more than the anti-social accumulations of grimy brick and mortar which they are today.'[11] The political means of transformation were actually at hand in the shape of local governing bodies and there was ample unworked power in municipal machinery to change the cities from ugliness to beauty. Social affairs should recognize the interdependence, as in tribal societies, of all the members of a community and municipal life should understand and obey the laws of good neighbourliness. Citizens needed not so much more votes and acts of Parliament but knowledge of how to use the powers they already possessed.

The municipality, he continued, was in effect a commune which should be administered collectively. Great strides had been made in recent years over the public control of gas, water, electricity, tramways and the markets and the success of these services suggested new areas for public enterprise which would have untold benefits for its citizens. The first of these should be control of working-class housing and he criticized the practice of heavily compensating landlords of condemned properties. Land laws would have to be reformed in order to find a just basis for taxation and the poor laws reformed. The degrading workhouse system should be abolished in favour of municipal industrial colonies 'where the backwash of our population might be exploited to rate-relieving ends rather than kept at great expense in the practice of generally wasteful labour.'[12] Jackson ended by quoting Walt Whitman: 'I will make inseparable cities with their arms about each others necks by the love of comrades'. By this comradeship the basis for greater individual growth should be laid, but it depended on the intelligent use of the municipal institutions by citizens who were aware that it was they who were the custodians of the life of the city.

This was a finely nuanced Fabian piece emphasizing the centrality of the term 'citizenship' which was to become a watchword in the Club's discussions. Significantly, whether or not he was a member of the Club is not certain, but certainly some of his close friends like Tom Heron were. The future deputy leader of the Labour Party, Arthur Greenwood, used the term as the title of a talk he gave to the TS branch in Leeds some years later. 'Citizenship' was to be a powerful rhetorical interpellation in the construction of Labour politics in the rising decades of the century.

His second lecture on the theme was given on 7 May with Orage in the chair. He introduced the title of his talk 'Democracy and the Individual' by denying the popular interpretation of democracy as the will of the majority, substituting instead the tolerance of individuality. The popular conception, he said, only reflected the decadence of the concept in implying abject subservience and tyranny.[13] Democracy was only important in so far as it tended to promote individual growth and the key to democracy was the notion of the union of individuals. He traced the historical development of 'union' from primitive societies to modern civilization and argued that it was a natural model. Life itself, after all, was the unity of atoms and death its disintegration for the purpose of newer and stronger combinations. Both religious aspiration and social consciousness made for unity, while love of god was only a higher phase of the love of man and fellowship (Morris's use). Democracy was merely the political application of this idea to social affairs and had nothing to do with equality 'save in the respect that there was an essential quality of kinship in all men, and its business as a legislative institution was to organise society in such a manner as to give the greatest opportunity for fellowship.'[14] (This marks an interesting gloss on the term which replaces its merely abstract quality of equality with the more fertile and full notion of fellowship.)

The failures of democracy, he continued, were not due to the idea itself but to the lack of development of the individuals who would in the end benefit from the intensified social life. Social affairs would change and progress but not without difficulty. Life depended on this change but each step was into the dark. Fellowship demanded more of its followers than its opposite since it was easier to slay one's brother than to tolerate and understand him. Tolerance and understanding were necessary not merely from altruism but because without them there could be no individuality. Men, he said, could not give themselves too freely because in so doing they realized individual life as one and indivisible with all things 'and that love comes to his own by union'. Democracy thus offered newer and more splendid possibilities of life.

This was the last lecture of the session and a lively discussion followed. One interlocutor suggested that Jackson's idea of democracy was coincident with the idea of a natural *aristocracy*, to which apparently he did not demur. Thus again it was a subtle and nuanced interpretation of a political concept which cannot simply be dismissed as anti-democratic so much as non-egalitarian, but even here not in opposition to comradeship but to foster it. It was hostile neither to individualism, because that was the point of the system, nor to collectivisim, since fellowship was what promoted this end. Rather it advocated a kind of social-individualism in which tolerance and understanding were the highest of values. There was little here to which socialists or liberals could object and by emphasis on tolerance and understanding little for the Christian to oppose.

This series of lectures constituted the core of the programme. They were supplemented by four lectures on literature, to which we shall come shortly, but also by the appearance of the Club's first guest speaker, Edward Carpenter, on the esoteric theme of 'Deities and Devils in the Light of Race Memory'. Carpenter was no stranger to Leeds, since he had been friendly with Tom Maguire and Isabella Ford since the earliest days of the Socialist movement in the 1880s and even before, when as a member of the Oxford University Delegacy, he lectured on astronomy in the city. As we have seen, Orage had consulted with him over his long poem 'Towards Democracy' for use in his Bookish Causerie in 1896 and friendship had developed from then. As an advocate of the New Life, Carpenter was also an established and influential figure by this time, having published *Civilisation its Cause and Cure* in 1889, *From Adam's Peak to Elephanta* in 1892 and his influential *Love's Coming of Age* in 1896,[15] as well as the four parts of *Towards Democracy* by 1902.

'Deities and Devils' took his audience through 'a resumé of the evolutionary steps in the production of those beneficent and munificent figures which dwell not in the ordinary consciousness but in the deeper or racial consciousness.'[16] At the back of our eyes as it were, 'are stored in the profound depths of the race (of which each individual is but a momentary point) the remote past of the world; and through our eyes look the eyes of dead ancestors'. Thus we see not only the bare objects of our gaze but we are also dimly aware of other effects. These effects form the halo or *glamour* in which objects appear and are basis for both deities and devils. This he named the racial memory, and was identical, he thought, with the *anamnesis* of Plato.

Another fragment of detail about this talk, or another of Carpenter's from the same time, comes from the unpublished autobiography of a schoolteacher called Marjorie Ingle. Though not a member of the Club she had been taken to hear Carpenter by her married cousin, also a schoolteacher, who was. She remembered that 'At the Club we heard a talk by Edward Carpenter, the philosopher, on his theory of a *middle* sex (called by him 'Urnungs') – possessing, if men, the qualities of women and, if women, male qualities. They were in fact mostly geniuses.'[17] Whether it was the same talk is not clear because the *Mercury* certainly does not mention 'Urnungs', but Marjorie Ingle dates it as the first half of 1904 and it is unlikely that Carpenter lectured twice in so short a space of time. The talks show just how popular spiritualist beliefs were amongst the membership and the strength of support from young women schoolteachers.

The first of the literary talks was given by a Leeds solicitor Frederick Jackson on Saturday 13 February on the subject of the 'Victorian Drama'. Orage had met him in the YMCA Literary and Debating Society in the previous year when he had opened a debate on disestablishing the Church of England. (Orage himself had taken part in a debate in December of the same year on 'Thought versus Action' where he had championed the thinker against the man of action, contrasting Napoleon unfavourably with Plato.[18] Fred Jackson was not however wholly in tune with the avant-gardism of the Club's founders for although he made an exhaustive review of the plays of the Victorian era he was severly criticized for relegating Shaw and Yeats to a postscript and omitting entirely any reference to the influence of Ibsen![19] He nevertheless became a staunch member of the Club and was involved in establishing the Club's offshoot, the Playgoers Society, in 1907 of which he was an assistant secretary until 1922 when it remerged with the Arts Club.

The second literary lecture, on Walter Pater (1839–1894), was given by Charles Smythe. Smythe apparently knew Arnold-Bennett and became one of the Club's most regular lecturers. Nothing else is known about him, although later he contributed to the *New Age*. This was a fairly vague summary of Pater's aestheticist theories, even then relatively unknown outside of metropolitan circles. Smythe argued that Pater owed his position at the head of English aesthetic criticism not merely to his style but because of his criticism of life.[20] He chose the line of beauty as a standard and carefully trained his sense of inward vision or 'Theoria'. Commitment to beauty rather than religion or politics was Pater's highest aim. His method of exposition through the medium of personality as in 'Maximus the Epicurean', rather than abstract exposition was very successful. His style was great because it conformed to his two canons; that it must spring naturally from the mind of the writer and that it must have scholarly restraint about it. Smythe concluded that we owe to Pater the best expression in our language of the doctrine that our lives are supremely important and can be made supremely happy by seeking meaning in beauty.

Arthur Hugh Evelyn Lee's talk on Browning, on Wednesday 23 March, was a more substantial offering in which he argued that Browning was a conscious and deliberate artist, a thing which might surprise the student fresh from the smooth periods of Tennyson and Swinburne.[21] The rugged nature of his verse was not the result of indifference to technical beauty but the result of matching it to his own thought. This fantastic style came from deep within Browning's subconscious in ways we could not yet understand and his obscurity was not because of vagueness but because to him his thoughts were obvious. Browning was a great demagogue but most at home in the short dramatic lyric in which he excelled. His method was to throw his entire intellect, feeling and imagination into the circumstances and experience of a character like St John or Fra Lippo Lippi. He would then think aloud in the person of the character conveying much of his own philosophy of life. He was an optimist who preached the gospel of becoming and developing. He taught that one should react strongly against the moral and natural environment and that love was the universal solvent: no love, no God. Lee concluded that, unlike the modern decadents, Browning believed that truth and justice were real and to be discovered in life and professed himself a Browning disciple.

Arthur Lee shortly became Chaplain of Emmanuel Church, the university's chaplaincy, and though an Anglican he still frequently lectured for the Theosophical Society. Later he contributed to the *New Age* and in 1910 also moved to London. He is best known as having co-edited the *Oxford Book of Mystical Verse* in 1917. He also translated and introduced the occultist text of de Sennevoy, *Magic Devoilee* in 1927. Lee clearly exemplifies another tendency within the Club, that of the mystical but socially radical Anglo-Catholicism which was to become so attractive to T. S. Eliot.

The fourth lecture on nineteenth-century writing was given by one of the Club's more established figures. He was the local architect, William H. Thorp (1852–1944), who was responsible for the design of Leeds School of Medicine and the Leeds Art Gallery. Leeds's only attractive police station, still standing in Chapel Allerton close to a number of Orage's old addresses, and combined with a free library, was also his. On Saturday, 9 April he gave a mostly biographical talk on Heinrich Heine in which he emphasized the poet's intellectual life and the unconventionality of his relationships.[22] His view of Heine as one of Europe's most gifted nineteenth-century writers marks a strong Eurocentric trait within the Club. Thorp also helped to organize the Club's exhibition for that session which was on modern domestic architecture and chaired the talk given by Albert Waddington on 'The Nature of Architecture' on its closing day. The exhibition consisting of photographs and drawings in colour of the work of Ernest Newton, Henry Wilson, Baillie Scott, Halsey Ricardo, C. F. A. Voysey, E. J. May, Basil Champneys and other wellknown architects[23] was hung at 18 Park Lane, from Thursday 21 to Wednesday 27 April. Tickets were one shilling.

This was the sum of the spring programme. The prominence of architects may have signified growing esteem and professionalization of architects now conscious of their difference from mere builders and engineers but also the emphasis on city life. Waddington was also a campaigner for the Garden Cities movement, with a Platonic attachment to the 'Ideal City'. It also marks a growth in civic consciousness which became central to the Club's project. Leeds at this time was experiencing enormous changes, not the least of which was the final destruction of the pre-Victorian town. Broderick's town hall, corn exchange and mechanic's institute had introduced grand civic buildings on continental models in the middle and later half of the century. Elegant shopping arcades now covered the old burgesses off Briggate, the redesigned market buildings with their exotic skyline minarets and domes were now nearing completion while Harding's City Square project had attempted to provide a new urban focus. 'So comprehensive were the changes from 1860 to the first world war that almost all the buildings which existed in 1860 had been demolished or replaced by 1914' notes Leeds historian Kevin Grady.[24] But the quality of renewal was piecemeal and enterprising starts so often failed to mature. Fine old buildings like the Red Hall were pulled down as well as those that deserved to be, while the new railway tracks and stations carved the city up without thought to community. Laissez-faire jostled uncomfortably with civic pride.

Autumn 1904

This is the first session for which a published syllabus has been found. It lists fourteen Saturday meetings, the object of the Club: 'to affirm the mutual dependence of Art and Ideas and to provide a meeting place for persons and societies interested in the same', the committee of management and the hon. secretary and his address: Holbrook Jackson, 9 Buckingham Mount, Headingly Leeds.

The first three names on the management committee are women's: Mabel Brunton, Isabella O. Ford and Margaret Proctor. Isabella Ford (1855–1924) was well-known and the two other women were probably amateur painters and the wives of professional men. Isabella Ford as we have already seen was a comrade of Orage's from ILP days and close friend of Edward Carpenter's since 1874. Not afraid to march with the Manningham strikers in 1880 and suffer the abuse of the honest citizens of Bradford, she had been militantly active in the trade-union struggles of the mill girls. In Leeds she had taken a leading role in the Leeds tailoresses strike and helped found their trade union, of which she was president until 1899. She was closely involved with Socialist League pioneers, Tom Maguire, Tom Paylor and Alf Mattinson and had been made a life member of the Leeds Trades Council. During the 1890s she had helped found the ILP in Leeds and had been a delegate to the Trades Union Congress and also to the women's meeting of the Second International in London. So now in 1903, at the age of 52, she was very much a respected elder stateswoman of the movement, though by no means finished with activism. She was elected to the National Advisory Committee of the ILP and was a delegate to the Labour Party annual conference.

Isabella Ford was a fine novelist and journalist. Her first novel, *Miss Blake of Monkshalton*, had appeared in 1890 and her second, *On the Threshold*, was reviewed in, as we have seen, only moderately glowing terms by Orage. Her third, *Mr Elliot*, a well-drawn indictment of a mill owner's inhumanity to his workers, had appeared in 1901. Now her energies were concentrated on woman's suffrage, about which she spoke at the Labour Party's annual conference in 1904. She also wrote an influential pamphlet for the ILP on 'Women and Socialism'. The presence in the Club of such a well-respected and authoritative woman of the left was an antidote to any potentially resurgent masculinism.

The male members of the committee included Orage, Holbrook Jackson, Albert Waddington, Rev. A. H. Lee, W. P. Irving and John H. Fearnley. Arthur Lee had taken a BA from Pembroke College, Cambridge in 1897 and an MA in 1901. In 1898 he had attended the Leeds Clerical School and was then living in Holbeck, but in 1905 he moved to Hilary Street, off Woodhouse Lane, in order to be near Emmanuel Church when he was made chaplain. As we have seen he was also involved in the TS where he had lectured on Browning, the Celtic races, Buddhism, Meister Eckhart, F. H. Myer's *Human Personality* and psychical research. According to Mary Gawthorpe he was close to Orage both then and later when he too moved to London.

W. P. Irving was quite different. The district manager of the County Fire Office Ltd & Alliance Assurance Co., he lived comfortably in a large terraced house in St Johns Grove, off Belle Vue Road, to the south of Hyde Park (as Woodhouse Moor had recently been renamed) and was probably one of Jackson's business acquaintances. An obituary in the *Yorkshire Post* by his friend Denis Botterill described him as energetic, high-spirited and a dedicated organizer; he was also a keen walker and rock-climber. 'Conservative at heart he was ever ready to listen to the arguments of the rebels; he liked men with ideas, and was ready with help and encouragement.'[25] John Fearnley was in the same mould. He was a company secretary to the wool manufacturers, Learoyd Brothers of Huddersfield, and a friend both of Waddington, who designed a house for him, and Father Walter Frere of the Community of the Resurrection in Mirfield.[26] He was also a talented amateur water-colourist and photographer. The committee therefore was composed of a mixture of artistically sensitive professional men, women, amateur painters, theosophists, ILPers and Fabians.

The key Saturday afternoon lectures were dominated by the contributions of Club members and a scattering of prominent national speakers. The most famous of these was G. K. Chesterton and, expecting a large crowd, the meeting was billed to take place in the Philosophical Hall of the Leeds Museum rather than the Arts Club rooms. Other speakers included a founder of the arts and crafts movement, T. J. Cobden-Sanderson, and the professor of history at Leeds University, A. J. Grant.

The Platonic core to the programme consisted of four talks on the Idea of Poetry, the Idea of Decoration, the Idea of the Novel and the Idea of Drama, given respectively by Orage, Waddington, Holbrook Jackson and Charles Smythe. Two sessions were concerned with painting: John Fearnley on the Renaissance, while the painter Gilbert Foster gave a demonstration of his method. Arthur Rowntree, a quaker headmaster from Bootham in York, lectured on Robert Louis Stevenson and Isabella Ford was to give a talk on Woman and the State but it was held over to the next session. The remaining three sessions were give over to a symposium on art and life, a *conversatione* for members and friends, and a general meeting.

Orage opened the session on the 'Idea of Poetry' on Saturday 17 September at 3pm. His argument was that the basis of poetry was 'rhythmic utterance', quoting Browning's 'Your brains beat into rhythm' in support. Having reviewed some theories of the origin of poetry, he concluded that the key to it lay in the primitive communal nature of man of which the most distinguishing elements were dance and cooperative labour. Out of this communion of joy and toil arose rhythmic and measured expression: rhythm was the mark of the tribe. The individual singer whose lyric was sung to the tribal accompaniment was an outcome of this. The reason why rhythm should have such significance lay in the nature of the human organism and its nervous systems. He believed that the sympathetic nervous system was related to emotion in the same way that the cerebro-spinal system was related to reason. All rhythmic expressions therefore, natural or poetic, would produce emotion in humans because of this association. The purpose of poetry was the healthy arousal and maintenance of such rhythms. Poetry could however be dangerously destructive and this led Plato to restrict the poet's writing to the simple rhythms of courage, endurance, joy and faith.

Healthiness was also stressed by Albert Waddington in his talk on the 'Idea of Decoration' the following Saturday. He began by dismissing the cheap commercial ornamentation that filled the shops as a costly piece of national folly which destroyed good taste. The desire for such decoration, he said, was akin to the drink-habit and about as healthy. True decoration, contrarily, was when something that was a joy for the mind was conjoined with what was useful for the body. A cup, for example, had a necessary size and shape determined by experience, but it was not something that could simply be beautified after mechanical construction. Its beauty and use had to be conceived in a single moment, like an acorn cup or flower: 'True decoration was the crowning honour paid by the mind to the thoroughly made object.'[27] Waddington concluded that the work to be done in restoring true decoration to objects was threefold: firstly, destroying false ornamentation; secondly direct and genuine construction with materials of simple outline and, thirdly, severely selecting from past and present traditions in order to create a firmer foundation for newer forms.

Holbrook Jackson delivered his talk on the 'Idea of the Novel' on Saturday 22 October to a large audience at the Club rooms. Following Orage, he saw the ultimate origins of the novel in tribal society or the moment of 'the birth of social intercourse and of solidarity in human affairs.'[28] As society became more individualized, so literature evolved different forms, but it was the growing isolation of the family unit that generated the need for the novel. Initially it was filled by letters and letter writing where gossip, or *good relationship*, was their content. The narrative of early novels was often carried by letters and the novel developed from the 'artistic letter' of the *Spectator* or *Tatler* under Addison and Steele, a highly civilized art form. Jackson characterized the development of the novel from Richardson and Fielding through Thackeray and Dickens to Hardy and Meredith as a movement from feeling to intellect. Before Hardy and Meredith novels were either masculine or feminine, but with them as with Balzac and Turgenev a philosophical and psychological position which embraced both in a wedding of intellect and emotion had been achieved. These thought Jackson were the high point of the novel which could go no further, because the individualization of life had reached its peak. The novel was dead; as life reverted to a more public and communal state, other forms of literary expression like the drama would predominate. Hardy's departure from the novel to the drama was indicative of this and even *Tess* and *Jude* were essentially dramatic themes.

The conclusion of Jackson's talk fittingly introduced the last of the series of four lectures on the essential ideas of the arts given by Charles Smythe the following Saturday on the 'Idea of the Drama'. He, too, used an evolutionary or historicist explanation but centred on Aristotle and Hegel. Drama was of three kinds – Greek, romantic and modern, and owed its origins to Greek religious festivals which developed into the dramatic productions of the Athenian stage. This process was repeated in medieval England culminating in the Shakespearian stage. Drama's central idea was conflict of the good with the good. He applied this idea to the three forms of drama. In Greek drama man was in conflict with fate which was neither good nor bad but merely logical and impersonal. With Shakespeare and the romantic drama we get personality or the conflict of forces making up the individual; Hamlet and Macbeth showing the waste of noble energies in ill-balanced personalities. In modern drama the individual was in conflict with the world around him. Ibsen showed this as social conflict in the *Dolls House* and ideological conflict in the *Master Builder*. However, because of the complexity of modern life, modern artists had been forced to abandon the purely descriptive method, or realism, in favour of *symbolism*. The present phase of English drama was decadent and ripe for an adequate new form.

Thus the four key talks were interrelated and purposive. All emphasized the evolutionary or historicist nature of the arts and the critical need to create new forms for the contemporary social epoch. In emphasizing the links of art to society's well-being they were suggesting a necessary political role for the artist not simply in terms of artistic content but in generating appropriate form.

When Chesterton arrived to give his talk on 'Man – The Great Man – The Super-Man', on 1 October, his audience was already accustomed to provocative and informed debate. The Philosophical Hall, hired for the occasion from the Phil and Lit, was packed and the meeting was chaired by Frederic Moorman, professor of English language at Leeds University. Chesterton did not disappoint his audience for his talk was no less than a subtle debunking of the Nietzschean superman theories so forcefully presented by the Club's founders (and pre-figured Orage's own change of heart some six or seven years later). Equality and solidarity of men, he argued, were fundamental ideas which could not be dispensed with. The challenge to this doctrine from Nietzsche, that humanity was merely a transitional stage from animals to supermen and had to be surpassed was mistaken. Tautologically, it would require 'a perfect man to produce the perfect conditions to produce the perfect man.'[29] The fact that Bernard Shaw and other brilliant men believed in this, he thought, could be traced to a belief in the idea of 'progress', which word he belaboured with 'genial vigour' as quite meaningless. The superman anyway would have to be judged in human terms and in the light of human solidarity. As for the great man or Carlylean hero, the lie was given to this by folk and classical stories, which always conceived of the hero as weaker than his superior opponent. In an illuminating shift of focus which suggested other influences for the superman cult, he continued:

> Mr Henly and Rudyard Kipling are perpetually calling on us to go back in the coarse and violent simple ways of mankind in order that we can worship strength and violence and success. But if you go back you do not find they worshipped strength and violence and success. They are perpetually insisting on the fact that what they are admiring is the little man who is prepared to fight the big man. That is the humanitarianism which is in all the old epics.[30]

He added that the old idea of the hero was an enormously intensified and extra passionate version of a human being, whereas the modern conception was a cold detached non-human being and that, said Chesterton, 'is an entirely modern feeling and I think a very decadent one'.

Significantly some elements of Chesterton's attack later surfaced in Orage's and subsequently T. E. Hulme's *New Age* pieces after 1910, especially the notion of man's imperfectibility. On 25 May 1911 Orage wrote that man was 'a fixed species' and two months later, on 27 July, that man was 'incapable of indefinite progress'. This major reversal of viewpoint marks a crisis in Orage's thought which we shall examine in more detail later, but implied a number of shifts, as on 'realism' and socialism which, John D. Coates argues, were suggested by Chesterton.[31] While Orage remained a humanitarian, his contributor, T. E. Hulme in 1912, was more hard-edged, holding that man was an extraordinarily fixed and limited being from which nothing decent would emerge without organization and tradition.[32] By coincidence on the following Wednesday the Headingley-born poet laureate, Alfred Austin, lectured favourably to the members of the Leeds Institute of Science Art and Literature on much the same views as Chesterton was denouncing. His theme, 'the dangers of progress,' was concluded by advocating that franchise be withheld from any man refusing voluntary military conscription.

The next nationally-known figure at the Club was T. J. Cobden-Sanderson, the father of the arts and crafts movement, who lectured on the history and aims of the movement on Saturday 15 October, in the central court of the Leeds Art Gallery. The occasion was an arts and crafts exhibition in the gallery jointly organized by the Club and the exhibition committee. Though the exhibition itself had attracted only about one-tenth of the numbers who had visited the permanent exhibition in the week (481 as opposed to 4,936 to the permanent exhibition) there is evidence that some of the city's leaders were there. Sanderson's talk was chaired by the gallery's architect, W. H. Thorp, and Holbrook Jackson's vote of thanks was seconded by the lady mayoress, Mrs Currer-Briggs, who considered it a privilege to second the vote of thanks to a man she had so long respected. With R. H. Kitson supporting the motion it was clear that respectable Leeds was indeed warming to the Club by way of its exhibitions, as Jackson later reported.

A similarly well-respected figure was the eminent historian Professor Arthur Grant (1862–1948) who on bonfire night lectured on 'Marcus Aurelius'. Grant was described by Norman Shimmin in his history of Leeds University as 'the completely civilized man'.[33] He had been recruited from the university extension movement to become professor of history in the newly founded university in which he played a large part in authenticating, and where he remained until 1927. His view of the Roman philosopher-emperor can be gathered from his *Outline of European History* published in 1907, in which he figuratively presents his stoicism as a 'noble and elevating creed' founded on brotherhood and cooperation. He believed that human will could be made independent of circumstances and that an unruffled calm was the highest good to which a man could attain.[34] He powerfully argued the case of democracy by relating the aspirations of the Labour movement to those of classical Greece.

> . . . inside all European states the democratic movement has made rapid advances and seems everywhere to move to assured victory. Its ideals may not be realised, its victory may not be complete; but the claims of the whole mass of the people to be considered and to exercise a decisive influence on the government of the state, is a dominant factor in every state in Western Europe. The labour movement – what may be vaguely spoken of as the Socialist movement – is but one phase of that. It is an effort to banish poverty and oppression, and the vice and crime that flow from them and to realize those dreams of social progress that have never been quite unknown since the days of Greece.[35]

The first of two talks on painting on 17 October by John Fearnley was on Giorgione, Titian and Tintoretto. Giorgione, he argued, was a pioneer of Renaissance technical advancement which the others had continued. It was in rejecting the archaic Byzantine tradition in favour of a deeply searching psychologistic representation that he was original and in this respect he gave the impression of modernity. Fearnley believed that it was only through the study of masters like Giorgione and his successors that critical touchstones for contemporary art could be assured. Two weeks later he also chaired the talk by the well-known local artist Gilbert Foster on 'Artistic Ideal and Realities' in which Foster demonstrated his own methods of work to the many local artists who were in the audience of the Chapter Hall of the Church Institute (not the Club rooms which were too small). His own practice was to make innumerable sketches outdoors and then paint in the studio from memory, as advised by Holman Hunt. The good picture always bore the traces of the painter's individuality, but should never be an excuse for shirking the study of nature. However, a literal transcript of nature as in a photograph was not satisfactory either, since pictures should be decorative and strongly designed. Finally in a refusal of modern trends, he said that the 'art' of the picture had to be totally hidden.

A similar artistic (though not social) conservatism was evident in the talk of the Quaker headmaster of Bootham School, York, Arthur Rowntree, on Robert Louis Stevenson on 17 December. In a celebration of the novelist's 'loveable nature' and his painterly eye[36] Rowntree showed that what animated Stevenson's writings was Nettleship's 'spirit of truth and spirit of charity'. Though this was possibly Rowntree's only talk for the Club, in 1918 he and a number of other Club members were involved in forming the Leeds Civic Society with the idea of advancing a garden city programme in the town. This received a certain amount of animosity from the city's elected representatives who felt the society was trying to usurp the council's function. Rowntree was reported as saying that it was time to 'begin to house the people of Leeds instead of trying to warehouse them.'[37] At about the same time he appears to have bought the magazine the *Atheneaum*, then edited by Arthur Greenwood, with the intention, according to John Carswell, of making it a path-breaking literary magazine with Middleton Murry as its editor.[38] Carswell was puzzled as to how Rowntree and Murry knew each other, but clearly the Club and Orage must have been the connection. (Equally puzzling though, is how Greenwood came to edit the *Athenaeum*. A freemason and Fabian, he lectured in economics at Leeds University and sponsored the formation of the Yorkshire District of the Workers' Educational Association of which he was chairman from 1914 to 1945. He also lectured occasionally to the Leeds Theosophical Lodge, once in 1917 on 'Citizenship'. He later found Herbert Read, an ex-student, a job in the Ministry of Reconstruction in 1919. So Greenwood too, in ways as yet still unclear, formed part of the Leeds-London axis of literary and political patronage.)

The only change to the published programme for the autumn session was in Isabella Ford's talk on 'Woman and the State', which was held over to the next session. In its place Albert Waddington took the opportunity to further examine Nietzsche's concept of the superman in a talk called 'Some Doctrines of Zarathustra'. This was a powerful and in retrospect chilling talk on the need to evolve the new race. Waddington maintained that Zarathustra was neither myth nor history but the *geist* of the Nietzsche, who, in his book, had tested the values of the nineteenth century for forming the future race and had found them wanting. Thus he had conceived of the concept of the 'beyond-man' who was to surpass man as man surpassed the apes. However he had discovered that one thing prevented this surpassing and that was humanity's lack of desire for evolution, as easefulness brought on by the old false doctrines of humility, poverty of spirit and prudence which had displaced the grand virtue of courage and turned the wolf in man into a dog. Waddington declared 'This is mediocrity; although it be called moderation!'.[39] Zarathustra's intention was to entice men from the herd and teach them how to fly – or else to fall faster. Virtue was activity of the soul, but goodness was non-activity of certain desires and this was the difference between master and slave morality. He declared that 'A new nobility is needed, proud not of their father's past, but proud for their children's future. Humanity must choose its star and give it birth'.

So the first full year of the Club's activities announced it as a truly Dionysian project in a city 'given over to the more sordid business of life' (as one of their circulars put it). The mixture of earnestness and egoistic flippancy that Mairet noted kept the audience by turns gasping and enthralled. However, the sessions were alternatively brilliant and modest, in a kind of provincial melange, though the exhibitions unequivocally raised the standard. Debate was generated around some of the most advanced social and artistic ideas of the time, and though national speakers were attracted, it was clear that its own members were neither ill-informed nor narrowly provincial. Nietzschean rhetoric rubbed shoulders with Fabian citizenship but, more ominously, Waddington's advocacy of the 'new nobility' signalled a current of militantly anti-democratic, anti-humanist and anti-Christian thought which in other hands later came to legitimize the charismatic élites of the interwar period. He wasn't to know that of course.

Notes

1. Millie Price, 'This Worlds Festival', p.112.
2. Mary Gawthorpe, *Up Hill to Holloway*, Penobscot, Maine, 1962.
3. Philip Mairet, *A. R. Orage*, p.25.
4. *Leeds Mercury*, 21 November 1903, p.7. My emphasis.
5. *Leeds Mercury*, Weekly Supplement, 12 December 1903, p.3.
6. *Yorkshire Weekly Post* (hereafter referred to as *YWP*), 12 December 1903, p.12.
7. *Leeds Mercury*, 28 November 1903, p.8. While rapturizing on the quality of the books and noting Ruskin's belief that no one properly appreciates a book unless it is obtained at some self-sacrifice, the reporter expressed 'the comforting mercenary thought that such books increase in value and form a safe investment'.
8. Holbrook Jackson Library Memorial Catalogue, p.75.
9. *YWP*, 13 February 1904, p.21.
10. *YWP*, 19 March 1904, p.17.
11. *Leeds Mercury*, 5 March 1904, p.3.
12. Ibid.
13. *YWP*, 14 May 1904, p.21.
14. Ibid.
15. By 1903 his influence had spread to New York where the anarchist Emma Goldman and the New York Modern School were indebted to him. See Linda Dalrymple Henderson, 'Mysticism as "The Tie that Binds": The Case of Edward Carpenter and Modernism', *Art Journal*, Spring 1987, vol.46, no.1, pp.29–37.
16. *Leeds Mercury*, 9 April 1904, p.3.

17. Marjorie Ingle, unpublished 'Reminiscences', 1964, in the possession of Catherine Thackeray, Greenwoods, Reaphust Road, Birkby, Huddersfield, West Yorks.
18. *Leeds Mercury*, Saturday 20 December 1902, p.3.
19. *Leeds Mercury*, 20 February 1904, p.3.
20. *Leeds Mercury*, 12 March 1904, p.3.
21. *Leeds Mercury*, 26 March 1904, p.3.
22. *YWP*, 16 April 1904, p.17.
23. Information from handbill in Leeds City Reference Library prints collection.
24. Kevin Grady, 'Commercial Marketing and Retailing Amenities, 1700–1914' in Derek Fraser (ed.) *A History of Modern Leeds*, Manchester University Press, 1980, pp.192–3.
25. I have assumed this was the *YWP* because of an internal reference. The obituary was cut out and inserted in the copy of Holbrook Jackson's *Bernard Shaw*, in the Brotherton Collection of Leeds University.
26. I am indebted to his daughter, Yvonne Fearnley of Broomfield Crescent, Leeds, for this information.
27. *YWP* 1 October 1904, p.22.
28. *YWP* 29 October 1904, p.21.
29. *Leeds Mercury*, 3 October 1904, p.3.
30. Ibid. quoting Chesterton verbatim.
31. See John D. Coates, *Chesterton and the Edwardian Cultural Crisis*, Hull University Press, 1984, chapter XI 'Conclusion, the Case of Orage'.
32. T. E. Hulme, *Speculations*, Routledge, Kegan Paul, London, 1924, p.116.
33. Norman A Shimmin, *Leeds University, the First Fifty Years*, Cambridge University Press, Cambridge, pp.125–26.
34. A. J. Grant, *Outlines of European History*, pp.97–98.
35. Ibid. p.359.
36. *YWP*, 24 December, 1904, p.21.
37. *Yorkshire Observer*, 2 October, 1918.
38. Carswell, *Lives and Letters*, p.156.
39. *YWP*, 3 December, 1904, p.21.

CHAPTER FOUR

1905: What is the Use of an Arts Club?

By comparison with what was to follow, the success of the Club's first year paled. 1905 was to be its *annus mirabilis* in which the founders and star guests like Bernard Shaw attempted to shock Leeds out of its civic complacency. The lecture series was itself announced by both the *Yorkshire Post* and the *Mercury* signalling a certain public interest, the *Post* going as far as to headline 'NEW SESSION'S INTERESTING PROGRAMME'!

The expanded programme again contained a core of talks around Nietzsche's superman called (borrowing a title from Pater) 'Imaginary Portraits of Beyond Men' by Orage, Waddington and Jackson. Orage opened the session with the first of these: the Philosopher, Waddington followed five weeks later on the Artist and Jackson concluded on the Saint. Orage and Jackson returned to argue out publicly a correspondence carried on earlier between them on whether the Critic should be impartial. They were supported in talks by Charles Smythe on Ibsen whom they saw as a fellow individualist and philosopher of life and Frederic Moorman on Browning. A third literary talk was given by J. E. Barton on Criticism. Isabella Ford's talk on 'Woman and the State' held over from the previous session was included as were talks on sculpture by the Leeds sculptor Caldwell Spruce and 'Street Architecture of Today' by Percy Robinson, architect, freemason and Club chairman. The two guest speakers were Cecil Chesterton, G.K.'s brother and George Bernard Shaw who, in typically *epater le bourgeois* style, told the citizens of Leeds what a rotten town they lived in. A major exhibition of modern paintings and sketches was held in March and a series of Friday evening discussions began in January. This series was heir to Orage's Plato Group in that he personally led the three sessions on Plato's *Phaedrus* and three more on the *Banquet*. There were twelve meetings in all but such were the popularity of them that a continuation series was announced in late March.

Orage began the session at 3 p.m. on 14 January on 'The Beyond-Man as Philosopher', explaining that his lecture was to be in the form of a utopian story, a fanciful construction of the circumstances necessary for the Beyond-Man's perfection.[1] The Beyond-Man was however not simply an ideal, for such characters had existed in the past and may be living today – Mommsen's account of Caesar and Plato's of Socrates were two such examples. The problem was that, as Plato revealed, such beings did not yet have a context in which they could work and were thus destined to obscurity or distortion. The distinctive feature of the Beyond-Man was that he was incapable of personal gain, he transcended ordinary personality. Lost in their work or their *idea* personality so called was abandoned and individuality absolutely gained.[2]

He then sketched a fictional community called *Sophiliaus* which was distinguished from ordinary nations by its possession of a single common purpose, the increasing and perfection of human life. Everything that made for the nobler and larger life they instinctively cherished and shunned all that reduced it. Into this community was born the Beyond-Man. Elected guardian and leader, he led the quest into unimaginable realms shaping his community through an education of which the two most important branches were, said Orage, 'out-sight' or exterior observation and 'insight' or penetration into motives and causes. These were followed by education in the spheres of civil and religious government. Orage quoted the philosopher-king's axiom as 'As the soul is to the body, so is the king to his people'.

The Platonic idea of philosopher-king as a version of Nietzsche's Beyond-Man also pre-occupied the Friday evening discussions, the first of which he had led the previous evening. Millie Price was a member of the discussion group which had studied Plato's *Republic* and *Symposium* and described how pathbreaking the group was. In the first place it broke the 'men only' rule for some of the discussions, even in theosophical circles, were regarded as too indelicate for women. They were, she wrote,[3] ranged around education, health, opinion and knowledge, communal child-care, capital punishment, democracy and the place in the community of poetry and the imagination. Plato, she said, was apropos of the times and in a very suggestive evocation of the contemporary mood wrote:

> The building of Utopian communities was in the air. The conception of the melting pot was very strong; racial religious and social conditions were set for change. The intellectuals of the time were discarding the materialist doctrine of the survival of the fittest, and turning towards a faith in the creative mind of man, capable of producing conscious and willed spiritual stature. There was no foreboding of wars which would decimate the thinkers, and largely reduce humanity to a dead level of docility, with material survival as the ruling aim.[4]

The role of imagination and will she describes, as opposed to deterministic strategies, marks a shift in the intellectual climate, coincident with a new optimism. Orage, it appeared, could dramatically convey this feeling of inner potential to galvanic effect. In this small circle there was no doubt that he *was* the philosopher-king. Indeed the great problem for so popular a leader as Orage was, in Millie Price's words, 'how to avoid dictatorship' giving added importance to the committee of management. Despite the fact that the committee had named elected members she presents it as much more informal. Once a week the committee met and every one present was ipso facto a member and organizational duties were allocated. As for Orage she presents him seated in an armchair puffing his pipe leading discussions like his great exemplar Socrates.

Interleaved with Orage's sessions on Plato were Nietzschean and other aphorisms, led by members of the Club. Not unfortunately reported, they were as follows: 20 January 'Thought Should End in Action' William Jones; 3 February 'The Most Despicable Man is He who can no longer Despise Himself', W. Allison Byrne; 17 February 'He only is Good who is Good for Something' Holbrook Jackson; 3 March 'The Right to Believe is Abused whenever it is not Constantly Challenged', W. P. Irving; 17 March 'All that hath its Fixed Browne is of Little Value', A. W. Waddington; 31 March 'Government is Best when it is Most', F. G. Jackson.

On Saturday 18 February Albert Waddington took the opportunity in his talk on the 'Beyond-Man as Artist', the second of the Imaginary Portraits series, to further his medieval guilds thesis. Taking up Orage's model of a utopian community, he discoursed on the role of the artist. The object of Art, he said, was to make 'work happy and rest fruitful'.[5] Since the old political economy had failed, a newer one, which would make life rather than gold the standard of wealth, must be attempted. Art was central to this. Every fine art had evolved from primitive utility through useful and decorative crafts but now had become decadent and morbid or commercial and paltry. Decorative arts merely covered shoddy goods with shoddy ornament and the crafts were sacrificed to the machine-finish. Thus a revived guild training should emphasize the training of the master even more than the apprentice. Division of labour should be reduced, hand and head work brought again towards a unity and the producer should once again attain priority. The great arts which had lost their moral properties of training our insight and emotions had urgently to be restored. Since no great artist was possible under the present commercial system it was not simply a question of individual expansion of consciousness, the emphasis given by Orage. Thus for Waddington the idea of the Beyond-Man as artist became inseparable from social revolution.

The final lecture in the series was not given until 7 April, with Holbrook Jackson on the 'Superman as Saint'. The delay of some weeks from the date printed in the syllabus may well have been because

Jackson differed quite sharply from Orage and Waddington about the nature of the superman. He contested that he would in fact express himself in the types of consciousness common to human beings and all attempts at a definition would fail because humans simply could not comprehend him. Jackson argued that art, philosophy and religion were merely human methods of expression which would be collapsed together in the transcendent being. Such unity was already represented in artists like Tolstoy and the real use of such divisions was to exemplify how far removed was present humanity from the cosmic type who would unite all three.[6]

Turning to the saint as a type however, Jackson maintained that what characterized him was the abnegation of physical desire and the intensification of spiritual life, a love of god rather than earth. He held though, that the 'super-saint', no doubt using the expression with his tongue in his cheek, would attain union with god not by negation of life but by affirmation. Enunciation rather than renunciation was the key to holiness or 'wholeness'. The saint's life would therefore be characterized by an affirmation of life which would teach by its example. A lively debate from the large audience at the Club followed in which all the speakers actually disagreed strongly with Jackson and supported the proposition that the superman would be recognizable in current human types.

This willingness of the group's founders to challenge each other's interpretations was also reflected in a meeting based on a correspondence between Orage and Jackson, on 'Whether the Critic should be Impartial'. The correspondence in question was in the form of a notebook which was passed between the two. Carswell's conclusion that it shows Orage's clear-headedness and avoidance of intellectual sloppiness is accurate[7] though his dating is not. It had to be written no earlier than October 1903 since Orage twice refers to Jackson as the secretary of the Arts Club.

The first salvo from Orage was that impersonality in criticism was impossible (except of course for the popular dailies where what passes for impersonality is really no more than absence of personality). Far from striving to escape personality the critic should treasure and display it. Similarly bogus is impartiality because every one has tastes which cannot be escaped. The critic's personality and taste (or partiality) are the only things of value to him and cannot be herded into the straightjacket of 'objective principles'. Jackson fairly easily disposes of this argument by levelling Plato's eternal verities at the arch-platonist himself. True criticism, he continued, begins where opinion ends by showing the reasons for the opinions held. Opinion and personality merely show 'how' not 'why', which is the function of reason. The critic, he concluded, should reason within the emotional medium (in passing he responded to Orage's jibe about the *Daily Mail*, commenting that that organ was 'merely the reflection of the passion and prejudice of the mob').

Orage was clearly stung by Jackson's weighing Plato at him, since the point about absolute standards was not one he wished to dispute and was cornered. But he responded by claiming that criticism depended on personality in the sense that the critic must possess a rich and interested mind from which criticism was far more interesting than from a critic with an everyday mind who merely applied principles. In a rhetorical flourish he concluded 'the opinions of the wise are nearer truth than the knowledge of the foolish'. While not disputing the value of wisdom, Jackson's reply was to say that the value of criticism was that it could say why one prefers this or that as opposed to merely stating a preference. Thus seeing or appreciating the worth of a thing and conveying this to another was different from loving or adoring it. He turned the screw further by attributing the ugliness and squalour of modern cities precisely to the partial critic whose prejudices were blind.

Though he was really on the ropes at this point, Orage rose magnificently to the occasion. He summarized Jackson's position as the difference between a critic with taste and a critic with taste and reason. Taste and reason was perfect, he said, but did not as Jackson implied equal impartiality. The impartial critic, who reasons where others feel, is a very dull critic. Reason must only enter the critical process *after* taste and felling, 'our perfect critic both feels *and* reasons. But notice, notice, that he reasons no further than he feels, not even as far'. This time Jackson was on the defensive and had to admit that taste was an affair of the emotions, but he replied criticism was not simply a matter of taste nor was taste the same as criticism. Criticism should be as logical as Euclid; it should be able to prove its conclusions through a process of reasoning capable of the same interpretation to different minds.

With some exasperation Orage concluded the correspondence by pulling out the Nietzschean ace from his sleeve. There were two kinds of critic; the first tells us what he *likes* and why while the second tells us what he *sees*. In ninety-nine times out of hundred the second kind of critic, the one Jackson had argued for, was sufficient, but one may say, never satisfactory. That could only be achieved by the *great* critic and he was of course of the first kind; what he likes is more important than why he likes it. Significantly Orage exemplified this by reference to the novelist Meredith (whom he always compared favourably to Dickens) concluding that taste could never depend on intellect. Orage thanked Jackson for the near oriental courtesy of his letters and signs himself your 'defeated but victorious friend'. It was an inconclusive skirmish that nevertheless displayed the contrasting personalities of the pair, Orage preferring the unsupported thought and passion of the Great Man while Jackson the patient process of reason. The epistemological subtext to the debate was a contrasted view of the nature of individual consciousness, for from his Nietzschean and occultist viewpoint Orage believed that the more the Great Man expressed his individuality the more he became universal. This relied on an idealist belief in a world *geist* or spirit which Jackson was far too much of a rational sceptic to wholly accept.

In a complementary paper on 'Criticism' which had been delivered the previous Saturday, 4 February, J. E. Barton M.A. of the *Saturday Review*, supported Jackson's tendency that the work of the critic was a professional discipline. The critic mediated between the vision of the artist and the public's reception of it. Following Addington Symonds, he prepared the way for the reception of the new work of art in the roles of judge, showman and scientific analyst. It was an informed and perceptive talk significant in that it signalled the prevailing movement of literary criticism away from the, possibly dilletante, *apercus* of the Great Man into the scholarly and increasingly university-oriented profession opened up by the new schools of English in provincial universities such as the one on the hill founded only the previous year. Leeds University ran in 1907, one of the first courses on tragedy entitled 'From Aeschylus to Ibsen'.[8]

The centrality of Ibsen to the new movement was further demonstrated by Charles Smythe in his lecture of 25 February. He said that despite Ibsen's being labelled an agitator for women's rights, a socialist and anarchist, he had no great zeal for setting up the ideal state. In fact he attacked conventions and shams because he considered that the great work to be done was the development of the individual. Every man and woman had a self, 'something whole united, certain and free',[9] a growth of the will to include the whole being which could only be developed by free action. Therefore conventions were positively harmful. In his plays tragedy arose when their heroes were broken by the conflict with the environment as in *The Master Builder* or when the conventions cherished by the ordinary individual became the instruments of his destruction, as in *Ghosts*. His later plays, however, were situated almost entirely in the higher plane of ideas and symbolism. Smythe classified Ibsen with Shakespeare as one of the philosopher-poets, men with large views and a single aim, 'who see life steadily and see it whole'.[10]

The last literary talk was given by Leeds University's immensely popular Professor of English Language, Frederic Moorman (1872–1919), on Browning's Art Poems on Saturday 4 March. Both Arthur Ransome and Herbert Read expressed their indebtedness to him whilst they were undergraduates, Read calling him 'perhaps the most inspiring teacher in the university'.[11] His radical and democratic sympathies ensured he was twice passed over in his desire for the chair of Literature, but he found expression for them in his extramural activities, such as the WEA and in collecting and establishing one of the first recorded dialect libraries. Unlike 'that severe woman-hating humanist' Charles Vaughan,[12] who held the chair of Literature, he was according to Shimmin 'neither explosive nor passionate', but like Vaughan he became attached to the WEA because 'he wished to reveal the treasures of scholarship to all members of the community'.[13] For a number of years he was chairman of the Leeds branch of the WEA and with Arthur Greenwood and George Thompson presided over the formation of the WEA's legendary Yorkshire District (under the enthusiastic eye of His Majesty's Inspector, John Dover Wilson) in 1914.

Despite an extraordinary physical fitness gained from cycling an average of 3,000 miles a year,[14] he died of a heart-attack, attempting to rescue his daughter Thea, in a swimming accident on his forty-seventh birthday in 1919. The local Labour Party paper wrote the 'whole Labour movement of Leeds and Yorkshire will have a sense of regret and loss'.[15] His collecting of dialect was no mere antiquarianism either, as a friend wrote, 'his great idea . . . was that through dialect and particularly through dialect drama that something of the old cheer and good fellowship might be brought about in our small towns and villages.'[16] Moorman was thus one of that radical generation of university intellectuals which acted as a bridge to the working class and labour movement. Sympathetic to their insistence on a right to the fruits of knowledge, he responded with generosity and warmth. Along with Grant, he was also the first member of the university to see the potential of the Arts Club for artistic expression and municipal reform, though he may have regretted its apparent exclusiveness. He became an active member and later hosted a number of its social gatherings.

His talk on Saturday 4 March, was an exegesis of Browning's poems, 'Fra Lippo Lippi', 'Andrea del Sarto' and 'The Bishop Orders his Tomb'. He followed Ruskin's interpretation found in *Modern Painters*, that the three poems form the most complete understanding of the Renaissance spirit in literature, saying in so many lines what had taken him thirty pages of the 'Stones of Venice'. Moorman demonstrated how 'Fra Lippo Lippi' showed the liberation of the Renaissance valuation of mortal life from the medieval doctrine of the prison house of the body. 'Andrea del Sarto' some three-quarters of a century later, while exhibiting all the design and colouring art of Raphael, lacks the value and significance of the soul and thus takes the first step towards decadence. In the 'Bishop' this decadence is in full flood of rococo prettiness and sentimentalism. With the decline of religion and art into fleshiness, the church had become a museum and art a devil's game. With Moorman's eloquent celebration of the triumph of Browning's realism the sessions literary sequence ended.

Painters were also the theme of W. H. Thorp's talk on 'Watteau and Chardin: A Constrast' on 28 January. This meeting was held in the Leeds School of Art around which the members were given a guided tour after the lecture. Thorp agreed with Pater's *Imaginary Portraits* that Watteau was 'the Prince of Court Painters' while Chardin by contrast was 'the bourgeois painter of the French bourgeoisie'.[17] Despite his glittering exteriors Watteau nevertheless failed to conceal an ominous melancholy. He died prematurely at the age of 37. The long-lived Chardin on the other hand gave us still-life interiors and the 'simple unaffected ways of french peasants and artisans'.

Earlier in the session Isabella Ford had delivered her lecture on 'Woman and the State', with Orage in the chair. She too developed her subject historically. Women, she said, now had less opportunities for free and natural development than at any time since the middle ages. They had had the franchise both in Greek states and in Celtic tribes, and in England they could hold public positions and take up corporate duties from which they are now excluded. She traced the decline of these rights to Sir Edward Coke. But the tide was now turning and women were once again demanding what was theirs by right. The masculine view of women as 'ministering angels' was responsible for much of their subordination.[18] Women had to throw off this sentimentality since the upbringing of the race was in their hands. They had in part their own passivity to blame, but women's involvement in recent reform movements had shown them the way to women's suffrage. So, with Isabella Ford too, the medieval and Celtic past became the inspiration for social reform and signified a rallying call to women's consciousness.

The great event of the session was George Bernard Shaw, who on Valentine's Day gave the key talk 'What is the use of an Arts Club?' He had broken off rehearsing his play *How He Lied* at the Royal Court to give his first lecture in Leeds for fifteen years.[19] The Philosophical Hall was filled 'with a large company of ladies and gentlemen who were thrilled by the critic's genial dogmatism and his satirical tilting at all conventionalism uninformed by artistic principles.'[20] Shaw talked 'wittily and brilliantly' for an hour and a half, insisting 'I dogmatically assert things. It saves a great deal of trouble, and is the only way you can really carry conviction.'[21]

He began by asserting that the superiority of art is that it appeals to, and can propagate, feeling, unlike reason which appeals only to the intellect. Intellect is unnecessary for the really vital person, who on wanting a thing, will take it. The real function of reason was to show how to carry out one's will, but it was not a spring of action. 'No amount of reading of documents on smoke abatement or treatises on art would inspire them with the desire to burn Leeds down and build a better town.' Warming to his theme, he continued:

> Art is thing that can finally make you believe that Leeds as it exists at present is a very intolerable place, that it is a place where no decent individual ought to live and that you individually have no right to be alive at all. It even has the power, finally, of driving you, under certain provocation, to burn down your town.[22]

Reflecting for a moment, he concluded that the best use of an Arts Club would be to get the people of Leeds to burn down the town and replace it with a better one, though to do that 'it would be necessary to get rid of the people of Leeds and replace them with a rather different sort'. If there was an uncomfortable silence or boos and catcalls they were not reported, instead there was a 'hearty laugh of approval'. Having immolated Leeds (and causing the art-critic of the *Yorkshire Post* to refer to him thereafter as George *Burnhard* Shaw) he moved on to other subjects. Education through the intellect rather than the feelings were merely a culture of lies (though perfectly harmless, because children immediately saw through them) and architecture had produced only that 'petrified wedding cake' the Houses of Parliament, despite the fact that it had more 'high art' to the square inch than any other building.

Despite the witty finesse with which Shaw gave his audience what they expected, there was also a serious element to his talk. Turning to the role of 'Ideas' in the work of the Leeds Arts Club he said:

> The Club is trying to cultivate the study of Ideas to induce people to think, and to shake themselves out of all that makes for commonplace, depressing conventionalism . . . Leeds people ought to be associated with a club which refreshes its soul, even in a city of machinery and smoke like Leeds, with ideas and imagination and feeling, all tending to purify thought and raise life, even the common everyday life to a higher plane.[23]

The neglected feeling for art had now urgently to be cultivated; ideas too had to be related to everyday life, thus the value of an Arts Club, he concluded:

> is that it directs attention to the beautifying and uplifting power of art. Every town should have some particular art centre in it. Without that centre you will not find your factories of great use in producing

> a high and noble life, and what is more you will not find your churches and schools of much use. If you have these things without art, you will have affectation, dilettantism, hypocrisy and brutality; but if you have art and can propagate the feeling out of which a noble life can come, the Arts Club in Leeds is the beginning of a centre for propagating that feeling.[24]

With such a powerful endorsement of the Club's work, Orage, who had chaired the meeting, gave the vote of thanks, saying that for such an intellectual treat the Club had already justified its existence. He hoped too that if, after another fifteen years interval, Shaw revisited Leeds, he would find it a more desirable place to live in. Shaw's talk was well covered in the serious press and it reverberated around Leeds for some time to come, though to what effect is inconclusive. Jackson claimed that it kept Leeds 'bubbling' for weeks. It certainly established the Club as a cultural landmark, if nothing else, and very few people concerned with the arts and theatre would now not have heard of it.

Shaw himself spent the next morning in the company of 'Kester' of the *Yorkshire Post* (J. Dodgson) looking round Kirkstall Abbey. Dodgson, a founder member of the Leeds Studio Club and a member of the Arts Club's management committee from September 1905 to 1907, reported that he had been favourably impressed by the rows of back-to-back houses along Kirkstall Road, for which Leeds is justly infamous, because they had no backyards. He admired the practice of hanging washing across the street as 'likely to raise the standard of wearing apparel' which struck Kester as a truly humorous idea.[25]

Both Orage and Jackson appear already to have known Shaw possibly through the Fabian Society, though Orage claimed he was at Shaw's marriage. This visit consolidated their relationship and in the end made possible their settlement in London. For it was Shaw along with a theosophical banker named Lewis Wallace who raised the £1,000 necessary for them to purchase the *New Age* in 1907. Its continued buoyancy also to an extent depended on his largesse and his frequent, unpaid, articles. In return Jackson's book was the first to celebrate his genius and the journal from time to time offered him an anonymous platform for politicking.

Shaw's insistence on the socially inspirational function of art was reflected in three talks on art and architecture and a major exhibition of modern tendencies in art. The first of these was given by the Leeds sculptor, Caldwell Spruce, on 'Sculpture' on Saturday 11 March. In Egyptian and Greek sculpture, he argued, one could see not merely a representational but a spiritual or religious conception of man which signified a positive educational function for sculpture. In the middle ages sculpture had a similar role and was regarded as a master craft.

For the health of the community sculpture must regain this status and he wished the Club all success in its attempts to bring 'the dignity of high art back into the lives of men'.[26] Despite Henry Moore's protestations to the contrary, sculpture was practised and taught in Leeds to a reputable degree, Spruce being one of the teachers at the School of Art to which he later came (though possibly after Spruce had retired). It was clear from Spruce's talk that many of the elements which so inspired Moore such as Egyptian and medieval sculpture were already well-known. Rodin was also well-respected.

Percy Robinson's talk on 'Street Architecture and its Defects' continued the theme of the need for arts education. Compared with the continent, there was a lack of 'collective appreciation of art' which had led to the unplanned ugliness of our cities.[27] The most striking feature of modern architecture was the absence of uniformity which resulted in buildings being jumbled together regardless of height and scale. Since architecture was an expressive art, all buildings should simply and straightforwardly express their purpose. Equally each building should take its proper place in the general scheme. Despite Leeds smoke-blackened exterior, more electric power was being used and with factories decentralizing, the worst was past. However, like the good architect he was, he denounced the municipal authority's lack of vision and the restrictions, petty and otherwise, which prevented the architect from maturing or revising his work.

Robinson (1868–1950) was in fact responsible for some of Leeds street architecture including Armley Public Library (1902), Rawcliffe's in Boar Lane just then being completed, Leeds Exchange in Briggate (1907) and Firemen's flats in Park Lane (1909)[28] not far from the Arts Club. Armley Public Library must rate as the prettiest in town and fulfills in a modestly arts and crafts way all the principles of internal expression and communal harmony he talked of. Its most marked feature is a carved triple-arched staircase from the street corner surmounted by a small clock-tower, dignified but not overdecorated. He was president of West Yorkshire Society of Architects for some years the Thoresby Society, and was on the management committee of the Arts Club from September 1905 to April 1909. He wrote and illustrated two books on Leeds, *Relics of Old Leeds* (1896) and *Leeds Old and New* (1926). A prominent freemason, he represents an interesting link between commercial interests and the artistic radicalism of Orage and co. One of five known architects in the Club, most of them well-established, he and his partner William Alban Jones were perhaps the only ones with national reputations. Other prominent freemasons included Bean the bookseller and Leonard Zossenheim who formed the first Jewish lodge, the 'Liberty', in Leeds. Arthur Greenwood, the economics lecturer and later Labour MP was also a freemason. Both he and Zossenheim were friends of Tom Heron of Cresta Silks who was a leading member of the Club ten years later. It's tempting to speculate on the relationship of freemasonry to Guild Socialist ideas then being developed in the Club by Penty and Waddington (both architects). The fascination of both for medieval formations and esoteric doctrines seems hardly coincidental.

It was in an additional series of four Friday evening discussions in April that Orage and Jackson came closest to outlining their literary principles. On 21 April Orage gave a talk entitled 'Sentimentalism, Romanticism and Realism'. He advocated realism because neither practicality nor romanticism on their own were sufficient artistic principles. There was an opposition between practicality and romanticism like that of the hand and the heart. The practical man had no use for imagination, whereas the ideals of the romanticist were too unattainable to be practically realized. Through the use of intellect, therefore, it was the realist who bridged practicality and imagination. Orage argued that realism was the highest artistic principle. It was possible to divide all works of art between the romantic and the realist. The former left the reader fatigued and langorous, while the latter would inspire activity. The realist was moreover the true reformer 'for he made heaven and earth kiss one another . . . All the greatest art was thus a battle cry; either Art played humanity into action or it called them into fatal slumber. Realist art was the bugle for charge'.[29] Sentimentalism, however, was a disease of drivelling novel readers, a pretence at romanticism but lacking genuine feeling. But worst of all was a 'sentimentalism of realism' which roused Orage into a damning indictment of some who might have been sitting in front of him. 'The majority of Ibsenites, Wagnerites and Nietzscheans', he said,

> were romanticists masquerading as realists. They never dealt a single blow for Heine's war of the Liberation of Humanity, and never intended to. They called themselves individualists in the secret hope that they might become individual. But like sentimentalists of other varieties a little push showed the buckram of their armour.[30]

From the animated discussion that followed it showed that Orage had started a few hares in the audience. He had never previously so angrily turned on his followers. He had never so clearly outlined the function of art before either. The concept of 'realism' was for him, like Lukacs and Brecht, an evaluation of a work's potential for progressive social transformation.

This theme was vigorously continued by Holbrook Jackson the following Friday in his talk 'Art and Conduct'. He spoke of the danger of the Club's aims being misunderstood. Club members should be exact in their understanding of art, beauty and citizenship, otherwise 'they might be led into the mistake of accepting prettiness for beauty, words for deeds and art galleries for decent habitations.'[31] The Club was for changing the world not sighing over it. Art was to urge men into action in keeping with the emotion it produced or it was worthless. People who were moved into rhapsodies over beautiful works of art without endeavouring to reform their own lives and surroundings in tune with them were quite sentimental and superfluous. A nervous shuffling. What was provoking this attack?

The lesson of the great modern teachers was that the true value of art might help us to realize for ourselves and our age some of the suggestions of the imagination. They dismissed the academic jargon about canons of taste and technical peculiarities and the like which was so far removed from life and reality. Instead,

> Modern philosophy aimed at making the individual an artist in life by teaching him to reconstruct his outworn ideas and institutions so as to give himself the greatest possible amount of freedom for growth and happiness. It despised all distinctions not the outcome of individual power and all wealth not invested in the common good.[32]

He cited William Morris as the supreme example of this idea, quoting his lines 'Dreamer of dreams, born out of my due time,/Why should I strive to set the crooked straight'. Both talks it seemed had been conceived to 'set the crooked' straight among the Club's enthusiasts. There was to be no misunderstanding or backsliding: the enjoyment of art must end in action.

The Club's exhibition of studies and sketches illustrating some tendencies in modern art was also conceived on an ambitious scale. Fortunately, enough records have survived to make it possible to piece together how the exhibition was devised and constructed.[33] Hung in the clubrooms in Park Lane from Wednesday 8 March to Saturday 18 March, it consisted of works by Whistler, Rodin, Lavery, Furse, Stott, Clausen, Orpen, Hornel, Mark Fisher, Shannon, Garth Jones, Ricketts, Rothenstein, Pennell, Holroyd, Byam Shaw, Wilson Steer, Le Sidaner, Moore Park, Conder 'and many others'. Season tickets which admitted one to both Spruce's and Herbert Thompson's lectures were two shillings and single admission, one shilling.

This was an impressive list for a small provincial club and was hailed by the *Yorkshire Post*, which announced: 'The Leeds Arts Club which promoted the lecture which made such a *succes de scandale* ('Burnhard' Shaw's)' had organized an exhibition of high quality, though to the admirers of the Burlington House gallery picture 'it may seem as subversive as Mr Shaw's views on Mendelssohn'. The following week's review continued: 'It says something for the advance of Leeds in artistic matters when even a small section of enthusiasts is able to plan and carry into effect a show of such uniformly high quality and containing nothing at all that appeals to the gallery.'[34] The reviewer was probably Herbert Thompson, who had an interest in these matters.

Despite being carried out in a remarkably short space of time, the planning of the exhibition was meticulous. A circular on headed Club notepaper was sent out to all 'Art members' (which suggests that there was an art subgroup) early in December 1904 'to consider arrangements for an Exhibition of a few selected sketches and designs to illustrate as far as possible the tendencies of Modern Art' and also to arrange for a lecturer on the subject 'in relation to the aims and objectives of Art Workers in the City'. Thus no exhibition without practical consequences.

It was probably at this meeting that William 'Billy' Alban Jones was elected organizing secretary. He then painstakingly drafted out a letter to artists and collectors asking for sketches or paintings which he sent to Orage at the Club for correction. (Even his note to Orage contains nervous crossings out lest the great stylist pillory him.) From an early draft it was clear that the Club wanted to emulate the International Painters, Gravers and Sculptors Exhibition, held previously in London. Another draft explains that the Club's aims had received support from Shaw, Chesterton, Carpenter and Cobden-Sanderson. The Club was also only approaching those artists whose work 'was in sympathy with its ethical aims'. Artists were at liberty to put their work up for sale. Orage must have knocked the drafts into final shape, though a glowing phrase from the original was included intact: 'The Exhibition is designed to further the object of the Club which . . . is the fostering of a higher taste both Literary and Artistic, in a provincial City largely given over to the more sordid business of life'.

The letter was finally signed by Holbrook Jackson and complete with the Club's peacock device and address, printed in fine copperplate. Encouragement was given by saying that local patrons had already loaned items by Clausen, Lavery, Stott, Le Sidaner, Wilson Steer and Priestman. The local patrons almost certainly included Sam Wilson and Charles Rutherston, the brother of William Rothenstein and the letter was sent, to among others, Gordon Craig. The final draft insisted that what was desired was a drawing study or sketch as opposed to a finished picture. Judging from the final size of the exhibition, there was obviously a very positive response to the letter.

On 24 February Jones then wrote to the packers, Messrs Bradley & Co. of Charlotte Street, Fitzroy Square, with a list of contributing

London artists for collection and delivery to Leeds by noon, Saturday 4 March. Bradleys agreed and charged the Club £13 for its services. Four days later Herbert Thompson wrote back saying that in a moment of weakness he had agreed to do the talk though he had to confess he hated public speaking. Moreover he might only expose his own poverty of thought after all the 'clever speakers on recondite subjects you have had of late'. So long as the organizers did not expect more than an informal talk, in the afternoon (to catch the light) all would be well. Thompson also generously offered to loan them a picture by Furse of 'calves in the ruddy light of late afternoon sun' and two 'brilliant' water colour sketches by the late Tom Collier. The only afternoon suitable was that planned for Holbrook Jackson's talk on the Superman as Saint' on 18 March, but he gladly gave way and Thompson gave his talk as planned.

The exhibition was, according to Jones's notes, a great artistic, if not financial, success but then that was not its aim. Sam Wilson, who had loaned some pictures, also bought two small studies, of an old man and female nude in sepia ink and charcoal, by William Orpen for eight guineas each (of which the Club took one guinea commission).[35] Jones's careful accounts show a loss of £11 9s. 2d. on total costs of £32 0s. 8d. and receipts including sale of pictures of £20 1s. 6d. Bradley's fee of £13 was the overwhelming outlay followed by Goodall & Suddick's printing of posters, tickets and catalogues at £5 3s. 6d. Other costs included picture hangers, insurance, carriage, correspondence, advertisements and a curator for the duration.

If the praise for organizing such a show had to go to the retiring Billy Jones, it was Herbert Thompson who offered it meaning. The son of a Leeds bank manager, Thompson had been art and music critic for the *Yorkshire Post* since 1886.[36] He was a highly respected and influential figure whose education in Wiesbaden had given him a strong taste for German music and culture. Though at Cambridge he had studied law and became a barrister, he held no brief for the bar and lived for art, music and his stamp collection. His diary entry for Saturday 18 March records that he left his home in Burton Crescent, Headingley, after dinner, caught the tram to Coburg Street in the centre of town and walked to the Arts Club in Park Lane to give 'an address on "the tendencies of Modern Art" as represented in the exhibition of studies and sketches now on the walls. The 2 rooms crowded out: W. H. Thorp (his next door neighbour) in the chair. Jaw for about 50 minutes or more.'[37]

Despite his diffidence, Thompson's 'jawing' was an accomplished outline of contemporary art trends exemplified by the exhibition. He began by asking whether there was a special tendency in modern art.

It was 'a departure from realism', pioneered by Turner, which showed one of two things; either 'an inability to make realism of sufficient aesthetic value' or 'a determination to make the picture clearly express what was half-hidden, and permanently to express what had appeared in a flash and then was gone'[38] (a *super-reality* Orage might have said). Today imitation and classic convention had been rejected in favour of 'a more individual and eclectic study, both of nature and the older schools'.

Thus the modern tendency could be defined as firstly, a daring individual freedom in subject and method, as in Whistler's 'Nocturnes', and secondly, a special development of design 'by which is meant something more than composition – something more subtle and less definable'. The modern was also characterized by other elements – a love of mystery 'the unexpressed often being the most beautiful', increased representation of movement 'due to a comparison of the artistic view with the scientific view' and the use of the camera 'especially in the vibrant qualities of atmosphere'. Modernity meant also greater dependence on imagination and on less accepted forms of symbolism and attendance to rapid first impressions such as 'the noting down of thoughts' illustrated in Rodin's sketches for sculpture.

'Design' in the way that Thompson meant it, became as important to younger artists like Kramer and Bruce Turner as the Club's earlier endorsement of the unfinished sketch had been. Through Thompson's talk members felt The Modern take shape. It entered the Club's discourses; they felt modern, Orage saw himself as consciously modernizing; Michael Sadler later addressed his audience as 'we moderns'; they were here to make it new.

The theme of modernity was also present in Holbrook Jackson's guided tour of Liverpool, an Arts Club outing some time the following summer. It was the second of two field trips to study street architecture in the light of Percy Robinson's talk the previous March.[39] The first had been to York whose medievalism they contrast sharply with Liverpool's modernity and both to the detriment of shop-soiled Leeds. As a scouser, Jackson was by no means impartial in his comparisons as he genially indulged his enthusiasm for his home town. Club members were struck by the way great commercial life co-existed with a distinguished civic life. As the gateway to the world, its citizens were conscious of this great purpose and proud to house its energies in a fitting manner. The signs of modernity, electric cars, underground and overhead railways and municipal steam ferries, marked Liverpool out.

For Holbrook Jackson, its street architecture was second to none in the land: fine proportioned avenues with towering stone buildings combined variety of design with harmony of effect. The lead given by the public buildings set a high standard which commercial building followed with pride. In fact it was in the commercial buildings, rather than in the, generally imitative, civic buildings that the best examples of modernity were to be found. Here were buildings that organically and elegantly expressed their purpose. Thus Club members, true to its principles, were invited to apply ideas to life and to find ways of making their own town a fit place to live in. They were encouraged to think in a holistic fashion about their own lives and environment and to see organic links between use and beauty, to see, crucially, the city as an expression of the soul and spirit of its inhabitants. Not just an exercise in civic pride, it was a moral duty to transform Leeds.

Thus the first half year's programme centred the Club on the imaginative revolution of civic life guided by new standards of taste and historical precedent. It advanced the future as a realizable project, made possible through will and imagination rather than as a fatalistic inevitability thrust upon passive citizens by remote and inexplicable forces. The key word was *Modernity*, the past existed to give lessons and examples but not simply to be imitated. The best domestic practices and European ideas were martialled for service, the new individualism heralded. But it was not an individualism of competition. Rather one that depended on the collective health of the community: Nietzschean transcendent man fused with Morrisian socialism. It was an exotic hybrid that bloomed in Leeds that Spring.

Notes

1. *YWP*, 21 January 1905, p.7.
2. See also T. S. Eliot, 'Tradition and the Individual Talent' in *Selected Essays*, Faber, London, 1932, pp.13–22.
3. Millie Price, 'This Worlds Festival', p.116.
4. Ibid.
5. *YWP*, 25 February 1904, p.17.
6. *YWP*, 15 April 1905, p.22 and *Leeds Mercury*, Weekly Supplement, 15 April 1905, p.3.
7. Carswell, *Lives and Letters*, p.22. I have since received an incomplete photocopy of the correspondence from Mr John Bunting who had the original in his possession for some years.
8. Raymond Williams, *Writing in Society*, Verso, London, 1984, p.181.
9. *YWP*, 4 March 1905, p.17.
10. Ibid., a phrase of Matthew Arnold's also adopted by Eliot.
11. Herbert Read, *Annals of Innocence and Experience*, Faber, London, 1946, p.86.
12. Storm Jameson, *Journey from the North*, vol. 1, Collins Harvill, London, 1969, p.50.
13. Shimmin, *The University of Leeds*, pp.123–4.

14. Frederic Moorman's Diary, 1913, Special Collections, Brotherton Library, Leeds University.
15. *Leeds Weekly Citizen*, 9 September 1919, p.8.
16. Letter from John Metcalf, Merlestead, Baildon in *Yorkshire Post*, 12.9.1919.
17. *YWP*, 4 February 1905, p.17.
18. *YWP*, 28 January 1905, p.21.
19. Letter to Florence Farr, 8 February 1905, in Dan H. Laurence, (ed.) *Bernard Shaw Collected Letters*, London, 1972, pp.509–10.
20. *Yorkshire Post*, 15 February 1905, p.5.
21. *Leeds Mercury*, 15 February 1905, p.5.
22. Ibid.
23. *YWP*, 18 February 1905, p.17.
24. Ibid.
25. Ibid.
26. *YWP*, 18 March 1905, p.17.
27. *YWP*, 1 April 1905, p.21.
28. Derek Linstrum, *West Yorkshire Architects and Architecture*, Lund Humphries, London, 1978, p.383.
29. *YWP*, 29 April 1905, p.21.
30. Ibid.
31. *YWP*, 6 May 1905, p.21.
32. Ibid.
33. From a scrapbook in the possession of Denis Mason Jones, son of William Alban Jones, Long Causeway, Adel, Leeds, to whom I am most grateful.
34. *Yorkshire Post*, Wednesday 8 March 1905.
35. I am grateful to Adam White for finding these which are now both in Leeds Art Gallery in the Sam Wilson Collection.
36. Mildred A. Gibb and Frank Beckwith, *The Yorkshire Post: Two Centuries*, Yorks Conservative Newspapers, Leeds, 1954, p.61.
37. Herbert Thompson's Diary, 1905, Special Collections, Brotherton Library, University of Leeds.
38. *YWP*, 25 March 1905, p.17.
39. Unheaded newspaper cutting dated only 1905, signed 'H.J.' in the miscellaneous clubs and societies box, Brotherton Collection, Brotherton Library, University of Leeds.

CHAPTER FIVE

The Discovery of the Future

At the Club's second annual meeting on 22 September 1905, Holbrook Jackson reported with obvious satisfaction that the year's work had been in keeping with the high standards aimed at by its founder.[1] Membership had exactly doubled to ninety and there had been only two resignations. G. K. Chesterton, T. J. Cobden-Sanderson, Edward Carpenter, George Bernard Shaw and Arthur Penty were made honorary members. The Club's library had been extended, thanks to the generosity of members and in turn was eagerly sought by others. Its activities had flowed out into the town. Jackson reported: 'several of the individual members of the club had so caught its inner spirit as to carry the work beyond the clubrooms into the broad stream of the city's life'.[2] As a result of Shaw's talk the club had circulated a questionnaire on how to beautify Leeds (as an alternative to immolating it) which had received many replies. It was intended to publish a report based on them in the form of a tract.

But in a move which was to signal a division of the Club's unity of purpose, it was decided to 'make the theatres of Leeds more interesting'. Attempts would be made to induce theatre companies to bring the 'better type of modern play' to Leeds, and the Royal Court Theatre was being approached about giving performances of some of its repertoire of Shaw's plays. There was no evidence that either of these moves was successful, though moving to this safer area of reform was perhaps more to the taste of its 'respectable' members than the directly political ambitions of its founders. However, the momentum gathered pace, culminating in the formation of the Leeds Playgoers Society, under the wing of W. P. Irving, two years later.

The lecture syllabus for the autumn session also lacked the concentrated sense of purpose of previous sessions. Though its aura prevailed, there were no expositions of Nietzschean philosophy as such and interest was more diffuse. In so far as a core theme was manifest it was 'Utopianism': Orage's lectures on 'Practical Imagination' and the 'Renaissance of Platonism' and Jackson's on 'The Uses of Freedom' all focused on the ideal society, as did Waddington's 'Impressions of Venice' on the city beautiful. These themes were, however, pursued in depth in the Friday evening discussions. In their talks, the Rev. Lee on Buddhism and Charles Whitmell, a schools inspector, on Clough's *Dipsychus* suggested some Nietzschean precursors, while Barton saw

Turgenev as a modern spiritual thinker. A more eccentric spiritualist, Stoughton Harris, gave an almost incomprehensible talk on the 'Fourth Dimension'. Arts and crafts were represented by a talk on porcelain by Alfred J. Sanders, a prominent Leeds collector, while Montague Fordham of the Arts and Crafts Gallery and the novelist, Oliver Onions both critically surveyed arts institutions.

Typically, Orage's lecture on 'Practical Imagination' crowded out the Club rooms. With Holbrook Jackson chairing the lively meeting and discussion that followed, Orage argued that the time had come for imagination to replace reason as a means to the truth. By perfecting the instruments of logic, the Greeks had raised the status of reasoning to the highest level. The question was: could imagination be trained in the same way? Orage thought so; take for example the plans of the architect. The trained mind could imagine a number of possible elevations and even completed buildings from them. This was practical imagination in operation. The same principles could be used in political thinking. Orage proceeded to divide utopian political thinkers into two categories: the fanciful and the imaginative. Bacon, Bellamy, More, Butler, Morris, Howells, Cabet and Campanella belonged to the former class because 'Their Utopias might be described as elevations without plans, and they were comparable to beautiful drawings made by artists of splendid buildings of fairy land, which, however, were architecturally impossible'.[3]

Only two utopian thinkers occupied the second class and they were, as master and apprentice, a surprising coupling: Plato and H. G. Wells. Orage's talk showed their common ground.[4] Wells, he said, 'demanded no revolution or impossible condition for his postulate, but assuming the world to be what it appears to be, he had endeavoured to trace the lines upon which things were moving'. Continuing the architectural metaphor, Wells projected elevations upon real plans and made his modern Utopia not so much an ideal as a deliberate forecast. Despite this Wells was 'defective in his fundamentals' – a theosophical phrase? – unlike Plato, 'It had never occurred to him to ask what Nature's plans were; or if it did he would probably dismiss the problem as insoluble'.

Before writing the *Republic*, said Orage, Plato had for years devoted himself to 'high speculation about the truths of nature' which were indispensible to any great art. So just as the postulates and axioms of reasoning were discoverable so, according to Plato, were those of the imagination. He defined them as 'The Good' as end and 'Justice and Beauty' as means. Anyone using these postulates would be able to forecast the future with certitude. In the discussion, Orage talked about Plato's 'splendidly dogmatic certitude about his findings compared with

Wells's personal reticence about his. This splendid certainty resulted from a trained practical imagination, which when put into practice would bring about 'the discovery of the future'.

Orage continued this reading of Plato two weeks later, when replacing the published talk on 'Thomas Hardy' by W. O. Peake, he lectured on the 'Renaissance of Platonism in England'.[5] He thought that the extraordinary current revival of interest in Plato owed a great deal to recent Platonic scholarship in, for example, fixing editions, settling the chronology of the dialogues and situating them historically. There was now as good a chance of interpreting Plato as even his contemporaries had. Moreover Jowett's translations of the dialogues were in excellent English and could furnish the bible of the Platonic Renaissance. It would be, like the influence of Herbert Spencer in the nineteenth century, a movement rather than a mere tendency. Significantly, he asserted, then everyone had been a materialist. The vast majority of people were evolutionists, agnostics, scientists and Spencerians, which was quite different from the closed scholastic or literary corporation which composed a school. But with the break-up of materialism as a movement the revival of Platonic idealism had become possible and because of materialism's real scientific achievements, Platonism had been able to learn from it.

Unlike previous revivals of Platonism, the mystical, symbological and theological elements of Platonism were of little interest to the modern mind. Rather the renaissance would be 'imaginatively sociological', using the *Republic* as chief source. This sociological colouring would derive from Platonism's insertion into the tradition of sociological thought of Carlyle, Ruskin and Morris. However, H. G. Wells, who had begun as a Spencerian, would be its chief architect. Orage claimed there was a general movement amongst intellectuals from materialist determinism to Platonism evinced by, for example, G. B. Shaw, W. B. Yeats, Thomas Hardy, Oliver Lodge, William James, Edward Carpenter, Myers and Voysey.

This shrewd interpretation of modern intellectual tendencies displayed by Orage, was continued in the Friday evening sessions. In these a subject was given for each discussion with qualifying aphorisms from the Club's favoured poets and philosophers with subtitles as follows:

> 17 November: Why the Artist is useless.
> 'Poets are the unacknowledged legislators of the world.'
> Shelley
>
> 24 November: Why the Philosopher is useless.
> 'The only hope for mankind is the reconciliation of Philosophy with the World.'
> Nettleship's 'Plato'

1 December: The advantages of telling lies.
'Good men never speak the truth!'
Nietzsche

8 December: What is Freedom?
'Liberty means responsibility. That is why most men dread it.'
G. B. Shaw

15 December: Utopianism.
'Proper creations of the imagination – and not of fancy – are universal verities.'
Emerson

29 December: Duty: social and individual.
'What others give as duties, I give as living impulses.'
Whitman

The discussion subtitles emphasized individual responsibility and agency, breaking conventions and personal response. Both Nettleship's and Emerson's introduced the pragmatic note signalled in Orage's talks, while the others suggested transvaluing values and inspirational action.

It was again Holbrook Jackson's part to reinforce the pragmatic, or as he put it, the 'point of view of practical sociology', rather than the philosophic idea of freedom, in his key talk on the 'Uses of Freedom' on 2 December.

Nietzsche's view that freedom was 'the will to be responsible for oneself' was undoubtedly profound but also entirely abstract.[6] Since the limitations of the power of the will were the limits of freedom and transcendent will-power was a negligible quantity, it followed that in the philosophic sense there could be very little freedom. He would therefore confine his talk to constitutional freedom or liberty. This was an entertaining version of the theories of the organic state developed by Bradley and Bosanquet, but most crucially T. H. Green, which signalled an end to laissez-faire political economy.

Liberty, he began, was the margin of free action given to the individual by the state (which itself was either the constituted enactment of the general will or that of a single will more dominant than the rest). Since this margin varies from country to country, he said, freedom, like morality, was 'largely a matter of geography'. Men were, quoting William Watson, 'such stuff as stars are made of', but unlike stars, they consciously sought their aim and destiny.

> We could not say for certain what was the end aimed at; what was the meaning of the populous heavens peopled with rotating worlds working out undreamed of destinies, but from careful listening to the music of the spheres we had concluded that the harmony was a song of growth.[7]

From this man and star may have the common end of growth towards a fuller consciousness of things and a firmer power to control them –

to lead fate rather than be fate-led. The problem today was that though men lived in a wide margin of liberty but were still in thrall to external conditions like disease that really should, in this stage of civilization, have been overcome, they lacked the will to be really free.

Whereas, he continued, social organicism had been more prevalent under the feudal economy, in contemporary capitalist society the economics of the Manchester School gave us more liberty than we knew how to use. Thus the 'social sense' had to be redeveloped urgently – 'a view of society not as a series of separate conflicting elements, but as an organism of units working to a common end'. He quoted Shaw's injunction that it was time to rein in the doctrine of live and let live and instead 'establish our rights by shouldering our share of the social burden'. However, social progress could only come from right feeling in which it was understood that individual growth corresponded to the growth of whole social organism. True economic freedom therefore lay in the proper use of growth, even to recognizing its rebels who were after all 'nothing but the heralds of a new dawn'.

If Orage and Jackson, in their talks, had begun to establish some of the principles of the New Republic, it was Charles Smythe who tackled the tricky problem of its poetry.[8] He too felt that a new age was dawning in which the 'cold hard materialism of the last century had run fallow and a new spiritual philosophy of the universe, to which the function of the poet was essential, was being formulated. Poets always expressed both the universal and the temporal in various measure in their work and, in particular, the essential truths which lay beyond reason. This was their primary value. The poetry of all ages had characteristics marked by, and in the end exhausted by, its epoch. New forms and themes had to be found. He speculated that these might be, firstly, man in relation to himself, secondly, the inherent poetry or symbolism of material things and, thirdly, poetry of will-power and personality. In some ways no bad selection, though he failed to predict the abrupt crisis of personality around the First World War, which shattered Romantic individualism and bundled the modernist poets willy-nilly into the fragmentation of masks and personae.

The poet as possessor of mystical insight was how J. E. Barton characterized his subject, Turgenev, on 28 October. Like Theophile Gautier, his stories showed an amazing perception of fine detail, but also a quality which separated him from both Gautier and his more intellectual predecessor Balzac, which was his ability to penetrate the surface things and infuse them with spiritual life: 'He saw the very bottom of human lives with a marvellous intensity, producing thereby in his reader a kind of indefinable calm'.[9] The specific qualities Turgenev revealed, said Barton, were 'the national fervour of love and of a soil'.

Complementing Orage's renaissance of Platonism, Arthur Lee drew attention to the European renaissance of Buddhism. He argued that the spiritual influences behind European writers like Turgenev came from even further east. The signs of Buddhism, he said in his talk on 28 October, could be seen all over Europe. Buddhism had deeply influenced Schopenhauer and Wagner (and they, in their turn, Nietzsche), but owing to the recent extraordinary rise of Japan – witnessed by its recent military humiliations of Russia – Buddhism was no longer merely a curious phenomenon. It had 'suddenly proved to be a factor of immense potency in the moral development of the race'.[10] The secret of Japanese heroism and self-restraint lay ultimately in the Buddhist denial of individualism. It had succeeded in subjugating private selfishness to public duty far more effectively than had the West.

Lee then outlined the relationship of Buddhism to science, saying that through the work of Frederick Myers, significant advances in understanding consciousness had come about. Myers had come up with a workable hypothesis about the subliminal consciousness which had enabled insight into the 'composite self' or 'multiple soul'. The reasons why this probing into the self was deeply distressing to those formed by Western-Christianity was because of its over valuation of individualism, a tradition which had run to seed in the moral and social anarchy of contemporary Europe. Buddhism on the contrary 'suggests a higher egoism in which the real "I" would be to the personal "I" what the ocean is to a dewdrop'. Similarly, glib Western notions like 'progress' were shown by Buddhism to be no more than a 'constant and terrible struggle against the massed efforts of countless inherited ghostly wills latent in all of us'. As Japan had borrowed the scientific inventions of the West, so Europe now desperately needed the spiritual truths of the East.

Of the three talks on the arts and crafts, the first by Oliver Onions also ended by seeing signs of a new awakening. Most of his talk on 'Modern English Black and White Art', 4 November, was devoted to the celebrated Leeds cartoonist, Phil May. Onions, though better known as the author of *Tales from a Far Riding* and *The Compleat Bachelor*, was also a black and white artist. May's greatest gift was his intellect and his art could stand comparison with the best, but May was now dead and ignoring new technological possibilities, the tradition of black and white art had decayed into conventional repetition. Onions blamed the institutions of art education for this decadence. Cheap education had encouraged mediocrity, he said, 'By means of scholarships hundreds of machine-made artists of the decorative school were being turned out yearly from the Royal College of Art, and the various Art Schools throughout the country'.[11] He demanded fewer scholarships and a more thorough training.

Though largely forgotten now, Onions (1873–1961), a Bradford born writer, was popular nationally. He was the same age as Orage but had spent three years at the RCA (or National Art Training School as it was then) and had then gone to Paris where in 1897 he was editor of the *Quartier Latin*. Despite writing The *Compleat Bachelor* in 1900, he married fellow romantic novelist Berta Ruck, celebrated for her quarrel with Virginia Woolf over the inadvertent appearance of her name in *Jacob's Room*. He was described as a typical Yorkshire man, capable of bitter attacks and no little misogynism. Clemence Dane called him 'a lone wolf in literature'[12] though politically he was a Fabian, a member of Herbert Bland's Anti-Puritan League and part of Chesterton's London circle.[13]

The second talk was held jointly with the Yorkshire Union of Artists in Leeds City Art Gallery, on 25 November, with Orage in the chair. The speaker, Montague Fordham, as director of the Arts and Crafts Gallery in London, also had a national reputation. Though nominally his talk was on the arts and crafts and their relation to everyday life, this too became an attack on art education institutions. These, he said, wasted large sums of ratepayers' money on schools of art and music, in a process that 'had created a large number of unemployed and unemployable people of certain technical capacity to compete with the few artists, and make life more difficult for them'.[14] The arts and crafts movement he said, was in crisis and in need of a new movement for both making and appreciating craft work. The necessity of solving the economic organization of the workshop and making things not only beautiful but moderately inexpensive, was *not* helped by William Morris, who was not only a 'plutocrat' himself, but worked for the 'plutocracy'. Though his own work was excellent, he left no tradition to help the impecunious craftsman who wanted to work for less wealthy people – a damaging criticism of one of the Club's household gods. Essentially, said Fordham, the artist was a mystic and art a mystery, a spiritual inspiration. But while the fine arts rested on individual inspiration, the crafts were a product of the workshop and so the problem became one of how to so build the workshop that inspiration might flow in and through it. The mere employment of money and energy to lift the workshop above the 'sordid struggle for wealth' was not enough. Both businessmen and municipalities had a responsibility to nurture and encourage the crafts movement rather than throwing away money on superficial training. This was sheer folly; if all work which was really suitable to be made by hand and was unfit for machinery was made by hand, there would be plenty of work for everybody.

Fordham's talk was well received and at the evening dinner at the Metropole for the Yorkshire Union of Artists it allowed Holbrook Jackson, who was replying to the toast, to promote the work of the Club. He said 'the aim of the Leeds Arts Club was to emphasise the philosophical side of art and the side of social utility (applause). Leeds had still a great deal to do to extirpate its commercial sins. It was still a blot on the fair face of the land'.[15]

What Fordham was saying was also intriguing territory for Orage, who with Penty was already working on what he called a 'Politics for Craftsmen' in an article published three years later. Penty, who now living in London and by this time probably a friend of Fordham's, was already drafting the first of forty drafts of his book the *Restoration of the Gild System*. Fordham, who published his own book, *Mother Earth* in the same year, became involved in the guilds movement from the earliest days and with Penty reacted violently rightwards to the Bolshevik Revolution in Russia shortly after he had published his second book *A Short History of English Rural Life*. As G. D. H. Cole commented at the time, of the National Guilds League, 'Our left wing is pushing us into Russianized communism: our right wing, in a panic lest something is really going to happen, is trekking at its best speed for the land of spiritual values, in which gross material things can be forgotten'.[16] While many left guild socialists, including Palme Dutt, Page Arnott, William Mellor, the Ewers, Ellen Wilkinson and Willy Gallagher eventually split off to found the Communist Party in 1920, Fordham and Penty collaborated in establishing the Rural Reconstruction Association.

How far A. W. Waddington actually contributed to Penty's formulation of guild politics and how far he was merely an enthusiastic follower is unclear, but his passionate articulation of it is plain to see. He concluded the Club's autumn session with a talk on one of the highest examples of guild craftsmanship, Venice, on 16 December. It was a fitting end to the term's work on utopian idealism since he managed to convey the material reality of Venice as the realization of an 'Idea'. He and his friend John Fearnley had recently visited Venice for the International Art Congress held there in September and John Fearnley's photographs illustrated his lecture. Since for him, Venice was the 'materialisation of the minds of Venetians', to find its true value, the traveller must convert it once again into 'mind' and relate it to his own situation.

Venice embodied the two great principles of church and state, and it was the united force of these two principles that made it into a city.

The patriotism that had welded them 'had two spheres of labour: the fitting of one's surroundings to become the germ of one's "Utopia", and the fitting of oneself to be a power therein.'[17] Venice had become a beautiful and renowned city because of common effort against a common foe and was a treasure city of art won by those who cared sufficiently to fight for it. The story of Venice had to repeat itself in all cities if they were to become beautiful. But before beauty there had to be cleanliness and before cleanliness, fighting. Thus his battle cry was 'Let your work be a fight; your peace a victory'! Did the assembled members conjure visions of Renaissance piazzas in City Square or even gondolas on the Leeds and Liverpool canal? Why not! Marshall's Mill in Holbeck already sported a Florentine campanile and elegant vaulted arcades were opening down the medieval burgesses off Briggate. Leeds, a Venice of the North . . . ? But it would be a fight of titanic dimensions with the artist-militant defiantly shaking his brush at faceless municipal bureaucrat and silk-hatted capitalist alike.

For those who wanted more, Waddington added a kind of coda to this talk at the Headingly Literary Society on 8 January. At this society, in the Methodist Church school room in Victoria Road, a couple of hundred yards from the house of Holbrook Jackson, Waddington talked on 'Cities: Real and Ideal'. It was another powerful demonstration of his idealism which began by introducing the work of the Garden City Association as 'not only an important experiment but as also the revival of important political creeds'.[18] The tenets of the creed were threefold: firstly, that all existing cities were incomplete; secondly, that cities did not grow by accident but 'like all vital organisms are the result of natural forces acting on living germs' and, thirdly, that within limits, cities were the exact counterparts of the effective mind of its citizens. Thus it followed, as in Venice, that the real city was the tangible result of an ideal city, unconsciously built, thought upon thought in the public mind. 'The science of politics therefore demands a psychological laboratory'. Since one could analyse the dominant thought forms that had created the great classical cities like Thebes, Rome and Athens, what belief did the modern city symbolize? He answered with a stunning metaphor:

> Nietzsche's 'reversed cripple' tells the whole story. The reversed cripple had too much of one thing or too little of everything else; the modern city is the reversed cripple – too much commerce or too little everything else. Commerce like a noble river has overflowed its banks, flooding houses, workshops, churches.[19]

From this inundation, he continued, the twin problems arose of how to redirect the river of commerce back within its true boundaries ('banks' perhaps) and how to raise church, state, art and industry above the highest floodline. The first could be achieved through the development of municipal thought and will, the second, by culture 'reaching down to the ancient crafts – as in the medieval guilds'. In conclusion, he poetically evoked the Arts Club's credo,

> But a reverence for beauty in Art and nature, both as road toward perfection and as a standard of success, is above all things needed; and the purifying of atmosphere and rivers, and the blending of the gardener's art with that of the builder are the first evidences that the city means 'business' in other ways than that of commerce.

On this poetic note Waddington prepared to assume the leadership of the Club. He would have known that Orage had already taken his leave from his school position on 22 December and was bent on the metropolis having come to the conclusion, despite their best energies, that 'Leeds and Dionysos would not work'. Jackson whose commitment to the provinces was stronger, held on for the time being, but resigned reluctantly the following April. He wrote:

> Leeds began to choke him (Orage). Its possibilities for expression and adventure suddenly seemed to fail. The dream of turning the dingy Yorkshire town into a modern Athens was broken, for our Socrates was going to leave us. Something had snapped and Orage seized the offer of a subsidy of £60 from Joseph Smith, a coal merchant from Pudsey who had sat at his feet both at the Theosophical Society and the Arts Club, to break with Leeds and its plain living and high thinking for ever. He would go to London and prepare the way for a newer and bigger campaign on the world's greatest platform and I was to join him as soon as possible. I thought the step premature. My plan was to achieve something in Yorkshire and the north of England generally before we knocked at London's door. I had imagined a battery of arts clubs all over the north, and the idea was developing – Halifax and York were nibbling and clubs were later formed in Bradford and Hull. Orage was convinced that all this could be done better from London. But that was an excuse. Something had snapped.[20]

Notes

1. *YWP*, 30 September 1905, p.17.
2. *Leeds Mercury*, 30 September 1905, p.3.
3. *YWP*, 7 October 1905, p.17.
4. Encouraged by the reception given to his talk on practical imagination, Orage decided to contact Wells directly and wrote to him enclosing a newspaper report. He told him how popular his ideas were with the Arts Club members in general and the participants in the Plato Group, which he said, had been running for five or six years (which dates its formation

as 1899 or 1900). The Plato Group had been discussing the same issues in the *Republic* as Wells had addressed (presumably in his *Modern Utopia*) and his solutions had greatly appealed to them. Orage thanked Wells for his stimulus to their imagination. Letter to H. G. Wells, 8 October 1905, H. G. Wells Collection, University of Illinois.

5. *YWP*, 21 October 1905, p.17.
6. *YWP*, 9 December 1905, p.21.
7. Ibid.
8. *YWP*, 14 October 1905, p.17.
9. *YWP*, 4 November 1905, p.17.
10. *YWP*, 28 October 1905, p.17.
11. *YWP*, 11 November 1905, p.17.
12. Kunitz and Haycraft, *Twentieth Century Authors*, Wilson, New York, 1969, p.1051.
13. Mrs Cecil Chesterton, *The Chestertons*, London, Chapman and Hall, 1941, p.58.
14. *Leeds Mercury*, 27 November 1905, p.6.
15. Ibid.
16. Quoted in James Webb, *The Occult Establishment*, Open Court, La Salle, Illinois, 1976, p.112.
17. *YWP*, 23 December 1905, p.21.
18. *YWP*, 13 January 1906, p.17.
19. Ibid.
20. Holbrook Jackson, *The Windmill*, no. 11, Heinemann, London, 1948, pp.47–48.

CHAPTER SIX

1906: The Celtic Revival and 'National' Socialism

Even before the spring 1906 programme had been drawn up Orage was no longer certain he would see it through. In November, after a Federation meeting, he had stayed over with a theosophical friend in Harrogate and written in the visitor's book under the heading *Where to*? 'God only knows!' and under *Remarks* 'Over a precipice. How far to the bottom?'[1] The previous August he had resigned from the discussions panel due to 'strain of over-work' despite having been co-opted onto it only three months before[2] and during July he had had three days off work due to neuralgia.[3] Plainly, he was exhausted. The demands of the Club, the TS, school, marital tensions, extramarital tensions, poverty and vaulting ambition had become unbearable. During the autumn term he had secured permission from the Leeds School Board for unpaid leave, though not apparently his resignation, and on 22 December his headmaster at Roundhay Road Boys recorded in the school log 'A. R. Orage ceased duties today having leave of absence for 6 months in order to write a book'. So, though his boats were not entirely burned, he was now a writer rather than a schoolteacher.

Though all accounts describe him as a popular and inspirational teacher under a relatively enlightened board, the school regime had taxed him. No description of Roundhay Road Boys from this time has survived, but Millie Price recorded her own schoolroom in Park Lane:

> Long desks, one behind the other, pierced with inkwell holes about a yard apart, provided seating space for sixty to seventy children in each class. There were other smaller rooms furnished similarly, but having a stepped floor so that the desks rose one above the other. The rooms were indescribably dingy; no pictures, no flowers, no pleasing object whatever on which to rest the eye.[4]

Though Orage's own school was less than ten years old and architect designed, the size of classes, inflexible routine and absence of anything except the utilitarian could not have done anything for his spirits. His walk from Potternewton Lane took him from an almost rural suburbia down Harrogate Road past spacious villas, or through Potternewton Park, into dense terraced and back-to-back housing. His knight-errantry would have been tested daily. To this was added, according to Mairet, the intense frustration that his meagrely paid profession increasingly prevented him from realizing his real vocation.

> To earn his living as an elementary school teacher whilst pursuing his real ambitions and applying all his greatest efforts elsewhere, was not only a division of his forces but in every way unsound. Whilst becoming a teacher – and something of a leader – of men and women, and clever ones at that his professional status was fixed at the lowest possible without hope of improvement. And now, with the attainment of considerable recognition in higher public activities, his position had become completely anomalous. That he had less than a bricklayer's income had never worried him enough in itself; but now it was a grave disability.[5]

Less than a bricklayer, maybe, but his income had remained at only £105 p.a. since September 1902,[6] and although he would ordinarily have received an annual increment of £5, failed to receive it, according to Millie Price, because of his persistent late timekeeping. But for Mairet,

> What made Leeds at last impossible for him was that the work by which he existed had become a mere obstacle to the powers which he wished to exercise, and which others, too, most valued in him . . . Nothing could now satisfy either of them but metropolitan life with all its mirages of mighty opportunity, and they thought they (Orage and Jackson) would probably work again in partnership, perhaps to repeat their provincial success on a wider stage of action.[7]

At Orage's funeral in 1934 Holbrook Jackson confided sadly to Millie Price that it was his introduction to Nietzsche that had been the unbalancing of his life. Mairet too thought that the impact of a really powerful thinker always had more than intellectual consequences and with Nietzsche this was particularly marked. Orage had increasingly believed that morality was a matter of individual style rather than religious or social regulation and since he had read Nietzsche he was now convinced that exercising his own will-to-power was the highest duty – 'one must seek if one *can*'. But he was bound by conventional ties of marriage and occupation to a life which contradicted this duty, as he saw it, to himself. Nietzsche was individual liberation from convention, but to be free was to leave this world in ruins. The atmosphere of the Club had more than encouraged the flouting of conventions and crucially for Orage had provided him with the laboratory for libertarian experiment in a 'school' context.

Inevitably not a little of this experimenting was sexual. Both Mary Gawthorpe and Millie Price have given accounts of his advances and one wonders how many more there were unrecorded. Mairet tells of an incident at the Club when 'a good and beautiful matron with three young children' had earnestly enquired of Orage how she could find her own way. When he told her that she could only find her way by having the courage to take it, she modestly asserted 'At least I have always tried to do my duty', to which Orage replied 'What a pity!'[8] Gerald Cumberland, a music critic, who had come over from Manchester on occasion to hear Orage lecture, commented on the swooning young ladies who lapped up every word[9] but this may well be little more than locker-room chatter. As for Orage's 'lover-comrade' who had become his wife, Jean, little is known except that she was an excellent needlewoman, sharp debater and strong theosophist. Millie Price thought that at about this time, unhappy in a childless marriage, she had left Leeds for Haslemere 'to practice her craft' in one of the flourishing arts and crafts centres there[10] and certainly some years later she was working on looms at William Morris's firm in Oxford Street. Mairet, however, says that the split did not come until they were in London, and Carswell incorrectly that she left Orage for Holbrook Jackson.[11] They did in fact separate on leaving Leeds but as late as 1915 Jean, a Roman Catholic, still refused to divorce him. Whatever, it was clear that the marriage was no longer compatible with Orage's belief that people should 'philander a little for the good of the soul'.[12]

For Millie Price, who had moved away from Leeds for a while, 'romantic tenderness had changed to physical desire' and though Orage was the magnet that drew her back to Leeds it produced only 'distressful meetings and agonised partings'. She was the direct beneficiary of his old friend Cyril Arthington Pease's attempt to induce Orage to help him set up a model school in Letchworth under Ebenezer Howard's aegis. Orage, who had already set his sights on London, gave her Pease's letter and recommended her for the job which she got, after which they met only a few times more. He had in the meantime anyway, been frequently in London for TS meetings where he met the woman who was to play a major role in the next phase of his life, Beatrice Hastings.

His role at the Club was much diminished and though he chaired meetings of other speakers, gave only one talk himself. However a new series of Friday discussions under the title of 'Events of the Week – Literary, Artistic, Political', echoing as they do his 'Notes of the Week' which became a feature of the *New Age*, may well have been his inspiration and the printed syllabus still listed Orage on the committee of management. Holbrook Jackson remained as Hon. Sec. until April when a note circulated to members announced that he had resigned and that A. W. Waddington would replace him. Jean Orage's cousin, Miss A. K. Kennedy, a headmistress and theosophist would be assistant secretary.

On Saturday 27 January the *YWP* announced the Club's spring programme as 'a most attractive list of lectures for the remainder of the winter season'. The programme seemed to lack the central core of Nietzschean themes but included no less than W. B. Yeats who would be lecturing on the 'Living Voice'. The opening session was on Saturday 20 January, the talk being 'The Necessity and Utility of the International Language of Esperanto' by F. L. G. Marechal, the secretary of the Esperanto Group in Leeds. Other themes included the Reformation, civic economy, modern art, Gregorian music, mass production, religious agnosticism, city growth, Holbrook Jackson on experimental life and lastly Orage on a new Magna Charta. One session was entitled 'Open Letters of Revolt' from various members. The two exhibitions for the session were of pastels and oils by Mark Senior, a locally established painter and the craft work of the Guild of Saint Michael. One last event which appeared neither on the printed list nor in the newspaper was the performance of six one-act plays over two nights by W. B. Yeats's, newly formed Irish National Theatre, including Yeats himself, John Millington Synge, and the entire company, an extraordinary coup.

On Saturday 27 January Orage chaired Frank B. Hutton's lecture on 'The Philosophical Significance of the Renaissance'. Hutton argued that the result of the reformation of the sixteenth century was the establishment of Protestant Christianity whose distinctive character lay in its protest against the dogmatic claims of Romanism.[13] Philosophically, protestantism replaced the Roman dualism, of faith in the supernatural order and reason in the natural order, with a monistic system. However, in the absence of external authority, the protestant world was compelled to make a choice between two forms of monism, either materialistic monism which amounted to atheism or idealistic monism, which was pantheism. These he concluded were in fact the two current philosophies in protestant countries today. It was unclear which he advocated, but it would have been consistent with the Club's dominant outlook to have been the second.

The following week Holbrook Jackson chaired J. F. Fearnley's lecture on 'An Omitted Chapter in Civic Economy'. This was a thinly veiled attack on the laxity of the city council in allowing commercial interests to continually defile the town. He argued that since wealth was not merely material riches but 'all things conducive to the health and welfare of the community' the bounty of nature, and works of art ought therefore to be included in the term.[14] These things were of course not recognized by mercantile economy with the result that the injurious discharge of smoke, chemicals and other waste was not controlled. Following William Morris's argument in 'Useless Toil and Useful Labour', he continued that labour was also compelled to perform useless and degrading tasks both by machine-making things which could be better made by hand and in the outrageous system of advertising which had recently developed. In the absence of adequate municipal action, 'All disinterested men of light and leading should form themselves into a committee of public weal to watch over these matters and let their voices be heard with no uncertain sound'. In the discussion that followed it was decided to set up a Committee of Public Taste with the intention of turning the Club's ideas into practical politics. In the Club's new manifesto various suggestions for reform would be incorporated. Although this project probably never got off the ground, twelve years later some members of the Club including Frederic Moorman, William Thorp and Arthur Rowntree did form a Civic Society. (A few days later another Club member, a schoolteacher called Sarah Foster, also carried Morris's message into what appeared to be another of the Club's offspring, the Headingley Literary Society, in a meeting chaired by W. P. Irving.)

Mark Senior's Exhibition of pastels and oils opened at the Club the following Monday, 4 February, and at the regular Saturday meeting he lectured on 'Two Aspects of Modern Art, Caricature and Landscape'. Senior (1862–1927) was the son of a wealthy Wakefield woollen manufacturer who had an established reputation as an English Impressionist painter. Recently interest in his work has revived and in 1983 an exhibition of his work was held at Wakefield Art Gallery. The catalogue foreword noted:

> Mark Senior belongs among that group of late 19th and early 20th century English painters of whom perhaps the most famous is George Clausen whose world was so violently challenged by the new vision of the Cubists and Post-impressionists, and whose work until recently was so unfashionable as to be all but invisible.[15]

Clausen was a lifelong friend and his greatest influence. What he most admired in Clausen also characterized his own work 'the same love of English landscape and of English peasant types, touching them with a glamour of fantasy which made him less interested in them as concrete individualities than as types'.[16] His friendship with Wilson Steer, Frank Brangwyn, Whistler and William Orpen may have facilitated the Club's exhibition of their work the previous year. He was also a member of the Chelsea Arts Club and a founder of the Leeds Studio Club as well as the Arts Club. While portrait painting of Leeds dignitaries provided him with a regular income in the winter, in the summer he would decamp with his whole family and numerous fellow artists to Runswick Bay on the North Sea coast where he could practise *plein air* techniques. Many of his most memorable paintings were made here. Though regarded by friends like Rowland Hill as a warm and generous man, he had no time for the new generation of painters. Later he was to have a furious public argument with Jacob Kramer, over his sketches for Sadler and Rothenstein's ill-fated Leeds Town Hall scheme, which he regarded as 'nightmare crudities' and 'distorted and chaotic effusions'[17] about which more later.

His talk to the Club was largely a celebration of the 'modern English School of painters' dating from the foundation of the Royal Academy in 1768 and initiated by Hogarth, Reynolds and Gainsborough.[18] Though it was still, in his view, not surpassed by any of the continental schools, it had in recent years developed two tendencies. The first of these was admirable in that it consisted of painters 'who were so by right of birth, instinctive masters of the brush, who felt and thought in the materials of their art and who found complete satisfaction in beauty of colour and in the vigour and variety of the appeal and massed and contrasting harmonies of good design'. Of the second tendency, of those painters whose aesthetic emotion always had a literary character, he had little more to say. But art was always a compromise in which the effort of representation required selection and omission consistent with the end in view. The truth was that the most advanced painting of the day was merely an old tune played in a new key in different time.

Not surprisingly, his talk occasioned lively disagreement from the audience. It was strongly argued that 'easel paintings were foreign to social life, things apart which bore no relation to the integrate order of society, being rather the expression of highly individualized moods rather than the record of that community of ideas upon which society was based'. His fierce interlocutor continued that 'The true social art was to be found in that of the decorative school whose work always bore a consistent relation to architecture and the building of the cities beautiful'. And, despite all the examples of pictorial art of the last hundred years our cities had become increasingly ugly and that the revival of architecture went hand in hand with that of decorative painting. The discussion, which went on long after the formal closing of the meeting, was a striking example of the heat the Club generated in aesthetic discussion and the passionate commitment to the unity of beauty and utility held by its founders. Senior's aesthetic conservatism, though well intentioned, was plainly out of tune with the Club's young Dionysians.

Significantly the Club's next exhibition, opened on Monday 19 February, for two weeks which was an Exhibition of the Craft Work of the Guild of Saint Michael, precisely expressed the thematic unity of beauty and utility. It was accompanied by a talk by Albert Waddington on 'The Cost of Cheapness', which, though unreported, almost certainly would have carried on the argument against machine-making what could better be made by hand. The exhibition contained fine examples of electric light and other fittings with silver and small work, church work and jewelry. 'Most of the larger handicrafts are of wrought iron and without exception very fine workmanship, the candlesticks in particular being worthy of attention. Some beautifully worked bowls and jars of beaten copper . . .' reported the *Yorkshire Evening Post.*[19]

The cult of the medieval was further reinforced when Father Walter Frere lectured on 'Gregorian Music'. Though no newspaper report exists, Mary Gawthorpe remembered the strange fascination of Frere's warblings. Frere was an authority on medieval music and contributed an article on it to *Grove's Musical Encyclopaedia* which is still used. Walter Frere was also a seminal figure in the history of Christian Socialism. Later Bishop of Truro, where he was denounced by the Cornish squires as 'nothing but a damned socialist!' he was First Superior of the remarkable Community of the Resurrection in Mirfield, on its removal from Oxford in 1898, until 1922. At Mirfield he had attempted to forge a new relationship between the Anglican church and the Labour Movement (the stronghold of non-conformity) by inviting prominent labour figures like Keir Hardie to dialogue.[20] His socialism, wrote C. S. Philips in 1947, 'was a very different thing from the modish socialism of today'.

> It was the 'Christian Socialism' of the early nineties – idealistic and religious to the core, ethical far more than political, rooted in compassion for misfortune as such: less the comfortable vision of a planned society than a call to self-sacrifice.[21]

A conference held at Mirfield in June 1906 led to the formation of the Church Socialist League, many of whose members like Archbishop Temple, R. H. Tawney, Maurice Reckitt and S. G. Hobson became deeply involved in guild socialism. Arthur Penty, whose talks with Orage in Leeds and York had laid the foundations of the guilds movement also became a member. Thus significant political and intellectual links ran between the Arts Club and the Anglican Community at Mirfield, which later had national consequences. An interesting example of which was the influence of the political philosophy of J. N. Figgis on the youthful G. D. H. Cole.

Figgis was both a member of the Mirfield Community and Cole's tutor at Oxford.[22] In 1913 he published *Churches and the Modern State*, which advanced a pluralist theory of the state, somewhat in opposition to the positive role of the state advocated by T. H. Green. He regarded the theory of state sovereignty as 'no more than a *venerable superstition*'[23] What interested guild socialists and particularly Cole was that

Figgis argued that the chief contradiction was not between the state and the individual but between the state and other groups, like for example the church and trade unions. As far as possible these other groups should be left free of state intervention. It was a magic formula which at a stroke cut through the hoary old problem of the freedom of the individual within the state, since it conceived of the individual not as the economic monad of laissez-faire economics but as constructed by intergroup relations. Thus what was most important for the security and independence of the individual was the survival and health of the group. 'In past history, Figgis argued, individual liberty had never been won except as a by-product for the right to exist of some particular group, often religious which the civil authorities did not want to exist.'[24] Kingsley Martin in his biography of another devotee of Figgis, Harold Laski, called this 'brilliant theorising' 'the classical justification for the theory of the corporate personality as applied to religious and industrial organisations'.[25] Figgis's *Churches and the Modern State* quickly came to be seen, paradoxically, as the 'very spirit of the National Guilds and [their] finest and clearest expression'.[26]

Though it is jumping ahead of the main story a little it is worth quoting Cole's own summary of the guild socialist movement because it makes clear the process of development that started in Leeds (though he modestly avoids mentioning his own role in it).

> Meanwhile in the *New Age*, a small body of intellectuals, ably headed by A. R. Orage and S. G. Hobson, was developing the new doctrines along another line. The *New Age* had long been an acute critic of orthodox Labour policies. It had supported Victor Grayson in the troubles of 1908, and had preached, at all events from that date, a doctrine which made economic rather than political action the key to social change. Gradually this emerged as Guild Socialism. It began as a plea by a medievalist craftsman, Arthur J. Penty, for a restoration of the gild system in industry. But after 1911, in the hands of S. G. Hobson and Orage it became a plea for the capture of control in industry by National Guilds essentially different from those of the middle ages . . . The proposed National Guilds were to be great corporations from the actual control and management of the various industries; and, according to the New Age plan, they were to be based on, and developed out of, the Trade Unions, which were to be widened to include all workers 'by hand and brain.' The workers, it was urged, should organise not merely for defence but for the winning of control; the protective Trade Unions should turn into great workers' corporations which should demand and secure from a reorganised State the whole responsibility for the conduct of industrial affairs.[27]

Cole added that though there were few direct adherents to the plan 'their skill and activity made them influential far beyond their numbers in the formation of working-class policy'.[28] The significance of this link between Anglo-Catholic and guild socialist intellectuals evidenced at first in Leeds and subsequently through the *New Age* and National Guilds movement appears little remarked. Yet the possibility of a political corporatism underpinned by ethical theory had widespread appeal in cultural circles, not the least for T. S. Eliot, who himself became an Anglo-Catholic in 1927.

In 1908 the Community of the Resurrection also began building an elegant gothic hostel in Leeds, designed by Temple Moore, to house its members who were taking Arts degrees at the university (and is now the dept of Adult Education). Its members here were also strongly committed to social reform. Storm Jameson, who was then an undergraduate at Leeds University, remembered falling in love with one of them and becoming naively involved in 'good works':

> Together we trudged about the slums beyond the filthy River Aire during a strike which had been going on for several weeks or months – what strike was it? – carrying tins of cocoa and other oddments given to us by the Charity Organisation Society. We walked about all day, and took back written reports to the Society: 'Room bare, all moveable objects pawned, wife pregnant, needs bedlinen, food.' What in decency's name can these half-starved women, sometimes lying in bed within a few hours of their time, have felt about the awkward smiling girl and the young man with a charmingly ascetic face who came in, sat down the tin of cocoa and asked politely, 'Do you need anything at once? Have you pawned all you can pawn? Will this be your first, second, seventh child?[29]

In early 1906 in one of those acts of fortune when the levelling and trivializing agents of commercialism so loathed by the Club members and academic researchers struck, the old Leeds Liberal paper, the *Mercury* was taken over by the Harmsworth brothers and the informative 'Weekly Supplement' discontinued, thus removing one of the two important sources of Club reports. However, occasional reports still appeared in the main body of the paper and the *YWP* still reported intermittently. After 17 February, though, there were no more reports for the rest of 1906.

The following lectures were advertised in the published syllabus. On Saturday 3 March, 'Religious Agnosticism' by Rev. W. C. Allan, An Anglican priest in Wortley who had received an MA from Glasgow in 1888. A week later on Saturday 10 March, Professor Clapham, the first Professor of Economics at the University of Leeds, lectured on 'City Growth its Past and Future'. Neither were the last three advertised sessions reported, which was a great pity because they may well have revealed much about the state of mind of the Club's founders as they prepared at last to quit Leeds. The first of these on Saturday 17 March was a talk by Holbrook Jackson which bore the significant title of 'Life considered as an Experiment'. The inevitable conclusion was that for Jackson the experiment in Leeds, though pregnant with immense promise, had failed, for in an epitaph to the venture written eight years later, he wrote:

> Those were great days. Orage and I put our heads together and evolved the Leeds Arts Club, whose ostensible but not admitted object was to reduce Leeds to Nietzscheism! We were very young, and very soon discovered that Dionysos and Leeds would not work. But were we downhearted? No! On the contrary we took it as a compliment and thought ourselves all the wiser! To have been popular in those days would have broken our hearts.[30]

How soon they discovered that 'Dionysos and Leeds would not work' is difficult to say. The Club had been established for less than three years and was easily the best thing Leeds had seen since the heyday of the Phil and Lit over fifty years earlier. Yet its membership still numbered less than a hundred despite the crowds that could be drawn to its lectures by the likes of Shaw and Chesterton and the face of Leeds had not visibly altered as a result of its activities. That they shunned popularity is also a clue to their style. It was a consciously elite group. 'We demanded a new aristocracy to guide a bewildered democracy into Utopia' he wrote on Orage's death.[31] The chiefs, apparently, had not attracted enough indians. This may have been the substance of the next unreported session which was entitled 'Open Letters of Revolt' from 'various members' held the following week, but equally it may have been the opening shots in a campaign about the state of Leeds. Orage was the last speaker on the programme: 'Wanted, a New Magna Charta', on 31 March. It may have been his last talk to the Club before, with Jackson's three volumes of Nietzsche in his case, 'the only ones in Leeds' he boarded the train for London.

But it was unlikely that he would have missed the Club's greatest coup to date: Yeats, Synge and the newly formed Irish National Theatre performing five one-act and one three-act plays over two evenings at the Albert Hall of the Mechanics Institute on April 27 and 28. This was to be Yeats's second visit to the Club in six weeks and Leeds's most major encounter with the Celtic Revival.

Yeats's talk on 'Poetry and the Living Voice', on Wednesday 14 March, was accompanied by Florence Farr, who gave 'an eloquent exposition of the art of speaking to a psaltery'. Orage chaired the meeting. Yeats prefaced his talk with a plea for the revival of the old organic community between the poet and the folk for 'the naive, vital close-quartered views of life that prevailed in the old days before printing disseminated news so far and wide, and inculcated a drab uniformity of thought and belief from which many of us now seek to escape'. So while the old culture came without effort, modern culture, by contrast, was the possession of only a few thousand 'who secure it through leisure and surrender and aloofness from life, rather than from life itself'. He then spoke of the Gaelic movement which sought to preserve the old culture as embodied in song and story. As the movement aimed to make modern lyricism not so much a written as a spoken art, the theatre was its vehicle. He said that he had recently secured a little theatre in Dublin for the purpose and hoped that before long the company would be seen in Leeds.

Yeats intended to revive the lost art of the minstrel for Ireland's many patriotic and other songs. It was an art that was neither speech nor song but somewhere between both, nor was it theatrical declamation for the reciter was not so much an actor as a messenger. Florence Farr was then introduced to exemplify the technique. She recited to a Dolmetsch-made psaltery whose peculiarity was that it used quarter tones and thus lent itself to the cadence of a line or a word. Though she never used the singing voice she employed 'a multitude of musical vocal inflections' in rendering translations from Homer and Euripides and poems from Yeats and Verlaine. It was plainly a moving experience as the *Mercury*'s reviewer (Orage himself ?) made clear.

> It was all very curious and subtle, and led one into an interesting unfamiliar world where only the music of the words and not their meaning seemed to count. Perhaps this was not quite what was intended, but music, whether it be musicians music or poets music, has an odd knack of absorbing the attention in whatever scheme it figures. But the harmony between the word and the incidental music was closer than one has experienced before.[32]

This concurs with Arnold Dolmetsch's own view, who had introduced her to the idea originally, of Florence Farr's performances:

> I once spent a whole night listening to Yeats reciting, and I came to the conclusion that he did not recognise the inflexions of his own voice . . . This did not interfere with the expression of his readings which was very beautiful, but it was useless from my point of view. I then tried Florence Farr, whose golden voice harmonized perfectly with the notes of the instrument. I taught her to play. In my own room with nobody but myself and Yeats present, it was delightful.[33]

But, Dolmetsch noted, in public halls, Miss Farr raised the pitch of her voice unconsciously, so that the psaltery could not follow it. He felt that the result was discordant and in the end a failure, so that it was shortly discontinued. Nevertheless, her performance was an enchanting evening for the large audience at the Institute, but like so many of the Club's productions almost instantly lost to memory.

Florence Farr was a fascinating figure. One of the original 'New Women' of the 1890s she had played the leading lady in the original productions of Ibsen's plays in English. She was also for a time Shaw's leading lady and had been instrumental in introducing him to Yeats at her salon in Hammersmith.[34] Her connection with Orage may well have been through theosophy of which she was a member or possibly its esoteric offshoot, the Hermetic Order of the Golden Dawn. Both she and Yeats were members of this mysterious organization and there may well have been a temple in Leeds, as there was in Bradford (Horus no. 5), perhaps connected with Orage's 'Alpha Centre'.[35] Her close, and probably intimate, connection with Orage continued in the following years. She wrote frequently for the *New Age*, on feminist and radical theatre issues and reviewed books on the 'new cosmic philosophy'. One such review was of Orage's book *Consciousness*, which she announced on 6 June 1907, with dramatic prophecy:

> England has been trembling on the verge of the Socialism that levels down for half a century; and the shade of Nietzsche, more powerful in death than ever in life, overshadows the great reforming movement and informs it with the aristocratic spirit.[36]

Very popular with the members, she returned to the Club at the end of 1908 with a talk on 'The Theatre and the Arts'.

Yeats returned to the Club the following month with John Millington Synge and the entire company of the newly-formed Irish National Theatre from the Abbey Theatre, Dublin, including Sara Allgood, Brigid O'Dempsey, Maire O'Neill, William and Frank Fay and Arthur Sinclair. As well, the group included the great Irish fiddler Arthur Darley, who played Irish airs in the intervals. Though the Club advertised the event in a large box advertisement on the front pages of both the *Mercury* and the *Yorkshire Post* for four consecutive Saturdays before the event, the Albert Hall was barely one-third full on both nights. But whereas the more expensive seats at 4s. and 2s. 6d. were empty, the cheaper gallery seats at 2s., were full.

The programme included on Friday, Synge's *In the Shadow of the Glen*, Lady Gregory's *Spreading the News* and Yeats's *Kathleen Ni Houlihan*. On Saturday Yeats's *Pot of Broth* was followed by Synge's *Riders to the Sea* and the evening rounded off with William Boyle's three-act play *The Building Fund*. The *Mercury*'s reviewer (Orage again?) deeply moved by the Friday night production, commented that the plays stand or fall according to a standard of literary excellence:

> There is an austerity about their mounting which would chill the heart of a London actor-manager, and the literary flavour is genuinely poetic, restrained and quiet. Theatricality as such is something which the authors have divorced from their writings. Atmosphere is every-

> thing, and it is well-realised. In their naked simplicity they transport the audience to the tender green hillsides, to the idyllic plains and whispering woodlands of Ireland.[37]

On the Friday, Maire O'Neill and the Fay brothers took the leading roles in Synge's *Shadow of the Glen*, acting with 'skill and subtlety'. Sara Allgood 'struck a note of sincere pathos' as the eponymous Kathleen ni Houlihan in Yeats's play and gave a 'virile and lively delineation' of Mrs Fallon in *Spreading the News*, ably supported by W. G. Fay.

The Post praised the Club for bringing to Leeds such an accomplished company.

> It was the first that Leeds had seen of that movement which, for want of a better name, is known as the Celtic revival, and which, through the Irish National Theatre Society, is working towards the noble goal of bringing back to the stage some of its ancient claim to be a platform of literature and a mirror of true life rather than a place where the pleasures of the eye are a paramount concern and where the talk of the players is a mere accessory to a picture . . . [38]

The plays exuded the spirit of the movement and the 'vividness and beauty of the tongue and talk of the common people'. They were pervaded with an ineffable sadness and a haunting melancholy. The characterization of the Irish people broke with the stereotype and through the 'slow easy natural bearing of the players and the poetic rhythm of their talk', it was good 'to get away from the noisy Pat swinging his shillelagh and dancing a jig, and see him, as he for the most part really is, quiet, quaint and homely'.

The following night's performance was better attended, though again only the cheaper seats in the gallery were crowded. The *Yorkshire Post*'s critic, probably with little justification, thought that if the company had played at one of the regular theatres it would have intercepted 'that great stream of theatre goers who in ordinary circumstances never think of gravitating to the Albert Hall', and the 'Celtic Revival would make itself known to a much wider section of the public'.[39] The *Mercury*'s reviewer offered no such balm to Leeds 'theatre goers', though the larger turnout of Saturday night allayed some anxiety that effort to enlist interest in the Celtic revival was doomed. 'The fault would have been on the part of the Sassenach, dull and unimaginative as the type has become under the corroding influence of commercialism'.[40] It continued in terms that could easily have expressed Orage's state of mind:

> Leeds people, we are afraid, require educating up to the subtle spirit and poetic expression of the Celtic message. Allowing for purely temperamental differences, a more sympathetic bearing towards the movement could have been expected. Still after 'A Pot of Broth', by

> Mr Yeats; 'Riders to the Sea', by Mr J. M. Synge; and 'The Building Fund', by Mr William Boyle, one is not without hope even in Leeds. To digress for a moment, it has often been regretted that the higher drama, the native product awakens but lukewarm interest in the West Riding of Yorkshire. Little encouragement, in its financial expression, is given to anything dramatic, be it either purely literary or poetic.

Nevertheless, despite this indifference, the reviewer added that the sheer musical beauty of Saturday's performances would inspire any heart not made of cast-iron. Synge's play, *Riders to the Sea*, was, especially, a small classic: 'Tragedy more simple and tense and quiet but with more soul-wracking, haunting expressiveness, has not been on the stage for many a year'. Yet, 'One feels perhaps that the sombre tone is too sustained, too harrowing in its poignancy to be truly artistic, from the dramatic point of view. And yet it is technically almost perfect. There is not a word that does not strike deep into the heart, not a word too many'.

With Sara Allgood's 'unfailing artistry' as Maurya creating convincing pathos, the curtain fell, leaving the audience lost in absorption. Seated in it were Millie Price and her fellow teacher and Club member, Alice White. They too were thrilled by the music of the voices and the simplicity of the sets. Yeats's *Kathleen ni Houlihan*, she wrote, 'carried me on the wings of patriotic romance, drowned beneath the Celtic Vision'.[41] Lady Gregory's broad farce *Spreading the News* broke the spell and Boyle's play was slight but the stark beauty of Synge's *Riders to the Sea* was 'poignant and unforgettable'. She remembers being as much moved by Arthur Darley's violin playing in the intervals: 'The Lark in the Clear Air', 'The Snowy Breasted Petrel', 'Lament for Michael Dwyer', 'Going to Kilkenny' and the reel 'Sally Gap' held her spell-bound. Millie also noted the formidable Annie Horniman 'who sponsored them and whom I saw seated at the table, stern and forbidding, taking and selling tickets',[42] a stern English corrective to the Celtic spirit.

Annie Horniman had poured several thousand of the Horniman's tea fortune into the theatre's cup over the last few years and her mood had not been improved by a sleepless night at the Trevelyan Hotel. She had been scolded, she later wrote to Yeats, by a tin trumpet being blown at 2 a.m. by some of the younger members of the company. 'The rowdiness had been encouraged by William Fay and Synge had encouraged it!'[43] Worse, the tour which had been mounted to raise money, had not gone well. Besides Leeds, they were also to visit Manchester and Liverpool in the spring and then Hull, Newcastle, Glasgow, Edinburgh and Aberdeen in the summer. But the tour lost altogether over £200 and 'Leeds was a miserable town for the company, for they spent £55 18s. 6d. on expenses and took £5 10s. 11d. from a handful of audience'.[44] If these figures are correct, then the combined audience in Leeds for the two nights could have been no more than fifty-five, which is even less than the reviews suggest.

Shortly after the tour, Miss Horniman, who, despite her largesse, was little liked by the company began to engineer the Fay brothers dismissal and they resigned two years later. The style and character of the company owed much to William Fay's pioneering work, but Miss Horniman thought him indisciplined and unprofessional. He was also too wedded to what she described as 'Irish peasant plays' from which she was also trying to wean Yeats himself and get him to write in the grand style to which, she felt, his genius must aspire. In what was clearly a disastrous move for a company so identified with the Celtic revival, she introduced an English manager to take over from Fay while Yeats engaged an English leading lady to take over from Sara Allgood, much to the company's alarm. Predictably, neither experiment succeeded and it was Annie Horniman herself who had to leave, moving to Manchester where she founded the Gaiety Theatre.

How the company decided to include the Arts Club in their tour is still a mystery, but the Golden Dawn, of which Annie Horniman was also a member, may well be the connection. Millie Price may have known little of the tension behind the scenes in what seemed such an ecstatic atmosphere. For her it was an extraordinary weekend of poetic drama, the like of which Leeds had never seen. It was completed for her and the other Club members by a visit backstage to meet the cast and the authors. While Synge, to whom she was presented, was warm and chatty to her, Yeats, on the contrary, 'moved away, a ghostly wraith in the gloom of the stage, preserving his poetic personality from the attrition of casual contacts'. Yeats, however, returned from the astral plane to maintain his connection with Orage over the next year or so and gave one of the first talks to Orage's Fabian Arts Group in London the following year.

So this was probably the last event organized by Orage and Jackson. It had been, appropriately, something for the dramatic stage, since the new drama provided a font of aphoristic inspiration. As Millie Price also recalled. 'In April 1906 . . . the founders of the club were seriously dallying with the notion of burning their boats, going to London, and, in the words of Ibsen so often quoted by Orage, "Living by what one lives for" '.[45] The powerful combination of moving drama and political purpose he had just seen in the works of the Irish playwrights and earlier in the works of Ibsen and Shaw had for him confirmed the centrality of the drama assigned by Nietzsche.

Orage was also deeply impressed by the force of the Irish Nationalist

Movement in which he perceived a force for social change more radically galvanic than anything offered by what he he had come to see as the timid and pedestrian reformism to which the English Labour Movement had succumbed. It was something that moved the spirit in a visionary sense and captured the feel of his early years in Leeds. It was perhaps in an attempt to convey this excitement to an English audience that he returned to write his first piece of political journalism for some years. It was an article for the *Leeds Mercury* of 6 March 1906 (and unmentioned in previous accounts) called, 'What is the Future of Socialism?'.

In it Orage foreshadowed his argument in 'Politics for Craftsmen' in the *Contemporary Review* of the following year. Socialism, he said, must be separated from its exclusive identity with the politics of the working class, labour and trade unions. If it was not then it would share the fate of the German Social Democrats, electoral defeat. Socialists should attempt to create a genuinely Socialist Party untainted by the gross material demands of the working man and inspired by a grander vision. In a rhetorical flourish Orage applauded the splendour, imagination, wholeness and sanity of what can only be called a . . . 'National Socialism'. The deeply troubling nature of this conclusion in the light of the political movement of that name formed in 1920 under Hitler is self-evident.[46] But Orage, though not a democrat in the conventional sense of the term was absolutely untainted by anti-semitism, racism or militarism. He was inspired by the apparent ability of nationalism to energize the poets and rouse the people, but neither he nor anyone else could foresee the kind of tiger he was attempting to ride.

Since this article is an extremely important and hitherto unknown statement of his politics, it is quoted in full in the Appendix.[47] In this complex of acute political prophesy, foreshadowing the totalitarianism of the 'actually-existing' socialist countries, and professional snobbery Orage imaginatively portrays what was to be the tragic 'eternal recurrence' of the Labour Party. The disgruntled exit of socialists from its ranks and the repeated cry for a true socialist party, has marked its progress ever since; at each crisis, it seems, Orage's claim that the Labour Party was the biggest obstacle to socialism has had to be wearily rediscovered by yet another generation.

Coinciding, as it does with Orage's decision to quit the known and familiar of Leeds for the great unknown of London, this statement is highly charged. He had at last found a politics which was both personal and professional. It was in a sense an articulation of the will-to-power for the professional class that had been produced by the 1870 Education Act. True socialism, he felt, belonged in some sense to the writers, artists, professional workers and educators to be found in the Arts Club and no doubt in similar organizations around the country. Like himself and D. H. Lawrence, soon to become an avid reader of the *New Age* under his editorship, the individuals had often come from working-class families. Unhappy with the style of either the manual labourer or the high street grocer, they were socially and politically adrift. Education and the pride of profession and craft had appeared to have allowed them a freedom of choice they had, Orage insisted, to embrace. Dreaming or imagining the future shape of mankind was their prerogative. Despite their insistence on individual freedom to create, they believed in a collective future, free of the evils of commercialism and capitalism in which their art could flourish and all humanity benefit from its nourishment. But they also believed that they, the artists, writers and cultural workers 'the professional proletariat' would provide the vanguard to take society there. This was the politics of Orage's superman.

In his early twenties Orage had been inspired by the socialist leadership given by Tom Mann, Tom Maguire, Edward Carpenter, Annie Besant and Isabella Ford. They had all been involved in working-class struggles out of which had been formed the great general unions and unskilled workers' unions such as the General and Municipal Workers, the Dock Workers and the first women's unions like the Tailoresses. It was a time when socialist vision guided and heartened the struggles and Orage had been a founder member of the ILP from which great things were expected. In their turn the new unions became an organized economic lobby but the better organized they became the more narrow and conservative their demands. They had often, understandably, exercised a 'new realism' in their dealings with their masters, in which the utopian aspirations of their erstwhile socialist leaders now began to look quaint and unreal. Sixpence a week more was something the new union leader might successfully negotiate, but the emancipation of humanity from the evil of capitalist exploitation took some organizing.

In the late 1890s, after the death of Tom Maguire the leader of the Socialist movement in Leeds, Orage had become dispirited by the timidity of the local ILP leadership. His own 'Bookish Causerie' had failed to change the taste of the *Labour Leader*'s readership and he had increasingly sunk himself into theosophy. In 1900 Holbrook Jackson had infused new life into him through the *Zarathustra* and together they had embarked on the Arts Club venture. Now this phase was at an end. They had not entirely failed to ignite Leeds but the town was, for Orage at least, too small a space. He thought he could create a 'new Samurai' in London.

Notes

1. Mairet, *A. R. Orage*, p.29.
2. Northern Federation of the Theosophical Society minutes, 12–13 August 1905.
3. Roundhay Road Junior School log book, 24–26 July 1905, p. 467, West Yorks County archives, Sheepscar, Leeds.
4. Millie Price, 'This World's Festival', p.107.
5. Mairet, *A. R. Orage*, p.28.
6. Leeds School Board Education Committee minutes, minute book 18, 25 Sept 1902, p.89, West Yorkshire Archives.
7. Mairet, *A. R. Orage*, p.29.
8. Mairet, p.27.
9. Gerald Cumberland, *Set Down in Malice*, Grant Richards, London, 1918, p.131.
10. Millie Price, p.119.
11. John Carswell, *Lives and Letters*, p.31.
12. Mairet, p.27.
13. *YWP*, 3 February 1906, p.17.
14. *YWP*, 10 February 1906, p.6.
15. Gillian Spencer, foreword to *Mark Senior Exhibition Catalogue*, Elizabethan Exhibition Gallery, Wakefield, 16 April – 2 July 1983.
16. Quoted in *Mark Senior Exhibition Catalogue*, Introduction.
17. J. D. Roberts (ed.) *The Kramer Documents*, Valencia, 1983, p.63.
18. *YWP*, 17 February 1906, p.16.
19. *YEP*, 19 February 1906 (in Leeds Cuttings, vol. 2, p.19, Leeds City Reference library). It thought that some of the domestic articles might make appropriate wedding gifts.
20. Fr. E. K. Talbot in C. S. Phillips, (ed.) *Walter Howard Frere a memoir*, Faber, London, 1947, pp.43–60.
21. C. S. Phillips in *Walter Howard Frere*, pp.32–42.
22. See Peter d'A Jones, *The Christian Socialist Revival*, Princeton University Press, 1968, who says 'of guild socialists specifically connected with Mirfield the most important were Father J. N. Figgis and Father Paul Bull' (p. 277).
23. Jones, p.279.
24. Ibid.
25. Kingsley Martin, *Harold Laski*, Gollancz, London, 1953, p.72.
26. Jones, p.278.
27. G. D. H. Cole, *A Short History of the British Working Class Movement*. 1789–1947, Allen and Unwin, London, 1948, p. 325.
28. Cole, p.325.
29. Storm Jameson, *Journey From the North*, vol I, Collins Harvill, London, 1969, p.57.
30. Holbrook Jackson, 'The Truth About Nietzsche', in *T. P.'s Weekly*, 31 October 1914, p.476.
31. Holbrook Jackson, letter in *New English Weekly*, 15 November 1934, p.114.
32. *Leeds Mercury*, 15 March 1906, p.6.
33. Joseph Hone, *W. B. Yeats*, Macmillan, London, 1942, p.191.
34. Carswell, p.38.

35. Anonymous article in *The Lamp of Thoth*, vol III, no. 4, Leeds 1985, p.33. The author emphasizes the role of *freemasonry* in what was 'a particularly active occult scene around this time in Yorkshire'.
36. *New Age*, 6 June 1907, p.92.
37. *Leeds Mercury*, Saturday 28 April 1906.
38. *Yorkshire Post*, Saturday 28 April 1906.
39. *Yorkshire Post*, 30 April 1906.
40. *Leeds Mercury*, 30 April 1906, p.9.
41. Millie Price, p.124.
42. Ibid., p.126.
43. Gerard Fay, *The Abbey Theatre*, Clonmore and Reynolds, Dublin, 1958, p.103.
44. Ibid.
45. Ibid., p.123.
46. Ernst Nolte, *Three Faces of Fascism*, Mentor, New York, 1969, p.404.
47. Published in *Leeds Mercury*, 6 March 1906, p. 4.

CHAPTER SEVEN

1907–1909: Expansion, Diversity and Division

Autumn 1906 – Winter 1907

Without Orage and Jackson the Club entered a new phase. A. W. Waddington took over as secretary and the addition of Miss Annie Kennedy as assistant secretary probably meant both that A.W.W. was not the most efficient of administrators and that the Club's activities were expanding. Only three newspaper reports survive and one of these indicates perhaps developing links with the university. This was in the shape of a talk by Pro-Vice Chancellor Arthur Smithells FRS (1860–1939), Professor of Chemistry, on the 'Modern Universities Movement'. Smithells believed that the new universities should not be based on Oxbridge models but instead should adapt themselves to the needs of modern industry. He noted with approval the great growth of popular education and the inclination of young people in industrial towns to seek higher education. He was also very popular with his students, one of whom was the novelist Arthur Ransome who described him as one of Leeds two 'notable professors'.[1] He had hoped to succeed Nathan Boddington as Vice Chancellor but in this he was disappointed when the university opted instead for Michael Sadler in 1911. Michael Sadler was to play a most important role in the subsequent story both of the university and the Club.

By 1907 it was clear that the Club had expanded its activities markedly. Apart from seventeen listed talks between January and April, the syllabus showed excursions to be arranged in the summer months, members groups including a literary group for the study of Plato's *Republic*, a sketching group with use of a model, a musical committee, a book club 'open to all' and library 'formed on the lines of the Objects of the Club.' There was also to be special discussion of recent events – 'Literary, Artistic and Political'. The committee of management had also changed and included, as well as Waddington and Kennedy, Holbrook Jackson, J. H. Fearnley, W. P. Irving, W. Alban (Billy) Jones, Arthur Lee, Percy Robinson, W. H. Lamb and Miss L. Wilkinson. Miss Louisa Wilkinson, the only new member of the committee, was a schoolteacher and Mr Lamb, who was now the hon. treasurer, a herbalist. Thus by occupation the committee comprised three architects:

Waddington, Jones and Robinson; two schoolteachers, both women: Kennedy and Wilkinson; a lace merchant cum freelance journalist: Jackson; an Anglican priest: Lee; a company secretary: Fearnley; an insurance manager: Irving, and a herbalist.

The central concern of the year was with philosophy, in relation to literature and Nietzsche. This was signalled in the second talk which was given by Orage on the subject of 'Apollo and Dionysos', on Saturday 19 January. Though no reports of the meeting have survived it is not unrealistic to suppose Orage had been reading Nietzsche's *Birth of Tragedy*. He was now living with Arthur Penty in Hammersmith and with Holbrook Jackson was deeply involved in the formation of the Fabian Arts Group in London. Using the Leeds Arts Club as a model, this group became the scourge of metropolitan Fabianism. In his study of Fabianism and culture, Ian Britain thought that they 'clearly saw themselves as missionaries of light attempting to save Fabianism from the powers of greyness',[2] but it was more likely that Orage's project at least, went way beyond merely reforming Fabianism. It was anyway seen as a great threat by the Fabian old guard of Pease and the Webbs, and strongly supported by H. G. Wells. As Eric Gill later wrote, the Arts Group made 'vague efforts to deprive Fabianism of its Webbed feet – vain efforts'.[3] As if to reinforce the Yorkshire connection, the *YWP* on Saturday 16 February, carried an announcement of the formation of the group, saying that its object was to 'interpret the relation of art and philosophy to Socialism'. It listed the management committee as A.E.R. Gill, Miss Murby, Holbrook Jackson, Alfred Orage, F. J. Richardson, Miss C. C. Townsend and Th. Wilson. As in Leeds, Holbrook Jackson became the hon. sec. and the list it gave of 'remaining fixtures' could easily have come from the Leeds programme: Edward Carpenter on 'The Chinese Academy', Will Rothenstein on 'Some Parallels between Art and Religion', Orage on 'Nietzsche contra Socialism'. This last was indeed a paper he had written in Leeds some time before. (Did Orage already know of Victor Grayson in Colne Valley, flexing his oratorical powers in preparation for his election as Independent Socialist by just over 150 votes in the July election of 1907? Grayson became his true model of Dionysian man in the heady days of 1908 when Orage opened an assault in the *New Age* on the Labour Party leadership. Grayson was, for a few months after his expulsion from parliament over the unemployment issue, his co-editor, but the mixture was explosive. Orage had harboured ambitions of Grayson and himself storming the Labour party but they soon faded.)

While Orage, with gifts of £500 from Shaw and a similar sum from a theosophical banker, Lewis Wallace, returned to London to negotiate the purchase of the *New Age* from his old ILP comrade Joseph Clayton, the Club carried on its new season. The second talk on philosophy was given by Frank B. Hutton on 'Scholasticism' on 2 February. He argued that Aristotelianism, the philosophy par excellence of the Catholic church, was undergoing a resurgence.[4] In its doctrine as to the nature, value and origin of intellectual ideas it held an intermediary position between materialism and absolute idealism. It was also profoundly critical of the notion of innate ideas or direct intuition of the deity. This was a corrective to the Club's more familiar diet of Platonism but that idealism returned in good measure in W. H. Perkins's lecture on 'Pessimism', of 16 February. His point was that philosophical pessimism, by holding life valueless, was a perfectly rational position to start from. Thus ethical schemes had to be formulated on the basis of one's own convictions, examples of which were to be found on the works of Omar Khayam and Schopenhauer: 'Omar, in his primitive civilisation had recourse to wine while Schopenhauer, with Plato and Kant to assist him, was able to construct a scheme which gained temporary relief in aestheticism and permanent relief in asceticism' from life's trials.[5] Perkins's talk thus supplemented some of the philosophical background to Nietzsche's thought. Little more is known of him except that he joined the management committee in 1908 and according to Geoffrey Woledge later became a friend of Jacob Kramer.

The theme of precursors of Nietzsche was followed in Arthur Lee's talk of 1 March on 'William Blake's *The Marriage of Heaven and Hell*' (also chaired by Perkins). This important lecture signalled the rediscovery of Blake as a Modern and an intellectual predecessor' of Nietzsche. Lee frankly acknowledged his debt to Orage in this observation. Imagination was for Blake, he said, the only reality while art was the only religion and energy the only expression of that religion. 'Blake was a visionary, and gloried in his twofold vision, praying always to be delivered from 'single vision and Newton's sleep' – i.e. the refusal or inability to see spiritual meaning corresponding to all earthly objects'.[6] He said that Christ was, for Blake, the symbolic name of the divine imagination, and the conflict between Christ and Satan, the eternal strife between the Reason that limits reality to 'nature' and the Imagination that liberates the mind from empty formulae and the dictation of the five senses. In *Heaven and Hell* Blake had declared the birth of his own imagination and the mystical marriage between 'the passive that obeys reason' and the 'active that springs from energy', which, said Lee, was his interpretation of the terms 'good' and 'evil'. Blake moreover saw Christianity not as submission but as revolt and gloried in the 'mental revolt and energy manifested in Christ'. Lee concluded that Blake's ideas and those of Nietzsche as outlined by Orage were clearly very close. Thus what was exemplified in Lee's talk was the process of absorbing Nietzsche into a known canon of cultural criticism and revitalizing it. Nietzsche was made palatable by his association with Blake, and in turn by producing a reading of Blake as a revolutionary he was made both modern and to an extent estranged. It furnished an important moment in understanding the formation of the 'rebel' art movements of the following years by creating a 'tradition' of revolt which could legitimate new practices (a strategy perfected by T. S. Eliot after the First World War).

In his talk on 'Teachers, Prophets and Heralds' on 9 March, Charles Smythe attempted to provide a theoretical structure to the theme of intellectual provenance. He began by suggesting that the conventional practice of estimating the value of artist's work only from the artistic point of view without reference to the artist's ideas was misguided. Great art was merely the expression adopted by the artist for the exposition of his ideas. As the title suggested, there were, he thought, three classes of great artist.

The 'Heralds', such as Shaw and Wells, were the acute critics and men of their age, who had adopted new ideas but without fully assimilating them. The 'Prophets' who came next, had seized and absorbed the new ideas and propagated them with greater skill – Shelley, Blake, Arnold, Ibsen and Nietzsche. They were men of intense zeal and high purpose, who had made spreading the word their mission. Ultimately, there were the 'Teachers' who were ahead of their age and marked out by their universal breadth of feeling and sublime serenity. Only Shakespeare, Dante, Virgil, Michelangelo and Wordsworth were in this category. In this taxonomy Smythe's grouping of Nietzsche and Ibsen with the British poets, Shelley, Blake and Arnold also incorporates them into a domestic tradition. His ranking of Shakespeare and Wordsworth with Virgil and Dante signified a 'Classic' universality, which was of importance to later debates. For example, while Eliot too would have agreed the primacy of Virgil and Dante, Wordsworth and Shakespeare he saw as too dangerously individual to be 'classics'. But clearly, efforts at establishing a structure of cultural authority (faltering as they were) were seen as important to the Club's project and part of a larger attempt to impose an order on cultural production.

The second most important theme was, loosely, civic and political consciousness, advertised as a series of lectures 'dealing with public questions of importance to artists and thinkers'.[7] Unfortunately no reports survive of Oliver Firth's lecture on 'Public Spiritedness' of 26 January, or Isabella Ford's talk on 'Woman's place in future progress' of 5 April, though Canon Stevenson's talk on the 'Ideal City' and Dr H. T. Calvert's on 'The Purification of our Rivers' were well-covered. Oliver Firth may well have been the same person who had been a member of the Bradford Horus Temple of the Golden Dawn, and who had resigned in September 1893. This would be another intriguing coincidence for it was none other than Annie Horniman, of the Abbey Theatre, who was sent to Bradford on behalf of the order to discipline an unruly 'Frater Firth' (either Oliver or Walter) who refused to respect the order's authority in matters of astrology and subjects of study.[8] The occultist network may well have been a more powerful undercurrent in shaping cultural trends than is conventionally acknowledged.

The Anglican overground however went straight to material facts. Canon Stevenson from Warrington focused directly on practical suggestions to make Leeds a more desirable place to inhabit opening with the remark that England contained some of the worst slums in the world.[9] He supported the Garden City ideal and the real achievements of the 'Beautiful Warrington' campaign in tree planting, smoke abatement and window boxes. For Leeds he suggested a great square on which would converge four main avenues and whose corners should hold a church, a museum, a library and a market with recreation and concert rooms. Behind this there should be parks and gardens and along the main avenues mixed large and small housing for all the citizens regardless of class. Factories should be re-erected away from the town centre and smoke done away with altogether since the technical means now existed. The talk occasioned a lot of laughter from the audience, no doubt sceptical of the municipal authority's and local manufacturers' desire to effect such changes.

Dr Calvert of the West Riding Rivers Board was similarly scandalized by the local ecology. Describing the growth of the Rivers Board and its legislative powers, he focused on the detrimental effects the discharge of chemicals by industry and the withdrawal of water by the canal companies had on the rivers Aire, Calder and Colne. The canals he said, were relatively clean and, if the will was there, rivers could be brought to the same standard. Tastelessly, he remarked: 'Leeds, with its River Aire, has tangible proof of what Bradford does with its sewage, but lower down the river, with its accumulated filth of Leeds and Bradford the stench is unbearable. Let him who doubts stand on Woodlesford Bridge in Summer.'[10] Unlike Leeds, Bradford, he said, was about to embark on an extensive sewage scheme and anyone who opposed scientific solutions to this and the related problem of smoke nuisance was truly ignorant.

The return of the Quaker, Isabella Ford, to the Club's programme was of some significance. Though no longer on the Club's committee, and still very active in the ILP and Labour Party she was now immersed in the women's suffrage movement. In 1907 she had become Vice-President of the Leeds Women's Suffrage Society and was elected to the Executive Committee of the National Union of Women's Suffrage Societies. The following year she was a delegate to the Conference of the International Women's Suffrage Alliance, Amsterdam. She was also writing extensively on women's matters, especially the condition of women workers. A notice of her article on 'Industrial Women' in the *Humane Review* of October 1901, commented: 'Against these conditions (of exploitation) the writer believes in preaching intelligent discontent, and reckons, among the influences which tend to keep things as they are, are conventional teaching, rescue work, and philanthropy'.[11] This demonstrated her decisive break with the Victorian Liberalism of her family for whom rescue work and philanthropy had been a daily diet. In her 1904 ILP pamphlet *Women and Socialism* she had addressed the question of the women and progress. She believed that the women's cause and the cause of socialism were directly related but, despite her concern for working women, she still appeared to think that women's causes were primarily about the home and childcare and traditional womanly concerns: 'Women's work is awakening people to see that society must be responsible for the welfare of the individual'.[12] However it was precisely women's experience of factory work that would enable them to be so effective in moral and welfare reform:

> At the heart of every woman who now asks for the vote in all seriousness, lies the conviction that until women possess this power, the deepest moral evils against which the world is battling can never be crushed or even touched. This is chiefly due to the increasing knowledge of industrial life and conditions which women have gained through their work as Guardians, Factory Inspectors, Sanitary Inspectors and so forth. It has shown with fearful distinctness, that the barbarous state of our marriage and divorce laws, our laws concerning the custody of children, illegal motherhood and fatherhood, the condition of our streets and factories etc.: all press most heavily on the lives of *poor* women. It is this knowledge which has stirred in so many women's minds an enthusiasm strong as religion – to many it is a religion – and a desperate determination that these things shall no longer continue . . . [13]

Undoubtedly, it was such a powerful and moderated argument as this to which she treated her Arts Club audience. Many women schoolteachers would have been there, including perhaps both Mary Gawthorpe and Ethel Annakin, who had met her future husband Philip Snowden only recently at the Club rooms. Significantly, the address was not so much to the working-class women she had been active with in the '80s as the middle-class professional woman who still believed, and with good reason, that there really would be 'future progress'.[14]

The Club's coverage of the expressive arts was still impressive but largely unreported. The Royal Academician painter George Clausen gave an 'Address on Art' on 20 February which was possibly the only session devoted to painting in the year. Photography was represented in a small exhibition and talk by the amateur photographer William Thomas called 'The Art Side of Photography: with lantern slides' on 15 March. Thomas argued that photography should be taken seriously as an art form and, with the aid of colour sensitive plates and multiple lenses, he rebutted charges that it could not deal with colour and perspective. The talk foreshadowed the experimenting that was to take place in the Club in later years – when Michael Sadler for example challenged painters and photographers to compete in producing the most realistic representation of a scene – and marked an important moment in the construction of photography as 'Art'. Another example of aestheticization was in the title of a talk on 'Art in Dress: with lantern slides, dress models &c.' given by Madame Naici-Peters, who was described as Secretary of the Scandinavian Dress Reform Association.

Either because of the success of its activities or because of conflicting needs within it, the Club was bifurcating. There was an expressed need for a society to promote theatre and opera which may have come from the less politicized members or alternatively from those who saw the stage as an appropriate political platform. Whatever the impetus was, it gave birth in the summer of 1907 to the Playgoers Society, a group which, at its height, grew to over ten times the membership of the parent body. Thus on 9 April, Waddington sent out a circular letter advertising a meeting for anyone interested in forming a new society to promote 'The Better Support of Opera and Drama in Leeds'.

Its formation was obviously prompted by, among other things, the poor response to the Abbey Theatre productions of the previous year. But it was clearly successful and through the single-minded devotion of two of its organizers, W. P. Irving and Charles Frederick Smith, changed the face of dramatic performance in Leeds. Irving who was the secretary for most of its fifteen-year existence, was, according to an obituary notice, responsible for raising the membership to nearly one thousand and before he left Leeds was near to establishing a Repertory Theatre. He also established kindred societies in Hull, Bradford and Sheffield.[15] His friend Denis Botterill's (Matty's son) description of him in another obituary (probably the *Yorkshire Post*'s) as a conservative at heart who was always ready to listen to the rebels and always ready with help and encouragement to men with ideas, seems to suggest that though this was more of an established middle-class enterprise, its potential for social reform was clearly signalled. The other man, Charles Frederick Smith, the son of Sydney Smith, a skirt manufacturer on York Road, was for many years the society's treasurer. He wrote a number of one-act social-comment plays which were performed at the Club in later years, including: *A Corner in Wheat* in 1911, *The Vessel of the Land* and *Mother Modernises* in 1920, the latter pair acted by the Arts Club's 'drama section'.[16] The Playgoers Society seems to have remerged with the Arts Club in about 1921 when Smith became the Club's co-secretary. When it became clear that the Club was in its terminal phase he seems to have been responsible for two new ventures, both of which had signal impacts on the Leeds theatrical scene. Firstly, the Leeds Arts Theatre of which he was secretary in 1921 and then Leeds Civic Playhouse of which he was director in 1925 (cf. Chapter 11).

As the Playgoers Society was taking shape in Leeds, Orage and Jackson were putting together the first editions of the *New Age* under their joint management in May 1907. But while Orage was now committed to the metropolitan project Jackson still found time to continue his provincial enthusiasms and returned to Yorkshire twice in the winter of 1907. The second time, 12 November, was in order to establish an Arts Club in Hull which he insisted should not be just another provincial literary society, but an institution to promote social change. The objects of the Club should be

> First, to provide a meeting place for the discussion of the various forms of art; second, to insist on the importance of art in daily life, and to combat the idea that money-making is the greater end; and, third, to discuss from its own point of view, and to form opinions on various aspects of public life, and to secure as much publicity as possible for those opinions.[17]

This statement could also provide a useful summary of the activities of the Leeds Arts Club to date, but there is no evidence that the club in Hull was as successful. Jackson also advocated something like the playgoers society but appeared to see it as the 'dramatic section' of the Club whose purpose it would be to represent the demands of 'the more intelligent playgoers' in Hull for plays of the modern school. It should cultivate a taste for the 'drama of ideas' by means of lectures, readings and debate, and then bring the plays themselves to Hull. Interestingly, the project Jackson seems to be suggesting here is less like cultivating home grown talent as in the crusading days in Leeds and more like importing the metropolitan product to an otherwise cultural desert. Whether this was because of the nature of the place, his developing role as a metropolitan intellectual or simply a 'new realism' is difficult to know.

When Holbrook Jackson returned to Leeds in October, his book on Bernard Shaw had just been published. The person who now came to address the joint meetings of the Leeds Playgoers Society and the Leeds

Arts Club on 'The Theatre and its Place in the Modern State' now spoke with the authority of 'the author' and 'the editor'. He did not beat about the bush. The state of contemporary theatre was a sad one:

> Plays that were prurient and suggestive were given a state blessing by the censor, and out of the hundreds of theatrical performances being given today there were barely a handful that were not an insult to the intelligence. Today there was too much playing to the gallery, which, after all, was not always the abode of the gods.[18]

If we were to have a real living drama, the censorship, he said, should be abolished and the establishment of municipal theatre a matter of practical urgency. Shaw's play *Caesar and Cleopatra* was exemplary in that by presenting Caesar as a modern, it was a bold break with dramatic convention. With Herbert Thompson's lecture on Verdi and Wagner of 4 December, this talk marked a heightening of the significance of the stage as a place for aesthetic education and reform. To what extent this indicated a growing predominance of one of the original aims of the Club over the others is unclear, but the very formation of the Playgoers Society betrayed a division of a once singular project.

1908–1909 Shaw: Municipal Theatre and Puritanism

The Club was established. It had outgrown its original rooms in Park Lane and in February 1908 moved to 8 Blenheim Terrace, Woodhouse Lane. Here the Club now rented the whole of a three-storey house in an elegant terrace about two hundred yards down the hill from the university, which was to remain its address until it closed in 1923. A caretaker, Mr Hardcastle, and his wife lived in and were from time to time the subjects of portraits by Arts Club members like Jacob Kramer.[19] Whether this was a symbolic move from town to gown is not clear. Certainly the Club's links with the university were to grow closer with the involvement of Michael Sadler, but that was not for a few more years. Academics like Frederic Moorman were enthusiastic supporters but the intellectual character of the Club was still largely formed by non-university men and women. The proliferating sections of the Club, which now included literary, sketching and musical groups as well as a book club, had more space for meetings and kindred societies like the Playgoers and Polyglot as well as the Fabians shared the premises. The *YWP* was agreeably, if wordily, impressed by the move:

> The entire premises have been taken, so that the clubman's (or woman's, for the membership includes both sexes) ideal of spaciousness no less than cosiness, has been pleasantly realised. The rooms

> are numerous to allow of separate sections meeting without inconvenience, and the scheme of decoration and furnishing conforms agreeably to one's notion of what the interior of a club with such an exacting title may fairly be held to demand.[20]

So the Club had become 'cosy'! This seems a far cry from the original intentions when Leeds 'was to be reduced to Nietzscheism'. But it was Orage himself, garlanded with the title of 'Editor of the *New Age*' who, on 15 February, gave the inaugural lecture. There was nothing cosy or even Appollonian about what he had to say. His theme was 'The Mystical Doctrine of Democracy' and he began by dismissing the popular notion of democracy, the rule of the majority, as wholly misguided. He said that it was a fact of the emotions or the feelings that all human beings belonged to the same family and were of the same blood. Once realized this fact would clarify our approach to the global problems of race. Secondly, despite the fact that no political party had been able to base a rational programme on it, all human beings had equal rights. This was an equality of value which underlay all differences of appearance. They could make claims on others by virtue of this rather than by rights obtained from the State (which was what contemporary political philosophy claimed). Rights were natural to individuals but the State had not the right to anything whatsoever. Individuals had the right to exercise their faculties in any way, nor was it abrogated by becoming injurious: human beings have the right to be tigers – but you have the right to shoot tigers also. It was also criminal to consider other people in anything one was going to do. If one set out to do someone good, the chances were that it would turn out to be a bad turn.

Finally, he said, mankind had conceived of God as a being like a man but now each man should be regarded as a potential god.

> That each man should be regarded as a potential god [he said.] is the driving force or can easily become the driving force, of a much more rapid reform than has ever yet taken place. You must not demand any human rights because we all have more than we deserve. The individual human being is worth nothing; even our race is worth nothing as human beings. But let human beings be considered as being of value for the future, as gods, as divine, then let them transfer themselves from the attitude of the worshipper to that of the worshipped, and they become valuable because of their futurity, and because of their promise. The Socialist is not merely concerned with the unjust distribution of wealth or the unhappiness he sees. What he is concerned with is the intolerable indignities suffered by human beings like himself.[21]

Rather than allow another human being to suffer indignity, he argued, he 'should be put out of his misery in a lethal chamber'. Russia, he said was the most democratic country in Europe from this standpoint, because they had the greatest conception of the value of human beings.

> They might do horrible things but they did not go through the form of sentencing a man to death. They did deeds which were passionate perhaps, but godlike, for there were good gods and bad gods – but they did nothing that was petty. England was the country of petty things.[22]

As reported, Orage's talk is difficult to interpret. It appears to be a kind of reckless egotism whose arguments while starting from perfectly acceptable premises conclude horrendously. And yet it is saved by a notion of political equality derived not from the state but from 'natural' rights. Once again, his conception of the individual appears to be profoundly Romantic and presocial, which he seems to have revived as a critique of the practice of Utilitarian democracy, the tyranny of the majority. The *Yorkshire Observer*'s report wryly concluded that a 'curious and indeterminate discussion followed' in which Orage was asked what was the difference between a good god and a bad one. Orage agreed with his questioner that he had no idea.

Orage was now the sole editor of the *New Age*, Jackson having resigned in January, one can't help thinking, because of the heat generated in the kitchen. The journal was rapidly becoming required reading for anyone who took art and politics seriously. The 'Chesterbelloc' debate had shown Orage's masterly ability to get established figures like Shaw, Chesterton and Belloc to debate their political differences publicly – and for free. New talents like Katherine Mansfield, Ezra Pound and T. E. Hulme were waiting in the wings. The circulation of the journal was rising and by October 1908, when Orage invited Victor Grayson to be political editor, it rose to an all-time high of 22,000.[23] It was during the blaze of controversy around Grayson, who had been suspended from parliament for insisting on a debate on unemployment and was currently barnstorming round the country, that Orage gave his next, and last, recorded talk to the Club. Entitled 'The Blessedness of Chance' it was given on 28 November and continued the radical individualist stance of his previous talk. But here the focus of his attack was on the notion of divine purpose. In a regrettably brief report the *YWP* summed up Orage's point as showing that people should remove from their minds any idea of purpose in the universe. Orage had said that few people had had the courage to throw themselves into the arms of chance, preferring to rely on their own puny efforts in the way of calculation. But those who did found that there was a 'blessedness of chance': 'Mr W. B. Yeats had said that where there was nothing there was God. I say', concluded the lecturer, 'where there is chance there is God; where there is calculation there is humanity, and there also is the devil.' (Laughter and applause.)[24]

He had, of course, taken his chance two years ago when he gave up a secure if poorly paid job with the Leeds School Board and his editorial boldness was already securing him an awesome status in London. But how far he was still in line with the aspirations of the Club members in Leeds was another matter. The Club had effectively bifurcated in the previous year with the formation of the Playgoers Society and its unity of purpose was no longer so evident. Though the proliferation of subsections betrayed the diversity of its members' priorities, the secretaryship was firmly in the hands of Albert Waddington who still pursued the radical intentions of its founding moment. None of his talks to the Club of this period was reported so we cannot be sure of the political leadership he was giving to it. However, his well-reported talk to the Halifax Arts and Crafts Society showed his missionary work for the Guilds Restoration League continued unabated.

Taking the title of his talk from his friend Arthur Penty's book *The Restoration of the Gild System*, published in 1906, Waddington made a strong plea for guild politics. Apologizing for the thinness of the audience, the chairman said that he had hoped that members of the Labour Party would be there in large numbers, but they did not seem to be interested in history. When Ruskin started the Guild of St George, Waddington replied, he knew it was bound to be a failure because the time was not yet ripe. The guilds had made it possible for common village masons and carpenters to produce such monuments of beauty as the churches and cathedrals of that age. The severance of the fine arts from the minor arts was in some cases the cause of the disappearance of guilds and the ugliness and misery of modern towns were largely the result of this severance. The guild might be defined as a society whose object was to produce greater values from human life by the twofold method of 'brotherhood and art'. The great problem of today was not to destroy the commercial 'idea' but to make it true, sane and healthy. We wanted not just a new guild system but a guild soul. The way to attain that was by right thinking on social questions and for this the artists would have to be politicians and fighters. 'Politics were the order of the day for artists'.[25] When he sat down, however, the chairman's comment that artists were not always the wisest persons in the world was seconded by Halifax's leading socialist, the treasurer of the ILP, John Lister of Shibden Hall, who said he did not think there was any connection between trade unions and guilds. Also since the labour movement was largely economic in motivation there was nothing artistic about it: 'The Labour party was no more concerned about art than were the Liberal and Conservative parties as parties'[26] and echoing back

Ruskin, he said 'Let everyone keep to his own last'. Since William Morris had spoilt himself when he took up sociology and politics, artists were better off sticking to their easels.

Holbrook Jackson also kept up an involvement in the Club during 1908 and 1909, despite his residence in London. In June he wrote to the architect Billy Jones on Fabian Arts Group notepaper asking him if he could use his drawing of Chesterton's, head done at the Arts Club, for an article he was writing on him in the *Idler*, which he was now editing. Saying that he hoped soon to return to Leeds, he wrote: 'I see Orage very frequently and although neither of us are making fortunes, we are making headway.[27] On 24 October 1908, he actually returned to talk on 'The Commonsense of Revolutionism' and in Spring 1909 gave a series of four weekly lectures on 'Modern Socialism' to the Leeds and County Fabian Society, in the Club's rooms. The first of these was on the 'Moral Basis of Socialism' but like the others was not reported. Jackson's involvement may have inspired an upturn in the Fabian presence in Leeds since a number of notices of their activities appear in the *YWP* at this time including a talk on 'England's Duty to India' and another on 'Socialism and Poetry' by T. Rudmose Brown. Orage and Jackson were still involved in the Fabian Arts Group in London where they earned the passionate hatred of Beatrice Webb for their support of H. G. Wells's attempted putsch on the Fabian old guard.[28]

The first of a group of talks on the theatre and politics was given by a fellow conspirator from the Fabian Arts Group, Milicent Murby, who lectured on 'George Bernard Shaw, Dramatist' on 4 April 1908. Miss Murby described Shaw as the most consummate of modern dramatists, his one drawback being that the ideas presented in his plays were so quick and dazzling that the audience did not have the time grasp them, to which a lady in the audience responded that Shaw's ideas were 'not worth the paper they were written on'[29] but she seemed the one dissenter in an otherwise pro-Shavian assembly. Miss Murby praised *Mrs Warren's Profession* as a telling sermon and the *Devil's Disciple* for revealing the old Puritan conception that true virtue is the denial of life. But she also felt that some of Shaw's female characters formed 'a gallery of inhuman types – all drawn from the outside and affecting us like very noisy and unpleasant clockwork', whereas Lady Cicely Waynflete 'is the high-water mark of his recognition of the superior civilisation and urbanity of our sex'.[30] She concluded that whether or not Shaw's plays survived on the stage, 'they would live as a permanent force in that literature which tended to make the race self-conscious'.[31]

Shaw knew Milicent Murby, who was an actress, well and had written about her humorously to Florence Farr three years earlier as expressing some anxiety on the subject of eugenics: 'Miss Murby, a Fabian', he wrote, 'is firmly persuaded that my views on the production of the Superman involve the forcible coercion by the State of selected women to breed with selected men and she, being a goodlooking and clever person, very likely to be selected under such a scheme, fears the worst'.[32] Whether she was so selected is not known, but fellow actress Florence Farr, who probably was, returned to lecture at the Club. Her talk on 'The Theatre and the Arts', given on 19 December 1908, inspired by Shaw's campaign, was largely devoted to practical considerations in designing and building a municipal theatre, for which she recommended simple low-budget productions without elaborate costumes or sets. She then turned to classical Greek theatre and gave examples of declamatory chanting as showing a more authentic mode of portrayal and concluded the evening by reading passages from Homer and Yeats while accompanying herself on the psaltery.[33]

Practical matters on the modern stage were also the theme of actor Martin Harvey addressing the Playgoers Society, on 2 April 1909, in the Philosophical Hall. In 'Some Reflections on the Art of Acting' the actor sometimes 'struck flashes of truth from a deeper consciousness'[34] and the longer the actor played the part the more his conception of the role deepened. However, the creative faculty had to be balanced by the critical, for in reaching to the depths for character it was possible to create something of a Frankenstein's monster which might devour its creator.

A sharply critical tone was introduced into the discussions by the *New Age*'s new theatre critic, Ashley Dukes, who came to the Club twice in this period. The earlier talk, 'The Drama and the Beards' on 16 October 1908 was not reported and 'Art and the Gravediggers' on 30 October 1909 not at length. He was scornful of both plutocracy and democracy. Art was prey to a number of dangers:

> . . . the half education of the mass of the people, the spirit of realism, and the spirit of the academy. But it is always found that with every revolution among the people of any nation art had a great revival. Art had never been really democratic . . . It had really been confined to the rich, to the governing classes, although the common people had had a certain form of art in their folk-lore, folk-songs, tales, etc., which had generally died out and not been recorded. Patronage in the old form had disappeared, and in place of the aristocracy which could, and did, support art, we had a plutocracy which has very little of their artistic taste and appreciation . . . The drama has become in the present day almost a gigantic form of novelette.[35]

Dukes concluded that he did not think in the near future the tendency towards democracy would be conducive to the regeneration of art, although it would most probably do so in the long run. An increasingly influential figure in modern drama, he was central to the *New Age*'s project to revitalize the English stage and, at Orage's insistence, had used the journal to acquaint its readership with the plays of contemporary Europeans like Chekhov, Strindberg, Wedekind, Gorky and D'Annunzio, the essays later published as *Modern Dramatists*. Strategically inserted into the collection were essays on Shaw, Galsworthy and Barker, the Court Theatre playwrights, for comparison. But Dukes was already beginning to swing against Shaw's too intrusive use of his characters to voice 'propaganda' and, with Cecil Chesterton, come out strongly against his 'Puritanism'. In a devastating review in the *New Age* in 1911 he wrote:

> (Shaw) carries Socialism to its furthest extreme. He nationalizes his men and women the instant they are created. He expropriates their imagination. He municipalizes their emotion. He confiscates their surplus value. And he renders compensation to each by the gift of a flickering cloud-halo of wit which sometimes illumines, sometimes obscures, the individual figure and the emminently social purpose . . .
>
> (Shaw is a Puritan, and Puritanism) sets ethics before taste, dessicates illusion, diverts all artistic emotion through the individual to a social end, creates a moral test of pure enjoyment, and offers a bribe of civic self-satisfaction to the artist as surely as Calvinism offers the promise of heaven and the threat of Hell.[36]

But Shaw, as ever, was crucial to the cultural revolution of Orage and the Club even if only as a doorstep over which the, as yet almost untranslated, European dramatists must tread. Accordingly the Club rolled out the red carpet for him when he made his second visit on Friday 10 December 1909.

This meeting was held jointly with the Fabian Society in the Great Hall of Leeds University, a most significant linkage of institutions, and chaired by Holbrook Jackson. The Club published an elegantly typeset four-page quarto brochure, printed by W. H. Bean and probably written by Jackson himself. It contained a fulsome tribute to Shaw, whom it described as 'the founder of a new tradition in our national drama, the leader of a new patriotism' and a new summary of the aims of the Club correspondent with the appreciation of Shaw. Shaw was celebrated less as a playwright and more as a prophet for his 'condemnation of modern civilization' as a 'frank and fearless critic of our social system and for seeing things so clearly that 'the utterance of his vision becomes a revelation'.

> He is a man of refined and fastidious taste, indignant at the ugliness, wastefulness and the cruelties of our social system, and his plays, essays, novels and lectures are all expressions of his indignation and suggestions for a way out. He is a hater of cruelty and a lover of

> order, and his denunciation of our foibles ranges from the wastefulness of free competition for financial profit, to corporal punishment and the eating of flesh.[37]

The Club itself is constructed as the ideal venue for the provocative airing and discussion of views such as Shaw's and 'many of the most eminent of living thinkers who have spoken before it'.

> It provides a platform for the free interchange and expression of modern thought. This expression of opinion is necessarily critical but not entirely destructive, for as the aim of the Club is the association of art and philosophy with actual life, it follows that however destructive its criticism of modern social conditions may be, their final aim is not destruction but construction.

Though less outrageous than on his previous visit, Shaw's talk nevertheless cited Leeds as one of the 'rotten towns' for theatrical endeavour, such that few serious theatre managers would bring a production there. Theatre was increasingly *the* source of modern ideas, thus if the people of Leeds cared for the health of their town they must establish their own.

> There should be in Leeds a theatre which belonged to the people of Leeds, which was maintained by the people of Leeds, and if necessary, endowed by the people of Leeds, not carried on with a view to commercial profit, but with a view to the edification and recreation, in the strictest and most solemn sense of those words, of the rising generation of Leeds.[38]

This emphasis on the ideological importance of the theatre in cultural renewal reiterated the Club's expressed views but he suggested that the university might well provide its location – a place where 'your souls are formed, and where your souls may be saved, and where, if it is conducted on too commercial lines, your souls may be damned', which the large audience greeted with rapturous applause. He concluded by suggesting an immediate campaign to establish a municipal theatre. In addition to plays selected from those performed at the proposed National theatre in London the municipal theatre should have drama 'acted by Leeds actors, written by Leeds authors, and dealing with Leeds subjects'. Thus Shaw re-emphasized the need for provincial renewal to be internally generated as well as stimulated from the capital. Here then was a project for the Playgoers Society which went far beyond merely attracting serious drama to Leeds and made the stage the focus for social criticism and civic renewal. It is difficult to believe that the Society's treasurer, Charles Frederick Smith, was not in the audience at this lecture, for the theatre he founded fourteen years later, the Leeds Civic Playhouse, exactly echoed these principles.

While political philosophy and the municipal theatre project provided the keynote sessions at the Club, the other arts were not neglected. Another Fabian Arts Group founder, William Rothenstein (1872–1945), had founded an Arts Club in Bradford in 1902, the year before the Leeds Club. The son of a wealthy German Jew, he and his son John had a considerable impact on the modern British art institution. William Rothenstein had studied at the Slade under Legros, at the Academie Julian under Doucet and Lefebvre and had exhibited in Paris in 1891. His friends and acquaintances included Degas, the Pissaro brothers, Whistler, Oscar Wilde and the poet Verlaine. Toulouse Lautrec had actually arranged his exhibition. He was well-travelled and highly cultured. He was made Professor of Civic Art at Sheffield University in 1917 and was an official war artist, but perhaps his greatest influence was exerted as Principal of the Royal College of Art 1920–1935.

Here, amongst other things, he championed the work of fellow Yorkshire artists Henry Moore and Barbara Hepworth, who arrived from Leeds for their first year almost simultaneously with him. (Indeed the Leeds connection was to become so strong, that the RCA soon had what was known as 'the Leeds table'.) His brother Charles had a large collection of modern paintings which he generously lent to both the Leeds and Bradford Clubs for exhibitions while his brother Albert, a member of the Chelsea Arts Club, was also a keen painter both in Yorkshire and London circles. Rothenstein's son John, after a brief spell as curator of Leeds Art Gallery, became the pioneering Director of the Tate Gallery. In his widely influential book, *Modern English Painters*, he noted that his father 'was shocked by the impoverishment of English provincial life by the progressive concentration of civilization in London and struggled to arrest it'.[39]

His concern for provincial life was echoed in his talk to the Club on 22 February, 'The Possibilities of the Fine Arts' especially in relation to city life. Concerned with the institutional underpinning of art in cities, he felt that municipal collections only acquired significance if they acted as serious adjuncts to a school of art, which largely they did not, but were instead 'generally cemetries where an occasional stranger with half an hour to while away before he caught his train enjoyed the saddest half hour of his journey'.[40] A municipal gallery should contain collections of all the good, sound, living work that was being done and regular exhibitions of not only paintings and sculpture but the crafts and photography should be arranged.

Ten years or so later Rothenstein was also involved in Michael Sadler's ill-fated Town Hall panels scheme in which Kramer, Stanley Spencer, the Nash brothers and Edward Wadsworth were each to design and paint a large panel to hang in the Victoria Hall, but this belongs to a later chapter. His brother Charles lent part of his collection for the Club's 1909 exhibition of 'Etchings, Drawings and Drypoints' by Muirhead Bone shown from 23 April to 1 May. Bradford's Liberal paper, *The Yorkshire Daily Observer*, reporting the exhibition, thought Bone's achievements as an etcher 'will challenge comparison with the greatest'.[41] Like its predecessors, the exhibition was a great success and showed,

> another instance of the manner in which an institution like the Arts Club may render service to the community. Art works of this kind can rarely be hung to their advantage in the ordinary gallery, but in the Club-house in Blenheim Terrace one is able to see them under more favourable conditions and to study them at leisure.[42]

Bone's sketches were largely architectural themes requiring precise draughtsmanship including drawings of the imagined erection of Westminster Abbey, Clare market and demolishing the Globe Theatre. The report comments glowingly on the sense of space and atmosphere achieved and of the way the minute detail was woven into a coherent whole. The favouring of the sketch over the finished object was a continuing feature of the Club's approach. The last sessions on fine art to be reported were by Frederick W. Jackson of the Staithes group of English Impressionists on 'Methods of training in Landscape Art' on 9 October 1908, W. A. Stewart of the Bradford Arts Club on 'Modern Landscape Painting' on 20 February 1909, followed the next week by Caldwell Spruce again on 'Sculpture'.

Discussion of literature followed the now familiar Nietzschean themes. Arthur Lee talked on 'Ecstasy in Literature' on 29 February 1908 in which he argued that the mark of a work's immortality was its ability to create ecstasy in the reader. Though it was not clear from the report, Lee seems to have had Nietzsche's criterion of the absolute distantiation of the reader from everyday life (a theme in Orage's reading of Nietzsche) in mind. He illustrated his argument, which was generally hostile to modern 'realism', with a comparison of Dickens and Thackeray. The latter he thought an excellent photographer of everyday life but lacked the ecstatic. Dickens's *Pickwick* on the other hand had it in abundance and ranked with Homer's *Odyssey*.[43] The following year he lectured on, appropriately, 'Faust' while on 13 February 1909 his fellow Anglican priest and graduate of Cambridge University, Fletcher Lamplugh, talked on 'Parsifal and the Grail'. Lee's esoteric approach however was articulated in his talk on 'Psychical Research and Mysticism' on 30 October 1908. Here he suggested that physical science's ability to reveal any more about the mystery of life was, now that the major landmarks of the nineteenth century had been passed, severely limited. Instead, psychical research, which while attempting to find a scientific basis for the belief in life after death had, almost in passing, discovered the extraordinary phenomenon of telepathy. Through telepathy 'communication with other souls and with the world soul once more becomes not only possible but actual'.[44] Thus that sense of the infinite which had inspired Plato, Dante and the master builders of the Gothic would be restored and religion and art could once again replace scientific materialism as the dominant mode of revelation. We can now see, I think, the significance of Lee's use of the term 'ecstatic' in relation to literature which was a literally held belief in a state of release from material life in which spiritual revelation could occur.

In the only other talk on literature. 'Romanticism and Classicism' Charles Smythe echoed Chesterton's differentiation and foreshadowed the debates in the *New Age*, which were to culminate in T. E. Hulme's famous formulations. However, he was not polemical and tried merely to show why Milton's *Paradise Lost* was Classical and Wordsworth's *Excursion* was Romantic. It is a pity that his earlier talk on 'Art and Democracy' of 7 March 1908 was not reported.

Musical performance had begun to play a much greater role in the Club's activities with the result that by 1909 a separate musical section had started publishing its own syllabus. In Spring 1908 there were performances of Brahms Opus 118 and 119 by Noel Bell and Hugo Wolf's songs by T. J. Hoggett (who possessed a copy of Nietzsche's *Contra Wagner*) and also an unreported talk on 'Musical Healthy Mindedness' by Miss Kate Whitehead, editor of *Musical World*. In the Autumn of 1908 there was a piano recital by Lloyd Hartley and a lecture recital of the later sonatas of Beethoven by C. W. Wilkinson, the Professor of Music at Leeds University and previous tenant of 8 Blenheim Terrace. The Musical Section's syllabus for Autumn 1909 (the only one discovered) advertised twelve musical 'evenings' including a Richard Strauss chamber concert, harp and cello duets by Jno. Walton senior and junior, a vocal and violin recital by Misses Beecroft and Appleyard, trios performed by Miss Lily Simms, Mr Marsden and Herbert Johnson, 'Enoch Arden with Incidental Piano Music by Richard Strauss' performed by C. W. Wilkinson, 'C. V. Alkan, with illustrations' by Leopold Jackson and E. Moxon, a song recital by E. J. Wilkinson, Hugo Wolf's songs again by T. J. Hoggett, gipsy music by A. Hague, 'Richard Wagner and the Sagas' by G. H. Cowling and a 'MacDowell' piano recital by Noel Bell.

Thus the period since Orage's and Jackson's residence in London was a process of expansion and variation on the original theme. Though the Club appears to have diluted the single-minded political project of the opening years, there was no lack of vitality in its offerings and the emergence of separate theatre and musical sections showed a widening of appeal. While direct commentaries on Nietzsche are less evident, German Romanticism is all pervasive. Orage's own politics appear to have become more extreme, while Jackson continued his practical and reasonable Morrisian Fabianism. Even Shaw was less ascerbic than on his previous visit and his argument for a municipal theatre in Leeds, reflecting his battle to establish a National Theatre, betrays a movement from open politics to cultural influence. The growing preponderance of actresses, actors and critics in the Club's programme pointed to the centrality the stage was to take, though Dukes's attack on Shaw's puritanism indicated that his own political theatre would shortly be challenged by European and expressionist avant-garde drama promoted, ironically by the very journal his finances kept afloat, the *New Age*.

Notes

1. *The Autobiography of Arthur Ransome*, Rupert Hart-Davis (ed.), Cape, London, 1976, p.63.
2. Ian Britain, *Fabianism and Culture, A Study of British Socialism and the Arts, c1884–1918*, Cambridge University Press, 1982, p.168.
3. *Eric Gill's Letters*, Walter Shewring (ed.), Cape, London, 1947, p.311.
4. *YWP*, 9 February 1907, p.17.
5. *YWP*, 23 February 1907, p.17
6. *YWP*, 9 March 1907, p.16.
7. *YWP*, 27 April 1907.
8. Ellic Howe, *The Magicians of the Golden Dawn*, London, Routledge, Kegan Paul, 1972, p.111.
9. *Leeds Mercury*, 3 December 1906, p.4.
10. *YWP*, 27 April 1907, p.21.
11. Scrapbook of cuttings relating to Isabella Ford's publications, West Yorkshire County Archives, Sheepscar, Leeds.
12. Isabella Ford, *Women and Socialism*, Independent Labour Party Press, London, 1904, p.9.
13. Ford, *Women and Socialism*, p.10.
14. Eric Hobsbawm, 'The New Woman' in *The Age of Empire*, Weidenfeld and Nicolson, London, 1988.
15. Cut-out (untitled) newspaper obituary notice dated in pencil 28 January 1930, but not signed, tipped in at page 13 of the copy of Holbrook Jackson's *Bernard Shaw* in the Brotherton Collection, Leeds University.
16. *Yorkshire Evening Post*, 14 December 1920. (In Leeds Cuttings, Leeds City Reference Library.)
17. *YWP*, 21 November 1907, p.19.
18. *YWP*, 12 October 1907, p.17.
19. Kramer's portrait of Mrs Hardcastle is in Leeds City Art Gallery. I am indebted to Mrs Hilary Brosh for this information.
20. *YWP*, 17 February 1908, p.9.
21. *The Yorkshire Observer*, 17 February 1908.
22. Ibid.

23. Wallace Martin, *The New Age under Orage*, Manchester University Press, 1967, p.62.
24. *YWP*, 5 December 1908, p.19.
25. *Yorkshire Daily Observer*, 30 March 1908, p.9.
26. Ibid.
27. Letter in possession of Denis Mason Jones, Long Causeway, Leeds.
28. In Autumn 1908 Wells resigned from the Fabian Society. 'He had gone but he left a scar. Beatrice was angry at what she felt to be an ill-judged, anarchistic, and impertinent attempt to swing the Fabian Society over to his own loosely defined purposes, to destroy the work of twenty years and to discredit its authors. She also disliked instinctively his views upon marriage and the relations of the sexes, as exemplified both in his own personal life and in novels like *Anne Veronica*.' Margaret Cole, *Beatrice Webb*, Longmans, London, 1945, p.116.
29. *Yorkshire Daily Observer*, 6 April 1908, p.9.
30. *Yorkshire Post*, 6 April 1908, p.6.
31. Ibid.
32. Letter to Florence Farr dated 8 February 1905, in Dan H. Laurence, (ed.) *Bernard Shaw Collected Letters 1898–1910*, London, 1972, pp.509–10.
33. *Yorkshire Daily Observer*, 21 December 1908.
34. *Yorkshire Daily Observer*, 23 April 1909, p.7.
35. *YWP*, 6 November, 1909, p.17.
36. *New Age*, VIII, 23 March 1911, pp.497–8, quoted in Wallace Martin, *The New Age Under Orage*, pp.77–8.
37. Brochure for Shaw's lecture in Leeds City Reference Library.
38. *YWP*, 18 December 1909, p.17.
39. John Rothenstein, *Modern English Painters*, vol I, Eyre and Spottiswoode, London, 1952–56, p.128.
40. *Yorkshire Post*, 24 February 1908, p.9.
41. *Yorkshire Daily Observer*, 26 April 1909.
42. Ibid.
43. An opinion he may have picked up from Orage. No Dickensian, Orage thought that Dickens began and ended with *Pickwick*, but one of the best talks Holbrook Jackson said he ever heard Orage give was on *Pickwick*, entitled 'the Iliad of London': Holbrook Jackson, 'A. R. Orage, Personal Recollections', *The Windmill*, London, 1948, p.45.
44. *YWP*, 7 November 1908, p.7.

CHAPTER EIGHT

Waiting for a Dancing Star

1910–1911: The Drama of Mystical Democracy

With what appears to be a renewed sense of urgency, the final two years of the Club's first period included not only the return of a number of nationally established figures like Chesterton, Yeats, Edward Carpenter and the actor F. R. Benson, but also newer influences such as William Poel and Haldane Macfall. Father John O'Connor, the original for Chesterton's 'Father Brown', lectured to the Club and also left an account of Chesterton's own lecture in the same year. Both Holbrook Jackson and Arthur Penty lectured, as did prominent figures in the socialist movement like Loftus Hare and Professor D. H. MacGregor. An exhibition of Frank Sutcliffe's and Frederick Evans's photography was the first shown at the Club. Perhaps because of the rapid growth and influence of the Playgoers Society, there was a continued emphasis on literary and dramatic themes with a number of the sessions jointly shared by the Club and its offspring. Music, the dominant feature of the previous year, plays almost no role except for a talk by Walter Frere on Medieval anthems and a demonstration by F. H. Evans on the pianola. Religion, politics and ecological issues occupy a substantial proportion of the programme. The Club was the focus of a debate in the Bradford liberal paper *The Yorkshire Daily Observer*, which has been preserved in the files in the cuttings books of Leeds City Reference library and forms an instructive insight into how the Club was seen by outsiders.

Syllabuses for spring and autumn 1910 and the only extant syllabus for the Playgoers Society, which covers 1910–1911, have been found as well as a handbill for Chesterton's talk. The spring 1910 syllabus contains a number of changes in form from that of 1909 including a significantly recomposed management committee. In place of the 'Object of the Club' paragraph printed on the back of the programme: a statement was inserted before the programme listings with the words 'The Leeds Arts Club Affirms' in bold capitals.

> That everyone in every place owes it to himself to make that place better and more beautiful. The divorce of Beauty from Life is disastrous: the existence of anything that does not add to beauty and truth is a stumbling block to the community. The Club values no

> enthusiasm for either Art or Philosophy which does not consciously react upon the ugliness, stupidity and chaos of modern civilization.

This purposeful and blunt statement replaced the more literary and idealistic formulation of the earlier paragraph, and may reflect the changes in the management committee. A. W. Waddington was succeeded as Club secretary by one R. E. Wilkinson about whom nothing is known apart from the fact that he lectured on this programme on 'Selfishness and Christianity'. Waddington was still a member of the management committee, though Miss Kennedy, the librarian, Rev. A. H. Lee (who had moved to a parish in London), Messrs Perkins, Robinson and Dodgson (Kester) are missing. New committee members included the bookshop owner, printer and leading freemason W. H. Bean as treasurer, Miss S. A. Foster and Miss Louisa Wilkinson who were schoolteachers, Miss Bertha Doyle, singer and artist, Billy Jones again and W. E. Pocklington as well as W. P. Irving who doubled as co-secretary with Frederick G. Jackson of the Playgoers Society. Perhaps the club was also feeling the pinch, financially, for the annual subscription leapt almost 50 per cent from 10s 6d to 15s., and an entrance fee of 5s. was required for new members, who were required to endorse the new affirmation. Non-members, however, could still come to lectures for 6d. The literary, sketching and musical groups (which advertised an extra syllabus) still met and occasional discussion of recent events, 'Literary Artistic and Political' was still a feature. Two furnished rooms in the Club were also available for rent from the resident caretaker or secretary. Very few reports are available so it is not possible to confirm how much of the printed programme actually went ahead, though one can assume it was substantial. The main meeting day seems to have changed to a Monday, and the time to 8pm.

The first meeting was given on Monday 10 January by the influential Quaker and Christian Socialist, the editor of *The Ploughshare*, H. Loftus Hare, on 'The Mysticism of Dante', but no report survives. Three days later William Poel (1852–1934), actor and founder of the Elizabethan Stage Society lectured on 'Shakespeare and George Bernard Shaw'. Poel was perhaps the most distinguished Shakespearian of his generation. His revivals of textually authentic productions in sparse sets revolutionized productions. Though no report survives of his talk to the Leeds Club, he also gave this lecture to the Bradford Playgoers Society a couple of years later. His view that Shakespeare like Shaw was the 'most modern mind of his day and the most progressive thinker of his age',[1] corresponded with Holbrook Jackson's. As Shakespeare was not respected in his own time as a prophet, classical writer, or man of letters so today Shaw was so neglected and the academic circle was unconscious of the world's greatest poet and thinker in its midst.

Shaw was probably also the subject of the next literary talk, on Monday 7 February, when Haldane Macfall spoke on 'The Puritan and the Theatre'. Macfall was a popular writer, art critic and an early admirer and patron of the sculptor, Gaudier Brzeska. He was also a friend of Holbrook Jackson to whom he presented a copy of his book on the painter Whistler in 1905.[2] Shaw was now regularly under attack in the pages of the *New Age* for his so-called 'puritanism', not only from the Chesterton group with whom Dukes and Haldane were associated but by some of the New Women like Storm Jameson, who described him a few years later as having 'the mind of a puritanical ratepayer', in one of her first contributions to the journal. Storm Jameson had recently arrived at Leeds University as an undergraduate in the School of English and also had strong opinions of her professor, Charles Edwyn Vaughan, whom she called 'that severe woman-hating humanist'.[3]

Vaughan, Professor of English Literature at Leeds University (1904–1913), was nevertheless highly regarded both in the university and in the town and on the Saturday following he spoke to the Leeds Playgoers at the Club rooms on 'Tolstoy and Shakespeare'. Inspired by T. H. Green at Oxford, 'Privilege and exclusion aroused his wrath; he wished to see the universities opened to all sections of the community and to every branch of study.'[4] It may also say something of the revision of Nietzsche's standing in the Club at this time, that Vaughan was profoundly unsympathetic to him and, for that matter, to Thomas Carlyle. Lecturing at the Swarthmore Centre, A Quaker Adult Education Centre in central Leeds, the following year, Vaughan roundly denounced the cult of hero-worship he found in both writers. The intellectual climate was turning against supermen in general and Nietzsche in particular, as war feeling against the 'Prussians' was notched up. Significantly the star of the philosopher Henri Bergson was rising who, perhaps because he was French and therefore allied, provided a more palatable form of evolutionist aesthetics. Bergson's name was starting to appear in the pages of the *New Age* in translations and commentaries by T. H. Hulme and he too appears to have been on the fringe of Orage's occultist network for his sister, Vestigia, was married to the leader of the Hermetic Order of the Golden Dawn, MacGregor Mathers.[5]

While Shaw may still have been too outrageous for the academy, the same did not go for his compatriot, and Golden Dawn magician, W. B. Yeats, who returned on 1 November 1910 to talk on the 'Modern Dramatic Movement in Ireland'. The meeting was held in the university's great hall with Vaughan in the chair. Yeats argued that the aim of aesthetic art was to express humanity and its permanent relations. That being said, Ireland was not the place it was and a new national movement had arisen to restore something of the 'ancient courtesy' to the new democracy which had to be taught and disciplined. He extolled the Gaelic League and its project of national revival. While in England there were libraries to educate the people, this was not the case in Ireland, so it was to the peasant that they returned for 'in the peasant's mind and not in any library is the national treasure.'[6] He and Lady Gregory had gone to the peasant for his stories and his fancies and had brought them to the towns. Yeats talked of how they had formed the Abbey Theatre – brought to the Leeds Club in 1906 he reminded them – for the purposes of putting before people who read little but newspapers, nobler things. He praised the work of his friend and fellow playwright, Synge, for its use of dialect 'which was a necessary part of the attack upon the imagination of that commercial Ireland which must be taught everything anew', but went on to say that a new 'realist' school of playwrights was emerging using methods similar to those of Galsworthy. He did not see the new realist as a threat to his own poetic drama though, as is often thought, 'I think' he said, 'they will win the battle for us and when the battle is won the plays of Synge and Lady Gregory will continue to be played'.

While Yeats saw the stage as pivotal to cultural renewal and, perhaps unexpectedly, embraced the new realism, the next major speaker, G. K. Chesterton, was sceptical. His talk was held on Tuesday 14 February 1911, also in the great hall of the university, chaired by no less than the Vice Chancellor, Sir Nathan Boddington. Chesterton asked 'What's Wrong with the Drama?' answering pretty well everything. Surprisingly no newspapers covered the talk, but by chance Father John O'Connor with whom Chesterton was staying left an amusing account of it in his memoir, *Father Brown on Chesterton*. Father O'Connor, who was not only the model for 'Father Brown' but Chesterton's spiritual mentor, recounted that his complaint of the drama was that

> . . . it is not dramatic. It is evolutionary. The characters are all possessed of private means, and not having to work for a living, they stay on the stage all the time, boring one another to tears, and there is a triangle, isosceles or equilateral, and sometimes one triangle inside another, and they keep on jarring until they get divorced and live happily ever after. This, being besides the opposite of the old drama which had a something to make for, aids in the annihilation of interest and even of thought, and fails of all object whatsoever, and is thoroughly inhuman. Whereas drama was invented to show how every man comes to a crisis in which he makes a free choice for good or ill, and the audience, allowed to suspect the tendencies, are

> held to watch how they work themselves out, teleology being the second deepest of all human instincts, causality being the deepest.[7]

There is no reason to suppose that this was not accurately remembered and not O'Connor's own gloss, since he recounts also that he and Chesterton had often talked about the history of drama. They agreed that while the 'Drama of the Heathen' (presumably the 'Dionysian' that Nietzsche describes in *The Birth of Tragedy*) was a demonstration of Blind Unpitying Fate, its Christian successor had based its drama on the 'great and difficult fact of Responsibility', but 'Modern Drama portrayed people as doing what they liked, and as nothing is so abysmally boring, it was decaying while it grew. Dried blossoms, empty fruits, if one thing is as good as another, where is the use of selection?'.[8] This was no doubt not the realism that Yeats had in mind but possibly the productions of Shaw and the other Royal Court dramatists. Chesterton's book on Shaw, published the same year, 1910, contained a devastating attack on his 'realism', his 'Puritanism' and even worse, his subservience to Nietzsche:

> This eloquent sophist has an influence upon Shaw and his school which it would require a separate book adequately to study. By descent Nietzsche was a Pole, and probably a Polish noble; and to say that he was a Polish noble is to say that he was a frail, fastidious, and entirely useless anarchist.[9]

This genial abuse, however, seemed to have been characteristic of the relations between Shaw and Chesterton, who otherwise had a great respect for each other. Orage had manipulated this relationship brilliantly in an orchestrated public debate on socialism in the pages of the *New Age* in 1908, in which Shaw had coined the name 'Chesterbelloc' to characterize the little-man anti-statist position of Chesterton and Belloc. During the first four years or so of his editorship there is strong evidence that Orage himself moved towards positions earlier asserted by Chesterton and away from the Nietzscheism he embraced in Leeds. In his book *Chesterton and the Edwardian Cultural Crisis*, John D. Coates convincingly demonstrates some of these shifts.[10] Coates argues firstly, that the *New Age* itself repudiated socialism in 1912 in very similar terms to those Chesterton had used in the first of his Chesterbelloc pieces in the *New Age* of 8 January 1908, 'Why I am Not a Socialist'. Secondly, after 1910 Orage gradually repudiated literary realism in terms similar to Chesterton's argument in the *New Age* of 25 January 1908, as 'missing men's inner life'. Thirdly, that Orage's *New Age* piece 'On Drama' of 18 May, 1911, came very close to Chesterton's long held views and those of Ashley Dukes who rejected Shaw in the *New Age* of 23 March 1911 as a Puritan who set ethics before taste. Both articles appear to owe a debt to Chesterton's book on Shaw, already cited.

Most strikingly, though, Orage appears to have altered his views on the limits of human development, from 1908–1911, directly in line with Chesterton's. His superman, capable of infinite transcendent development, of a few years earlier had been reduced to 'a fixed species' in the *New Age* of 25 May 1911, and was 'incapable of indefinite progress' in the *New Age* of 27 July 1911, where he further declared that the modern crisis stems from lack of human definition. In the same piece, Orage also accepted the doctrine of original sin and redemption as the only theory which accounted for 'all these cross purposes of the world', which echoed Chesterton's *New Age* essays of 22 February and 31 December 1908. But perhaps even more significantly in terms of the British modernist debate, these expressions also pre-date T. E. Hulme's more widely celebrated versions in the *New Age* by a year, though, as Wallace Martin notes, while Hulme fervently embraced original sin, he was conspicuously silent on redemption.[11] Coates believes that, in his blend of cultural conservatism and radical reforming politics, Orage was in fact politically closer to Chesterton than Hulme, though even he lacked Chesterton's warmth, tolerance and geniality. The boundaries though are not clear. Hulme's aesthetics appear radical, revolutionary even, in their assault on humanism and realism and demand for geometric form in which he was prepared to go much further than Orage who, though discontented with superficial 'realism', in arguing that art should have a concern for man's inner life, was nevertheless proposing a form of realism. What Orage actually seems to have objected to is what Georg Lukacs would have called 'naturalism'. For Orage, art that was concerned with man's spiritual life would reveal a deeper realism and like him was profoundly distressed with the fragmentariness of the new decentred subject, which seemed to be emerging.

But there is something about this formulation of the 'deeper' or 'inner' which is easily overlooked. In looking 'below the surface' for 'the true reality of being' or some such phrases, Orage was tapping an enduring vein of metaphysical speculation which tries to differentiate between an underlying or essential reality and a merely transitory appearance. Lukacs's Marxism also made this kind of discrimination. Orage was echoing not only the symbolist preoccupations of Walter Pater but the related spiritualist ones of theosophy, contained for example in Annie Besant and Cyril Leadbetter's theosophical text, *Thought Forms*. Though for many these were the esoteric and by now archaic fancies of the nineties, they were, in fact, to reappear in the debates around abstractionism in 1914, as we shall see. It is arguable that in some respects some modernist arguments about the importance of formal structure, imagery and even to an extent the notion of an 'objective correlative' rely on the belief in a mystically or unconsciously structured substratum of life. This is the unspoken agenda for many of the succeeding debates both in the *New Age* where they are the focus of Hulme's attack on Kandinsky's theories and Herbert Read's discussions on Jacob Kramer in the Arts Club. We shall return to this debate later, but what we see here in Chesterton's attack on Shaw and on Nietzsche is evidence of the continuing debate over aesthetics from the nineties which was to erupt in the fierce polemics of 1910–1914.

Chesterton remained an avuncular and respected figure in the Arts Club which he still occasionally visited and when he finally converted to Romanism in 1922 it was O'Connor who received him into the church. O'Connor himself discussed the poetry of the dissident Catholic poet Francis Thompson, who had died three years earlier, at the Club on 14 October 1910, but no report has been found of it. The priest of St Cuthbert's Church, Bradford, he also translated and published *Art Scholastique*, by the French neo-Thomist philosopher, Jacques Maritain, in Eric Gill's Ditching Press in 1923 for which Gill provided the Introduction. In his own wrestling with faith, T. S. Eliot seems to have been drawn close to Maritain's position in the years following the book's publication.[12] (By coincidence, Eliot was in Yorkshire in 1916, when he gave a series of lectures for Oxford University Extension Delegacy on 'Modern French Literature, tendencies in modern French thought', in Ilkley, about twenty miles from Leeds in which the return to the Catholic Church was the subject of his fifth lecture.)[13]

A variety of unreported talks and events relating to drama organized by the Club or the Playgoers Society included a dramatic reading of the poetic drama *Herod* by the actor/poet Stephen Phillips (1864–1915) on Thursday 6 October 1910, by the Rev. Dr Warschauer. On Thursday 17 November there were 'Operatic Selections' under the direction of Miss Lily Pearce, with Introductory Remarks by Arthur Grimshaw. The pieces chosen were from Beethoven's *Fidelio*, Wagner's *Flying Dutchman* and Mozart's *Don Giovanni*. The vocalists included Ada Beecroft, a Leeds organist who, with Grimshaw, had recently been instrumental in promoting the work of Debussy among resistant Leeds musical patrons. 1 December saw Frederick Whelen of His Majesty's Theatre talk on the 'Work of the Stage Society', the Fabian-inspired experimental theatre group, which was chaired by another Community of the Resurrection member, the vicar of Leeds, Cyril Bickersteth.

An 'at home' of the Playgoers Society on Thursday 9 November was reported, when Frederic Moorman and his wife received the guests at the Leeds institute Cafe for a lecture on 'Drama and the Art of Life' by the actor F. R. Benson, currently appearing in a play at the Grand

Theatre. It was chaired by Councillor E. R. Philips of the *Yorkshire Post*. Benson held that drama was the art form that most completely expressed life and to some extent had an almost mystical relationship to it: it was a holy well around which the people gathered to learn of the future and what the gods held in store. A fortnight later he gave 'a short but eloquent address' to the Bradford Arts Club on 'Beauty in Town Life' when he called drama the true popular democratic art but he also felt that the future of 'the race' would depend more upon the activities of clubs like the ones in Bradford and Leeds than on anything that was happening in parliament.[14] This was another example perhaps of what Orage meant by 'the mystical concept of democracy' in which theatre as the expression of 'the folk' and the Club as the concentration of the elect, revealed the true spirit of demos. Perhaps the Club members took Benson's thespian hyperbole with a pinch of salt.

Other theatrical events in 1911 included the pioneering Elizabeth Bessle Comedy Company which gave three performances in the Albert Hall of the Leeds Institute, playing Ibsen's *Pillars of Society*, Shakespeare's *Comedy of Errors* and *Admiral Guinea* by W. E. Henley and R. L. Stevenson, described blandly by the *Yorkshire Post* as a 'pleasing break in the long spell of pantomime'. On 2 March E. T. Heys of the Gaiety Theatre, Manchester, which had been recently founded by Annie Horniman after her break with the Abbey Theatre, talked on 'The Irish National Theatre' and on 6 April there was a 'Special Shakespearian Lecture, In Shakespearian Atmosphere', with lantern slides, given by Patrick Kirwan. E. Kitson Clark of the Philosophical and Literary Society chaired a discussion on 'Old Comedy and New Humour', the first evidence of any link between the Club and the Phil and Lit. Herbert Thompson again talked on opera and the London impresario, Nigel Playfair, on 'Theatre Organisation'.

At least four sessions were devoted to social and political matters during these two years. Two of them involved the return of inspirational founding figures, Edward Carpenter and A. J. Penty and Leeds University economist, David MacGregor, who was also an inspirational force in worker's education in Yorkshire. Penty's lecture was on 'The Revival of Apprenticeship', but went unreported. In his seminal 1906 work, *The Restoration of the Gild's System*, Penty had claimed that he owed its underlying philosophy to Edward Carpenter's *Civilisation Its Cause and Cure*. Carpenter returned to the Club to talk on 'Beauty in Town Life' the following autumn. Though this was also unreported, a talk given the following autumn, Monday 23 October 1911, may have been similar. On this occasion Carpenter spoke of 'Beauty in Civic Life' and the meeting was chaired by his and Penty's old friend, Albert Waddington, who had known Carpenter from as far back as 1886 when he was secretary of Carpenter's newly founded Sheffield Socialist Society.

Carpenter, in terms now very familiar to the Club members, attacked the dereliction of beauty of such a wealthy country and the spiritual impoverishment of the masses at the hands of the wealthy. He maintained that the old towns produced by craftsmen were inevitably more beautiful than the products of the modern industrial system and it was vital that the crafts should be restored. Following Penty's argument he recommended the restoration of a guild system but also spoke approvingly of the French Syndicalist movement as involving the idea that 'workers should carry on their industries co-operatively' and that 'if that came about it would result in a different kind of production, artistic and not mechanical in character'.[15] He also suggested that nationalization could lead to shorter working hours and thus free the workers to develop 'their own free and spontaneous industries in which the elements of beauty would again exist'. This is a significant yoking of the two political movements of guilds restoration and syndicalism, and it is interesting that Carpenter's emphasis was on 'workers' while Waddington, Penty and Orage would have favoured 'artists and craftsmen'. Clearly in Carpenter the refusal to divorce the political interests of craftsmen from those of the workers was still strong and tied to democratic organization, whereas those inspired by him, now found those attachments sentimental and sought more charismatic solutions.

Something of the organization and social milieu of the club at this time is revealed in two postcards Edward Carpenter sent to Alf Mattison, now in the Brotherton Collection. The first one, dated 27 August 1911, appeals to Mattison: 'Can you tell me anything about the "Arts" Club? I wrote to them a fortnight ago about a lecture – but – no answer!' A month later he appears to have confirmed his booking and would also be in Leeds to talk to the Clarion Scouts the previous evening. He asks Mattison if he can stay with him the Sunday or the Monday night. The Ford sisters had asked him to stay the Saturday night and he notes that they would have to miss the Arts Club lecture because 'they always have a girls class on Monday' – presumably a night class for women textile workers. (These classes were started by their mother in the 1850s and were possibly the first ever evening classes for workers.) Carpenter ends by asking Mattison if he will come to Sheffield to give a lantern slide lecture on 'Life in the Olden Time'. (The lecture to the working-class activists of the Clarion Scouts, on the 'Prospect of a General Strike' was, by contrast with Arts Club talk, a full blooded advocacy of Tom Mann's industrial syndicalism in which he does not appear to have mentioned the guild system as an alternative.)[16]

The reconciliation of the crafts movement with modern industrial methods was also implicit in a meeting of Leeds' sister club in Bradford. This was held on Saturday 2 December 1911, when the founder of the arts and crafts movement, T. J. Cobden-Sanderson, opened an exhibition of arts and crafts in the Bradford Club rooms. Chaired by Charles Rothenstein, Sanderson's talk on 'Art and Industry' was prefaced by a short autobiographical account of his meeting with William Morris in the revolutionary fervour of 1882 when 'we thought we were going to revolutionise the world' and how Janey Morris had turned him towards the, not so revolutionary, craft of bookbinding. The core of his talk was on the *reconciliation* of arts and crafts with industry in which he dismissed the claim that the movement was hostile to industry per se. He was reported as saying that machinery was one of the most marvellous things in the world: 'You should not despise it. I think it is a prolongation of man himself'.[17] Further, the artistic work of cloth manufacture was the real art and craft of Bradford, and the object of the Arts Club there should be to put itself in touch with the city's industry. The function of the arts and crafts exhibition was to demolish the academic notion of art as being merely the production of paintings sculpture and architecture, since 'Art' embraced the whole of life, it should embrace industry too.

Thus, in reflection, while Edward Carpenter was refusing to encourage the separation of the political interests of the craftsman and manual labourer, so urgently pursued by Orage both in his *Leeds Mercury* article of 1906 and in 'Politics for Craftsmen' of 1907, Cobden-Sanderson, in Bradford, was seeking a reconciliation of crafts and industry. Certainly Sanderson's constructive reconceptualizing of the traditional categories followed the Leeds Club's belief in the need for unity of art and life and was aimed at preventing the formation of an elitist coterie (suggested by the correspondence in the *Yorkshire Observer*, as we shall see). Later in the following year, the newly appointed curator of the Leeds Art Gallery, Frank Rutter, re-emphasized Sanderson's talk to the Bradford Club with practical suggestions of his own. Perhaps Leeds and Bradford, historical rivals, were different. For example Bradford's most celebrated modern writer, J. B. Priestley (1894–1984), recalled with affection that Bradford before World War One 'was the most progressive place in the United Kingdom.' This was due in part to its 'flourishing arts club' of which he was a young enthusiast, 'So I grew up with two equally strong tastes: one for what is truly urban – for concerts and theatres and arts clubs and cafes to argue in'[18] – the other, of course, for the Yorkshire countryside. Though Priestley appears to have adopted Orage's 'reactionary Radical' stance his other poses of 'grumbling patriot, cosmopolitan Yorkshireman, professional amateur, cultured philistine'[19] constantly reasserted the 'common sense of the common man' so markedly absent from the Leeds Club's deliberations.

Professor David MacGregor's talk on G. Lowes Dickinson's *Justice and Liberty* took place on 19 December 1910. Denounced as 'subversive' by the Professor of Education at the time, MacGregor had succeeded Clapham as the professor of the recently formed department of economics at Leeds University, 1908–1919. But known as 'God' among WEAers, he tutored one of the Leeds Branch's first courses, in 1907, entitled 'Competition, Association and Communism'. MacGregor was one of that generation of socialist intellectuals who attended to the detail of socialist reform, rather than the utopian transformation of humanity as proposed by Orage and others. In his influential political handbook *The Evolution of Industry* of that year, 1911, and reprinted four times between 1917 and 1922, he gave an impressive summary of the progress of the labour movement and assessed the problems currently facing it. Contrary to Orage, he believed that the main obstacle to reform was the British cult of leadership, such that, in crisis, even amongst the more advanced socialists weak solutions were too willingly accepted.

> This result is due largely to the tremendous personal repute that has come to be attached in England, perhaps more than anywhere, to political leadership. It is a leadership not simply of causes, but of men and the thoughts and purposes of men. It has established so strong a grip on the people that it has created nothing less than a new English aristocracy. The opinion on any issues whether closely or only remotely connected with politics, of a great political leader has a power over the minds of the people greater than that of the expert. Theology and Literature and Social Science can furnish well-known examples of this. It is against the personal force of this new aristocracy that democratic causes strike and fall back in a weaker wave.[20]

Thus for MacGregor the interests of working-class democracy were linked with those of the professional expert against the political leader, whose expertise should be confined to politics. In tune with the general intellectual reaction against the superman cult, it must have been an interesting corrective to a club that within the last few years had responded to calls for a new aristocracy, to find that MacGregor had identified one and found it lacking! He added that 'Democracy, of course is not forbidden to trust great personalities, but it is forbidden to submit merely to great names. Its spirit requires a real power of initiative and a constant power of check on public policies.'[21]

The presence of democratic socialist perspectives such as MacGregor's in the Club, as opposed to the charismatic socialism of Orage, may well be the result of greater university involvement, as evidenced by Professors Moorman, Vaughan, Cohen and Vice-Chancellor Boddington, bringing increased academic 'objectivity'. However the lack of university representatives on the committee suggests that it was still controlled by non-university teachers and professionals. It might also have been due to a climate of anti-Nietzscheism and increasing pessimism about the limits of human possibilities, already noted in Orage's writings; a New Realism perhaps. MacGregor's talk, however was a clear example of the 'professional' intellectual warning the amateurs off his patch. A stream of moderate but purposeful debate had always paralleled Orage's more arcane pronouncements and it was to this that J. B. Cohen, Professor of Chemistry at Leeds 1904–24, contributed. In his illustrated talk on 'The Smoke Nuisance' he argued that the volume of smoke and smut that disfigured everyday life was indefensible since the scientific means of reducing it was available if only Leeds manufacturers would adopt it. Here again the expert felt that his knowledge and advice to the city fathers was being ignored.

The remainder of the sessions was something of a collection of loose ends. In two lectures on religious themes, R. E. Wilkinson, the new Club secretary talked on 'Christianity and Selfishness' and the Rev. J. G. Melling spoke on 'Devil Worship: Ancient and Modern'. Nothing is known of either talk, but Melling, according to Crockford's, was at this time the vicar of St Mark's, Woodhouse, where he remained until 1921. One of the young, well-educated Anglicans in the Club's orbit, he had graduated from Selwyn College, Cambridge in 1901 and had enrolled at Leeds Clerical School in the same year.

The remnants of the arts programme contained renderings of William de Morgan's 'The Official Chimney Sweep' and 'Symbolism' by Arthur Machen. The ceramicist and potter, William de Morgan (1839–1917), had been a close friend of William Morris and only late in life had started writing fiction, this being one of the short stories. Arthur Machen (1863–1947), famous for his supernatural tales of evil and horror, was also a member of the Hermetic Order of the Golden Dawn and an actor in F. R. Benson's Shakespeare Repertory Company, 1901–1910. 'Symbolism' was a literary critical essay from his 1902 collection *Hieroglyphics* and illustrates the close correspondence of symbolist aesthetics to occultist thought. During this session Charles Smythe also talked on 'What is Poetry?' and there was a practical session on 'Stencilling' by Bertha Doyle who had recently joined the management committee. She subsequently married the secretary R. E.

Wilkinson and set up a mill run on guild socialist lines in Collingham, North Yorks.[22] Lastly E. W. Smith talked on 'Heating and Ventilation'.

The Club's only exhibition was held between 21 February and 7 March, 1910, of photographs by the now famous Whitby photographer, Frank Sutcliffe, and Frederick H. Evans. Sutcliffe contributed a weekly column to the *Yorkshire Weekly Post* on photographic matters and the Club's interest in photography as an art-form dates from this time. Evans, who also later received recognition for his work, also lectured on the exhibition's opening night on the 'Pianism of the Pianola' illustrated on the obscurely named 'Themodist'. The last discovered report for 1910–11, also musical, but epochally distant from Edwardian technology, is of a meeting on 2 December 1910, when the Rev. Walter Frere, lectured on the 'Medieval Evolution of the Anthem'. Tracing the development of harmony, he referred to a species of song which he described as 'elaborate warblings' and proceeded to illustrate them.[23] So much laughter ensued that Frere reminded his audience that the Pope in 1322 had put a stop to this kind of warbling. This was succeeded by measured music as opposed to plainsong which included the first carols and England, he said, in the fifteenth century, had led the world in the development of musical composition.

'A Cultured Coterie': the Press Debate on the Arts Club

A remarkable set of cuttings in the Leeds City Reference Library's cuttings files shows a vigorous debate being conducted in the pages of Bradford's *Yorkshire Observer* about public life in Leeds. This mentions the Arts Club and Playgoers Society a number of times with varying degrees of respect or disdain and provides an insight into how their activities were judged at the time – at least, that is, by the readers of the liberal *Yorkshire Observer*. The collection of cuttings itself must also signify the importance attached by the librarian who compiled it, T. W. Hand, to the Club's activities and indeed his name occurs a few times later in connection with them.

The correspondence is begun by someone signing himself 'Forward' in a letter dated Leeds, 9 January 1911, who bemoans the fact that such a great and wealthy city like Leeds cares so little for the arts that the only progress which most Leeds people seem to be concerned about is that of a soulless materialism in which the finer purposes of life have no place; 'this rank growth of commercialism' he says, 'has brought a blight upon the public life of the city, dissipating the great ideals which ought to animate municipal government; and it has all but smothered the great arts which we see flourishing so vigorously in other more favoured cities'.[24] Bewailing the lack of public patronage for painting and music, he describes the present civic policy as 'cold neglect' and despite its roaring factories and teeming mills the walls of the art gallery wait in vain for gifts from its rich citizens. Referring then to Shaw's 1909 talk to the Club, he says,

> George Bernard Shaw told us not long ago that Leeds was included in the list of 'rotten towns', and who should gainsay it? I admit that, thanks to the activities of the Playgoers Society, some little improvement has been apparent of late, but even that society has to struggle valiantly to keep itself alive, and after an existence of three years or so musters a membership of about only three hundred on an annual subscription of half-a-crown![25]

On 12 January 'A Stranger within the Gates' replied bluffly that however much he agreed with 'Forward's' criticism of Leeds he could not see much hope of salvation in the Leeds Arts Club and he cautioned: 'Rather let Leeds remain unenlightened than that it should become the hunting ground of cultured coteries of wholly tiresome persons obsessed with two or at most three ideas'.[26]

The following day the *Observer* featured a long interview with Holbrook Jackson, who was in Leeds to give a lecture on Maeterlinck and was introduced by the paper as a leading writer on modern developments in art and literature. (The Playgoers Society programme records the talk as 'Maurice Maeterlinck and Dramatic Symbolism', Thursday 12 January at 8pm.) Since October 1910 Jackson had been the de facto editor of *TPs Weekly*. Though less explosive than the *New Age*, *TPs Weekly* shared many of its contributors and maintained a high standard of reviewing, which contributed to his independent reputation as an editor.

Jackson was very warm about Leeds, one of the most sociable towns he knew, 'where people talked to perfect strangers but appeared to have no idea how to pull together in the realms of civic life', and gave his assessment of the Club he had co-founded.

> One of the most useful clubs Leeds ever had, the Arts Club, has always been starved, not for lack of argument but for lack of public support. I know it has been suggested that the failure of the Arts Club to exert a definite influence on Leeds is partly due to the fact its members are inclined to be over intellectual. But what would you have? A Club of that kind must take up a strong position in one direction or another. If it threw in its lot with the purveyors of popular art, drama and music it would soon find itself in the old groove supporting financially inspired art. The only alternative was to take up a strong position of thorough opposition to financially engineered arts of the day. In creating this point of view the club has been eminently successful, and thanks to its exertions many of the leading thinkers of the day have lectured in the city. The attitude

> of the members has not been entirely critical, and by means of exhibitions of pictures, arts and crafts, bookbinding, printing and so on, they have tried to show Leeds people what they would like to become popular.[27]

He reminded readers that it was through the Club that Yeats and the Irish National Theatre had visited Leeds and that the 'vigorous baby of the club, the Playgoers Society' had invited many other leading theatre groups to play, but all this had failed to move the populace. Leeds was simply a second-best town and the people only had themselves to blame. He had some praise however for the public library (one reason perhaps for the debate to have been covered so exhaustively) and for Brangwyn's panels in the art gallery. When pressed by the interviewer on the subject of drama, he said that it was thoroughly degraded not only in Leeds but nationally due to its commercialization. Echoing Shaw he said the only help for the drama in Leeds,

> . . . is that Leeds people themselves should create their own drama; that is to say, write their own plays about their own locality, paint their own scenery, design and make their own costumes, and produce a play with their own local players. That ought to be the one definite aim of the Playgoers Society.[28]

Some rude things about the Leeds musical festival followed – one of the 'greatest farces in modern musical life' and for that reason he was glad it did not pay. But as to the future, he became almost rhapsodic:

> I hope great things of Leeds as I hope great things of Russia. That is to say Leeds like Russia is a thoroughly barbaric place! There is an element of wildness about Leeds that appeals to me very much. An eminent philosopher has said that unless you have chaos within you cannot give birth to a dancing star. It must be obvious to all those who have not lost the faculty of looking frankly and recognising a fact when they see it that Leeds has chaos within. For that reason it certainly will give birth to a dancing star, which will be a new Leeds with resplendent streets, great libraries and art galleries, a fine musical centre and a great theatre. But in every instance these temples of the arts will be the expression of the local life; not of the ideas of London, Germany or any other place, but simply of Leeds and Yorkshire.[29]

Despite his Nietzschean aphorism, Jackson's sybilline pronouncements failed to sum up the correspondence. The next day someone from Headingley wrote that he agreed that the average Leeds citizen simply wanted to be left to make his brass in peace without worrying about his fellow man or the lack of beauty and dignity of the city and he doubted whether the Arts Club or any similar institution was doing much to remedy that! 'The members talk and talk: many of them have high and beautiful ideals, but their influence is little felt outside their club walls. Example is better than precept'. 'Fabius' in another letter bemoaned the lack of a Jowett or a Priestman (founders of the Independent Labour Party) in Leeds, as there were in Bradford, no doubt rubbing with relish salt into Bradford's rival's wounds. Fred Jowett, in particular, was an inspirational politician who after some years as a reforming Bradford councillor, was one of the first Labour MPs and one of the very few, nationally, to be elected against Liberal opposition.

'Forward', the correspondent who opened the debate, was allowed to close it,

> 'Stranger' is mistaken in supposing that I look to the Arts Club for salvation. Such a club organised on really broad lines, might do really excellent work, but with all due respect to Mr Holbrook Jackson's eulogising of the existing Arts Club, I think its lack of influence is due, not to the irresponsiveness of the public, but because the club has failed to come into contact with the common life of the people. Apart from a few lectures by men of national repute, the discussions of the club have nearly always been on an academic plane – using that word in its worst sense – quite out of the mental reach of the ordinary working man or woman. Latterly, indeed, the energies of the club have seemed to be exhausted in preaching a curious doctrine compounded of the writings of Ibsen and GBS. In my opinion the club would have done far more good if its activities had been directed to the organisation of public lectures, simple in character but well informed and authoritative and designed to reveal to uncultured minds something of the meaning and beauty of the various arts.[30]

Thus though the Club had clearly made an impression upon Leeds it was seen as marginal to the needs of ordinary folk. In the difficult task of finding a line between offering genuine intellectual leadership and appearing as a merely elitist fringe of eccentrics, public perception decided it was the latter. Even some artists shared this view. A damning indictment from 'Brooks of Sheffield' in the *Yorkshire Evening News* the following July put the concluding stroke to the canvas, but also revealed the hidden agenda of the debate:

> As for the so-called Arts Club, that is simply a congregation of 'cranks'. Such artists as belong to it were driven out by the 'anti-everything' faddist. Some of its most active supporters are men who would not spend a farthing on art . . . Of course such a coterie would be laughed at, if people knew anything about art, just as, if there were a real Arts Club in Leeds, this question of the appointment of a curator to the Art Gallery would be made a live question, and the education of the artistic taste of the city would not be sacrificed in the interests of a huckster-like economy.[31]

Art, at least, as John Rothenstein later said, was a battleground in Leeds, unlike Sheffield and roused high emotion. The agitations around the issue of who should be the new director of the art gallery resulted in the appointment of a man who had a decisive influence on the next phase of the Arts Club's life, and put post-impressionist art squarely on its agenda, Frank Rutter.

Notes

1. *YWP*, 19 October 1912, p.20.
2. Holbrook Jackson Library, Memorial Catalogue, Elkin Matthews, Cambridge, 1952, p.92.
3. Storm Jameson, *Journey From the North*, vol. 1, Collins Harvill, London, 1969, p.54.
4. Norman Shimmin, *The University of Leeds, the First Fifty Years*, Cambridge University Press, 1954, pp.122–3.
5. Though interested, Bergson was not very impressed. 'I have shown him everything that magic can do', Mathers said of his brother-in-law, 'and it has no effect on him'; quoted in Ellic Howe, *The Magicians of the Golden Dawn*, Routledge, Kegan Paul, London, 1972, p.113.
6. *Yorkshire Daily Observer*, 2 November 1910, p.4.
7. Father John O'Connor, *Father Brown on Chesterton*, Muller, London, 1937, p.92.
8. Ibid., p.94.
9. G. K. Chesterton, *George Bernard Shaw*, John Lane, London, 1914, p. 203.
10. John D. Coates, *Chesterton and the Edwardian Cultural Crisis*, Hull University Press, 1984, pp.235–244.
11. Wallace Martin, *The New Age Under Orage*, p.219.
12. Peter Ackroyd, *T. S. Eliot*, Abacus, London, 1985, pp.155, 157.
13. Ronald Schuchard, 'T. S. Eliot as Extension Lecturer, 1916–1919, *Review of English Studies*, New Series, vol. XXV, Oxford, 1974, pp.166–8. Eliot felt that his audience 'showed a highly intelligent interest . . . and followed the lectures with closer attention than they merited'.
14. *Yorkshire Daily Observer*, 10 November 1910, p.10.
15. *Yorkshire Daily Observer*, 24 October 1911. Unpaged cutting found in the Mattison Collection of the Brotherton Collection.
16. The *Leeds Weekly Citizen*, 28 October 1911. Cutting found in the Mattison collection, the Brotherton Collection, University of Leeds. The *Citizen* was, and still is, the Leeds Labour Party's weekly paper and was established in 1911, with support from D. B. Foster, the ex-proprietor of the *Forward* which Orage had edited in the nineties, and now first secretary of the Leeds Labour Party.
17. *Yorkshire Daily Observer*, 4 December 1911.
18. J. B. Priestley, Preface to *Socialism over Sixty Years, The Life of Jowett of Bradford*, by Fenner Brockway, Allen and Unwin, London, 1946.
19. See the entry on Priestley in Margaret Drabble (ed.), *The Oxford Companion to English Literature*, Oxford, 1985, p.788.
20. D. H. MacGregor, *The Evolution of Industry*, Williams and Norgate, London, 1922, pp.244–5.
21. Ibid., p.245.
22. Information supplied by Denis Mason Jones.

23. *Yorkshire Daily Observer*, 3 December 1910, p.4.
24. *Yorkshire Daily Observer*, 12 January 1911, p.38.
25. Ibid.
26. *Yorkshire Daily Observer*, 13 January 1911.
27. *Yorkshire Daily Observer*, 14 January 1911.
28. Ibid.
29. Ibid.
30. *Yorkshire Daily Observer*, 18 January 1911.
31. *Yorkshire Evening News*, 13 July 1911.

PART THREE
1912–1923: Metropolitan Intellectuals and Modernity

CHAPTER NINE

Sadler, Rutter and Post-Impressionism

While for the previous nine years the invigorating genius of the Club had been largely home grown, two new appointments to public positions in 1912 brought considerable change. The first of these was that of Michael Sadler to the post of Vice-Chancellor of Leeds University. A leading educationalist, he was also a compulsive collector of paintings and thanks to his wife's largesse had accumulated one of the largest private collections of modern paintings in the country. His move to Leeds also stimulated Frank Rutter, a freelance art critic and organizer of the Allied Artists Association, to apply for the post of director of the Leeds art gallery. Also because Rutter had noticed in London that interesting modern works were being sent to Leeds he assumed that the municipality had a progressive art policy. He was soon disabused but rapidly cemented his relationship with Sadler whom he co-opted onto his newly formed Leeds Art Collection Fund – a charitable body formed to purchase works of art otherwise frowned on by the gallery committee. Together they appear to have focused the Club's activities sharply on the theory and practice of post-impressionist painting. It was a significant shift of emphasis towards modernist painting and theory and one which in his own words was to be 'decisively influential' on a new recruit to the Club, the young undergraduate Herbert Read.

The source material for this phase of the Club is markedly different from previously. Now the detailed reports of its activities in the *Mercury* and *Post* from which its discussions could be reconstructed, had virtually disappeared. Instead we have had to rely on memoirs and published letters, diaries and secondary material. So it has not been possible to create a detailed picture of the annual programmes. Instead, because of the higher public profile of the leading members and larger amount of their own published writings we can see more clearly the broad directions of their thought, the networks which linked them to the metropolis and the disputes which embroiled them in Leeds politics. It was no less exciting than the first phase and in some ways, because of the eruption of movements and manifestoes in the apocalyptic pause before the War To to End All Wars, more so. If ever there had been a time when, in the conduct of cultural affairs, it had been possible to assume a gentlemanly consensus, as Virginia Woolf had suggested, it was not now. The tone of discussion, as evidenced by, for example, the Imagist manifestoes and Wyndham Lewis's *Blast* and, not least, the unblinking assertiveness of the *New Age*, left little room for tentative disagreement, a process illuminated in George Dangerfield's *The Strange Death of Liberal England* (1935).

Voices raised in anger were not confined to the metropolitan cultural sphere. For the working people of Leeds it was a time of renewed industrial militancy. They underwent another major municipal strike, this time fuelled by rumours of syndicalism and revolution. It was a strike that Michael Sadler and the university with, he claims, the support of the 'Bradford Socialists' was instrumental in breaking. Art and politics were not to be kept in discrete boxes and for Sadler and Rutter the energy and dislocation of cubism, futurism and abstractionism were definitive signs of the times. In a speech in October 1913 to the Conference of the National Union of Women Workers Sadler had remarked 'In their present mood, the arts of painting and of music were like voices prophesying war.'[1]

Michael Ernest Sadler had been born in Barnsley in 1861, the son of a general practitioner and the great great nephew of the reforming MP for Newark and Aldborough, Michael Thomas Sadler. In 1875 he went to Rugby and then in 1880 to Trinity College, Oxford, where he developed enthusiasms for the poets Algernon Clough and Robert Browning (both celebrated in the Club) but also a deep and lifelong devotion to John Ruskin. In 1890 he refused an offer from C. P. Scott to become assistant manager of the *Manchester Guardian* because he was committed to the great cause of Oxford University Extension – the extension of university education to the working classes. It was at great personal cost but this commitment to the ideal of extension earned him not only the respect of his colleagues but of many working class leaders. Tom Mann, the leader of the Dockers Union, for example, who had been invited to speak at the Oxford delegacy's summer meeting wrote on his return to London that 'there are many not directly classed as "workers" who have the welfare of humanity at heart'.[2]

Despite his enthusiasm, Sadler's appointment at Leeds was a career sidestep. For some years he had worked under the deeply unpopular Morant ('an early arrival of the Fascist mentality'[3]) at the Board of Education and on Morant's resignation had hoped to replace him as Permanent Secretary. He was thought by many to be the leading educationalist in the country, and probably saw himself in that way, but because of suspicion of him adopted an almost 'King over the Water' posture. In 1916, for example, he wrote to his son that education in Britain was in the throes of another great crisis and that he was taking a leading part in the decision making, adding 'I must go on as practically the leader of the teaching profession. I couldn't shirk what now has to be done without abdicating.'[4] Despite being denied the highest post in education, he nevertheless threw himself into the work at Leeds and was in the main responsible for completing the conversion of the institution from a technical college into a fully-fledged university. Sadler also directed much of his great energy into the town of Leeds by sponsoring many charitable and cultural bodies. He created bodies like the Leeds Luncheon Club for drawing together local businessmen and leading professionals to discuss the issues of the day, hoping to engender a kind of shadow cabinet of opinion alongside the municipality – much to its distrust. In this way Sadler both fitted Orage's ideal of a Platonic 'Guardian', a great man prepared to wholly submit himself to the duty of public service and also reinvigorated the ghost of the old Leeds Liberal elite of the early nineteenth century which had been responsible for the creation of the Phil and Lit and the Mechanics Institute. It was not surprising therefore that the Arts Club attracted his interest and patronage.

Shadowing Sadler the public man and leader of opinion though, was a frequently acutely depressed figure whose despair was only assuaged by bouts of compulsive consumption of art, generously sponsored by his wife's inheritance. Sadler's enthusiasm for modern art dated however only from 1909 under the influence of a Dutch dealer called van Wisselingh. Through him he bought over thirty works by the painter Mari Bauer described by his son as financially 'modestly disastrous' and was launched as a collector of modern art. He was totally unversed in impressionism and had not even visited the Luxembourg but his passion was undiminished. His son commented, 'that making acquaintance with Bauer's work was literally his first contact with Impressionism. Yet within four years he was in the van of appreciation of the great Post-Impressionists, so swiftly and assiduously did he contrive self-education.'[5]

For the next two years Sadler bought paintings and sculpture catholicly, including works by Steer, John and other members of the New English Art Club, but occasionally with a misplaced belief in the genius of certain contemporary artists, like one J. Havard Thomas, which induced further financial crisis. His introduction to the work of the painter Wassily Kandinsky was occasioned by Frank Rutter's Allied Artists Assocation's exhibition of 1911 in the Albert Hall, where Kandinsky exhibited some woodcuts which were seen and bought by Sadler's son (Michael Sadleir) who noted: 'They were strange productions, semi-representational, and with an element of hieratic rigidity which presumably appealed at that time to some Schwarmerei of my own.'[6] Intrigued, Sadleir wrote to make Kandinsky's acquaintance and he invited them to visit him at his country cottage near the town of Murnau in Upper Bavaria. Accordingly, in the summer of 1912 father and son embarked on a picture-buying tour of Germany with Murnau a stop on the way. Significantly, from the train window, Sadler's own comment on the differences between the English and German bourgeoisies bore echoes of the Ruskinian sentiments voiced in the Club.

> It is interesting to see in this Rhineland, with the succession of big towns coming quickly one after another, the German counterpart of our Lancashire and Yorkshire industrial region. One feels that *this* is much the older civilisation – with a stronger tradition of the amenities and discipline of city life. The country side of things is much less socially attractive than with us. The merchant is a merchant in these great German cities, with a city patriotism. In England he becomes a country gentleman.[7]

At Murnau, the Sadlers were so fascinated by Kandinsky's religious and mystical outlook that they missed the last train and had to stay overnight in the station hotel, Kandinsky's cottage having no spare room. But it cemented a relationship in which Sadler bought several paintings and drawings and Kandinsky was to send him several others over the next few years. Sadler's son felt that it was a highly significant meeting

> Kandinsky later became a painter and teacher of international repute, whose work – painted and written – had immense influence on the progressive young. I believe that (my handful of woodcuts apart) the pictures bought by MES at this time were the first specimens of Kandinsky's work to be seen in England.[8]

The Sadlers also planned a *Blaue Reiter* exhibition in London to promote the work of Kandinsky and his group but it had to be abandoned on the grounds of cost. Sadler's pictures attracted some attention however, when they were exhibited by Roger Fry in March 1913. Another important aspect of their promotion of Kandinsky was the translation and publication of his work of aesthetic theory *Uber Das Geistige* as *The Art of Spiritual Harmony* by Sadleir in 1914. This not only attracted the admiration of some of the leading English avant-garde painters like Edward Wadsworth (and even poets like Ezra Pound) but was roundly condemned as we have seen as 'a romantic heresy' by T. E. Hulme in the pages of the *New Age*. Thus within a few years, from a position of near ignorance, Sadler became deeply embroiled in the passionate controversy over the direction of English modernist art.

Frank Rutter (1876–1937), on the other hand, had virtually been born into controversy in modern art. In his childhood his father had been John Ruskin's solicitor when the latter had accused Whistler of 'hurling a pot of paint at the public' and had been sued for it. He was born in

London and was educated at Merchant Taylor's and Queen's College, Cambridge, where he took oriental languages in 1899. Then, as a result of his extensive involvement in Parisian Left Bank circles, he was one of the first critics in England to press the claims of the French Impressionists by setting up the French Impressionist Fund to buy pictures for the National Gallery in 1906. By coincidence he was for a short time, until 1905, the editor of Jerome K. Jerome's magazine *To-Day*, a title revived by Holbrook Jackson in 1916. In 1908 having become art critic of the *Sunday Times* he established the Allied Artists Association which was intended to emulate the Societé des Artistes Independants, in allowing subscribers to exhibit their works without submitting them previously to a jury – an attempt at breaking the power of the Royal Academy. It was at one of these that Sadleir bought his Kandinsky woodcuts. The AAA was successful for a few years when it enjoyed the support of Sickert, Pissaro and others and despite inevitable unevenness in quality allowed the younger generation of subsequently established English painters their first chance to come before the public. It closed however because of what Rutter described as 'the incurable snobbishness of the English artist.'[9] It was perhaps altogether too European an institution.

His decision to apply for the post of Director of the Leeds Gallery appeared to have surprised himself no less than his friends. On his own account, apart from four years at Cambridge his entire life had been spent in either London or Paris and he was 'completely ignorant of the provinces.'[10] He had no knowledge of the manufacturing and commercial classes since his parents' friends were all professionally employed as stockbrokers, barristers, architects, physicians, musicians and so on and his own friends were all artists and writers. However, family pressure to secure permanent employment became the spur, and pausing only long enough to secure a quantity of beads and baubles to placate the warring hill tribesmen of the West Riding, he took the next mule train north. His decision to apply for the Leeds post had been influenced by noticing labels on some paintings he liked in recent exhibitions the notices 'Bought for Leeds Art Gallery'. In particular Orpen's portrait of his wife known as 'The Red Scarf' took his attention. (It had also been two Orpen pen and ink sketches at the Arts Club's exhibition of 1905 that had taken Sam Wilson's eye.) 'In my ignorance I imagined that Leeds must be a go-ahead place, and that there was chance to build up a really fine collection of modern art.'[11] Arriving at the Leeds Gallery in 1912, he found to his dismay he had fallen amongst philistines and far from welcoming the advice and support of Sadler and other collectors the art gallery committee resolutely cold-shouldered them. Rutter had never before come into contact with the kind of men who became councillors and was instantly appalled by their 'grossness, their ignorance, and general lack of manners'.[12]

To give the flavour of his employers he recounted an incident when he had the privilege of conducting three members of the committee around a spring exhibition at the gallery:

> In gloomy silence they passed along walls hung with paintings by Orpen, Sargent, Wilson Steer, Nicholson and other modern painters. Without a pause we progressed to the last room devoted to local artists, that is to say, artists resident in the city whose work could not be rejected without fear of losing a vote. Here the trio at last came to a standstill before a portrait worthy of a place on the lid of any chocolate box. Immersed in aesthetic thought before this painting of an attractive young woman, they stood awhile in silence: and then one councillor nudged another, remarking, 'Eh! A wudna mind takin' yon t'Blackpool for a week-end.'[13]

Not one penny was devoted by the committee for the purchase of works of art (though they did vote a sum of money for a portrait of a previous chairman of the committee by Herkomer). If Rutter wanted to buy works he had to raise money from outside. An exhibition of Gordon Craig's stage models and designs was arranged by him only through personal guarantees from Michael Sadler, Sam Wilson and F. H. Fulford. But he circumvented the art gallery committee by establishing the Leeds Art Collection Fund in November 1912, a few months after he was appointed. It was chaired by Sadler and included a number of Arts Club members and associates including W. H. Thorp, the *Yorkshire Post* art critic Herbert Thompson, the Vicar of Leeds, Cyril Bickersteth, Kitson Clark and William Rothenstein's friend, the ceramics collector Alfred J. Sanders. It was responsible for buying many works some of which were amongst the gallery's best pieces. However, according to Rutter, when another private body of subscribers presented the gallery with a fine collection of original drawings by the Leeds-born cartoonist Phil May, the gallery committee's response was to censure Rutter severely for spending five pounds advertising the generous gift without being consulted.

It was against this background of municipal recalcitrance that Rutter's involvement with the Arts Club flourished. It became an alternative centre for artistic and cultural policy. Though hard evidence of his activities is hard to come by, David Thistlewood has constructed an account in his recent study of Herbert Read.[14] According to Thistlewood, Rutter significantly affected both the understanding and artistic practices of Club members. In 1912 Rutter brought with him from London an already developed theory of art he called 'significant form' which had also attracted Clive Bell's attention. To the Club members already existing preference for quick expressive sketches rather than finished paintings

> Rutter now urged that such sketches need not necessarily be pictorial, and he encouraged attempts to represent musical sound and composition by means of reflex painting, and to correlate words with drawings representing nothing other than the emotions the words aroused.[15]

These experiments apparently began as soon as Rutter arrived, as part of a programme of general education rather than geared to a specific style of abstract art. His achievement, according to Thistlewood, was to focus argument and debate upon individual creativity and emotional argument 'matters quite outside the narrow conventions of contemporary criticism.'[16] the objectives of these experiments were not dissimilar to those of Kandinsky and the conjunction of the arrival of abstract paintings by him, which were exhibited at the Club, together with the translation of his theoretical work by Sadler's son, Michael Sadleir, provided an inspirational workshop. Sadler held monthly Club meetings at his home in Buckingham House, Headingley Lane, where his collection, by this time including Gauguins, Van Goghs and Klees as well as the best of the modern English painters, was housed. To this aesthetic seminary Rutter's friends from the Camden Town Group, Charles Ginner and Harold Gilman, also contributed from time to time as did members of the Rothenstein circle including brothers Albert and Charles.

Rutter apparently also encouraged the Club's usual practice of debating the editorial matters of Orage's *New Age*, which, since the cultural explosion of the first post-impressionist exhibition in 1910 was also noticeably changing direction. In the five years since he and Jackson had assumed control of the *New Age*, Orage had established himself as the leading editor in London. Jackson had left to form an independent editorial career within a year and with him Orage's last links with a more gradualist Fabianism. The journal had moved into an increasingly anti-Fabian and anti-labour stance and although Orage still saw it as the vehicle for debating socialism, a strongly independent line was emerging. Contributions by Chesterton and Belloc attacking labour 'statism' had reinforced his own distaste for centralized bureaucracy and attacks by them and others on collectivism encouraged the non-possessive individualism he had nurtured in Leeds. Though his and Penty's attempt to launch a Guild's Restoration League in 1908 had failed, the idea had not and through the articles of S. G. Hobson the politics of guild socialism was evolved to a higher stage. Hobson and later G. D. H. Cole, by downplaying Penty's medievalism and intensifying the role of trade unions, sufficiently modernized the idea to make it politically attractive, at least to the more revolutionary edge of the labour movement, like for example, Jim Larkin[17] and later the more philosophical, like R. H. Tawney.

Orage's ertswhile collaborator, Joseph Clayton, the Christian Socialist from whom he had bought the *New Age*, however, held a somewhat jaundiced view of the new tendency. He believed that guild socialism though attractive to some of the younger trade union officials was little more than a middle-class deviation from socialism,

> ... but it was in the Fabian Society and amongst the 'intellectuals' dissatisfied with the average standard of intelligence in the ILP that Guild Socialism flourished. Dislike of the state, contempt for representative institutions, hatred for bureaucracy, despair of parliament – all these things were favourable to the Guild Socialist of the middle class ... The average Trade Unionist was no more persuaded by the writings of Penty and Cole, Orage and Hobson to give up the Parliamentary Labour Party and turn his trade union into a company for the ownership and control of industry, than induced by Tom Mann to turn Syndicalist.[18]

Orage felt that with the death of Edward VII in 1910 the end of the Victorian age, so often prematurely announced, had at last arrived. In oracular mode he had asked 'If it is felt, as it is clearly felt, that the era of Victoria is indeed at last over, who is so bold as to dare forecast the nature of the epoch that is now opening?'[19] Various *New Age* writers, like Galsworthy, predicted an imminent renaissance in Britain. Ezra Pound thought initially that it would come from the United States but by 1915 had settled for England. Orage was more Delphic in his pronouncements and in October 1912 wrote:

> If I were asked upon what I rely for the renaissance of England I should say a miracle. But it does not follow that because we cannot define the nature of miracles, miracles are not therefore to be understood. They can be understood easily enough if they are regarded as works of art instead of works of logic ... The miracle that may therefore be confidently anticipated in England is not necessarily one that we cannot sense in advance or cannot deliberately create. We can both divine what it will be and prepare for its coming.[20]

Rutter's AAA shows and the post-impressionist exhibition of 1910 had signalled the release of new kinds of artistic energy. 'Realism', the standard of Orage's early criticism faltered under the celebration of a newly discovered 'expressionism'. Katherine Mansfield for example felt she could write stories like Van Gogh painted – with 'indigo skies'. The representation of the ext rnal, however impressionistically, was becoming subjugated to the expression of internal states. George Calderon in a review in the *New Age* saw post-impressionism as 'a revelation, the visible manifestation of deeper levels of consciousness.'[21]

This belief in 'deeper levels of consciousness' had, as we have seen, occupied Orage since earlier days and much of his experimenting in the theosophical society had been to find ways of access to it, as evidenced by his study of Myers's theory of personality. This quest led him, before virtually anyone outside the specialists, to see the significance of Sigmund Freud's new theory of psychoanalysis and he shortly introduced this major innovatory theme and its advocates into the journal. Rowland Kenny (later editor of the *Daily Herald*) remarked that,

> With his remarkable flair for spotting new ideas of significance in almost any field of human endeavour, Orage had grasped the importance of psycho-analysis, and given space to Dr M. D. Eder, one of the pioneers in this country . . . and to others interested in it . . . When the *New Age* began to deal with the subject openly in its columns psycho-analysis was anathema.[22]

Freud's name was first mentioned in the *New Age* in 1912 and Eder's articles, the first to introduce Freud to a non-specialist audience, began in the following year.

A third new mode of investigation into the unconscious and intuitional sources of creative energy (alongside post-impressionism and psychoanalysis) to appear in the *New Age* after 1910 was the philosophy of Henri Bergson. This was introduced by the most vigorous of the new contributors to the journal, T. E. Hulme, philosopher, art critic and the writer of five imagist poems. Although he anticipated by one or two years the positions on classicism and romanticism associated with Hulme, Orage, perhaps over-highly, valued his talents. Jacob Epstein, for example, wrote:

> Orage was a man of extraordinary mental vigour. He had a magnetic personality, attracting people by his conversation. His charm of voice and manner drew listeners to him and he went about like a Greek philosopher or rhetor, with a following of disciples. As between the two, Hulme was the more solid man – the more profound mind. Orage was undoubtedly under the influence of him at one time.[23]

Hulme's presence in the journal in the next few years was explosive. Something of a pugilist (he had a set of knuckledusters made for him by Gaudier-Brzeska and once declared that the best method of dealing with one of his intellectual opponents would be 'a little personal violence') his pronouncements on art and poetry were like so many hard jabs in an ageing culture's kidneys. Between 1912 and 1914, he edited a famous series of drawings by Epstein, Wyndham Lewis, Gaudier-Brzeska, Bomberg, Nevinson, Edward Wadsworth and William

Roberts, vigorously defended Epstein against his critics and wrote a series of seminal essays on 'Modern Art'. These made the *New Age* the key journal for the discussion of modernist tendencies in the pre-war years and no artist could afford to ignore what it said or afford, like Sickert, Orage's resident art critic, not to reply in its pages.

Hulme's arguments were closely followed by the members of the Club and in the weekly discussions three young members of the Club took prominent parts. These were the painters Jacob Kramer and Bruce Turner and Herbert Read, who a few years later himself became a regular contributor and was given the task by Orage of editing and publishing Hulme's posthumous papers. Thistlewood argues that they looked to Hulme's presentations 'not so much for an explanation of abstraction as for a theoretical account of the creative process'.[24]

Hulme argued that human creativity consisted in intellectually grasping fleeting fragments of imagery first glimpsed intuitionally. 'The creative artist, the innovator', he said, 'leaves the level where things are crystallized out into . . . definite shape, and diving down into the inner flux, comes back with a new shape which he endeavours to fix.'[25] Hence abstract forms were wrought from the vast mass of intuitional material into simpler mental constructions which were valid artistically. Hulme concluded that hard-edged geometrical imagery would be the appropriate form for the modern, mechanical, age. He demanded this return to what he called classical form (in a modern context) as a necessary antidote to the decadent romanticism of the late nineteenth century.

The Club members, particularly Herbert Read, however, could not see that romanticism and classicism were mutually exclusive but rather dialectically held in tension. They saw in the concept of the romantic the necessary Dionysian element that Orage had so persuasively argued for between 1900–1910 (the classical being identified with the Apollonian mode). Read held faith with romanticism throughout his life once musing on the paradox of his long friendship with T. S. Eliot who had declared himself a classicist in art, Anglo-Catholic in religion and royalist in politics while Read saw himself as romanticist, atheist and anarchist. Thistlewood concluded that through Hulme's articles in the *New Age* Bergson was 'the major influence' on Read and the proceedings of the Arts Club at this time, while Nietzsche was 'the occasional provider of decisive insights'.

Though this is probably right, it may ignore the deep bedrock of Nietzschean thought upon which the Club's discussions rested as well as its continuing reinforcement in the pages of the *New Age* through the contributions of Nietzsche's translators, Oscar Levi, J. M. Kennedy and Ludovici. The *elan vitale* had not entirely replaced the will-to-power though arguably Nietzsche's stock amongst the avant-garde had fallen because of rising anti-German xenophobia. Certainly he was a caricatured figure in the middle-brow weeklies. Holbrook Jackson, who, it will be remembered, was responsible for introducing Nietzsche's ideas to Orage noticed, however, something even worse to the 'intelligentsia' (a word freshly coined in the *New Age*) than popular ignorance of the Great Man, would have been popular acceptance of him! Since the publication of Orage's pioneering books on him, he wrote, many others had followed:

> and the philosopher of aristocracy and exclusiveness has become one of the most familiar 'stunts' of the popular Press. People came to talk Nietzsche as M. Jourdain talked prose – without knowing it. But the 'intellectuals', fearful of such popular acceptance, scuttled to new gods, many of them ranging themselves under the banner of Bergson. I caught even Mr Orage biting the hand that fed him in the 'New Age'. Then came the war, and Nietzsche, so nearly become famous – became infamous. Now he lies there, and none so poor to do him reverence![26]

The popular significance of Nietzsche, it might be argued, was really as the last tribune of romanticism. Even before Hulme's articles on Bergson, the term 'classicism' had appeared in the *New Age*, as part of a critique of romanticism, by Chesterton and Hilaire Belloc, but only became an article of faith after 1915 when a generally 'neo-classical' approach was fostered by Orage. Orage's debt to Chesterton has been well documented by John Coates[27] but Belloc was also influential. Through his book *The Servile State*, published in 1912 but based on articles in the *New Age* from 1910, he had a great impact on a new generation of disillusioned Fabians flocking to the *New Age* like Maurice Reckitt.[28]

As if to reinforce the links between the *New Age* and the Arts Club, in February 1912 Belloc lectured on 'The Classical Drama' (in one of the few talks reported) to the Playgoers Society at the University. According to a reminder card sent out to members it appears that it was by no means his first visit. In his talk he regretted the period of artistic romanticism and was grateful it was nearing its end.[29] But tragically, he saw no sign of a new dawning of the classical spirit, which was essential if the European nations were to persist as civilized communities. The problem with romanticism was that because it saw human emotion as an end in itself, it became increasingly violent. The classical spirit was, alternatively, a means to an end, namely to complete what was lacking in man. Thus Belloc was simply reinforcing the new note that he, Chesterton and Orage had already introduced in to the *New Age*, that a man was a 'fixed species' requiring classical discipline – a far cry from Orage's superman days! Only two years later did Hulme with characteristic pugnacity take up the phrase and say that man was a fixed and limited species and it was only by 'tradition and organisation' that something decent could be made of him, converting a conservative doubt into a reactionary platform.

Following Belloc's talk, the vogue for the classical was reinforced by the visit of Penelope Wheeler's Greek Play Company to the Headingley Parochial Institute in November, arranged by the Playgoers Society. The company performed Gilbert Murray's translations of *Iphegenia in Tauris* and the *Hippolytus* of Euripides.

Belloc's attack on romanticism was re-emphasized in the next talk by Frederic Moorman who was now, informally, coaching Herbert Read in literature. His lecture on Monday 11 March was on 'Poetry and Life', chaired by a new light in the club, Tommy Lamb. Moorman traced the decline of romanticism during the earlier part of the last century in favour of a new spirit of realism as exemplified in the work of Dickens.[30] The *fin-de-siecle* romanticist revival had also, in turn, given way to the vigorous realist movement in all forms of art, particularly in the prose drama of Shaw, Galsworthy, Synge and Masefield, but not in poetry. What the Club needed therefore was a non-romanticist poetry-writing section which would deal with present-day life in Leeds. After all, he said, Whitman had written a poem about a pork factory in Chicago and the last thing they needed was romantic poetry about the 'golden age of martial men'.

In 1912 the Club has therefore to be seen as entering a new phase in which the dominance of already established metropolitan intellectuals like Michael Sadler and Frank Rutter is combined with the influence of the *New Age* itself. To be sure, Shaw, Chesterton, Yeats and others had linked the Club to metropolitan ideas previously, but always under the shaping influence of Orage and Jackson, who provided as it were, a placing commentary on their contributions, in the wake of their determined polemicizing of Nietzschean ideas. Now Orage and Jackson had themselves become metropolitan leaders of thought and their visits to the Club less frequent.

The role of Club members, also previously so prominent in advancing new ideas, is hard to gauge, since many like Arthur Lee and Charles Smythe were also now in London and contributing to the *New Age*. Since Thistlewood argues that the theory of neo-realism which appeared in the pages of the *New Age* in 1914 under Charles Ginner's name had its origins in the Club's discussions, it appears that it had lost none of its vitality. But with Nietzsche's star eclipsed by rumours of war, the superman had perforce given way to the fixed and limited species, the Dionysian tempered by the Apollonian. The evolutionary realism of the Club's earlier aesthetic, where art was the hand maiden of man's creative attempts to reach a higher stage of evolution, now responded to an expressionism in which the inner, the spiritual and the unconscious took priority over external representation. Those who had kept up with Orage knew anyway that 'reality' was not a simple matter and as much a product of the construction of the idea or the will as dependent on material laws. The ending of the Victorian age promised strife and division and in the previous years the Club appeared to have lost the promise of its founding fecundity; its catholicity in danger of petering out into esoteric fads. Its creative intuitional chaos needed to be given form and Michael Sadler now appeared to fit this role both by temperament and conviction. Art was central to his educational aims, as subsequently it became for Herbert Read.

If Sadler was to provide some of the charismatic leadership hitherto associated with Orage, Frank Rutter had the organizational energy. None of Rutter's talks to the Leeds Arts Club were reported but his determination to take art out of the gallery was reflected in his talk on 'Art and Industry' to the Bradford Arts Club. He said that he hoped he would have the assistance of Sadler and his fine collection in his aims which were to make the connections between art and industry meaningful and to destroy the notion of art as merely a leisure pursuit.[31] The following month he returned to the same theme in the first of two talks at the Leeds Art Gallery, noting that the export trade in British wallpapers had increased because of a renaissance in taste and that now because of mass production, we were all in a sense patrons' of art. While he allied himself to the arts and crafts movement's adherence to the unity of utility and beauty, he refused to place the blame for ugliness on industry:

> We were inclined to blame modern machinery and manufacturers for the ugly things turned out, but it was a question whether manufacturers were less to blame for producing ugly wares than the public which set up the low taste . . . The evil of bad taste might be traced to snobbery which was the failing of every class and certainly not the privilege of one class. Beautiful furniture was not necessarily expensive, or fantastic, and in many houses the artistically furnished room was the kitchen, where the furniture supplied the needs.[32]

Rutter thus embraced modernity in a populist vein and set a new tone at the gallery which was perhaps carried to the Club's members, still smarting from being dismissed as 'cranks' in the newspaper controversy of 1911. He also organized the Club's next major show, the keynote of the new age, its 'Post-Impressionist' exhibition of June 1913. This ambitious project, based on pictures lent by Sadler, Rutter and the Lord Mayor of Scarborough, one A. M. Daniel, included works by Cezanne,

Gauguin, Matisse, Serussier, Kandinsky, Asselin, Rodo, Doucet, Picart Ledoux and Fournier.

One report of the show came from the pen of Tommy Lamb, the Club's new secretary, who had been appointed temporary keeper of the paintings for the show's duration. A 'humorous' piece it nevertheless gives a flavour of its reception by visitors paying the one shilling entry fee and Lamb's own Yorkshire scepticism as to their value. One of these asked Lamb to explain to her the meaning of the Kandinsky woodcuts (presumably lent by Michael Sadleir). He described them variously as 'Aeronautics in the Stone Age', 'A Japanese Giantess Wading', 'The Giraffe at Home' and 'Pit Ponies' to which she replied 'How wonderful'. She then pointed to Kandinsky's signature and asked what that was. Lamb explained that it was his signature and that artists often signed their pictures with adopted names like 'Kester', the local cartoonist and Arts Club member, James Dodgson. The young lady asked whether Kester was also a post-impressionist. 'I could not resist an impulse. "He's generally looked upon as an Evening Post-Impressionist," I ventured.'[33] Lamb worked as a compositor on the *Evening News* and contributed occasional pieces like this one. Later Blackwell published two volumes of his short stories. One based on his wartime experiences at the munitions factory at Barnbow was called *T.N.T. Tales* (1919) which contained well-observed vignettes of the women workers. The second was called *Quilt Takes* (1922), though what experiences these were based on is not known. In the portrait by his friend Kramer, now in Leeds Art Gallery, the stiff collar, perky face and balding dome reveal a somewhat Dickensian figure.

An accompanying lecture to the exhibition was given by Michael Sadleir, whose talk on 'Post-Impressionism and Public Galleries', 12 June, reinforced Rutter's view that the exhibition would not have been welcomed by the Art Gallery Committee. Sadleir (1888–1957) was not resident in Leeds though he often visited his parents and no doubt the Club. Educated at Rugby and Balliol College, he had recently taken a second in History but had won the Stanhope prize for an essay on Sheridan. He instantly graduated to the London art world and publishing and persuaded his father to back *Rhythm*, the newly launched aesthetic journal of Middleton Murry. (Much to Orage's displeasure, since although by her own admission, he had transformed Katherine Mansfield's writing, Murry had snatched up her stories for the journal and she had installed him in her apartment.)[34]

Sadleir's talk in fact made a plea for the purchase of post-impressionist paintings by the municipality before the prices rose, which they inevitably would. Leeds now had a sympathetic art gallery director he told his large, and apparently 'contentious', audience and offered four pieces of advice: firstly not to be afraid of making mistakes in purchasing new work, secondly not to hamper the director with committees, thirdly, not to buy haphazardly but to choose a coherent historical line of development and fourthly at all costs avoid the academy![35]

The exhibition itself was opened by A. M. Daniel the Mayor of Scarborough described by the reviewer of the *Yorkshire Post* as 'a connoisseur of high repute in matters of art'.[36] In an extensive preview of the exhibition, which mentioned that the catalogue was written by Sadleir, the reviewer gave a fairly full account of its 63 exhibits, as well as a somewhat sceptical view of their value. Picasso's *Portrait of Mr Kahnwheiler* was not entirely to his taste; Cezanne's large landscape rather 'clumsy', Van Gogh's landscape, on the other hand, was on a 'higher plane' as were five photographs of his work also on display. Lucien Pissaro's two offerings *The Brook* and *L'Escalier* were 'realistic enough to be almost reactionary' while Gaugin's *Poemes Barbares* was 'a remarkably fine example of this strange artist'. He approved of Anne Estelle Rice's *Negress*, Toulouse Lautrec's *Portrait* and Henri Doucet's *Child's Head.* Charles Ginner's *Still Life* was 'rich and brilliant', while Duncan Grant's untitled piece was sweeter and more tender in tone. Theodore Schindler's untitled piece 'was only saved from violence by the power with which the high pitch of colour is sustained' but Ethel Wright's flower picture was the finest on show. He thought that J. D. Fergusson's *Girls Head* showed the germs of cubism and that Wolmark's *Bretonne* and Doucet's *Girl's Head* both displayed 'a beautiful pattern of refined colour'. Though he passed without comment over Maurice Asselin's *Cargo Boat Quaie de Louvre*. Ludovic Rodo's *Lande Bretonne* and Henri Geusel's *Rue a Draveil*, Paul Emile Pissaro's two *Markets* evoked 'a vivid effect by the simplest possible means'.

For the *Post*'s reviewer, the true villain of the 63-piece exhibition was Kandinsky, whose two water colour *Compositions* demonstrated that he was truly 'the advanced guard of the extremists'. He was nevertheless moderately encouraging and though it would probably be productive of much strong language, still deserved attention from Yorkshire folk. The exhibition seems to have created only a modest uproar among practising artists and craftsmen some of whom wrote to the *Yorkshire Post* in strong but not apoplectic terms, though reminiscent of Ruskin's feelings about Whistler's *Nocturnes*, one correspondent, 'A Craftsman', did contribute an amusing anecdote about trained monkeys with paintpots. The Club members ably rose to the paintings' defence and letters from Tommy Lamb, and local artists Ernest Forbes and Frank Dean, who both contributed to the Club's next show in 1914, showed a desire to welcome the radical new directions.

After his visit to Murnau, Sadleir began translating Kandinsky's major theoretical work of aesthetics, *Uber Das Geistige*, which was published in 1914 by Constable, of which he became a director, as *The Art of Spiritual Harmony*. He later recalled it as 'a gallant effort which paid a sincere and prescient tribute to Kandinsky and his work' but 'Aesthetic theory was then as much beyond my comprehension as it still is – with the difference that I am now aware of the fact'.[37] Nevertheless, the book was read in avant-garde circles. Ezra Pound wrote 'when I came to read Kandinsky's chapter on the language of form and colour, I found little that was new to me. I only felt that some one else understood what I understood, and had written it out very clearly'.[38] Edward Wadsworth, a native of Cleckheaton in the West Riding who had exhibited at the Bradford Arts Club before he entered the Slade was also very impressed. In an article in *Blast* vol. 1, he wrote about it in terms that would have been familiar to the Club members:

> This book is a most important contribution to the psychology of modern art . . . Herr Kandinsky . . . is a psychologist and a metaphysician of rare intuition and inspired enthusiasm. He writes of art – not in its relation to the drawing room or the modern exhibition, but in its relation to the universe and the soul of man. He writes, not as an art historian, but essentially as an artist to whom form and colour are as much the vital and integral parts of the cosmic organisation as they are his means of expression.[39]

According to Richard Cork, Kandinsky's ideas had a liberating effect on Wadsworth and his contemporaries since it instantly freed their art from the limitations of the representational tradition. They went on to paint in a freer and for a while almost wholly abstract way. Roger Fry was also impressed enough to write an early appreciation of Kandinsky's most abstract work calling it 'pure visual music'.

But the new found enthusiasm for abstract expressionism did not impress T. E. Hulme. Condemning this 'romantic heresy', he grumbled:

> In this instead of hard structural work like Picasso's you get the much more scattered use of abstractions of artists like Kandinsky . . . Lacking the controlled sensibility, the feeling for mechanical structure, which makes use of abstractions a necessity, it seems rather dilettante.[40]

Hulme felt that the new movement was not destined to survive. This, as we shall see is arguable, but according to Herbert Read, the *Art of Spiritual Harmony* was much read and discussed in Leeds by students of art and later Henry Moore himself was undoubtedly aware of the book.[41] David Thistlewood concluded that Sadleir's translation of *Uber das Geistige* and his father's willingness to introduce members to Kandinsky's abstract painting had a profound effect upon the thought and practices of the Club:

> It was this climate of opinion then, which nurtured an expressionist realism, for example in the work of Jacob Kramer and Bruce Turner, young members of the Arts Club, and which encouraged Read to paint a succession of 'futurist works' and some entirely non-representational compositions.[42]

But another twist in the tail of this story about the influence of avant-garde European art and metropolitan intellectuals upon a small provincial Yorkshire club was of course that some of these ideas were *already* familiar. Kandinsky had based his theories of colour and emotion on theoretical material from a source the Club knew more than ten years earlier. This was Annie Besant and Cyril Leadbetter's theosophical text, *Thought Forms*, translated into German in 1908 and described by Sixten Ringbom as 'One of the most important of Kandinsky's theosophical sources',[43] to which when he was a leading member of the Bauhaus group ten years later, he still referred. Thus an ideological loop was completed when a version of the theosophical ideas from which Orage and the founders of the Arts Club had derived much of their inspiration, returned via the Russo-German avante-garde and the metropolitan intelligentsia to its own provincial roots.

Notes

1. Michael Sadler, 'Premonitions of the War in Modern Art', 26 October 1915, Brotherton Collection, Leeds University.
2. Quoted in Michael Sadleir, *Michael Ernest Sadler*, Constable, London, 1949, p. 115.
3. Ibid., p. 195.
4. Ibid., p. 274.
5. Ibid., p. 223.
6. Ibid., p. 237.
7. In a letter to his wife of 12 August 1912, Sadleir, *Sadler*, p. 235.
8. Sadleir, *Sadler*, p. 239.
9. Quoted in his obituary notice, *The Times*, 19 April 1937, p. 16.
10. Frank Rutter, *Since I was Twenty-Five*, Constable, London, 1927, p. 200.
11. Rutter, pp. 200–201.
12. This was not merely a southerner responding badly to northern bluntness or symptomatic of class disdain for social inferiors. Rutter soon became involved in the newly formed Workers' Educational Association and commented 'With the working people of Leeds I got on a great deal better than I did with their employers. Generally speaking they were much more intelligent, more refined in thought, more civil in manner'. (Rutter, p. 208.)
13. Rutter, p. 204.

14. David Thistlewood, *Herbert Read, Formlessness and Form*, Routledge, Kegan Paul, London, 1984. Thistlewood however relies heavily on a letter sent to him by Club member Tom Heron (father of Patrick Heron) shortly before his death.
15. Thistlewood, pp. 25–26.
16. Ibid.
17. 'Larkin had imbibed his social doctrines from no less a source than the *New Age*, for whose editor, the persuasive A. R. Orage, he had a profound regard.' George Dangerfield, *The Strange Death of Liberal England*, Paladin, London, 1970, p. 279.
18. Joseph Clayton, *The Rise and Decline of Socialism in Great Britain 1884–1924*, Faber and Gwyer, London, 1926, p. 152.
19. *New Age*, VII, 12 May 1910, quoted in Martin *New Age Under Orage*, p. 129.
20. Quoted in Martin, *New Age Under Orage*, p. 130.
21. Martin, p. 132.
22. Quoted in Martin, *New Age Under Orage*, p. 140.
23. Jacob Epstein, *An Autobiography*, Hulton Press, London, 1955, p. 61. Epstein also described Orage as 'a loveable spirit' and remembered meeting Paul Robeson with him in New York.
24. Thistlewood, p. 29.
25. Quoted in Martin, *New Age Under Orage*, p. 138.
26. Holbrook Jackson, 'The Truth about Nietzsche' in *TP's Weekly*, 31 October 1914, p. 476.
27. John D. Coates, *Chesterton and the Edwardian Cultural Crisis*, Hull University Press, 1984.
28. Maurice Reckitt, *As It Happened*, Dent, London, 1941, pp. 107–8.
29. *YWP*, 10 February 1912, p. 17.
30. *YWP*, 16 March 1912, p. 24.
31. *Yorkshire Observer*, 4 November 1912, p. 12.
32. *YWP*, 7 December 1912, p. 20.
33. Cutting found in 'Leeds Clubs and Societies' box in the Brotherton Collection, dated 24 June 1913. The *Yorkshire Evening Post* was the evening partner to the *Yorkshire Post*.
34. Claire Tomalin, *Katherine Mansfield, A Secret Life*, Viking, London, 1987, pp. 80–87.
35. *Yorkshire Post*, 13 June 1913, p. 9.
36. *Yorkshire Post* 7 June 1913, p. 8.
37. Sadleir, *Sadler*, p. 240.
38. Quoted in Richard Cork, *Vorticism and Abstract Art in the First Machine Age*, vol. 1, University of California, Berkeley, 1975, p. 214.
39. Cork, *Vorticism*, p. 215.
40. 'Modern Art II' in the *New Age* of 26 March 1914, quoted in Cork, *Vorticism*, p. 214.
41. Herbert Read, *Henry Moore*, Thames and Hudson, London, 1965, p. 31. Moore said: 'I'd had the luck to know Michael Sadler who was then Vice Chancellor of Leeds University, a man who had bought Cezanne and Gauguin before 1914, and translated Kandinsky, and really knew what was going on in modern art' in Philip Jones (ed.) *Henry Moore on Sculpture*, London, 1966, p. 32.

42. Thistlewood, *Herbert Read*, p. 27.
43. Sixten Ringbom, *The Sounding Cosmos, A Study in the Spiritualism of Kandinsky and the Genesis of Abstract Painting*, Abo Akademi, Finland, 1970, p. 62.

CHAPTER TEN

Interventionist Patronage: the Sadlers, Kandinsky and Kramer

In 1913, just as Sadler and Rutter had established their credentials in Leeds society, the whirlwind broke. For Sadler it was the municipal strike, while for Rutter it was the escape of the suffragette Lilian Lenton from his house, where, under the 'Cat and Mouse' Act, she had been recovering from a hunger strike at Armley Jail. The newspapers covered the story for weeks afterwards and Rutter and his wife were never freed from suspicion of complicity in the escape. Sadler organized students to man services and transport during the municipal strike. Despite the fact that he was convinced that he had acted with a deep sense of civic responsibility, he admitted he was 'the best hated man in Leeds and in the trade union circles of the north'.[1]

Sadler was no ordinary strike breaker and his belief in his civic, even socialist, responsibility beyond what he saw as the narrow sectarian interests of the strikers was genuine. In December he wrote to his son:

> Leeds is on strike. Gas is giving out, trams precarious, electric light threatened. The Goya streets are full of swirling paper; the class war is preached – so far with uninterrupted kindliness of feeling in personal intercourse . . . I don't *think* there'll be very serious trouble, but there may be. There is no revolutionary feeling in Leeds *as a whole* though much of it is gathering . . . There *are* grievances which should be put right; but a lot has been done and the trouble is partly due to the Lord Mayor's abrupt Norman Warrior approach.[2]

Shortly before he wrote this, he had gone to hear the Irish socialist leader, Jim Larkin, address a huge meeting at Leeds Town Hall. He was greatly impressed by him, feeling that there was a touch of Synge and A. E. about him, with a note of poetry and pathos that roused the young people. In true patrician style, however, he declared him 'just the sort of man who would have been a leader in a (WEA) tutorial class'.[3] Like his other mentor, Matthew Arnold, Sadler clung tenaciously to the belief that education and culture would save the working class, and hence his own, from the nightmare of anarchy and revolution. The real danger, he insisted, was not the 'small group of politically motivated men' characteristic of *Yorkshire Post* editorials, but 'the revolutionary temper of the times' and he proposed positive measures to end the dispute amicably. He advocated an authoritative standing commission to enquire into wages and conditions in the municipality with the power to make recommendations: 'To get this new idea realised, to prevent reprisals and injustice to the workers, is our chief job and preoccupation now'.[4] He thought he also had the backing of the 'chief Socialist leaders in Bradford and here' for this proposal despite the hostility of the rank and file. It was not the last time that 'socialism' had come into conflict with 'narrow trade union demands' but he was not wholly convincing. Even the members of his own economics department, who were identified with the Workers Educational Association, did not see it his way. Professor David MacGregor and lecturers Arthur Greenwood and Henry Clay publicly demanded, and received, his resignation from the Leeds branch of the WEA of which he had recently become honorary president. It was a salutary lesson for Sadler, who never meddled so directly in municipal politics again.

It is worth dwelling on the WEA for a moment because there are interesting personal connections with the Arts Club at this time which were quite unexpected. Not only were Greenwood and MacGregor leading lights but so was Frank Rutter. He lectured frequently, took groups round the art gallery and on at least one occasion appears to have been 'lent' by the branch to the newly formed branch of Victor Grayson's British Socialist Party for a course of lectures in modern art.[5] For a while he was even chairman of the Leeds branch, a post which Frederic Moorman also held until his death in 1919.

MacGregor, who had also lectured for the Arts Club was, as we have seen, an inspirational figure and had, with Greenwood, pioneered the creation of the radical Yorkshire District of the WEA in 1914. His friend, the Shakespearian scholar, John Dover Wilson, then His Majesty's Inspector in Leeds noted 'the awe which he inspired may be gauged by the question which the secretary's little son put to his father, who passed it on to me. "Daddy, is Professor MacGregor God?" '[6] George Thompson, the charismatic secretary of the Yorkshire District,[7] whom they had 'discovered' in an economics tutorial class in Halifax, accompanied Sadler on a deputation to the Master of Baliol's Oxford Conference on Education in 1916 in which, Sadler noted, they heard prophesies of social revolution in England after the war.[8]

Arthur Greenwood, who later became a minister in the first labour government was the chairman of the Yorkshire District and close confidant of Thompson until the latter's retirement in 1945. Though there is as yet no evidence of Greenwood's direct involvement in the Club, he did lecture for the Leeds Theosophical Society in 1916 on a familiar Arts Club theme 'The New Citizenship'.[9] (The meeting was chaired by Joseph Smith, president of the Leeds Industrial Co-op. Could this have been the same Joe Smith who gave Orage the £50 which saw him safely through his first weeks in London?) Through his membership of the Fabian Society, he was also a friend of Frederick Keeling and Tom Heron, who was during the war a committee member of the Club and whom we will hear more about later.[10] Greenwood taught Herbert Read, who had attended WEA evening classes in political economy while a bank clerk, economics at Leeds University and found him his first job after leaving the army. Thus the network of connections between the Arts Club, university and WEA, seems to have been of some complexity.

Art patronage in Leeds was by no means as securely established as in more prosperous industrial towns like Manchester. In the mid-century interest was shown by men like Thomas Plint who commissioned *Work* from Ford Maddox Browne and had bought Pre-Raphaelite painting, while later Sam Wilson's collection of contemporary English painters was noteworthy. But little of this had impressed the art gallery committee as Frank Rutter discovered. One of his successors, John Rothenstein, later wrote,

> Leeds might have been compared to a battlefield in which serious art had been hard pressed and on balance defeated, but Leeds had however been a battlefield and at least as early as 1912 when Frank Rutter, a consistent advocate of modern French painting and of the New English Art Club, had been made Curator, and even earlier good pictures were occasionally acquired and progressive ideas current.[11]

Rothenstein was also impressed by the relative fecundity of the West Riding in artistic terms and how the conditions of life and, implicitly, the lack of patronage, made the ultimate emigration of the artist inevitable:

> Yorkshire, in particular the West Riding, has made a unique contribution to British art in the past century or so. Matthew Smith, Edward Wadsworth, Henry Moore and Barbara Hepworth were all born within a few miles and less than twenty-five years of one another but the grimness of life ensures that the flowering shall be elsewhere.[12]

In the absence of liberal and constructive support for painting, artists were forced to move south. Elsewhere, he noted how his Bradford born father, William Rothenstein, had been 'shocked by the impoverishment of English provincial life by the progressive concentration of civilisation in London and he struggled to arrest it'.[13] This was why he founded the Bradford Arts Club in 1902 and opened the Bradford Art Gallery in Cartwright Hall in 1904. In 1915 he became Professor of Civic Art at Sheffield University and in 1920, as we shall see, he became involved with Sadler in his ill-fated scheme to decorate Leeds Town Hall. Subsequently he was instrumental in promoting the careers of

Barbara Hepworth and Henry Moore when they graduated to the Royal College of Art in 1921, the year he was made principal. On his only recorded talk at the Leeds Arts Club, in 1908, he had described municipal art galleries (though he did not specifically name the Leeds gallery) as places where one might spend the most depressing half-hour of one's life while waiting for a train.

Michael Sadler therefore played an important role. As a patron, he was extremely generous. Very few societies in Leeds, it appeared, did not actually benefit from his largesse or promotion as a *Yorkshire Post* cartoon mourning his departure in 1923 showed. But more than any other it was, perhaps, Jacob Kramer (1892–1962) who felt the benefit of his patronage. Born in Klincy in the Ukraine, Kramer emigrated with his parents to Leeds in 1900, the year Orage met Holbrook Jackson and discovered Nietzsche. (Orage might even have taught him, but didn't. Kramer was a pupil at Darley Street School while Orage was teaching at Roundhay Road Boys.) His mother was a trained singer and his father had been a court painter in Russia. With little opportunity of following this occupation in Leeds, he earned a meagre living colouring portrait photographs. Jacob ran away from school a number of times and like his father made a living from retouching photographs, then he worked for a Leeds printing firm and did 'rather well'. His draughtsmanship had been recognized at school by his teacher, a Miss Poyser, and she encouraged him to attend evening classes at the Leeds School of Art. He soon won a junior art scholarship and remained there for two years, despite several threats of expulsion.

Kramer met Michael Sadler in 1911, almost as soon as he arrived in Leeds, who was immediately struck by the energy of his painting. He encouraged him to try for a place at the Slade, which he won and regularly bought paintings and drawings from him over many years. He commissioned a portrait from him, however, which he all but disowned since it showed him not so much as a Great Educator but, in his wife's words, as 'a tired old man with a bad temper'. He regularly offered Kramer critical comments on his work and advanced him money, other than for his paintings, amounting to £30 by mid–1916 for example.[14] Kramer took the advice with grace and the money with enthusiasm (though it may well have been more than repaid in gifts of paintings). In 1917, to quote Christopher Sheppard, 'the patron's advice turns to unqualified praise for a mature artist'. Sadler's view of some pictures Kramer had sent him was that 'No finer imaginative work has been done in Leeds within living memory'.[15] He seems to have attempted to secure Kramer some teaching in the university on one occasion but dissuaded him on another, on the grounds that it would hinder his creative work. Kramer, on the other hand, was keen to get a regular income and it may be significant that Sadler to an extent always held him at arm's length. As Kramer's nephew, John Roberts, remarks in his published edition of Kramer's letters, Sadler's letters always begin 'Dear Kramer' rather than 'Dear Jacob'.[16] Through his personal contact with the editor, Wilson Barrett, Sadler was also instrumental in getting some of Kramer's paintings reproduced in the art magazine *Colour*.

At Oxford Sadler had been heavily influenced by John Ruskin whose lectures he found 'inexpressibly splendid, like seeing a jewel talking to coals in a coal hole'[17] and it was no doubt from him his view of patronage was learned. Ruskin, he told a WEA audience in 1913,

> would allow no bar of humble birth to shut out a lad of genius from the training which would fit him for leadership and honoured rule. He warned us to leave no Giotto among the sheepfolds. But he believed in breed and no words meant more to him than *noblesse oblige* . . . [18]

In the same talk he remarked with some relish that Ruskin was no democrat and that his mind was 'disposed to an almost hierarchical organisation of national life' (a view which would find resonances in sections of the Arts Club but unlikely to go down well with WEA members). If Kramer was to be Leeds's Giotto, was Sadler its Medici? He seemed again to applaud Ruskin's romantic fantasy of 'A group of followers, faithful in their allegiance to a noble self-sacrificing leader':

> Ruskin believed in the clan. Loyalty to a brave leader seemed to him to be one of the greatest things in human life. To organise society in such a way as to bring great leaders to the front and to impel men to follow them, through suffering and self-sacrifice, to death, was the message which in his later and more prophetic years he gave to the world.[19]

Certainly the measured and archaic phrasing of Sadler's linking of Ruskin's medieval 'ideal settlement' and the life of the West Riding, in what followed, seemed almost unduly pointed:

> But within the broad lines of status [Ruskin] would preserve (as in feudal England it was preserved, and as in industrial Yorkshire it still lingers) great familiarity of intercourse between men of different stations in life . . . [20]

This would certainly have enshrined the relations of patronage within a quasi-Nietzschean discourse already familiar to Arts Club members but his quaintly phrased 'men of different stations in life' were rapidly turning to bitter class warfare. There can be no doubt that Sadler, ensconced in his university 'court' overlooking the town, nursed a fantasy of the second coming of the great man of culture and learning in ways not dissimilar from Orage's earlier Zarathustran vision of the superman/shepherd. He assumed the role, not with ostentation but with becoming modesty. For example, though he leased the largest house in Headingley for his residence, Buckingham House, it was not so much to display his status as his pictures, on the available interior walls. Moreover, on his letterheads, he dropped the name Buckingham House with its overtones of rank and opted simply for '41 Headingley Lane'. It was a genuine, if often misguided, concern for the 'common folk' and to an extent echoed that of Ruskin himself.[21] Ruskin had been taken up with enthusiasm by the local liberal press in the 1860s when the *Leeds Mercury* under Forster's friend Wemyss Reid had published his 'Time and Tide' essays and the *Bradford Observer* under Byles had done the same for 'Unto this Last' despite the screams of execration from reviewers.[22] But Sadler was also keen to distance himself from Ruskin's medievalism and to demonstrate his modernity in aesthetic matters. Ruskin, he said, never saw the beauty of the industrial landscape. He could admire the tall medieval towers of San Gimigniano or Bologna but he failed to see the same beauty in the tapering chimneys silhouetted on the skyline of Morley or Pudsey. His talk to WEAers continued with an awed, oddly futurist, paeon to the mystical power of the new machine age:

> [Ruskin] failed to see that for us moderns strength and power show themselves in the great arms of travelling cranes, in the gossamer beauty of scaffolding, in the gaunt severity of Lancashire mill sheds and in the intense and silent power of dynamoes and turbines. Where there is force, there is beauty.

It was for those of *us moderns*, inspired by Ruskin's teaching, he said, to see the beauty of the industrial landscape and fight for it to be cleansed of the squalor and the smoke which alone were the true ugliness and waste. This was clearly a new inflection of the Arts Club's initial project, which implied the aestheticization of life. Implicitly, a healthy community was an aesthetically satisfying one (or was it the other way round?). But it also continued the project a stage further, for the Club's dedication, through Orage, Waddington and Penty, to the craftsman had relegated industry to an unrealistically, subordinate position. Both Sadler and Rutter, by embracing an ecologically cleansed industry with open arms, had in effect opened the doors of the Club to modernity. The effect was probably galvanic; many older members hastily left by the back door and like Mark Senior, as we shall see, subsequently engaged in rancorous disputes with its new young turks like Kramer.

The sense of mystical urgency apparent in Sadler's talk to the WEA delegates, becomes almost apocalyptic when discussing the work of Kandinsky and other modern artists. For him artists were visionaries whose best work captured a spiritual reality not apparent on the surface of life. He told a conference of the National Union of Women Workers in October 1913 that 'in their present mood the arts of painting and of music were like voices prophesying war'.[23] In a later talk, he exemplified this by reference to a purely abstract painting he had received from Kandinsky in December 1913, in which the artist

> ... had expressed himself in free non-representational design. The pattern of the composition had broken free from orthodox decoration as vers libre departed from conventional metre. The design, strong in structure and balance, suggested hurtling masses in impending collision. The dominant colours were vermillion, purple, black, sulphur yellow and blood red. Some of the lines of the picture called up thoughts of swift arrows, aircraft and exploding shells.[24]

Sadler had written to Kandinsky asking if he had in fact foreseen the impending world war, to which Kandinsky had replied that he had been conscious of 'a terrible conflict going forward in the spiritual world'. The mode of his approval of Kandinsky might easily have been framed by Orage's own intuitionist discourse. He noted that Kandinsky, '*in the spirit of Nietzsche*' wrote that: 'every artist working under an impulse from within must go along a path which in some mystical manner had been laid out for him from the beginning. His life is nothing but a fulfilment of a task set for him, not by himself.'[25]

Continuing with a very interesting interpretation of what artists might be saying about the postwar settlement, Sadler appeared to prefigure the totalitarian states of the twenties and thirties. He suggested that the artists' preoccupations with 'certain geometric, especially cubist forms' could be seen as indicating 'a reaction from the vaguer generalizations of the historical method . . . and a preference for the more exact and axiomatic truths, which in the sphere of politics, would have their counterpart in the strict discipline of the sternly regulated state'.[26] This is a curious judgement since strict discipline and stern regulation smack more of the schoolroom than the artist's studio. Would his Nietzschean reading of Ruskin have predisposed him to such an interpretation or was it the product of the new authoritarian intellectual climate, that actually desired such a state?

Kandinsky was a key figure for both Sadler and his son. Alongside his paintings, they promoted his theoretical approach in order to 'explain' and 'understand' them. Though a planned *Blaue Reiter* exhibition in London had to be abandoned on the grounds of expense, Sadleir's translation of Kandinsky's *Uber Das Geistige* went ahead. As we have seen this was to be widely read by artists both in Leeds and

London; it circulated round the would-be Vorticists and was adopted by Wadsworth, was approved by Ezra Pound, denounced by T. E. Hulme and was aired in both the *New Age* and *Blast*. Herbert Read vividly remembered hearing Kandinsky's name spoken for the first time in the great hall of Leeds University in the presence of Sadler's son[27] and Jacob Kramer had a copy of the *Art of Spiritual Harmony* (Sadleir's title) on loan from Sadler as late as 1920.[28]

For our purposes Sadleir's book[29] is valuable not just for its translation but for his Introduction, which, *pace* Eliot, also suggests how Kandinsky's dramatic abstractions might be seen as part of a great tradition and thus accommodated. Although he later rejected this Introduction as an error of youthful ignorance, it provides a fascinating insight into his and, presumably, Sadler's thought at this time. Its main thrust is to advance Kandinsky's work as the expressionist vanguard of the post-impressionist movement.

For Sadleir post-impressionism had been thrust on a public who had hardly realized what impressionism was; presumably he was referring to Roger Fry's 1910 and 1912–13 exhibitions. Kandinsky was the leader of a new art movement in Munich which included painters, poets, musicians, dramatists, critics all working to the same end, which was: the expression of the soul of nature and humanity, what Kandinsky called the *Innerer Klang*. The tradition of true post-impressionism was a modern expression of the ancient symbolist antinaturalist ideal which was dedicated to the expression of inner feeling rather than outer reality. This tradition could be traced from the primitive Italians, Greeks and Egyptians forward to Byzantine art and Giotto. However, the tradition had been halted when the 'naturalist' revival in the Renaissance had subordinated symbolism to representation and hence downgraded the religious in favour of the humanist.

Though representational art had dominated European art ever since this time and had fallen into increasing decadence, the symbolist tradition had carried on. Firstly, through El Greco, who had passed it on to Goya and the Spanish school which in turn had influenced Daumier and Manet. In Northern Europe it had been carried by Rembrandt and Brower, who had also influenced the French, by way of Delacroix, Decamps and Courbet; they in turn had opened the way to Cezanne and Gauguin. Thus both northern and southern lines of symbolist influence had converged at the moment of maximum pressure on the dominant representational, or naturalist, tradition in the late nineteenth century. The characteristic element of the symbolist tradition's re-emergence, Sadleir continues, was radical simplicity, or rather *discrimination of vision*, a process which could begin only when the naturalist process had run its course.

At the end of the nineteenth century both Cezanne and Gauguin represented the modern expression of the symbolist tradition, but the differences between them, though subtle, ran very deep. Both painters centred on the 'ultimate and internal significance' rather than the 'momentary and external'. However Cezanne who had emerged from the northern tradition showed the 'architectural mind of the true Frenchman' in his profound sense of the *structure* of rocks and hills (in landscape). But since structure depended essentially on reality, the material of his art was drawn from 'the huge stores of actual nature' and thus, at base, still representational.

Gauguin showed 'greater solemnity and fire' than Cezanne and his pictures were 'tragic or passionate poems' rather than structurally revealing. His art always tended much more to the 'spiritual' and always came closer to complete rejection of representation than Cezanne. Thus Cezanne's art was tied to the actual in ways that Gaugin's was not and his successors did little more than exaggerate his technique until the first signs of cubism emerged. Picasso merely carries on this tendency to its logical conclusion. He mastered Cezanne's structural treatments of nature to the extent that representation all but disappeared, but it was still *based* on a natural object.

Gaugin's work, on the other hand, was 'intensely spiritual'. He was 'a preacher and a psychologist, universal by his very unorthodoxy, fundamental because he goes deeper than civilisation'.[30] But with the comparative failure of Gauguin's immediate followers to develop his work, the baton had passed north, as evidenced by the development by the Munich group of the *Neue Kunstlervereiningung*, of Gauguin's use of curves. Kandinsky took up the succession. His 'final abandonment of all representative intention' was an even greater achievement than Gaugin's. By combining the spiritual and technical tendencies of one great line of post-impressionism, he represented the culmination of the symbolist tradition, and was the true leader of non-representational art. Standing before one of Kandinsky's canvasses, his feelings answered to Kandinsky's spirituality; 'there was no question of looking for representation, a harmony had been set up'. Sadleir's concluding critique of Picasso was that because his art was structurally based and owed its existence to matter rather than emotion, it was no more than abstract mathematics. Picasso's 'Futurist' error, he said, lay in attempting to harmonize one element of reality with a surrounding aura of angular projections which inevitably resulted from, or in, conflicting disharmonious impressions.

Sadleir concluded that Kandinsky was fundamentally a religious painter though one who had not yet achieved perfection. Though he was the prophet of the art of spiritual harmony, he had yet to attain his end of spiritual abstraction wholly liberated from representation, in other words, to achieve the quality of music. Unless he did this he would be condemned as indecipherable 'by those who did not have the key to the cipher'. He intended this introduction as testimony of one to whom Kandinsky's art had spoken.

Jacob Kramer could have become aware of these arguments either in Leeds or in London, where in the autumn of 1912, with assistance from the Jewish Educational Aid Society and Michael Sadler, he entered the Slade School of Art. Here he was a misfit. Unlike Mark Gertler, whom he met there, he did not collect his passport into Bloomsbury society, nor, as Frances Spalding pointed out, did he 'immediately follow his fellow students David Bomberg, William Roberts and C. R. W. Nevinson in their experimentation with a cubist language'.[31] Wyndham Lewis thought highly enough of him, in 1915, to ask him to exhibit with the Vorticists, to which he contributed four pictures, but reviewed his work, *Earth*, in *Blast* with some caution: 'Mr. Kramer shows us a new planet risen on our horizon . . . It has fine passages of colour, and many possibilities as a future luminary. Several yellows and reds alone, and some of its more homogeneous inhabitants, would make a fine painting. I have seen another thing of his that would confirm me in this belief' wrote Lewis.[32] Frank Rutter, though excited by the painting, was similarly reserved: 'This mad medley of dancing figures indicating different races, may be to some extent expressive of the madness which rules the world for the moment; but its powers would not have been impaired by its having a more coherent design'.[33]

More enthusiastic about Kramer's work was Augustus John, whose strong advocacy of his *Mother and Child* ensured it a prominent position in the New English Art Club's 1915 exhibition. Its radically simplified formal structure moved Bill Oliver, the *Yorkshire Post*'s art critic, some years later, to speculate that it must have been 'one of the first Post-Impressionist paintings to emerge in this country'.[34] Kramer applied for membership of the London Group in 1915 and despite the Club's refusal of, amongst others, Horace Brodzky, John Currie, Mark Gertler, William Roberts and both Albert and William Rothenstein, he was elected. He may have been helped by Edward Wadsworth who was still enthusiastic about Kandinsky and as secretary of the London Group, informed Kramer of his election.

Though he was based in London until 1918, he returned regularly to Leeds where he had taken on a number of commissions for portraits of Leeds worthies, because, with his father's death, the burden of family upkeep now fell on him. These were necessarily less avant-gardiste though, even so, not as traditional as the sitters, or their wives, would have preferred. His portrait of the Leeds surgeon Berkeley Moynihan, for example, suffered exactly the same fate as that of Sadler. Sadler, nevertheless, regularly sent him money and saw all his new work. Perhaps, more importantly, he discursively suggested their significance to perplexed audiences. In a speech opening an exhibition of over fifty of Kramer's drawings at the Leeds School of Art in November 1916, he said that

> Among the many things Mr Kramer had done for them was this: he had interpreted to them the humanity, the romance, and pathos of the life of their city. There lay behind some of the drawings an intensity of family feeling, and a recollection of old far-off unhappy things, which gave to the work a depth of meaning which more and more appealed to them as they knew the drawings well.[35]

In this way Sadler, almost mystically, confirmed Kramer's identity with Leeds which may have made it all the harder for him to settle in London. Equally, the exhibition was already charged with heavy emotion since it also included his *Descent from the Cross* and the widely praised *Death of my Father*. A third painting was described by Tommy Lamb as '. . . apparently symbolic: an old man, with a strange expression of yearning and questioning, is kneeling in semi-darkness; on the neck, shoulder and body are patches of light, with a mysterious sense of exudation; while beyond the figure infinite space and the great unknown are suggested with extraordinary effect . . .'.[36] For Lamb, too, the key to his work was its intense spirituality.

Although he continued to show paintings in London, 1916 marks the beginning of Kramer's regular exhibiting in Leeds and Bradford. In December he exhibited 23 items at the Bradford Arts Club which drew the praise of the chairman of the art gallery committee, W. H. Brocklehurst. In May 1917 Frank Rutter was delighted to welcome him to membership of the Allied Artists Association where he exhibited the following year. However, his painting of *The Jew* which was reproduced in *Colour* was vigorously attacked by another Jewish painter, Frank Emmanuel, as a cardboard cut-out. This provided another occasion for Kramer's patron to intervene and Sadler replied to the criticism in his most fulsome terms yet. His letter, printed in *Colour*, noted that he had been intimately acquainted with Kramer's work for some years,

> . . . and I can only say that the longer I live with his pictures and drawings the more they mean to me, and the more intensely do I feel the power of his creative insight. Day by day I compare them with the great works by painters of other schools, and find that they and Mr Kramer's imaginative pictures and drawings, however much they may differ in methods of presentment, in pattern and in colour, have in common the supreme qualities of sincerity, vision and truthfulness to personal conviction.[37]

Although Sadler felt that Kramer's genius might well blossom into greater things in the future, it did not prevent him from asking Kramer to add a line or two to his hair in his portrait of him to indicate waviness; the principle being, presumably, that there is a point where genius and truth to external reality occasionally part company. Whatever the result it did not unfortunately improve Mary Sadler's opinion of the painting and she asked Kramer to exhibit it untitled. But Sadler's help and encouragement continued undiminished.

Kramer was now spending much of his time in Leeds, and entering into his most fruitful period, unhappily all too brief. Jacob Epstein, who modelled a bust of him at this time recalled that he 'seemed to be on fire. He was extraordinarily nervous. Energy seemed to leap into his hair as he sat, and sometimes he would be shaken by queer tremblings of ague'.[38] The bust, now in Leeds Art Gallery, stands in mute confirmation. Increasingly, he not only exhibited his work but also lectured on art, the earliest of these talks being to the Leeds Arts Club on 22 January 1918 (chaired, incidentally, by Tom Heron). Evidence of the Sadler/Kandinsky influence was most marked in his use of the keywords 'expression', 'spiritual' and 'form'. All great art, he believed, was 'an expression of spiritual feeling'. It was, therefore, 'his endeavour to create a purely spiritual form, and in his work he had the greatest satisfaction when he was able to separate the spiritual from the actual outward form. He did not regard faithful reproduction as expression'.[39] Kramer was already mining the same terminology as the the Kandinsky translation and it seems unlikely he did not know of it by now.

He must have expressed something of the same in his, now lost, letter in early 1918 to Herbert Read, then with the 2nd Battalion The Yorkshire Regiment at the war front. Kramer had written that the more conscious he became of the element of spirituality in everything the more he became filled with a sense of abiding happiness. The philosophically rigorous Read criticized this on the grounds that the element of spirituality lay not in the things themselves, but in the image of the things in his mind, a significant move from the objective to the subjective, with which Kramer did not probably agree. But despite this disagreement Read entirely reinforced Kramer's view of the nature of realism (as opposed to naturalism) which was that 'in my estimation symbolism and realism are almost interchangeable terms because I express in form the absolute reality as I perceive it'.[40]

Thus, for both Read and Kramer at this time, the absence of naturalistic representation was necessary for the expression of reality. Formally, both saw themselves as realists (this formal distinction between 'naturalism' and 'realism' is important to hold on to in these debates) but while Kramer appeared to believe in the direct apprehension of the thing in itself, or essence of the object, Read maintained a sceptical idealism. With much contemporary philosophical opinion, he held that the object itself was unknowable and that the only knowable things were the contents of the mind. Hence he concluded his discussion of Kramer's ideas on symbolism and realism with a key statement of his own position: 'You see how that sentence fits in with my generalisation: *the mental image or intuition is the only reality*' (my emphasis).[41]

In another letter to Read in the following year, while he was in the process of painting *The Day of Atonement*, he expanded on what he meant by symbolism:

> . . . only through symbolism could I express all the ideas accumulated in the ordinary channels . . . When the natural and spiritual elements impinges itself upon my consciousness, a terrific struggle invariably ensues, and it is by the greatest effort that I am ultimately able to transcend the base substance of detailed naturalness into the essence of spirituality. The latter always predominates, owing to its essential vigour and direct appeal . . . [42]

In his most forthright statement of his views to date, he also told Read: 'As you know, the degree of expression in a work of art is the measure of its greatness – a spiritual discernment is more essential than the reproduction of the obvious . . . it is my endeavour to create a purely spiritual form'. Clearly the notion of 'a purely spiritual form' is one fraught with difficulties and later the same year sees Kramer, in an article in Yiddish, later translated into English, attempting to clarify it by making a Platonic distinction between 'form' and 'shape': 'The shape is not yet the form itself, but only the outward and accidental manifestation of the form. On the other hand again, form in its transcendental sense is that inner and eternal essence of the object which indicates and determines all external shapes and aspects.'[43]

His letter to Read must have been the basis for a talk on 'Symbolism in Art' he gave to the Bradford Arts Club, in 1919, since it contains the same argument and many of the same phrases. Significantly, the problem of language is raised again: 'Owing to the comparative modernity of the symbolical phase in art, and the consequent rather limited vocabulary it was difficult to convey in words the spiritual idea he had in mind'.[44] (It should be born in mind that Kramer's native language was, like Kandinsky's, Russian, and that he also spoke Yiddish.) He went a stage further however by linking the notion of 'spiritual form' to his 'conception of expression' or, in other words, for him expression *was* the creation of spiritual form. He described how this process felt:

> To one who felt the essence of things very deeply the scope of most art as exemplified in the work of the conventional artist, was not sufficiently broad to include the more mystic tendencies – if he might

> so name them – in order to translate these crude desires into pure symbolism. In his case the symbolical expression followed a comprehensive study of the natural form.

For Kramer, then, to express his feelings meant portraying the 'spiritual' essence of the thing he was painting, thus linking subject and object transcendentally. He attached the greatest importance to expressing his deeper feelings since 'such a method denoted life and all of the multitudinous activities'. Echoes of the Great World Soul. He felt that all the modernisms such as impressionism, cubism, futurism and post-impressionism were but different ways of expressing the innermost meaning of things. Again, for the artists who painted in this way, the expression of their own feelings produced the 'fullest symbolism'. Philosophically unsatisfactory as this statement is, as Read instantly saw, since the unity of subjective feeling with objective reality suggested was by *mystical* intuition, it nevertheless dramatically revealed Kramer's intentions when creating his most moving works such as *Jews at Prayer, My Mother, Hear Our Voice, O Lord our God*, as well as *The Day of Atonement* which were all produced in 1919. Curiously, none of them could claim to be non-representational but all contain a high degree of simplification and formality.

During 1919 Kramer had exhibited both at Rutter's Adelphi Gallery in London, and with the Glasgow Society of Painters; his *Day of Atonement*, which had taken nine months to paint, was presented to Leeds City Art Gallery by the Leeds Jewish Representative Council and five other works presented to the Bradford Art Gallery. He was well established with a growing national reputation, but he was determinedly based in Leeds. In 1920 this identity was to be confirmed by Sadler and Rothenstein's Town Hall panels scheme, which would have included his painting of miners but, as Leeds and Dionysos had not mixed earlier, so Leeds and modernism were shortly to part company and the scheme was abandoned. Kramer's activities centred on the Leeds Arts Club. Here he opened an exhibition of children's art, where perhaps remembering his own school experiences, he counselled parents and teachers to treasure children's art work. They were he said 'often priceless because they were the key to latent powers which might be allowed to die by sheer neglect or even ridicule'.[45] He condemned cinemas for crushing the imagination of the young much in the same way as later generations were to condemn television, but worse was Leeds itself, since 'throughout the city there was terrible evidence that love of beauty was either crushed or allowed to die'.

An example of the direct collaboration of patron and painter was on 8 March 1920, when Kramer demonstrated 'Colour in Relation to Music' at the Club. Michael Sadler, who chaired the meeting, lent

Kramer his copy of his son's translation of Kandinsky as well as some of Kandinsky's abstract paintings for the lecture. (He was later, by post, to request the return of both, reminding Kramer that on a previous occasion one of his Gauguin's had come back damaged.) Musical illustrations were provided by Kathleen Frise Smith, on piano, whose interest in the subject was largely inspired by Kramer's researches. The basis of Kramer's argument was the romantic assumption, elaborated by Kandinsky, that music was the most authentic condition of all the arts, since it was entirely divorced from the problem of representation. The aim of all the other arts, therefore, was to become like music. Music, he said, denied its true function when it attempted to become descriptive or realistic: 'A musical piece and a picture have justification only when they bring our consciousness into mystical union with the inner transcendental essence of reality, and not merely when they photograph its petty external details'.[46] Kramer illustrated his thesis from a large collection of 'cubist and futurist' works hung on the wall of the lecture room while Kathleen Frise Smith attempted to decode the colour values into sound. The report of the meeting suggested that in a general way the audience were able to recognize some resemblance between the music and the paintings, and apparently the coloured drawings that Kramer was making, but when it came to illustrations of concrete and abstract symbolism exemplified in Scriabin's music 'a severe test was imposed on the imagination of all but the erudite in such matters'. Sadler and Kramer apparently organized a number of such experiments at the Club and on at least one occasion invited painters and photographers to compete over representing the same scene.

Kramer appears to have been very loyal both to Sadler and Leeds. Shortly before the town hall panels escapade, in a letter to the *Yorkshire Post*, holding up Sadler as a paradigm, he attacked the city fathers for their neglect of art patronage. Since this was to be Sadler's last foray into city affairs it is doubtful whether he welcomed it. Kramer claimed to have moved in many circles and that no city outside London could claim a deeper interest in matters of art than Leeds 'in spite of the Art Gallery' but the deplorable fact was that it was concentrated in a handful of individuals and even the intelligent mass of the citizens were left cold by it.[47] He described Sadler's collection as magnificent and famous in three continents, but wholly without honour in Leeds itself. Sir Michael, he said, had never once been approached by the city fathers, who in other cities would have fallen over themselves to co-opt him. His unique collection, comprised in addition to works of masters of all periods, 'a magnificent collection of modern works of a catholicity that leaves nothing to be desired'. The sins of the city were compounded, he said, in neglecting to purchase the collection of the head of the Leeds School of Art, Haywood Rider. This included a superb Rembrandt, a fine example of Titian's best period and a fine Gainsborough, all about to go under the hammer at Christie's.

The distrust that the Leeds City Council held of Sadler and for that matter, the university, is in itself a complex issue of town and gown. Historically, the bones of it lay in the formation of a self-appointed liberal elite of manufacturers, businessmen and bankers in the early nineteenth century, who created the Philosophical and Literary Society in 1818 and then set up the Mechanic's Institute. The Phil and Lit had become a centre of opinion making and 'civic consciousness'. Though it had declined as the elected municipal structures had risen, it had erected the principle of a local aristocracy of leading families such as the Baines, Kitsons, Gotts, Luptons, Marshalls, Fairbairns, Becketts and of course Sadlers.[48] This in turn had spawned the Conversation Club in 1849, but by the 1870s the old elite was split over the question of education and in any case most of its original members were dead. Others, like the second generation Marshalls had joined the landowning squirearchy of Westmoreland (giving weight to Sadler's observations on the greater civic consciousness of the German bourgeois). To an extent the vacuum created by the demise of the old vigorous, civically and culturally aware elite had allowed the formation of the Arts Club itself, though from a lower social stratum (not gentlemen but supermen) and allied to different social forces. The vigorous interest the Club and its members showed in municipal affairs and its forthright criticisms of the municipality were not welcome. So, when Sadler joined the fold, the spectre of the old elite appeared to have risen to haunt it once again.

Especially ominous for the city council had been the founding in 1918, by a group of Arts Club members including the architect W. H. Thorp, Professor Frederic Moorman, the Vicar of Leeds and Sadler himself, of the Leeds Civic Society. Descendants of the old elite included Kitson Clark, Gott and F. M. Lupton, who rather ingenuously remarked at the society's foundation, that 'the society should not cause any jealously on the part of the City Council'.[49] Worse, Arthur Rowntree had declared 'Let us begin to house the people, instead of trying to warehouse them!' and Kitson Clark had read a litany of the council's dereliction of civic duty:

> In Leeds we disfigure our magnificent site by rows and rows of houses that we can only deplore, we blacken everything with smoke, we carry our traffic through mazes of ill-connected streets, we disfigure the latter by ugly decoration and poor buildings, we litter them with tram tickets; with little regret we destroy a charming 17th century building like the old Grammar School, we neglect the Red Hall, we scarcely recognise the duty we owe to our unequalled

> Abbey, we are guilty of poor memorials of our gallant dead, and further, we are dreadful cowards – we fear to avow that our reason for doing anything is, because it is beautiful.[50]

Thus when Sadler, inspired by designs commissioned for the Imperial War Museum, suggested a scheme to decorate Leeds Town Hall in 1920, the city council was justifiably suspicious. It was, as it were, to strike at the very heart of the municipality, its own black wedding-cake temple of civic neglect. But Sadler, who had the ear of Lloyd George himself was not to be dissuaded by mere aldermen. Two influential considerations were the fame and value of Ford Madox Brown's murals in Manchester Town Hall, always a red rag to Yorkshiremen, and the fact that it would not cost the ratepayers a penny. He proposed that a number of modern artists should design panels for the interior of the Town Hall, the Victoria Hall, on the theme of Leeds, its people and its industries. He won the council's consent for initial sketches to be made, undertaking to pay up to £200 of the initial costs himself. The artists were chosen by the directors of the three national galleries: Jacob Kramer, Edward Wadsworth, Paul and John Nash, Albert Ruthersden (William Rothenstein's brother), Stanley Spencer and Percy Jowett.[51] They would get £21 for their rough sketches which would remain the property of Sadler and William Rothenstein was responsible for approving them. Sadler would then submit them to the city art gallery committee. If they were acceptable to the city council, Sadler hoped to secure individual donors to present the completed decorations to the city.

The scheme was announced in the *Yorkshire Post* in the summer of 1920, along with the published sketches, the *Post* adding its own instructive commentary. Ruthersden's *Building* and Jowett's *Woollen Mills* showed 'clean drawing' and had the charm of old architectural prints. Paul Nash's *View of the Aire from the Leeds Bridge* (later called the *Canal*) and John Nash's *Landscape and Trees* (later called *Rhubarb and Coal*), both landscapes, were more or less acceptable, while Paul Nash's second design *The Quarry* was described as 'Blakelike' and much the best drawing. John Nash's *Kirkstall* (later called *Millworker's Landscape*) 'sought for ugliness of form at the expense of truth' and was not acceptable. Kramer's *Coal Mine* which was paired with Wadsworths's *Leeds* (later *Slag Heaps*) was 'unrestful while Wadsworth was 'accused of depicting Leeds being blown to bits by a heavy gun or possibly a Bessemer converter'. Both were 'too discordant'.[52] In truth, they could have been painted in the trenches of the Somme at the height of battle and contain powerfully Vorticist motifs, but all the paintings showed Leeds as a smoky and energetic chaos with glimpses of a more pastoral side.

Stanley Spencer's washing day scene, arguably the most impressive of all, was by common consent not in keeping with the more distant subjects of the rest. It was a product of a very moving visit to Leeds by Spencer, who was taken on a guided tour by Kramer. Spencer wrote to him a few days later thanking him copiously for his help, saying, 'I should have seen nothing of the side of life in Leeds that I most wanted to see unless you had shown me. You were like a link between me and the people of Leeds which somehow joined me to them'.[53]

Predictably the publication of the sketches drew a storm of abusive letters, not the least of which was from an Arts Club founder member, Mark Senior. This in turn drew fire from Kramer, the match illustrating the enormous gap that had opened up in aesthetic matters between older and younger members. Senior was by now, well-established and exhibited regularly at the Royal Academy, though Sam Wilson was still his most consistent patron, having bought no less than eighteen works. His letter to the *Yorkshire Evening Post* which began with an assault on the 'nightmare crudities' and 'distorted and chaotic effusions' of modern art, declared that this sort of stuff must not be allowed to disfigure the town hall.[54] He did not doubt that specious arguments by the silver tongued would claim the revelation of deep symbolic essences in the works but this was so much fatuous jargon:

> Futurist, cubist, vorticist and impressionist art is as ephemeral as the fevered times in which we live. The grandeur, the eternal sanity of things, the underlying purposes of creation, are entirely lost by these artistic Bolsheviks . . . We want pictures in the Town Hall of merit and balance, and not such as in years to come will reflect the abnormality of the times, and will bring a smile of derision to the men who can discern good art from bad, true from false.

It is not hard to imagine who the 'silver tongued' might be, nor which particular 'artistic Bolshevik' he might have had in mind. Indeed Jacob Kramer lost no time in replying, personally, while his patron, sensibly, kept quiet. Kramer attacked the artists of the traditional school who were badly imitating the shape of traditional British art without ever catching the soul of it. The implication, as in Eliot's recent essay 'Tradition and the Individual Talent', was that he and his fellow modernists were actually more traditional than those who only appeared to be. He defined the task of modern artists as the expression of 'spiritual realities', their method . . .

> . . . to get beyond mere technique to the hidden essence to which technique is subordinate. In the process they have eliminated a good deal of the technical complexity of traditional art, its crowded detail, its multiplication of the trees which prevented it seeing the wood. They have leapt at reality, and reproduced it with as little complexity as possible.[55]

Though he calculatedly glanced at the 'academy type of picture' with its niceness, frills and flounces, he claimed to have admired Senior for the way he stuck to his own work and begged him not to be ungenerous with the 'young artists of the modern school'. In all, the letter was an articulate defence of his position and drew a somewhat mollified reply from Senior, who wished that 'these artistic pioneers . . . could infuse as much clarity into their canvas as Mr Kramer has managed to do in his prose'. Nevertheless he was not convinced that the sketches had any merit and his and other onslaughts in the press appear to have shaken Michael Sadler badly.

Amidst much acrimony from the artists themselves, Sadler declared that the sketches were not harmonious enough for the Victoria Hall and withdrew them. Alderman Willey, chairman of the art gallery committee, who had not even seen them, had no hesitation in condemning them in the most aldermanic terms. 'I think my committee, judging from the photographs, believe the designs to be most inappropriate. The Victoria Hall is a magnificent building, and I, for one, would like to see it decorated, not by a discordant group of young experimenters, but by an artist of proved powers . . .'.[56] Needless to say, none was sought and the whole scheme was swiftly entered forgotten until Michael Sadler presented the drawings to the town over twenty years later. It was, Alex Robertson suggests, 'one of the few schemes of private patronage on such a scale this century',[57] but in its near farcical collapse, it appeared typical of Sadler's grasshopper enthusiasm of skipping from one visionary scheme to the next, without seeing it through.

However misguided his attempts to intervene in the life of the city, there can be no doubt that Sadler's role in art patronage was instrumental in licensing an actively experimental art in Leeds. Kramer, Henry Moore and many other local artists benefited from his studied encouragement and regular purchase of paintings and drawings. His promotion of Kandinsky's painting and his son's introduction to his theory gave encouragement to artists to reject conventional representation and plunge into a world of abstraction and expression, which as we have seen was vital to Kramer's work, and as we shall see, formative for Herbert Read's theorizing and possibly, even, of critical importance for the early development of Henry Moore. Roger Fry, who had long taken note of Sadler's activities, but was ignorant of the context of it, saw him only as a missionary of light in a benighted outpost of empire:

> Every time I came to Leeds I got more and more impressed with the work Sir Michael was doing. He had civilized a whole population. Since I went to Leeds the first time more than ten years ago, the entire spirit has changed from a rather sullen suspicion of ideas to a

genuine enthusiastic intellectual and spiritual life. He has shown what *can* be done – but rarely is, – by education.[58]

Jacob Kramer's role in advancing the new art should not be underestimated. His passionate promotion and defence of his own work, as well as his generous support of others, was vital in keeping open space, of which the Arts Club was the institutional embodiment, of experimentalism. It was hardly justified of Roger Fry, after another visit to the Sadlers, to write off Kramer as 'a bloody fraud' who 'takes them all in by his high falutin'',[59] but not unexpected, after all Kramer was only one of the natives.

Notes

1. Sadleir, *Sadler*, p. 260.
2. Ibid., p. 257.
3. Sir Michael Sadler's Diaries, 7 December 1913, Bodleian Library, Accession 252, p. 46.
4. Sadleir, *Sadler*, p. 258.
5. Leeds WEA branch minute book, 1914, Leeds University Adult and Continuing Education Department Archives.
6. John Dover Wilson, *Milestones on the Dover Road*, Faber, London, 1969, pp. 79–80.
7. See Tom Steele, 'From Class Consciousness to Cultural Studies, George Thompson and the WEA in Yorkshire' in *Studies in the Education of Adults*, vol. 19, no. 2, October 1987.
8. Sadler's Diaries, 25 August 1916, p. 155.
9. Programme of lectures for 1916 in the archives in Leeds TS Lodge, Queens Square.
10. E. Townshend, (ed.) *Keeling Letters and Recollections*, introduced by H. G. Wells, Allen and Unwin, London, 1918, Appendix II by Arthur Greenwood.
11. John Rothenstein, *Summer's Lease*, Hamish Hamilton, London, 1965, p. 221.
12 Ibid., p. 206.
13. John Rothenstein, *Modern English Painters*, vol. 1, London, 1952, p. 128.
14. Christopher Sheppard, 'Jacob Kramer in his Correspondence' in *Leeds University Reporter*, vol. 30, 1987, p. 209. This is a valuable source on Kramer, written on the occasion of the purchase by the Brotherton Library of Kramer's letters.
15. Sheppard, p. 209.
16. J. D. Roberts, (ed.) *The Kramer Documents*, Valencia, 1983, p. 10.
17. Quoted by Bill Oliver in his introduction to the catalogue of the Commemorative Exhibition of Sir Michael Sadler's collection, Leeds City Art Galleries, 1963, p. 5.
18. Typescript notes for a talk 'Reminiscences of Arnold Toynbee and Ruskin' read to WEA delegates at Leeds University, 18 October 1913, Bodleian Library, Accession no. 252.

19. Ibid.
20. Ibid.
21. Ruskin had in fact developed a special relation with the 'Yorkshire Operatives', whom he had in mind while writing his *Fors Clavigera* essays. See Malcolm Hardman's excellent archaeological work *Ruskin and Bradford*, Manchester University Press, 1986, p. 10.
22. Hardman, p. 7.
23. A newspaper cutting entitled 'Premonitions of the War in Modern Art' dated Leeds, 26 October 1915, of an address by Michael Sadler, Brotherton Collection, Leeds University.
24. Ibid.
25. Ibid., my emphasis.
26. Ibid.
27. Michael Sadler Commemorative Exhibition Catalogue, p. 6.
28. Letter from Sadler to Kramer, 25 November 1920, Brotherton Collection, requests its return which Kramer had borrowed 'some time ago' as he needed it for a lecture.
29. Wassily Kandinsky, *Uber Das Geistige*, translated and introduced by M. T. H. Sadler (Michael Sadleir), Constable, London, 1914. All following quotations are taken from the Introduction pp. x-xxv.
30. Significantly the phrase 'deeper than civilisation' was also used a few years later by Eliot in his review of Wyndham Lewis's *Tarr* in *The Egoist*, September 1918, p. 105. The use of the word 'psychologist', also picked up by Edward Wadsworth in his review of the book, in *Blast*, to describe Kandinsky signalled a significant shift in aesthetics.
31. Francis Spalding, Introduction to *Jacob Kramer Reassessed*, a catalogue for an exhibition at Ben Uri Art Gallery, May-July 1984, p. 3.
32. Quoted in Roberts, *Kramer Documents*, p. 15.
33. Ibid.
34. Quoted in Sheppard, p. 206.
35. Quoted in Roberts, p. 19.
36. Ibid., p. 18.
37. Ibid., p. 28.
38. Quoted in Spalding, p. 4.
39. Quoted in Roberts, p. 33.
40. Letter from Herbert Read to Jacob Kramer, 6 April 1918, Brotherton Collection, Leeds University and quoted in Roberts pp. 34–35. The Brotherton Collection purchased the bulk of its collection of Kramer's correspondence at Sotheby's auction, 11 July 1986.
41. Ibid.
42. Quoted in Spalding, p. 4.
43. Quoted in Spalding, p. 9. In this essay, by criticizing the 'so-called realist or rather naturalist school in painting', he again implies that he is a realist.
44. Undated press report in Roberts, p. 41.
45. Untitled newspaper report, 26 January, quoted in Roberts, p. 52.
46. Newspaper report, 9 March 1920, quoted in Roberts p. 54.
47. Quoted in Roberts, p. 57.
48. G. Kitson Clark, 'The Leeds Elite', *The University of Leeds Review*, vol. 17, no. 2, 1975, pp. 239–240.
49. *Yorkshire Observer*, 2 October 1918, cutting found in Leeds City Reference Library, Cuttings Book, vol. 7, p. 204.

50. Leeds Civic Society, founding document, 17 July 1918, in Thoresby Society archives, no. 22B6.
51. Alexander Robertson, 'The Leeds Town Hall Decoration Scheme', *Leeds Arts Calendar*, no. 74, 1974, p. 12.
52. All quotations from Robertson, p. 17.
53. Roberts, p. 72.
54. Letter dated 6 May 1920, quoted in Roberts, p. 63.
55. Letter dated 7 May 1920, quoted in Roberts, p. 64.
56. Quoted in Robertson, p. 19.
57. Ibid., p. 22.
58. Letter from Fry to Lady Sadler, quoted in Sadleir, p. 333.
59. Letter to Vanessa Bell, 14 February 1923, in Denys Sutton (ed.) *Roger Fry's Letters*, vol. 2, London, 1972, p. 531.

CHAPTER ELEVEN

The Sorcerer's Apprentice

Out of the Vortex, Herbert Read

If the painter most indebted to the formative influence of the Arts Club was Jacob Kramer, then the writer was Herbert Read. While Kramer had benefited from the patronage of Michael Sadler, Read was to discover a collaborator in Frank Rutter and in Alfred Orage a mentor. The *New Age* was for Read, as it was for his fellow undergraduate Storm Jameson, a bible of taste and ideas. During the war years he followed its arguments and debates assiduously and occasionally contributed to them. On leave from the front, he made the acquaintance of Orage and his circle. Ezra Pound, T. S. Eliot and Wyndham Lewis. Orage was so impressed by his literary talents that, when he decided to cease editing the *New Age*, he asked Read to take over. He had already handed over his own coveted 'Readers and Writers' column to Read and asked him to edit and publish the papers of T. E. Hulme. His first published piece was a letter to the *New Age* in 1913. Later Read acknowledged that 'Orage encouraged me and gave me liberal advice until he thought I was fairly launched.'[1]

In some respects they were remarkably similar.[2] Both were born into Yorkshire farming families where the deaths of their fathers caused the uprooting of the family and strong-spirited mothers had to work for a living to maintain the children. Read was born near Kirby Moorside about thirty miles east of Dacre, Orage's birthplace, in 1893, twenty years later. On the death of his father in 1903, his mother took a job helping to manage a laundry and Read was sent to Crossley's School in Halifax. He left there in 1908, with a second class honours in the Cambridge Junior Certificate and having received some encouragement for his literary abilities. Like Orage he came to Leeds seeking work but unlike him there was no Howard Coote to send Read to college and at the age of fifteen or sixteen he found himself working as a bank clerk. Orage had left town three years earlier, but Read knew of him as 'a name and a legend in Leeds'. In 1908 his mother had moved the family to Leeds, hoping that a city of that size would offer better opportunities for her sons' careers. Initially they lived in the Woodhouse area but by coincidence, or design, in 1912 she leased 7 Buckingham Mount, the house next door to Holbrook Jackson's, the one that witnessed Orage's fateful introduction to *Zarathustra*, and here they remained until they left Leeds.

Herbert Read's first job was with the Skyrac and Morley Trustee Savings Bank but, like his friend T. S. Eliot, it was not an ultimate career move and after three years the Tory farmer's son underwent a profound change. His graphic Road to Damascus passed through the smoke-blackened heart of Leeds:

> For three years, with only one week's break in the year, I walked these streets – I could not afford a tram fare. From my home on the outskirts to the Bank in the middle of the city; from the head-office of the Bank to the branches at Armley, Beeston and Chapeltown, I passed through areas in which factories were only relieved by slums, slums by factories – a wilderness of stone and brick, with soot falling like black snow. Drab and stunted wage-slaves drifted through the stink and clatter; tramcars moaned and screeched along their glistening rails, spluttering blue electric sparks. These same wage-slaves brought their savings to the bank – we accepted deposits of threepence and upwards – greasy coins which blackened the fingers that counted them, and were then entered into pass-books permeated by grime and sweat. For a year or two my way home passed through the City Square, where a political agitator sometimes drew a crowd around him; and sometimes I would stop and listen. In one way or another, this environment gradually penetrated the armour of my inherited prejudices. Ugliness and poverty, dirt and drabness, were too universal to be ignored. The questioning intelligence which was slowly awakening in me began to question the material things before my eyes. I found that other people had questioned them: not only Disraeli but Carlyle, Ruskin and Morris; and that they were being questioned by people round about me.
>
> Plato has written about the windows that open in the mind, and it is very true image. The mind of youth is a room without an escape: there is perhaps a dim inner light, and an endless succession of pictures flicker on the walls. Then suddenly, on one side the shutters are drawn and through an open space the youth looks out on to the light and landscape of the real world.[3]

He began to attend WEA evening classes taught by the proselytizing members of the university's economics department, MacGregor and Greenwood, and shortly cashed in the savings books for academic texts. In 1912 he managed to borrow enough money from an uncle to enrol at Leeds University as an undergraduate. Having initially taken the first year of a BA course he changed to economics, where David MacGregor and Henry Clay taught him classical economy and Arthur Greenwood social economics and economic history. Read claimed that, ironically, economics, the only subject he had a thorough grounding in, was the one he made least use of. Nevertheless the campaigning Fabianism and commitment to working-class emancipation through education of his tutors powerfully reoriented his politics. Inevitably, he transcended the ideological parameters of his tutors and began reading Marx's *Capital*, Kropotkin's *Fields, Factories and Workshops* and pamphlets on anarchism. But most decisive of all was Edward Carpenter's *Non-Governmental Society*.

Even more inevitably, it now seems, other extra-curricula signposts, Ibsen, Strindberg, Shaw and Orage, led him to discover Nietzsche, 'a central exchange of intellectual tendencies' that fired his philosophical imagination. Orage had sown his seeds well, Common's translations of Nietzsche and possibly his own introduction (for they are still there) had found their way into the university's library and a course in tragedy from Aeschylus to Ibsen had been taught at the university as early as 1907.[4] 'Zarathustra' wrote Read of the young undergraduate, entered deep into his soul, so deeply that he has never wholly departed'.[5] Nietzsche, rather than his friends or tutors, he claimed, was his real teacher during these years.

But one tutor who did take a special interest in him was Frederic Moorman, professor of English language for whom Read wrote some poetic dramas in dialect. Dialect dramas were Moorman's own speciality and his most famous one, *Potter Thompson*, an Arthurian romance, was performed some years later at the Arts Club.[6] Moorman, who was already impressed by his academic essays, was so delighted by Read's imaginative work that he encouraged him to write more and Read contributed a number of poems to the student's magazine *Griffon* which were also well received. Moorman was still actively involved with both the Arts Club and also the Workers' Education Association, being at this time chairman of the Leeds branch. He also organized a number of *converzationes* for the Playgoers Society and lectured on Shakespeare as a democrat. It may well have been he who introduced Read to the Club. Read recounts how he had wished he could resume his relationship with Moorman, whom he described as his 'mentor' after the war, but Moorman died tragically, in 1919, in a swimming accident.

Though one of the early members of the Club, Moorman was also infected by the new post-impressionist atmosphere encouraged by Sadler and Rutter. His diaries recount how in 1913 he went to hear Roger Fry lecturing on principles of design 'in reality an exaltation of the Post-Impressionist school of painters'[7] (he does not say whether it was at the gallery or the Club). But he was more impressed by Sadler's defence of post-impressionism in a debate at the university the following month. He also felt that Rutter spoke very sensibly about the French impressionists and post-impressionists at a lecture a few days later.

Moorman may well have taken his protegé to one of these lectures because Read later recalled being very impressed by Rutter's lectures on the post-impressionists. Here, in 1912, he met Jacob Kramer, Rutter and through him, the Camden Town Group painters, Harold Gilman and Charles Ginner. Both Kramer, the first painter he had met, and Rutter strongly influenced him. With Kramer as we have seen, he corresponded on abstract theory and with Rutter he collaborated on the briefly brilliant journal *Art and Letters* (the forerunner to T. S. Eliot's *Criterion*) and while Kramer was to introduce him to the mystery of artistic production, Rutter showed him the techniques of criticism. 'It is my delight', wrote Read in his 1917 diary, to get him into a quiet corner in some cafe and over coffee and cigarettes to listen to him whilst he talks Meredith and Henry James by the hour'; he was the 'perfect critic'.[8]

The Club that Read joined in 1912 was, as we have seen, now powerfully committed to the values of artistic experiment. That these values were not simply confined to its more well-known incomers but were rapidly assimilated by the members themselves was exhibited by their spirited defences in the wake of the Club's 1913 post-impressionist exhibition. Several of them had replied to a correspondent in the *Yorkshire Post* who described post-impressionism as a 'mental disease'. They included Tommy Lamb, and Mrs F. R. Dale, Ernest Forbes and Frank Dean, who were painters. Mrs Dale, who had attended the first post impressionism exhibition in London, strongly defended Van Gogh, while Ernest Forbes stated that great art of necessity must be experimental. His letter to the *Post* suggests having read or heard Sadleir on post-impressionism's provenance since he mentions Rembrandt, Velasquez, El Greco and Goya as part of its tradition. And further,

> We believe that the Impressionist movement of 1870, begun by Pissaro, Cezane (sic), Sisley, Monet and other men, got nearer still (to the soul) and that this particular movement was about the healthiest experiment in art for more than four hundred years. Encouraged in such a belief, men like Gauguin and Van Gogh have advanced the theories of the other men, and have given us something which, fed as we have been upon a brown past, is not at first taste palatable.[9]

Forbes found in the Van Gogh 'a vibrating light such as in no other picture we can call to mind' which danced 'in all the joy of pure colour'. Significantly his defence is in both the quasi-religious terms of spirituality and the quasi-scientific terms of experiment and theory; the artist as seer and technician. His metaphor of food suggests digestion and excretion but it is light and colour, so patently absent from the urban environment which must have dazzled the Leeds artist.

Frank Dean, on the other hand, saw the work of the post-impressionism as part of a global ideological cataclysm: 'What is very like a revolution seems to be taking place in various fields of thought. In religion, science, politics, music and in art we have it. Its efforts may be as far reaching in the field of art as a great social revolution in the field of politics'.[10] He too argued that post-impressionism had its roots in the history of painting and in particular in primitive symbolism to which, he felt, the new generation were attempting to return.

> Painting has for some 500 years or more concerned itself almost altogether with the imitation of Nature. Realism has gone as far, perhaps, as it can, and has done it remarkably well, but in the doing it has lost certain qualities essential to great art, the dignity, simplicity and the intensity of faith of the early men. Now the inevitable reaction sets in, and we find a body of men who throw over all tradition, and are content to go back to what we might call the infancy of art, and start again, giving us a view of things uninfluenced by all the conventions of centuries and a view which is distinctly personal.[11]

Leeds offered so few occasions to witness anything beyond the ordinary and mundane it should be grateful to the Club for this exhibition. So Dean reinforced the importance of the symbolic and the pure in a way Kramer might have done (but not making Kramer's distinction between realism and naturalism). He was less interested in experiment than in the cosmic upheaval the new art represented. These too were familiar themes within the Club from its earliest times and part of an apocalyptic vein which saw art as just another manifestation of some other colossal change.

Frank Dean, Ernest Forbes, Mrs F. D. Dale, Emily Ford, Elsie Lawrence, P. M. Teasdale, Herman Hildesheim (later Hilton), H. H. Greenwood, and A. J. Sanders were amongst the artists regularly meeting to discuss and display their work at the Club. Their keenness to experiment was encouraged by Rutter and Sadler, who urged them to adopt, as we have seen, notions of significant form and explore the relations between abstract painting and music. This was the environment Read was introduced to. Although Kramer was by now much of the time in London, there was another artist, whose work though now almost entirely lost, was regarded by Read as very important. This was Bruce Turner, whom Read recalled at an exhibition of his work on his death, fifty years later. Read believed that had he not been imprisoned as a conscientious objector and his spirit broken, he could have been one of the leading artists of the period. Bill Oliver, Read's friend and art critic for the *Yorkshire Post*, believed that some of his early paintings were in style, as advanced as any of the great innovators in Paris during the same period.[12]

Almost nothing is known of Turner except that he attended Leeds School of Art. In 1911, shortly after finishing art school, he met Tom

Heron. Heron began buying his paintings and introducing him to his circle which included, according to his son, Patrick Heron, not only the Arts Club but Orage's Cafe Royale circle.[13] After the war which for him was a spell of brutal imprisonment for conscientious objection, Bruce Turner was employed by Tom Heron as a designer, along with Paul Nash and McKnight Kauffer, in his Cresta Silks factory. As a child, Patrick Heron found Turner's work inspirational. Fifty years later on his death Tom and Patrick Heron, Bill Oliver, Herbert Read and the curator of Leeds Art Gallery, Robert Rowe, arranged a posthumous exhibition of his work at the gallery. Many of the paintings were from Tom Heron's collection but some were from that of Tom Laughton (Charles Laughton's brother), his other major patron. Patrick Heron's opinion of Turner's work was that 'it was an utterly avant-garde art', 'the brilliantly original and gifted expression of a talent quite remarkably attuned to the most creative explorations of the time.'[14] He especially liked Turner's *Pavlova* which he described as a cinematic vision of the moving dancer. Though others, like his *Boxing Match*, also had this quality, most of his paintings between 1911 and 1916 were 'unusually static presentations of their subject'. Heron describes the writhing pine-trunks, the irregular lumpishness of stones in dry-stone wall, the carved contours of a sleeve or a face or a rising field, which were, he said, all simplified into forms suggestive of carved wood derived from Fauve and early cubist rhythms. He makes the very large claim that 'Turner, in those early works, showed a boldness, an intelligence, and a thoroughgoing professionalism, which it seems to me in retrospect, must have been unparalleled in the England of 1914: by comparison Wyndham Lewis seems unpainterly, and Ginner or Gilman too conservative.'[15] All the more frustrating, therefore, that so little of his work remains.

Turner's work has also been mentioned by Richard Cork who saw him as one of those minor talents 'in isolated provincial centres such as Leeds' who were fired-up by the uncompromising abstraction of Vorticism. He had 'translated the violence of a *Boxing Match* into a formalized design that conveyed *all* the dynamic vitality of its theme'.[16] However, though the signs are that Turner's use of formalized design pre-dates Vorticism, Wyndham Lewis may well have been directly influential.

In May 1914, shortly before he announced the Vorticist movement, Lewis opened an exhibition at the Arts Club of 'Cubist and Futurist' art. The exhibition contained sixty works including paintings by Cezanne, Gauguin, Bomberg, some of his own, *Marble Group* by Jacob Epstein and prominently exhibited was the work of Edward Wadsworth. The substance of Lewis's address was that at the moment there were three movements in modern art namely: futurism, cubism and expressionism, the two latter being the first in date. His hopes were that eventually the divisions would cease and that modern art would be unified – presumably in Vorticism, though the word was not used. He said that in the last thirty years academic art has been entirely discredited and that now the struggle was no longer between academics and futurists but between those who wanted to get what they could out of modern art, but remain safe, and those who sincerely believed in it.[17] In the discussion following Lewis's there was an incident which revealed the enduring indebtedness of some of the members to theosophical notions of abstraction. A Mr Howdill asked Lewis to comment on drawings of his own which, he said, were of 'thought forms', a reference to Besant and Leadbetter's concept which so fascinated Kandinsky. Lewis's blunt reply was that they were not thought forms but flowers and he could see the stalk.

How Lewis came to be in Leeds with this exhibition is not clear but both Rutter and Kramer knew him quite well at this stage and could have been responsible for inviting him. Orage himself may have been involved. Whatever, it is a mark of the significance he attached to the Club to have lectured there at such an important moment in the movement's history. Herbert Read, now twenty-one years old, was probably in the audience. In the year or so before the outbreak of the Great War, Read was therefore assailed by an extraordinary battery of aesthetic ideas, from theosophical speculation on 'thought forms', Rutter's view of 'significant form' and Kandinsky's *innerer klang*, to Fry's promotion of cubism and Wyndham Lewis's nascent Vorticism. Added to this the Club discussions which had closely followed T. E. Hulme's pronouncements on modern art in the *New Age* and Sickert's replies, were instrumental, according to David Thistlewood, in informing Charles Ginner's doctrine of neo-realism[18] which attempted a compromise between formalism and figurative art. With Nietzschean and, increasingly, Bergsonian ideas common fare in the debates, the last great upheaval of European romanticism was, in the Club, settling into the sandbed of English modernism, a romantic modernism which was to become Read's trademark.

Aesthetics were never wholly separate from politics. Though one could clearly detect a Nietzschean tendency to aestheticize politics within the Club – democracy subordinate to the most 'beautiful' ideas, for example – the reverse was also true – art must serve society: art as evolutionary or spiritually nourishing. That aesthetics and politics could be synthesized, not surprisingly, became an enduring feature of Read's thought. While he developed a critique of collectivism along the lines of the Club's non-possessive individualism, he still embraced socialism as an end. But before he adopted guild socialism 'the most logical and attractive form of socialism', he flirted with syndicalism, so recently persuasively advocated by Jim Larkin in Leeds. A few years later syndicalism also came already packaged with aesthetics in the pages of the *New Age* and subsequently in Hulme's translation of Sorel's *Reflections on Violence* in 1916. He was swept along as much by Hulme's presentation of the ideas, as by Sorel himself, but had grasped them sufficiently well to write an eloquent defence of them in the *Yorkshire Post*. In this the would-be pacifist views war as a necessary evil. He sympathizes with Sorel's view that a great European war would have the effect of accentuating class difference, because its resulting quickening of commercial interest would give the middle classes new life and spirit, while the poverty and disorganization of labour would inspire the proletariat with heroic and revolutionary spirit.[19] He concluded that syndicalism had its equivalent in aesthetics.

> It is hopeless for anyone to attempt to understand this new social doctrine unless he rid himself of every post-Renaissance humanistic prejudice in his thought. Syndicalism is not the babblings of a lot of ignorant workmen. It is the political equivalent of anti-Romanticism in literature. It is the social manifestation of anti-humanistic revolt – of a return to a classical and pessimistic conception of the universe.[20]

As he admitted later, this was virtually a paraphrase of Hulme's introduction to Sorel's work and rested on a confusion of the notions of romanticism and humanism, views he later strongly advocated, but his keenness to assimilate political to aesthetic ideas is all too plain.

Read may well have followed Hulme's Bergsonian proposal that abstractionism enabled a return to pre-Renaissance classicism for a while, along with T. S. Eliot, but there is no evidence that this was anything more than a modification of a still seductive romanticism, for the abstractionism of the Club had much more to do with romantic notions of essential spiritual realities than with classical form. However, for Read like Kramer, attention to formal criteria did produce a radically simplified art which gained much from divesting itself of superfluous detail and gushing sentiment. Also, according to Thistlewood, Read accepted the Leeds argument that evolutionary stages in the development of human consciousness were always individual achievements and that the evolution of consciousness was the chief purpose of existence, to which art was subordinate.[21] This belief, along with a reaffirmed romanticism, remained with Read for the rest of his life.

What may have pulled Read back from his flirtation with the 'classical' anti-humanism and anti-romanticism in the views of Sorel, Bergson and Hulme was almost certainly his experience of war itself. But it now appears that his exchanges with Kramer were also significant. As we have seen in the previous chapter Read had met Kramer in 1912 and from the front corresponded with him about art. In March 1918 Kramer had written him an eighteen-page letter about individual expression and spirituality to which we have already referred. Read had replied at that stage, with impeccable rigour, that the element of 'spirituality' lay not in the things themselves but in the image of the thing in the mind. Some years later, however, he confessed to having missed the point: 'I think that, in my reply to this letter, I must have defended Cubism and the formal values of art, for I was not at that time sufficiently familiar with the alternative values which Kramer was expounding – those values we now call Expressionism. Kramer is and always has been an expressionist.'[22] Read felt that because of his excessive attachment to theoretical precision, he had missed what Kramer was actually trying to tell him about his own struggles to create. He subsequently re-appraised the letter as 'a remarkable self-realisation of a young artist's aims' in which Kramer had demonstrated that he was fully conscious of the movements surrounding him but had dismissed them as inadequate modes of expression; 'He had the strength', said Read, 'in that time of disruption and reorientation, to stand on his own ground'.[23]

It was ironic therefore that Read, tainted by that 'romantic heresy' that Hulme had sniffed on the wind from Leeds in 1914, should have been the one to edit and publish the posthumous papers of the arch-classicist himself. But it does put in context his developing friendship with T. S. Eliot, who following Hulme's lead, was a self-confessed 'classicist', but nevertheless retained a strong romantic element of spiritual yearning and individualistic expression disguised in the notion of an 'objective correlative', a term he appears to have borrowed from Nietzsche.[24]

In 1914 Read had joined the Leeds University OTC along with Frank Rutter and in 1915 had been called up (the Club was divided on the issue of the war – both Tom Heron and Bruce Turner were conscientious objectors). He had published essays on Disraeli, Francis Thompson and Strindberg in the Leeds University magazine *Gryphon* and was granted a degree without taking his finals (though considering the range of his studies at Leeds, two would have been more appropriate). In 1915 he published his first volume of poems, *Songs of Chaos* and continued to read voluminously and to write to the *New Age* while at the front. He also corresponded with a fellow student at Leeds, Evelyn Roff, whom he married after the war. As the record shows, the war made an enormous impact on him for despite the bravery which earned him the Military Cross and the Distinguished Service Order, he became a convinced pacifist. He was increasingly determined to become a journalist or artist and in 1916 wrote to his Uncle Ernest that he had decided not to return to Leeds but to study art in London and Paris for a year or so.[25] Several of his drawings and paintings, which ranged from trench caricatures to abstractions were sent to Rutter's Allied Artists Exhibition in 1917 or 1918, two of which were sold.

Frank Rutter was perhaps his most important collaborator at this time and, together with Harold Gilman and Charles Ginner, they conceived the idea of a literary journal to rival the *New Age* which in 1916 Read thought, had become stale and dull partly because the best writers were in the army. The first appearance of *Art and Letters* was predictably savaged by Orage in the *New Age* causing Read to describe him/it as 'a despot among the moderns', but it found lively response from its readers and subscriptions instantly appeared. They published poetry by Wilfred Owen, Isaac Rosenberg, Siegfried Sassoon, and others more associated with Georgianism than imagism,[26] including some of the finest war poetry. Laurence Coupe notes its continued fascination with romanticism:

> It is fascinating to read *Art and Letters* simply as a student of Herbert Read's career. The key to Read's total contribution is the understanding of modernism as a further working out of the Romantic movement in poetry, philosophy and politics. The attention of the imagists to the pure, value-free image was tactically effective, he argued, but any valid aesthetic must rest on some deeper notion, such as Coleridge's 'organic form', and a wider view of poetry which recognizes the pervasive importance of rhythm – understood as expressive of the poet's relation to nature and history – which carries and synthesises the imagery.[27]

This is an important insight which presages what might be called a more mature modernism, or possibly the demise of the hard-edged proto-classicism of the pre–1920s. Though short lived, folding in 1920, it set the tone for its successor, T. S. Eliot's *Criterion*, in which modernism's romantic provenance was allowed fuller reign. Was this, in the end, the denial of modernism's revolutionary potential in favour of incorporation within a modified conservative hegemony, which was the question we began this history with, or merely the necessary reassertion of humanist cultural liberalism, which reminded the rapacious dominant order of the need to desist from its worst excesses in the name of social harmony? Perhaps it was simply the voice of the provinces quietening the roar of the vortex.

On leave from the front Read would return to the Club which although hit by wartime austerity and loss, still offered him relaxation and stimulating conversation. It now sadly lacked the energy of Frank Rutter who was sacked in 1917 from his post, allegedly over a disagreement with the art gallery committee about purchasing a Pissarro painting and Michael Sadler, who had left for India in October 1917 for an eighteen month residency at Calcutta University. Other members were also at the front or, like Bruce Turner, in prison as conscientious objectors. Ernest Forbes ('the Hermit' cartoonist of the *Yorkshire Evening News*) who had also joined Leeds University OTC with Read was severely gassed in 1918 and never fully recovered.

Tommy Lamb, the Club secretary, kept a skeleton programme of events going. In 1917 Read could have heard recitals by Kathleen Frise Smith and others, lectures by Tom Heron on 'Reconstruction', Albert Waddington on 'Creation and Recreation' and Clutton-Brock, editor of the TLS, on 'The Ultimate Belief'[28] or joined in a discussion about 'Form'.[29] Read could also have seen Kramer's new paintings and drawings at one of his regular one-man exhibitions or talk dialect with Frederic Moorman. Though Kramer too was planning to join the army he did not actually enlist until the war was virtually over, and after an unsuccessful attempt by Michael Sadleir to get him a job as a war artist he was demobbed in February 1919.[30] After the war it was Kramer's energy that kept regular exhibitions of contemporary painting coming to the Club, including those of the Glasgow Society of Artists and Painters to which he was elected as the only non-Scot in 1919.

In other leave from the front Read became increasingly integrated into Rutter's and Orage's London circles. *Art and Letters* was a success and he and Rutter, in ways reminiscent of Orage and Jackson, were planning another joint enterprise for after the war. This was the Allied Authors Association, a kind of trade union for writers based on the same principles as the Allied Artists Association. But instead of pictures, the committee of the Allied Authors Association, which would be open to anyone 'who had the cheek to claim that he is an author' would select works by members to be published. Both AAAs would get together to find premises for a gallery and a bookshop where the work of their respective members could be bought. 'The idea is the democracy of Art', said Read, and 'the show as a whole to be the centre of all modernist activity'![31] The thing ought to buzz he insisted:

> The havoc wrought by capitalism in industry and the life of the workers is obvious. The havoc wrought by capitalism in Art is less obvious but no less vital. It is not too much to say that for the last two hundred years or so, Art has been strangled to death in Europe. No work of art, however great a masterpiece it may be, has a chance today unless it can be guaranteed 'to pay.' We shall alter all this . . . [32]

Only four months before the Bolshevik Revolution everything seemed possible, but the idea came to nothing. He read Penty's *Old Worlds for New* in October and declared that it was really important: Fabian collectivism was dead and decentralization was the only way forward,

'He pleads for revolution and not the evolution advocated by the *New Age*'. But Read who was strongly in sympathy with Penty, felt that the change of heart required for his system could be brought about only by a change in the economic base of society first, and then through education. So the *New Age's* promotion of guild socialism had to be the only feasible strategy. It was fascinating that Read should have picked up on the simmering quarrel between two of the Club's founders about the function of the guilds, but hardly surprising. Penty had by this time wholly distanced himself from the guild socialist strategies then being developed by Orage. Sidney Hobson and G.D.H. Cole because of the role the political state would play. He refused the name socialist and stuck instead to nationalist, advocating a National Guilds League. It was a tragic split: guild socialism lost that commitment to art and culture that had inspired is creators in Leeds, while Penty turned aggressively against trade unionism. In the early 1930s, shortly before he died, he joined Mosley's British Union of Fascists, which by then saw him as one of its own inspirations. Guild socialism was burst asunder by the news of the Bolshevik Revolution and many of its activists left to found the Communist Party of Great Britain. However, it remained a lasting influence on the Anglican Christian Socialist movement where men like Maurice Reckitt were to assimilate it to Orage's more recent preoccupation, social credit.

In February 1918, Read's 'flagging socialist heart' had been revived by the Report of the Inter-Allied Labour and Socialist Conference even though he thought Henderson was 'too much of a TU official to be a revolutionary' and wished the British had men of the quality of Vandervelde and Camille Huysmans. However his despair of organizations and his belief in individualism was turning him steadily towards anarchism: ' "A beautiful anarchy" – that is my cry. I hate mobs – they fight and kill, build filthy cities and make horrid dins',[33] and he was beginning to feel that their salvation was none of his concern. He still felt that Nietzsche's idea of the superman and the evolution of a higher race was both possible and desirable, he even felt that eugenics or birth control was a method of achieving it (so close this individualism came to totalitarian solutions) but stepped back from the brink of advocating state action. In the end he said it was for the civilization to adapt to the culture and not vice versa; what was necessary was the *vivid* life where fully cultured individuals could make their own decisions about the future of the race.

Read was now being taken seriously by the 'older generation' of modernists like Wyndham Lewis, Ezra Pound, T. S. Eliot and Ford Madox Ford, whom he had met in Rutter's company. He had also got to know the Sitwells, Nina Hamnett and other Fitzrovian painters whom he regarded as his own generation, though the Sitwells were rather too comfortable to be really modern. In his relations with Wyndham Lewis, there was a marked mutual admiration, while Pound declared that the younger men must serve a ten-year apprenticeship before they could relieve the older generation of its burden.[34] Read was clearly prepared for it and in December 1918 wrote Orage a long piece about his experience of the war for publication in the *New Age*. Orage rejected it in that kindly, forceful way of can-do-better, insisting that as it stood the *detail* of Read's war was not interesting, what he had to bring into consciousness was what his *unconscious* thought of it all. 'What,' he asked, 'did your *soul* learn in the Great War?'[35] Read took the advice to heart and pared down his prose in the way Kramer had simplified his painting.

A war hero, he quit the army in January 1919 and went to see his old economics tutor, Arthur Greenwood, about a job. Greenwood was now in London at the beginning of a political career, as secretary to the Ministry of Reconstruction. He liked Read from the Leeds days when he had been a bright student and was especially impressed by his skills in deftly summarizing complex reports. Seeing a political future for him, he advised him to take up a post in the Labour Party which might eventually lead to a parliamentary seat (Greenwood's position as a leading freemason could probably see to it) or if he preferred he could recommend him for a promising post in the Ministry of Labour. Read opted for the latter and by the summer of 1919 had become private secretary to the Controller of Establishments. However, like his friend T. S. Eliot now working in Lloyds Bank settling German war debts, routine administrative work imposed too much on his creative energy and he grew restless. He contemplated moving back to Yorkshire as a freelance local writer but was dissuaded by Ford Madox Ford and eventually in 1922, he was appointed to a post in the Victoria and Albert Museum in the department of ceramics which was congenial to artistic and literary vocation.

His craft apprenticeship was also proceeding well. Though *Art and Letters* had folded in 1920, he continued to write for the *New Age* under his master Orage. Orage was preparing to unship his way of life in London as he had fifteen years earlier in Leeds and was looking for someone to take over his coveted 'Readers and Writers' column, if not the editorship itself. There was no lack of takers, but Herbert Read was the writer Orage chose. In a series of letters written in the summer and autumn of 1921, that Read kept because they so well illustrated Orage's 'creative conception of an editor's function', Orage trained him in the trade of literary causerie.[36] Let one thing suggest another in a kaleidoscopic manner, he advised; take pains to be right but let it look effortless; surprise readers pleasantly, but keep their attention slightly strained; announce a new critique of which the living should stand in awe; be dogmatic, concern yourself with solutions rather than problems; beware of writing essays 'Everything divine runs on light feet', neither subject nor treatment in the abstract; cultivate your relations with your unknowable readers intuitively; enlighten them about things they *think* they already know; the quality by which a book survives is *force* – like a spinning top. But, beware of the dangers of the causerie style, want of compression, on occasion, introduce a few chiselled sentences just to assure yourself that you are not in slippers automatically. And so on. Read took the medicine and was soon producing work which a delighted Orage would celebrate as 'Critical lyricism'. He was properly launched.

Thus a circle worthy of a medieval guild was completed. The craft master had passed on the secrets of his trade to the apprentice and retired to Gurdjieff's Prieurie at Fontainebleau to seek God. The apprentice, twenty years his junior, had first heard of the master in the smoky chaos of Leeds to which they had both come in their time to practise a safe profession and both had left to chance it in the metropolis. Read had joined the Arts Club which Orage had founded and been nourished by the stew of ideas and culturing he had found there. The *New Age*, reconstructed in 1907 in the Club's image and by 1912 returning the favour to the Club, was first his bible and then his instrument. The mixture of openness and dogmatism, the esoteric and the rational, the revolutionary and the conservative had proved addictive to him. Through the Arts Club, the *New Age*, Orage and the Nietzschean traces scattered along the way, Herbert t' Read(er) discovered the writer.

Herbert Read, Henry Moore and Barbara Hepworth, a postscript

Despite T. S. Eliot's opinion of him as the best poet of the First World War, Read is probably best remembered as an art critic and theorist, and one of the most persuasive advocates of art education. From the early 1930s he became the leading apologist for 'modern art', its painters and sculptors, and more than any other writer, perhaps, created a space in the national culture for its acceptance.

His more than thirty-year advocacy of the sculpture of Henry Moore was an unquestionable achievement. It would have been a triumphant conclusion to announce the work of Henry Moore, the most internationally respected British artist of the century, as the fulfilment of the Arts Club's project to relate art and ideas to life and to seek spiritual truth in non-representational art. But there are no grounds for this whatsoever. Yet there is an argument, which is reliant on seeing Read as preparing a place for the acceptance of Moore's art, as in a sense creating a language through which it could be read. More than anyone else, his books and articles on Moore have established a way of approaching the sculpture, which has rendered it accessible and, it could be said, meaningful. For Read's treatment respects both its artistic autonomy and its social responsibility, asserts that it is at the same time formally coherent and expressive, and, that it establishes a vital relationship of 'Man' to 'Nature'. Read, helped create, so to speak, an 'international' space for the acceptance of Moore's art by utilizing a language, elements of which are recognizably those of the Arts Club.

Henry Moore was born in Castleford in 1898, the seventh son of an educationally ambitious miner. At Castleford Secondary School his artistic talent was first noticed and encouraged by his art teacher, Alice Gostick, a woman in her mid-twenties who was appointed in 1910. Though Castleford is only fifteen miles away from Leeds and well-serviced by public transport there is no evidence that Miss Gostick ever attended the Arts Club. On the other hand, young women teachers sensitive to the most recent developments in art, as she was, were active committee members of the Club. It was almost impossible for her not to have heard of it or Michael Sadler and there is every reason to suppose she could have visited its exhibitions and listened to the lectures, even if she was not a member. Examples have been found, as in the case of Mary Ingle, of young women schoolteachers from Huddersfield, about the same distance, taking their friends and relations to Club meetings. Alice Gostick also took the magazine *Colour*, which had featured Jacob Kramer's work and *The Studio*, and showed them to Moore and Albert Wainwright over sunday afternoon tea.[37] She could therefore have established the earliest contact between Moore and the Club's ambience.

There was also the sculpture of the Serbian, Ivan Mestrovic, which Moore remembered his father who 'was very excited about Mestrovic's work'[38] showing him photographs of in a magazine when they were exhibited at the Victoria and Albert Museum in 1915. Though this is well-known, what has received little comment is that as a result of seeing the exhibition in London with his son, Michael Sadler invited Mestrovic to Leeds where he lectured in the university's great hall on 5 October 1915.[39] In December Frank Rutter arranged for the entire exhibition to come to Leeds Art Gallery and, as one of the pieces was broken in transit, Mestrovic returned to repair it. Might not his father or the very aware Miss Gostick, not have taken their protegé the short ride to Leeds to see the exhibition or hear the talk? Moore therefore, at the age of seventeen, had an opportunity of seeing both the sculpture and even the sculptor himself in Leeds.

Despite his enthusiasm for art, Moore's father was reluctant to let his son gamble a living from it and insisted he trained as a schoolteacher. But, in February 1917, after an unhappy spell as a student-teacher Moore joined the army and served at the front. While recuperating from severe gassing in hospital, he continued to correspond regularly with Alice Gostick and when he was demobbed in 1919, it was she who encouraged him to apply for an ex-serviceman's grant to train as a sculptor. He duly enrolled at Leeds School of Art in September 1919 where, on his own account, he spent an uninspiring two years:

> I was very glad I didn't go to an art school until I was twenty-one. Art schools especially in the provinces had a terribly closed, academic outlook. When I got to Leeds School of Art in 1919, there were students who'd gone there at fourteen or fifteen, and any excitement or freshness they might have had had been deadened or killed off.[40]

This account of his time in Leeds has often been advanced to prove that little development in his sculpture took place until he left Leeds in 1921 for the Royal College. But as we have seen from Kramer's accounts Leeds Art School was not necessarily the dull place Moore portrays. It also omits consideration of his extracurricular activities, which, as Herbert Read notes, took in visits to see Michael Sadler's collection, which excited him as his first real contact with modern art, sketching medieval carving at Methley and Adel churches and his regular rambles through Adel Woods to sketch the awesome two-piece rock outcrop heaving out of the ground like one of his recumbent figures. There was much of the material here for his early drawings and carving. Ann Garrould also felt sure that he had read Sadleir's translation of *The Art of Spiritual Harmony* and that possibly Alice Gostick had introduced him to it.[41] Would the spiritually starved art-student then have missed Jacob Kramer's talks and demonstrations of Kandinsky's themes at the Club in 1920? It is suggestive that his own relatively few discussions of art were often framed in terms current in the Kandinsky/-Sadler/Kramer discourse. For example, David Thistlewood remarks:

> On the subject of abstraction Moore had said in 1930 that an art devoid of representational imagery, analogous with music and architecture, could be regarded as a legitimate objective. In 1934 he had enlarged this argument, suggesting that non-figurative art might offer deeper penetrations into reality than might the imitative.[42]

This defence of abstraction as analogous with musical and architectural form, and the notion of a deeper reality underlying phenomenal forms and unrevealed by naturalistic art, was, as we have seen, perfectly familiar to Arts Club members at least fifteen years earlier and its theosophical/symbolist version ten years earlier still. Moore was not compelled to have learned it in London though it may have there he became conscious of it.

So the question arises when did he meet the critic who deployed this vocabulary so effectively, Herbert Read? Although their paths *might* have crossed in Woodhouse Lane, in the Leeds Art Gallery, before Sadler's paintings or in the rooms of the Arts Club, both have seemed reluctant to date their friendship to before the 1930s.[43] Read had of course left Leeds in the same year as Moore began art school in 1919, and conventional accounts say they first met only when Read settled in Hampstead. Certainly by 1935 Read had introduced Moore to Hulme's notes on Worringer, which had had such an impact on himself some ten or twelve years earlier.

Though Read's influential two-volume introduction did not appear until after World War II, the first of Read's persuasive accounts of Moore's work, *Henry Moore, Sculptor: An Appreciation*, was published in 1934, and revised and expanded in 1938. Various articles, catalogue introductions and appreciations continued the work of establishing him and his reputation was consolidated in his 1965 publication, *Henry Moore A Study of his Life and Work*. A valuable summary of his appreciation of Moore was published in The *Philosophy of Modern Art*, 1964. Though he would no doubt say that Moore's work spoke for itself, Read's remarkable achievement was in inscribing his fellow Yorkshireman into a tradition which could be read as at once English and international and at the same time romantic but also classical. It was both particular and universal; the particular English sensibility, grown from and reflective of the national soil but universal in that it suggested both *ancient* (as in medieval carving and the ethnic primitivism of African and South American masks) and *modern* (as filtered through the work of Brancusi, Rodin and Picasso).[44] It was romantic in as much as it expressed the soul and the emotions but its truth to geological and human forms and relations suggested classical discipline.

Read was nevertheless obliged to support this persuasive aesthetic discourse by an appeal to moral purpose, which was to say that Moore's art was conditioned by 'a certain philosophy of life' a deep rooted humanism held 'in common with artists of his type throughout the ages.'[45] The substance of this deep-rooted tradition in which Moore was written, was the familiar Arts Club doctrine that 'behind the appearance of things there is some kind of spiritual essence, a force or immanent being which is only partially revealed in actual living forms'.[46] This suggested simplicity of form rather than complexity and perhaps was to explain why Moore rejected the constructivist path of modernism in favour of the organicist or as he was to put it (unsatisfactorily for Read) the *vitalist*. (It is worth remembering here that Hulme's dismissal of Kandinsky's tendency in 1914 as 'a romantic heresy' was precisely to prevent such a deviation. But perhaps even more noteworthy is that the forms of the landscape which Moore so movingly invokes in his work do not for a moment include Sadler's chimneys on the horizons of Morley and Pudsey, no less than the silent power of dynamoes and generators.)

In a devotional moment Read quoted Moore's 1934 *Unit One* pronouncement as having a special significance which should be carefully pondered. While Moore makes prominent use of the term 'vitality', not an Arts Club word, it is important to note just how much the key words 'expression' and 'spiritual' are brought into play and how the familiar rejection of naturalism in favour of a deeply penetrated realism, is used. Moore argues that a work of art must have a vitality of its own, not merely a reflection of life but in itself (what Kandinsky might have called 'inner necessity'). He calls this a 'spiritual vitality' which was not merely 'beauty', went deeper than the senses and is essentially the function of 'power of expression'. The object of art, as understood here, could be read as a powerful restatement of the Arts Club's manifesto, in Moore's words: 'not just the exercise of good taste, the provision of pleasant shapes and colours in pleasing combination, not a decoration to life, but an expression of the significance of life, a stimulation to greater effort of living'.[47] This statement can be interpreted as belonging to a continuity of thought or, to use Raymond Williams's term, 'structure of feeling' generated in the Arts Club and it is in turn important to note how Read interprets it. He rejects any idea that it might have been a product of a 'learned' discourse: 'These are' he says, 'the words of an artist – an artist who has had no truck with metaphysics or aesthetics, an artist who speaks directly out of experience'. How then did the words frame themselves?

One suggestion is that Moore, no simpleton, was so deeply saturated in the dominant aesthetic discourse of the time that the words he used seemed to have been imbibed with his father's tobacco smoke. What I am suggesting is a modified version of this, namely: that a specific local, *provincial*, conjuncture was forced by a particular relationship of the Arts Club with the *New Age*, cut with the Sadlers' promotion of Kandinsky's painting and ideas and its atavistic recalling of local theosophical doctrine (as exemplified by Wyndham Lewis's interlocutor) and over-determined by Kramer's forceful yoking of currents in Russo-Jewish mysticism. Read, more analytically close to the threads of discourse, a wordsmith rather than a sculptor, created a synthetic resolution out of them which could agree a 'meaning' with Moore's actual creations, partly because the syntax and key terms were already common to them both.

However, Read chose not to see it this way because he was convinced that in some mysterious way the artwork itself possessed the power, the life, or the vitality of the artist, that reification was a fact and not merely an explaining myth. Thus even the atheistic Read was forced back into what in the end was a numinous justification of the work: 'The work of the artist of Henry Moore's seriousness', he said, 'is always religious: though it is not necessarily Christian or sectarian, but rather mystical . . .'[48] Undoubtedly Read was struggling for a non-religious interpretation of the religious in this passage. He talks in other places for example of the 'the mystery of life' or 'the psychic depths of the organic process' or how the theological word *numinous* would be more exact but it seems to me that his struggle is actually frustrated by the limits of the discourse itself. The terms 'spiritual' and 'expression' were, and possibly still are, too powerfully held within the grip of an essentialist usage to be released into the arena of structurality that Read was attempting. Thus, ultimately to find meaning in Moore's work he had to resort to what Hulme had called 'the spilt religion of humanism', the religion of humanity, with all its stereotypes of earth-mothers, primitives and paternalism.

Somewhere in that long shadow cast by Henry Moore wasn't there a woman sculptor experimenting with abstract forms too and wasn't she at college with him in Leeds and London? Ah, yes, Barbara Hepworth, mentioned just three times in all in the *Philosophy of Modern Art*. She was quite good, wasn't she? Read thought a letter she wrote to him in 1948 was 'a very revealing explanation of the creative process'. Surprisingly, she did not appear to need to invoke the religious at all. Working realistically or abstractly, she said,

> It all feels the same – the same happiness and pain, the same joy in a line, a form, a colour, – the same feeling of being lost in a pursuit of something. The same feeling at the end. The two ways of working flow into each other without effort . . . Working realistically replenishes one's *love* for life, humanity and the earth. Working abstractly seems to release one's personality and sharpen the perception, so that in the observation of life it is the wholeness of inner intention which moves one so profoundly: the components fall into place, the detail is significant of unity.[49]

One can't help feeling that this language of feeling in explanation of what an artist is doing might have offered a way out of the discursive impasse of the magisterial and portentous rhetoric of spirituality, but then she always kept quiet when the men were talking. After classes at

Leeds Art School, she caught the 9.30 train home to Wakefield each night and probably never went to the Arts Club at all.

Notes

1. Letter to *New English Weekly*, 15 November 1934, p.112.
2. The detail of Read's life that follows is drawn from Robert Parrington Jackson's 'Herbert Read The Yorkshire Background' in *A Tribute to Herbert Read 1893–1968*, Bradford Art Galleries and Museums, 1975.
3. Herbert Read, *The Contrary Experience*, Secker, London, 1973, p.200.
4. Raymond Williams, *Writing in Society*, Verso, London, 1984, p.181.
5. Read, *Contrary Experience*, p.62.
6. It is not known whether the choice of the hero-potter's name was influenced by the charismatic leader of the Yorkshire WEA, George Thompson, whom Moorman knew well, but the blunt Yorkshire artisan who rouses Arthur's knights to throw off the yoke of the oppressor bears a strong resemblance. Moorman, legend has it, was also responsible for rediscovering *Ilkla Moor bar t'at* and popularizing it at a WEA summer camp.
7. Frederic Moorman, diary entry, 25 February 1913, Special Collections, Brotherton Library, Leeds University.
8. Read, *Contrary Experience*, p.103.
9. *Yorkshire Post*, 26 June 1913, p.11.
10. *Yorkshire Post*, 24 June 1913, p.11.
11. Ibid.
12. *Yorkshire Post*, 10 October 1964, p.15.
13. Patrick Heron, Introduction to Bruce Turner Exhibition Catalogue, Leeds Art Gallery, 1964, p.3. Tom Heron later served on the editorial board of Orage's *New English Weekly*. He also shared a friendship with T. S. Eliot through this and Anglo-Catholicism.
14. Ibid., p.4.
15. Ibid., p.7
16. Richard Cork, *Vorticism*, p.277.
17. *Yorkshire Post*, 18 May 1914, p.8. See also Cork, p.332. Cork also notes with metropolitan surprise how well-informed the *Yorkshire Observer* was on the state of modern art, quoting its comment of 15 June 1914, that 'Futurism in this country had hardly been born before it has budded off into Vorticism'.
18. Thistlewood, *Herbert Read*, p.27.
19. Read, *Contrary Experience*, p.205.
20. Ibid.
21. Thistlewood, *Herbert Read*, pp.32–33.
22. Herbert Read in Millie Kramer (ed.) *Jacob Kramer a Memorial Volume*, E. J. Arnold, Leeds, 1969, p.3.
23. Ibid.
24. Cf. Friedrich Nietzsche, *The Birth of Tragedy*, Anchor Books, New York, 1956, p.103. Eliot also appears to have borrowed Nietzsche's discussion of *Hamlet* in these pages.

25. These biographical details are taken from 'Herbert Read – His Life and Work' in *A Tribute To Herbert Read.*
26. Laurence Coupe, in Alvin Sullivan (ed.) *British Literary Magazines, The Modern Age 1914–1984*, Greenwood Press, Connecticut, 1986, p.32.
27. Coupe, p.33.
28. What it was was not reported, but Frank Rutter noted 'In one of his charming essays the late Mr Clutton Brock referred to a growing belief that man is a machine "and should be conscious of the fact that he is one". Jacob Epstein expressed his consciousness of the fact in his statue *The Rock Drill*, but before August 1914, the masses were not familiar with this belief, and his sculpture consequently was not understood' (*Evolution in Modern Art*, p.124).
29. Information from an Arts Club syllabus for February-March 1917, found in Leeds City Reference Library (cat no. T LIL Arts). It lists the committee as Miss S. A. Foster, Mrs. H. H. Greenwood, Miss L. Wilkinson, Frank Dean, Tom Heron, H. Hilton, W. P. Irving, C. F. Smith and J. Harrison. By occupation they included three school-teachers, two small clothing manufacturers, an artist, an insurance manager and two unknown. Mr. Hilton, a German Jew, had changed his name from Hildesheim in 1915.
30. Roberts, *Kramer Documents*, p.40.
31. Read, *Contrary Experience*, p.106.
32. Ibid.
33. Ibid, p.124.
34. Ibid., p.141.
35. Letter from Orage dated 17 December 1918, quoted in Wallace Martin, *The New Age Under Orage*, p.280.
36. Quoted in Wallace Martin, p.52.
37. Ann Garrould, 'Henry Moore 1898–1922', in *Henry Moore Early Carvings 1920–1940* catalogue, Leeds Art Galleries, 1982, p.15.
38. Ann Garrould, p.15.
39. Sadleir, *Sadler*, pp.265–267.
40. P. Jones (ed.) *Henry Moore on Sculpture*, Macdonald, London, 1966, p.32.
41. Ann Garrould, p.18.
42. Thistlewood, *Herbert Read*, p.99.
43. See Moore's contribution to *Homage to Herbert Read*, Canterbury College of Art 1984, p.40: '(we had known) each other from early years, we were dear friends for more than fifty years'.
44. A similar strategy had been used by T. S. Eliot in relation to the work of Wyndham Lewis, whom he described, in review of *Tarr*, as possessing the energy of the caveman and the thought of the modern: 'The artist, I believe, is more *primitive* as well as more civilised than his contemporaries, his experience is deeper than civilisation, and he only uses the phenomena of civilisation in expressing it. Primitive instincts and the acquired habits of ages are confounded in the ordinary man. In Mr Lewis we recognise the thought of the modern and the energy of the cave-man': *The Egoist*, September 1918, p.105.

45. Herbert Read, *The Philosophy of Modern Art*, Faber, London, 1969, 2nd ed., p.203.
46. Ibid.
47. Ibid., p.207.
48. Read, *Philosophy*, p.212.
49. Quoted in Read, *Philosophy*, p.98.

CHAPTER TWELVE

Epilogue: Experimental Drama

By the close of the First World War experimental art and ideas had suffered severely, but Leeds's modern romance was not yet ended. Though many of the Club's leading figures, like Herbert Read and Frank Rutter, had by 1919 left town, Michael Sadler was freshly returned from Calcutta, and Jacob Kramer was actively campaigning against the pogroms in Poland with his expressionist posters (*How Long, O Lord, How Long?*). Sadler's return had quickened the pulse a little, as we have seen, with the town hall panels scheme but it had misfired. He had one last adventure in civic art before he too finally packed his bags for the more congenial southern climate of Oxford.

In memory of the many young men of the university who had died in the war, he commissioned a war memorial from the sculptor Frank Gill. The design he chose was of Christ driving the money lenders out of the temple, which Gill had submitted to London County Council in 1916. The council had turned down the design, on the grounds, Gill thought, that they had taken fright 'or were insulted at the awful suggestion that London were a commercial city or that England were a Temple from which a money-changer or two might not be missed.[1] Sadler must surely have known there was a lighted fuse here but maybe he misjudged the times in attempting another skirmish with the philistinia.

Gill's own motives for constructing a war memorial on a not obviously related theme were mixed. The idea had come to him, he said, when having his portrait drawn by William Rothenstein. He believed that it was the one occasion on which God in the form of Christ had used violence to enforce his will, not on the surface a particularly apt subject, since it appeared to be justified violence in the last resort. What made it even more bizarre was that Gill appeared to have approved the German destruction of the cathedral of Rheims with its wonderful medieval statuary, because the commercial system had changed temples from places of worship into treasure houses. The German guns were God's means of depriving the money-changers of the temples of France: 'The sculptures of Rheims are gone. Good. If we cannot construct a Christian Europe in this age, we are certainly not fit to be the guardians of the evidences of the Christian Europe of the past. The whole thing should be wiped out. It would be completely just.'[2] He further urged that artists should be God's instruments in completing the cleansing of the temples. So it is hard to avoid the conclusion that Gill wholeheartedly embraced the Nietzschean view of war as the catastrophic cleanser, the bloody purging, and in this respect his sculpture had to read as a celebration of war rather than a memorial to the dead.

With the exception of Christ's timeless priest's alb, Gill had decided that the memorial's figures should wear modern dress, adding that they should represent 'Leeds manufacturers, their wives & servants' and confessing, with relish, 'as "citizen of this great country" and a member of Christ's Bride, I rather like the job, the revolutionary job of turning out the money changers'.[3] Christ wears thick boots because he is 'a Priest for ever'. His lash is a seven stranded cord for each deadly sin with which he is portrayed driving out a fashionably dressed woman, her pawnbroker husband, his clerk carrying his account books, a politician and two financiers. A seated woman holding a child to her breast looks on knowing 'that this is not her funeral' and a dog with a burning brand in his mouth, the eponymous *domini canes* of his order, the Dominicans, capers after him. Running along the cornice of the sculpture is a biblical inscription in Latin from *James* V.1 which, translated, reads 'Go to now, you rich men, weep and howl in your miseries which shall come upon you. Your riches are putrid'. In a letter to his friend Father John O'Connor, Gill's comment was, 'If they stick that they'll stick anything.'[4] A further inscription from *John* II.15 describes the scene.

Even before it was unveiled, on 1 June 1923, on the outer wall of the great hall in University Road, a storm of protest was predictably gusting through the newspapers. Diplomatically abroad, Sadler missed it. Though they argued that the crude modernism of the design desecrated the memory of the fallen, it seemed more likely to Gill that those who found it so distasteful, bore a little too close resemblance to the silk-hatted millionaires and their molls bending under Christ's lash, many of whom had, in truth, done very well out of the war.

On his return Sadler also seemed to enjoy the spectacle of civic discomfiture and, though cursing Gill in private for having altered the design, rose magnificently to defend the work in public. But his defence of Gill's modernism was again curiously paradoxical. What he admired in it was its old/newness, its contemporary archaism, its 'Gothic' vitality. In its design, he said, 'ancient and modern things are combined'.[5] It was a Christian view of war derived from the gospels where Christ recalled the words of the Hebrew prophets who 'bode men do righteousness and thoroughly execute judgement between man and his neighbour'. Though he did not condemn 'honest traffic', it was a reminder that sacred things (such as higher education) should be kept apart from monetary gain, a point even more forcefully reiterated by

Wilfred Childe and J. R. R. Tolkein in their own contribution to the debate.[6] For Sadler this signified the timelessness of the moral law.

Despite this effort to justify modernity in terms of the immemorial and soothe the impassioned civic breast, Sadler was not aided by Gill's own comments. He had published and circulated a little pamphlet, which in a flippant and almost childish way interpreted the memorial's meaning in the ways already outlined.[7] But in a more serious and disturbingly incoherent passage, he pointedly comments on the nationality of the money-changers, as if sensitive to comments on that point. Their nationality, he says, is 'not definitely ascertained' . . . 'There are money-changers in all civilized countries, and modern war in spite of the patriotism of millions of conscripts and their officers is mainly about money – for the "white man's burden" consists chiefly in the efforts to bestow the advantages of "civilization" upon "those unenlightened 'natives' who happen to be living where gold or oil is available" '.[8]

Despite the orthodox socialist analysis of this odd passage, it is difficult not to hear a discordance in what it is saying. In the first place, it does not correspond with his earlier Nietzschean viewpoint, which celebrated war; secondly, though ultimately about imperialism, *this* war was not a colonial war and the 'white man's burden' piece is simply a non-sequitur, but, perhaps most importantly, by suddenly raising the issue of nationality, the natural assumption that these are English money-lenders becomes problematized. What is he trying to avoid saying? What reading, by clumsily discouraging it, is he actually emphasizing?

It seems not impossible that the relief could have been perceived by the large Leeds Jewish population as antisemitic. This would have raised the subliminal issue of 'nationality'. Already sensitive to their 'foreignness', Leeds Jews had not only anglicized their names because of widespread wartime persecution, but had experienced terrifying race riots in 1917[9] and were still agitated about the Polish pogroms. Was the pawnbroker's sign, then, held between the woman and the second man of the relief, a reference to 'Jewish' finance? There were after all no Leeds 'manufacturers' represented, despite Gill's apparent intentions and in the original biblical story Christ was perforce driving out Jewish money-changers. His references to re-Christianizing Europe and his justification of violence cannot have eased Jewish feeling one whit. It could just be Gill's insensitivity, but the discordance of this passage and the ambiguity of the relief itself, suggests the powerful antisemitic undercurrents in Roman Catholicism of which Gill himself was only half-aware (though not so his friend Chesterton), and which contributed to the storm over its installation.

Ironically, Sadler even more than Gill was held to blame for what seemed a wilful insult to the honest burghers of Leeds. Various attempts at sabotage were made and Sadler's successor, the conservative, James Baillie, even gave orders to the university's gardeners to plant ivy in such a way as shortly to obscure it, but as Michael Sadleir reported, 'once the ivy began to flourish an unknown hand snipped the climbing stems with scissors'.[10] Though the incident caused a rift between Sadler and Gill whom he later described as a 'vain poseur', Gill's relations with other Arts Club members, especially Father O'Connor, improved. His Ditchling Press published O'Connor's translation of the French Catholic philosopher, Jacques Maritain's text, *Art Scholastique* in 1923 to which Gill provided an introduction, while O'Connor himself converted G. K. Chesterton to Roman Catholicism in 1922. However if Gill did betray any conscious antisemitism, it was not apparent to William Rothenstein, who as principal of the Royal College of Art had warmed to Henry Moore's advocacy of Gill as professor of sculpture. Gill also never lost contact with Alfred Orage, with whom he had been involved in the Fabian Arts Group days and had contributed to the *New Age*. As a testament to him, he carved the headstone for his grave in Hampstead cemetery. As for the university's war memorial, after many years of neglect, when the soot of Leeds manufacturers succeeded where James Baillie's gardeners failed, it was finally cleaned up in 1961 and installed in the entrance to the new arts block of the university where, though it can now be seen, is studiously ignored by undergraduates ignorant of its subversive iconoclasm.[11]

Everyone was changing places. In the metropolis, Herbert Read was now writing Orage's 'Readers and Writers' column in the *New Age* but had declined to take over his editorship. In this respect, the apprentice failed his master, but Orage was anyway casting off the *New Age* skin to enter his next reincarnation as Gurdjieff disciple. Sadler had been offered the mastership of University College, Oxford and, despite malicious rumours of incompetence, went gladly to assume it, leaving the Arts Club, as Orage had once left it, and was now leaving the *New Age*, in the hands of lesser mortals.

In Leeds, Kramer who had decided at last to stay put, in fact sustained the last years of the Arts Club by organizing a number of exhibitions of contemporary art, including that of the Glasgow group, already mentioned, in 1920 and the Contemporary Art Society in September-October 1921, which had been offered to the Leeds Art Gallery but had been turned down by the committee. The last known exhibition at the Club which included work by Augustus John, Wilson Steer, Muirhead Bone, Spencer Gore, and Kramer himself, as well as Matisse's *Paysage* and *Walk by the Sea* and Cezanne's *Bathers* and a landscape, was in July 1923, probably shortly before the Club closed. An 'American auction' of its books was its final event sometime in the winter of 1923.

Lamented only by a few writers and artists the Club slipped from the stage. In the absence of Orage, Sadler and Read, and the deaths or disability of many other members in the war, Kramer's attempts to keep it alive failed. But from its ashes a number of cultural institutions immediately sprang, including Kramer's famous Yorkshire Luncheon Club. Welcoming the initiative, Sadler wrote to Kramer: 'You are carrying on the tradition of the Leeds Arts Club, which had a brilliant flickering history and inheartened, if it did not help to breed, a number of eminent men – Orage and Frank Rutter and many others whose names are held in honour'.[12]

A number of literary groups, which more or less owed their origins to the Club sprang up in its wake. Geoffrey Woledge, who was then an undergraduate, poet, and later librarian at the London School of Economics, had joined the Club in 1920 or 21, when, he says, it was only a shadow of its former self. One of its less formal successors, he remembered, was the Wednesday Club presided over by the Tory Catholic poet William Kerr, a brilliant and provocative talker as well as Wilfred Childe, fellow Catholic poet and the socialist economist H. D. Dickenson 'a forceful but candid disputant', which met in the *Cock and Bottle* or the *Guildford*.[13] There was also Murray's Bitterary Club, a largely journalistic association, which met in the *Packhorse* in Briggate.

However, although as we have seen, its discursive formations in art theory were to be lingeringly resonant, the most enduring institutional tradition of the Club was the drama. In a kind of Sophoclean moment the Club's 1907 gigantic offspring, the Playgoers Society, was reunited with and all but consumed its parent sometime after the war and at the beginning of 1920 became the basis for the Leeds Arts Club Dramatic Society.[14] Under the enthusiastic direction of its leader, Charles Frederick Smith, who shortly became the Club's secretary, it staged a number of impressive dramatic productions. His own plays, *The Vessell of the Land* and *Mother Modernises* were both well reviewed in December 1920 and there were also productions of John Galsworthy's play *The Pigeon* and scenes from *Othello* and *Much Ado About Nothing*. Geoffrey Woledge himself produced Synge's *Shadow of the Glen*, though wholly unaware of the fact that Synge himself had overseen its production at the Club fifteen or sixteen years earlier. Its successes inspired the dramatic section to secede from its ageing parent and form a repertory company, thus, according to him, mortally weakening it.

The impetus to form a separate theatre company had been present at least since the visits of Shaw and Yeats to the Club in 1905, 1906,

1909 and 1910. Both had argued that the stage was the most potent medium for the propagation of ideas through its power to dramatically condense and mythicize social issues. While Shaw perhaps more pragmatically saw immediate and local issues as available for dramatization, Yeats had the grand mythic vision of national regeneration. When Shaw had addressed the Club in 1909 on his campaign to create a National Theatre he had also, as we have seen, proposed a regional network of municipal theatres which could feed off it. But in particular, he said, there should be in Leeds a theatre which belonged to, was maintained by and endowed by the people of Leeds, 'not carried on with a view to commercial profit, but with a view to the edification and recreation, in the strictest and most solemn sense of those words, of the rising generation of Leeds'.[15] Holbrook Jackson had reinforced this in his interview in the *Yorkshire Observer* in 1911, after his talk on Maeterlinck, where he claimed that the British stage was so thoroughly degraded by finance, that any attempt to alter it from within was bound to fail. The only hope for the drama in Leeds was for Leeds people to create their own drama and, inspiring other Playgoers Societies, bring about a renaissance of drama throughout the country.[16] After his three years in London literary circles, Jackson was even more committed to the belief that a national resurgence had to be provincially based.

In the intervening years the Arts Club and the Playgoers Society appear to have met with considerable success in inducing national managers to bring serious plays to Leeds and in encouraging the performance of opera. They had also arranged talks by leading playwrights and critics like John Galsworthy, Ashley Dukes, G. K. Chesterton and Hilaire Belloc. As we have seen, the insurance manager, W. P. Irving had been largely responsible for organizing this side of the Club's affairs. But it was now Charles Frederick Smith who stepped into the limelight.

In 1921 Michael Sadler, himself, had been involved in discussions to launch a repertory theatre, mentioning £40,000 as a necessary sum, but they came to nothing. His thoughts were stimulated by the successful production by Edith Craig of Shaw's *Blanco Posnet* for a Leeds Repertory Season at the Albert Hall in November 1921 almost certainly organized by Smith, who then engaged her as artistic director of his newly formed Leeds Art Theatre.

The Leeds Art Theatre was the first of the new theatrical movements to emerge from the Club's declining years. Smith, son of a successful Leeds shirtmaker, was its inspiration and almost certainly its financial backer, while the business manager was L. B. Ramsden, son of the musical instrument retailer Albert Ramsden. It was an extremely impressive venture into experimental theatre performing plays by leading European and American contemporaries as well as home grown playwrights which attacked naturalist conventions and experimented with expressionist effects. Edith Craig, the daughter of Ellen Terry and sister of Gordon Craig, was very impressed by the quality of people she had to work with. Though she felt that she had never been in a town where social distinctions were so marked, she found many enthusiastic amateurs 'ordinary workaday folk' who needed help, who knew their Shaw backwards and had good taste.[17]

The Art Theatre's policy in choosing its plays appeared to be threefold: first, European drama, second, leading English drama and third, locally written and produced plays. In the opening season, 1922–1923, plays were performed by Maeterlinck, Strindberg, Chekov, Quintero, Suderman and Chapin as well as Shaw, Drinkwater and George Calderon (Ashley Dukes's predecessor as *New Age* drama critic). In addition there was 'a new work of considerable promise' by Beatrice Mayor, a dialect play by Yorkshire poet J. R. Gregson and an opera by Dame Ethel Smyth directed by herself.

The following season the list was even more ambitious, including works by Eugene O'Neill and Hugo von Hofmannsthal and a version of his novel *The Secret Agent* by Joseph Conrad. In all, eleven plays were performed between 19 October 1923 and 8 April 1924, including those performed by three visiting companies, Hull and Sheffield Playgoers Societies and the Everyman Theatre, Hampstead. The list included: Hofmannsthal's *The Great World Theatre*, Conrad's *Secret Agent*, Bjornson's *Beyond Human Power*, Martinez-Sierra's *The Romantic Young Lady* (trans. Granville Barker), Wilde's *Lady Windermere's Fan*, Galsworthy's *Punch and Go*, Anatole France's *The Comedy of the Man who Married a Dumb Wife* (translated by Ashley Dukes), Gordon Bottomley's *King Lear's Wife*, O'Neill's *In the Zone*, and *A Night at an Inn* by Lord Dunsany. It was a bold list for a provincial town; Wilde was still regarded as scandalous, Bjornson, Ibsen's contemporary, Martinez-Sierra and O'Neill were virtually unknown, Conrad's play was surrealistic and disturbingly evocative of the prewar anarchist terror and Dunsany was associated with the Irish Nationalist movement. Though well-established as a novelist, John Galsworthy's recent social and moral dramas were less well-known and more directly critical.

Undoubtedly the most extraordinary achievement was the production of Hofmannsthal's *The Great World Theatre*. It was only the second time this modern medieval mystery play had been played since it was produced by Max Rheinhardt in Salzburg in 1922. Hofmannsthal had written it for the Salzburg Festival and it confirmed his movement towards a Roman Catholic religious art with social significance. Since it was set in a church, the Art Theatre staged it at Saint Thomas's church in Holbeck, an industrial suburb of Leeds south of the river, rather than at their usual venue of the Albert Hall in the Mechanic's Institute. It ran to rapturous audiences from 7–19 January 1924 and because of its success was held over another week; Madge Pemberton, its translator, and various other celebrities attending the performances in what was a permanently full house. The *Yorkshire Post* reviewer commented on the atmosphere of deep reverence and spirituality in which the play was performed and the excellent articulation of the local players. He picked out as 'a masterpiece of characterization', the ex-Arts Club member H. Hilton's Beggar and congratulated Edith Craig on such a superb production.[18]

Spurred on by this success another ambitious season was planned for 1924–25. The venue was transferred to the Blue Triangle Hall leased from the YWCA in Cookridge Street opposite the Mechanic's Institute. Its programme was again threefold: European drama included Ibsen's *Berkman*, Pirandello's *If You Think So* and Gogol's *Inspector General*; British drama: Lady Gregory's *Mirandolina*, Chesterton's *Magic*, Masefield's *Philip Thinking* and Yorkshire plays by Frederic Moorman, Dorothy Una Ratcliffe and Lascelles Abercrombie, who wrote the footnotes for the programme. Lascelles Abercrombie (1881–1938), who became professor of literature at Leeds University in 1922, had an established reputation as a Georgian poet and man of letters and became a significant figure in Leeds literary life during the decade. He wrote that 'one more successful season and we feel that the Leeds Art Theatre will be firmly on its feet and will have taken its proper place in the forefront of experimental theatre in the country'.[19] Lennox Robinson, the London *Observer*'s theatre critic, agreed, writing, 'we are proud of the fact that the renaissance of the drama has been largely fostered by the provinces' and, of the production of Ibsen's *Berkman*, he had seldom enjoyed an evening more. Further, the company was to break into the commercial theatre with a production by Edith Craig of Shaw's *Androcles and the Lion* at the Grand Theatre (legend, 'the home of pantomime'). The programme noted ominously that its success was vital to the future of the Leeds Art Theatre. Thus it seemed that the utopian aims of the Arts Club's founders Orage and Jackson and its inspirers Shaw and Yeats appeared at last to have flourished in an enthralling display of socially vital drama in the heart of the city.

Smith intended the Leeds Art Theatre to be 'the Experimental Theatre', a permanent place for dramatic expression and experiment. Its ends were neither to simply entertain nor educate but 'a spiritual quickening, a mental stimulating, an increased consciousness'.[20] The drama had the direct appeal only shared by music and ceaseless experiment was essential to discover the new forms relevant to the postwar world. Even in England, always 'the last to feel a new artistic impulse' a new mood was emerging. While he acknowledged the triumph of Ibsenian realism over the prevailing nineteenth-century sentimentalism, even this once liberating form had become imprisoning. On the continent there was 'a riot of new forms all seeking in some way to express the spirit of the play', like Ernst Toller's *Machine Wreckers*. Also the technical excellence of stagecraft had outstripped the dramatist 'and all manner of curious and impressive effects are possible in a well-equipped Theatre, which demand a new type of play for their exploitation'.[21] The Art Theatre aimed to present the work of the younger generation of European dramatists who were alive to these new possibilities. In a remark reminiscent of Billy Jones's 1905 description of Leeds as 'a provincial city largely given over to the more sordid business of life', Smith said the enthusiasm of the amateurs' work for the Art Theatre, was inspired by the 'leaven' which was 'required in a solid commercial town to humanise its crude industrialism' and concluded, 'A community with pretensions to culture cannot dispense with a live theatre without ultimate detriment to its civic life'.[22]

The financial side of the theatre was in the hands of L. B. Ramsden, its business manager, and run on a subscription basis. The season's subscription for all seven plays was 25s. (£1.25) for area seats, 19s. (95p) for the centre gallery and 10s.6d. (52.5p) for the side area. There was no advertising and the promoters relied on subscribers to attract others by word of mouth. The 1923–24 programme printed a list of 383 subscribers from the previous year (of whom at least twenty-three had been prominently identified with the Arts Club as speakers or committee members, including Orage's theosophical schoolteacher colleague, Miss A. K. Kennedy, Billy Jones, the newly knighted Michael Sadler, 'Father Brown', Frederic Moorman, Tommy Lamb and one of its last members, Geoffrey Woledge). There were apparently 700 other subscribers who had joined under the auspices of the Leeds Schools Music and Drama League (which may have been a form of covert municipal subsidy).

The private subscription basis and the choice of plays betrays the mark of the London Stage Society, a group formed by Fabians at the turn of the century to perform plays fought shy of by the commercial theatre because of their political standpoint or shocking content. It had been responsible for the first production of some of Shaw's more pointed plays including *Mrs Warren's Profession*, *Man and Superman* and also *Captain Brassbound's Conversion*, which was included in the Art Theatre's first season. Later the Stage Society was a testing ground for the Royal Court Theatre under the management of Harley Granville

Barker. Its founder, Frederick Whelen, and Milicent Murby had both spoken at the Arts Club or Playgoers Society in previous years and the whole venture was closely related to Orage and Jackson's Fabian Arts Group. Initially determinedly experimental, by the 1920s it had become rather staid, which made the Art Theatre's radicalism, more dedicated to contemporary European theatre than to Fabian drama, even more significant.

Like all experimental institutions it was short-lived and closed after only its third season. Smith was certainly keen to find a more popular audience for serious theatre, so while earnest but safe amateur operatics and drama was retained by Ramsden as the Little Theatre, Smith launched what was intended as a radical/popular theatre, the Leeds Civic Playhouse in the Art Theatre's original home, the Albert Hall of the Mechanic's Institute. Seen as a public intervention, this was an even more ambitious venture than the Art Theatre, though the compromise for popularity may well have harmed the original cause.

The most remarkable aspect of Smith's Civic Playhouse was that entrance was entirely free, the only free theatre in existence, it claimed. A silver collection, however, was taken at the end of the performance with contributions asked for according to means, but this still inserted a principle of access not possible in the commercial theatre. There was also a subscriber system for those who could afford to support the venture financially. Their privilege would be to book seats in advance, but even so, a 'democratic' figure of 6s. (30p) for the series of five productions was not unreasonable. Inevitably the poor would have to sit at the back, but at least they would not be turned away. Smith had secured the patronage of more than thirty city dignitaries including its Lord Mayor, the four MPs, the Vicar of Leeds, the surgeons Maxwell Telling and Berkeley Moynihan and many alderman, councillors and city guardians. He himself was the director, as he was also now, of the York Everyman Theatre. The style of the programme bore his unmistakable imprint: 'The Theatre is the most potent cultural influence of modern life. Its appeal is immediate and direct and no community can allow it to be debased or disregarded without permanent injury.'[23] It should be as much the city's responsibility as the provision of libraries and art galleries. The word 'civic' in the title was used to show that it should have a wide appeal and not simply be a theatre for the cultured few but also in the hope that 'some day its efforts to provide Drama for the masses will justify direct municipal support'. Similarly 'playhouse' was preferred to 'theatre' because they intended to make it a place of entertainment and amusement for all those who loved the art of the theatre.

The opening season offered less serious productions alternately with advanced drama. Smith thought that although the chief use of the drama should be to enlarge the mental life, it also had to cater for the emotions, and no play was of any value if it did not hold the audience's interest. Half the programme, therefore, was occupied by comic or light drama, including a translation from the Italian, Laurence Housman's *Little Plays of St Francis*, a Yorkshire comedy by James Gregson, Shaw's *Caesar and Cleopatra, Overture* by Sutton Vane and a poetic comedy from Petronius's *Satyricon* by another Leeds writer, T. Wray-Milnes, but even these were substantial pieces. The more serious matter was nonetheless ambitious for that, including Sophocles *Oedipus Rex*, the fifteenth-century morality play, *Everyman, The Machine Wreckers* by Ernst Toller 'the most hopeful portent that has emerged out of German theatre since the war', a Norwegian play (author not given) called *The Witch*, a Hungarian play called *Liliom* which had been produced by Edith Craig and Elmer Rice's caustic expressionist drama, written in 1923, *The Adding Machine*. There was certainly no concession to provincial taste in this selection, and Smith's strategy was to hook the newcomers on the comedy in the hope that they would come to the serious stuff in their own time.

Since, alone among theatrical ventures, the Playhouse survived through the twenties and thirties, the strategy was successful. At length it achieved Smith's objective of municipal support in 1945, when it was taken over by the local authority and, ironically, renamed Leeds Civic *Theatre* – on the aldermanic assumption, presumably, that if it's good for thee it can't be any fun! Nevertheless, following the Second World War it housed a number of small amateur groups including a remarkable all-Jewish company, The Proscenium Players, directed by Alex Baran whose production of *The Dibbuk* received acclaim.

But not everybody felt that the Playhouse had maintained its commitment to experimentalism and by the early thirties a dissident group argued that, regrettably, economic necessity had compelled the Playhouse to adopt the policy of the professional Repertory Theatre, which though understandable had left a vacuum for serious experimental theatre. So began the short but exotic career of the last of the Arts Club's progeny, the Eyebrow Club.

The Eyebrow Club was opened on 11 October 1931, in one of the Playhouse's rehearsal rooms in Dorrington Street behind Miles's Bookshop in Woodhouse Lane. The ceremony was performed in the best possible taste by Sybil Thorndike, recently relished in Leeds as Shaw's 'Saint Joan', in one of the rare serious productions to be mounted at the Grand Theatre, and who had returned to have her portrait done by Jacob Kramer. She was followed by Edith Craig who read letters to her mother, Ellen Terry, from G. B. Shaw.[24] The sign of the raised eyebrow denoted the fact that it was an avant-garde theatre dedicated to plays banned by the censor, but the connotation of *highbrow* was not entirely lost on its members. It advertised itself as the only theatre club of its kind outside London and seems to have been unique. The rooms were in a basement of a warehouse, expressionistically decorated and hung with Kramer's paintings. Although its small auditorium contained one of the most advanced lighting boxes available, the means of powering its unique revolving stage consisted of a man on his back pushing with his feet to the hissed urgings of offstage thespians. The club immediately became the centre of Leeds Bohemia where distinguished patrons like Berkeley Moynihan mingled with artists and actors, watched risqué plays and indulged in the odd spot of illegal gambling.[25] At Dickie's Bar you could get cheap meals and interesting cocktails at almost any hour of the day and meet some of Leeds most exotic characters.

The Club saw itself as carrying the torch for minority experimental drama and, in the somewhat overblown rhetoric of enthusiastic amateurs, declared that 'Only such organisations as the Eyebrow Club can hope to keep alive and vigorous these vital contributions to Drama without which the Theatre cannot advance or rejuvenate itself from time to time' though of course 'This does not infer nor imply that the spices of frivolity, nonsense, and sophistication must be entirely absent from our programmes . . . Only that which is stale, flat, and profitable need be taboo' etc. etc.[26] Though its reported aim was to perform 'plays of exceptional quality but limited interest' a good deal of its productions were little more than agreeably smutty farce.

Its boldest venture may have been a production of *Salome*, starring Sheila Tomey, then fresh out of high school and at eighteen the youngest Salome ever. Certainly the press went wild, hailing it as the Club's most ambitious production and greatest success. In the scramble for seats blood may well have been shed. A disgruntled PBM of the *Mercury* wrote

> The play drew to the Leeds Eyebrow Club last night one of the biggest recorded audiences. So big indeed, was the audience that the present writer's seat was 'jumped' and in any event could not be approached owing to the crowd. He was consequently condemned to stand in some discomfort at the back of the theatre with only occasional glimpses of the stage. From these glimpses it seemed that the performance was well up to the standard set by the Eyebrow Club . . . As Salome, the dancing princess daughter of Herodias, Sheila Tomey very successfully encompassed a part that demanded unusual versatility.[27]

Cheerfully echoing these sentiments another reporter, with a better view, wrote that *Salome*

> stands or falls by the figure of the impulsive sensual daughter of Herodias. Herod himself may be a brilliant character study but without an actress who is not only intelligent but physically suited to the title role, the tragedy becomes meaningless. Miss Tomey missed nothing of the physical possibilities, and her interpretive powers were remarkable.[28]

Miss Tomey went on to have a long and successful career in amateur dramatics, but unlike her son who is a member of the musical comedy troupe 'The Grumbleweeds', never left Leeds. Other members like Basil Lord went on to Brian Rix Whitehall farce while Hamilton Dice went into television. Miss Tomey also remembered a play about Nazis and Jews by Alan Peters being performed. The Club also held playreading circles and occasional symposia. One such 'Banquet of Philosophic thought' was entitled 'If I were Mussolini' in which several well-known persons were asked to give their panacea for present national and international problems if they possessed dictatorial powers. One of those who agreed was Leeds novelist, Lettice Cooper, but sadly, Dickie's promotion of gambling was an excuse for a police raid and the Club was closed in March 1935.

With demise of the remarkable Eyebrow Club in 1935, the avant-garde tide in Leeds ebbed but left small but prolific seas of Bohemia washing round public houses like Whitelock's and the Victoria. Jacob Kramer's Yorkshire Luncheon Club which met in Whitelock's in Briggate continued as a centre of discussion and a meeting place for artists and writers. Old Arts Club members like Father O'Connor, Tommy Lamb and Denis Botterill, who ran the Swan Press, now mixed with a new generation of writers sucked in by tales of ancient glory. One of these was the playwright R. C. Scriven who was 'more in awe of Jacob than a minnow of a whale', of whom he wrote:

> About him he drew a great circle into which he drew every big and little fish of those shoals which crowd the sea-coast of Bohemia. Whitelock's in Briggate was his footstool, and over the Victoria he threw his washpot. There was scarcely a celebrity of the stage who, passing that way, did not gladly swim into Jacob's aquarium of big and little fishes. Eminent men in the worlds of medicine and music found their relaxation in what was not a club but a fellowship.[29]

So the traditions of the *old* Arts Club as it came to be known were sluiced out in a silver age twilight in the pubs and bars of the town with Kramer their master of ceremonies. This was Leeds's Fitzrovia, a cultural underground that persisted remarkably through the thirties and forties and into the fifties, where town and gown interfaced, sometimes with a frisson of criminality. In the fifties it offered spiritual sustenance to the producers and directors of the newly established BBC studios and eventually writers like Stan Barstow, John Braine, David Storey, Keith Waterhouse and the poet Tony Harrison.

Undeniably, the work of the Arts Club and its successors had changed the cultural climate. By World War Two, theatre in Leeds was well-respected; under John Rothenstein and Philip Hendy the Art Gallery built up a substantial modern collection, and music advanced well beyond light opera. This change is attested by the poet Vernon Scannell, who after exemplary service in the war deserted when it was over and had to go underground. In London a friend advised him to go north and hide out in Leeds. Leeds?

> Perhaps I had a mistaken notion of what Leeds was like. People from down south seemed to think it was nothing but factories, fish-and-chip shops and Rugby League football. Not at all. It was culturally stimulating. There was a university, regular symphony concerts at the Town Hall, lunch-time recitals at the museum, a repertory cinema and a theatre where first-class companies tried out first-class plays before the London run. There were plenty of civilized people. Away from the flashy distraction of the metropolis I would be able to concentrate on being a writer.[30]

Here he thrived. He became part of Scriven's Bohemia where through Kenneth Severs, then editing a magazine called *Northern Review*, he met Professor Bonamy Dobree, still connected with Orage's *New English Weekly*, Herbert Read and T. S. Eliot, and G. Wilson Knight who encouraged his poetry and let him in to their lectures. And here he would have stayed had not the long arm of the law felt his collar. He was court-martialled and, as desertion was clearly a form of madness, convicted to a term in a military mental hospital. On his release he returned to Leeds and tried to start again, meeting up again with R. C. Scriven, Wilfred Childe, John Braine and Robin Skelton. With this stimulating company, he hoped to settle but for him, as for Orage and Jackson and Read and Rutter, Mary Gawthorpe and Storm Jameson and so many more, its nourishment, at first so satisfying, now only famished the craving:

> I still found beauty in its ugliness, I still felt gratitude for its warmth, but it seemed smaller now and too constricting. There were times when I felt I had to get away from its voice, its manners, its features. Some of my friends seemed too readily satisfied with what Leeds could offer them, assuming too easily that no other place could offer them more. Some, without knowing it had been defeated by Leeds, been reduced and exhausted by it, afflicted by that most insidious of provincial diseases, a complacent impotence. I felt disloyal and a little guilty, but I had to go. And of course there seemed only one place to go to and that was London.[31]

Of course.

Notes

1. Quoted in Malcolm Yorke, *Eric Gill, Man of Flesh and Spirit*, Constable, London, 1981, p.221.
2. Ibid.
3. Ibid., p.222.
4. Ibid.
5. *Yorkshire Post*, 26 May 1923, p.8.
6. Letter to the *Yorkshire Post*, 30 May 1923, p.4. Tolkien, who had been appointed to replace Frederic Moorman after his tragic death in 1919, and Childe, said that Christ condemned the placing of commercial values where only spiritual values should reign.
7. Eric Gill, 'War Memorial', Welfare Handbook No. 10, Ditchling, 1923.
8. Ibid.
9. Nigel Grizzard, *Leeds Jewry and the Great War*, Jewish Historical Society of England, Leeds Branch, 1981. In this pamphlet the author mentions large scale anti-Jewish riots in Leeds beginning Sunday 3 June 1917 and lasting for three nights. On the first night 1,000–2,000 youths, many from the Bank attacked Jews, smashed shop windows and looted them. The following night 3,000 repeated the scene and stoned police. Jewish leaders complained of police delay and inaction; the riot was never properly investigated and 'for many better forgotten'.
10. Sadleir, *Sadler*, p.329.
11. But not all the professorial staff, one of whom in a recent *Leeds University Reporter* thought that since the university was now holding out the begging-bowl to the very figures Gill would drive out, it was time for the sculpture to be removed once and for all.
12. Michael Sadler, letter to Jacob Kramer, 5 December 1934, Brotherton Collection, Leeds University.
13. Presidential address to the Thoresby Society, Clarendon Road, Leeds 3, given by Geoffrey Woledge, printed in Annual Report, 1980 and interviews with G. W. November-December 1983.
14. *Yorkshire Evening News*, 16 April 1920, reviewing its production of *The Younger Generation*, notes its formation a few months earlier.
15. *YWP*, 18 December 1909, p.17.
16. *Yorkshire Observer*, 14 January 1911.
17. Interview with Edith Craig in *Yorkshire Evening Post*, 3 November 1921, see Leeds newspaper cuttings, vol.10, p.30.
18. *Yorkshire Post*, 14 January 1924, p.11.
19. Leeds Art Theatre programme, 1924–25 season, Leeds City Reference Library.
20. 'A New Era in the Theatre' in Leeds Art Theatre programme, 1923–24 season, p.10, Leeds City Reference Library.
21. Ibid., p.11.
22. Ibid., p.12.
23. Leeds Civic Playhouse 1925 programme, Leeds City Reference Library.
24. *Yorkshire Evening Post*, 5 April 1975, p.2.
25. Most of the information on the Eyebrow Club is drawn from interviews with, and the scrapbook of, Sheila Colville (nee Tomey), 385 Otley Road, Leeds 16, to whom I am extremely grateful. Ms Colville remembers Moynihan frequently invited members to his own home, where amongst

other things he refused to keep white linen – all tablecloths, napkins and sheets were black.

26. Fragment of a membership circular, signed by Claude Pycroft, 1933 in Sheila Colville's scrapbook.
27. Sheila Colville's scrapbook.
28. Ibid.
29. R. C. Scriven in Millie Kramer, *Kramer*, p.24.
30. Vernon Scannell, *The Tiger and the Rose*, Hamish Hamilton, London, 1971, p.34.
31. Ibid., p.106.

CHAPTER THIRTEEN

Conclusion: From Leeds Permanent to National Provincial

So what do these tales of provincial life signify? Are they merely the mock-heroic exploits of small-town characters or a major vein in the pulse of the national life? Alfred Orage and Herbert Read were undeniably influential figures in the national culture, while Michael Sadler was a major art patron and leading educationalist. Jacob Kramer was probably an undervalued painter as Francis Spalding has argued, and Henry Moore's reputation continues to grow. Did the Leeds Arts Club significantly influence the character of modern, or modernist, English culture or was this a school of provincial supermen whose wings would have melted in the heat of the metropolis, as Kramer feared his would?

In attempting to answer these questions, I have tried to argue that the modernism of the Club and its leading players was heavily romanticized in character. It opted for a modernity based on spiritual values, medieval organicism and a supercharged romantic individualism. Many of these characteristics can also be identified in the national culture where certainly by the 1920s, the more hard edged, deconstructive and technological modernism of the continent had been decisively rejected in favour of an expressionist 'vitalism'. But a national culture is composed of many contradictory strands in which the notion of single individuals or even groups imposing their will on something so *nebulous* is not acceptable. It could never be, for example, Bloomsbury writ large. What this study has discovered, or slightly illuminated, is part of this nebula, a network of communication and influence.

But the very size of the metropolis, London, and its concentration of institutions of commerce, government, culture and of course wealth has had an unbalancing effect on the rest of the country, the 'provinces', the 'regions'. As early as 1822 William Cobbett had perceived it as a 'Great Wen' sucking in the life and vitality of the country for its own ends, and it has become a persistent image. Provincial vitality however has been essential to the national health.

If London had too much of everything, Leeds, it appeared to the founders of the Arts Club, had too much of just one thing and too little of everything else. It was, said Albert Waddington, Nietzsche's inverted cripple, a city overbalanced by an excessive concentration on industry and commerce and too little art and culture. Its citizens lacked, in an image that reflected the desired pastoral economy, nourishment. Art and culture should nourish the vitality of the spirit as commerce fed the body. But while some metropolitan institutions such as the Fabian Society and the Arts Guilds offered partial models, inspired by the Celtic revival. German romanticism, oriental philosophy and the pre-capitalist past, the Club itself set the tone inviting Chesterton, Shaw and others to add sparkle. The national culture, as filtered through the metropolis to the provinces, itself appeared as academic, lacking in vitality, prosaic, introverted and decidedly provincial.

When Orage and Jackson decided on a Club as the best means of regenerating the culture life of the town they were of course choosing an approved kind of organization in Leeds. The Arts Club precursors included the Philosophical and Literary Society, which from the 1830s aimed at self-help for the town's entrepreneurial and engineer aristocracy and its offspring, the Mechanics Institute, which intended to pass on the fruits of science and rationality to the labour aristocracy of artisans. Later in the nineteenth century the socialist Clarion Club and the central ILP Club in Briggate, which Orage had joined, were important centres of discussion which brought working-class militants, both men and women, into contact with socialist middle-class intellectuals like the Ford sisters and Edward Carpenter. In addition there were the Fabian Society branches which sprang up briefly in the 1890s which were Jackson's preferred sphere of activity, while for Orage what were most important were the lodges of the Theosophical Society. In the TS's mode of discussion of contemporary events and issues in the light of the 'higher' knowledge, there was the model for the Arts Club. Orage's role in the TS was already that of an established seer and in many ways the Club's early rationale was for the promotion of his ideas. Carried over also from TS was more than a whiff of freemasonry and indeed a number of freemasons, which may have added to its cultish and semi-mystical atmosphere.[1]

But the Club was also a relaxed and informal meeting place open to both men and women and tolerant of race and creed which, as Millie Price says, was both a leftish base for the more culturally aware ILPers and Fabians and also attractive to the more open-minded of the local business community. Fundamentally, from the founders' point of view, it practised and developed the art of conversation. Although all discussions were led and nationally known speakers often took the rostrum, the ordinary members were themselves encouraged to debate the issues and take issue with the speaker. This was inherited from the democratic environment of the socialist and working-class movements rather than, say, the Phil and Lit where only polite applause was expected. The great men invited to the Club were expected also to join in the Club's socializing after the talk as the Leeds socialist pioneer, Alf Mattison, remembered in his memoirs:

> To the Club in Blenhein Terrace came G.B.S. and both my wife and I still have vivid recollections of his being seated and for the space of an hour and a half listening to the conversation he rattled off, the while we stood and sat around him. One or two more venturesome plied G.B.S. with questions – leading him on to our enjoyment. Oh but it was a treat of a time to see the big man sat at ease in the Club's armchair and playing upon us like a fiddler on his strings. It was amusing to see the expressions on some of his auditors faces. Some of them sat at his feet and open mouthed drank it all in. Others with a look akin to awe; the more knowing, like myself gave each other a knowing wink.[2]

Club members were also expected to lead discussion groups and give lectures fostering a self-confidence and the skills of reasoned argument which were to stand many of them in good stead in public life. As Mary Gawthorpe attested, the Club was a source of nourishment to those who were politically active, both in terms of being a place to recoup energy and to gather new ideas for the struggle. For the businessmen it was the only culture-club in town where mixing with artists and writers with dangerous ideas offered more than a frisson of excitement.

Part of the Club's excitement was its dedication to 'life as experiment', to quote the title of one of Holbrook Jackson's talks. No Victorian shibboleth, it seemed, was safe while Orage and his companions were speaking. Gerald Cumberland remembers Orage's 'divine flapdoodle' as rather dangerous, but the received nostrums of art, religion, morality and sex were there only to be questioned and, if found lacking, discarded. All values were to be transvalued and nothing that was neither useful nor beautiful was to be allowed through the doors. All were held to be utterly responsible for their own lives as condition of their emancipation from conventional morality and in place of duty there was only the aweful but inspiring infinity of existential choice.

This experimentalism, as we have seen, extended from the ontological and theological (despite or perhaps because of the large number of young Anglican clerics in the Club) into painting and drama. In painting the virtues of continental and English impressionism were both celebrated and contested, firstly by voices from the arts and crafts movement who would have nothing to do with 'easel art', and then contemporaneously with continental developments, by the advocates of post-impressionism. A curious exception to this experimental modernism was cinema and photography. Though the photographers Frank Sutcliffe and F. H. Evans both exhibited their work and spoke about it, and competitions were held between painters and photographers as to whom could best capture a landscape, the Club it seemed was suspicious of the camera as a means of art. More significantly it ignored cinema altogether, despite the fact that Leeds was, through the inventions of Louis Le Prince, whose studio had been literally four doors down Blenheim Terrace in what is now the BBC television studios, a leading centre of film technology. There was not a little of Ruskinian snobbery in this pointed aversion to such a popular form (though later the Eyebrow Club did in fact plan to have an Art Cinema). Club members, like the best avant-gardistes found it hard to see spiritual values in something that so obviously bore the taint of commercialism;'popular culture' is a term that would have made no sense to them.

Following Nietzsche they regarded the drama as the most potent cultural weapon. Initially the Club's approach had been inspired by the Ibsenian revolution in realism, more particularly by Shaw's interpretation of it. Because of Ibsen's fierce dramatizing of domestic and social relationships, it could not be separated, of course, from their life experimentation. The 'Life Force' was for many members not simply a metaphor. This preference for realism in the drama coexisted, paradoxically, with a predilection for the mythicism of Wagnerian opera. Again for many Ibsenian/Shavian realism was but the other side of the coin from Wagner's vast mythic structures which suggested the hidden agenda of the collective unconscious. Wagner's adaptation of Celtic myths like *Parsifal* and *Tristan* anyway linked him with the theatre of Shaw's *Man and Superman* and more especially with Yeats whose resignation from the casual comedy of the time in discovering the folk beauty (and Nationalist potential) of the Irish peasant was all part of the great revelation they expected from the Celtic Renaissance.

Later, in the Playgoers Society it appeared as if this radical thrust were being dissipated into simply getting serious theatre and opera to visit Leeds, but it is clear that the campaign for a locally representative drama and a revival of the dialect drama were also successful innovations. The keenness with which the Club took up modern European drama, partly through the championship of Orage's *New Age* drama critic, Ashley Dukes, was notable. Finally the bold attempts at staging expressionist and modern mystery plays showed that the centrality of experimentalism was also the key to the Club's successors. Playwrights like Ernst Toller and Hugo von Hofmannsthal were hardly known outside Germany in 1922, while Eugene O'Neill and Elmer Rice were the leading edge of the New York avant-garde (even then crowding into Orage's lectures above Jessie Dwight's Sunwise Turn bookshop on Forty-fourth Street).[3]

Alongside this experimentalism another concept was being pursued: citizenship, a political novelty for a newly enfranchised working-class and a desired goal for the excluded class of women. Citizenship, for Holbrook Jackson at least, was to be one of the consequences of freedom from Victorian moralism. It did imply duties, but they in turn were the consequences of democratic reform. Its focus, in that fluid turn-of-the-century Fabianism, was less the national state than the local state, and for Jackson and more particularly Waddington it was the city. For them, citizenship was bound up with creating the 'City Beautiful', a two-way process in which beautiful cities were the materializations of beautiful ideas, and ideals, which, in turn, produced beautiful people. The city was the building block for the decentralized state, autonomous and democratic, it would be a noble, dignified and above all healthy environment for its citizens of the future.

Naturally, the urban models were Italianate and medieval, mystical unities where the lives of their citizens were to be nourished and symbolized. Not unnaturally, their leading advocates were architects but modern technology, however, would take second place in the new utopia to the skills of the craftsman. The transition from arts and crafts to Bauhaus made by Gropius and Kandinsky was too late for them. Percy Robinson for example proposed a scheme of out-of-town cottages for workers' families with gables and gardens (though in the shape of Quarry Hill flats, in the thirties, Leeds did erect the most celebrated development in mass housing in Europe. Its damp and crumbling remains were pulled down forty years later). In campaigning for the city beautiful the Club operated as a practical non-party intervention into municipal politics which became the model for later civic societies and environmental groups. Its own offspring, the Leeds Civic Society, had an important, though largely conservatory, role in the town's affairs.

The social stratum of the Club and the *New Age* was the creative and educational lower-middle class. More precisely it was composed of professional workers at a time of crisis of status of the professions. Teachers, architects, journalists, typographers, illustrators, photographers, professional painters and musicians and clergymen made up the bulk of the membership. The crisis these occupations were undergoing was because of late Victorian demographic and technological changes. Changes in working practices introduced by transmission belt production, Taylorism, and the conversion of previously self-employed groups of the old petit-bourgeois into wage-earners[4] had created virtually a new social stratum, what Orage called the 'professional proletariat'.

The teaching 'profession' had undergone elephantine development as a result of the 1870 Education Act and the board school system, Leeds having the largest board outside London. Teachers were now being drawn from the class that was being newly educated like Mary Gawthorpe and Orage himself. Many middle-class graduates like Cyril Pease also came into the profession for ideological reasons and membership of socialist organizations was common. Thus a compounding of craft protectionism against dilution in the quality of teachers and policized trade-union militancy made teachers a highly volatile group. (A rally against Balfour's 1902 Education Bill brought between 70,000 and 100,000 onto Woodhouse Moor, the demonstration taking two hours to move through town, where it was addressed by sixteen MPs speaking from six platforms.)[5]

With the rapid growth of municipal functions and the colossal building programme in Leeds between 1860 and 1910, which had replaced almost all the buildings in central Leeds and added entire new suburbs, architects too were sensitive about their status. The building was often unplanned and poorly controlled and in the municipality untrained engineers were often given responsibility for building design. The Club contained both architects of an established reputation like W. H. Thorp and younger members like William Alban Jones who had had no formal training but who considered himself an artist. The formation of RIBA to assert professional status was strongly supported in Leeds and Yorkshire generally and led by Club members like Percy Robinson. Arthur Penty and Albert Waddington, also architects, campaigned politically for the rights of the craft enshrined in a guild system, inscribing the fight for professional status into a formation which was both medieval and modern. As we have seen this strengthened the prevalence of a desire for medieval models in architecture and city planning.

Journalists and allied trades were also suffering from trade disruption as the result of modern printing processes and new cartels in publishing. In the *Yorkshire Post* Leeds had an almost unique well-established local Tory paper of national significance, owned by Yorkshire Conservative Newspapers until quite recently. During most of the Arts Club's life it was under the relatively liberal editorship of Ragland Phillips and was only too keen to publish in full the reports Orage and Jackson sent in, as was the *Leeds Mercury*, Baines's well-established and even more highly celebrated Liberal newspaper. Both papers reported the early years of the Club at length. Orage and Jackson were freelance contributors to these papers and other members were like Herbert Thompson, art critics or like James Dodgson (Kester) and Ernest Forbes, cartoonists. While some, like Alf Mattison were photographers, the expansion of reprographic technology had opened up new areas of practice for painterly skills, for example Jacob Kramer had for a while followed his father into colouring photographs for a living, and painters now found employment as poster makers, a help in Kramer's anti-pogrom campaign. For all these the Club's debates about representation, realism, naturalism, symbolism and expressionism, were in a sense in-service training. They learnt about new techniques, new movements, techniques of simplification and expression and so on, which were all relevant to the business of writing and illustrating newspapers and journals.

A last category perhaps surprisingly suffering from a crisis of status was the clergy. Though a large number of clergymen were still the second or third sons of the well-to-do who were not much good at law or unfit for the army, increasingly they were young well-educated radicals who had come to Leeds with a sense of mission to the poor and the working-class. Already well-known as a centre of high church Anglicanism, or Anglo-Catholicism, Leeds also benefited from the establishment of Bishop Gore's Community of the Resurrection in Mirfield which became a centre of Christian socialism. (Its links with the university were to create several generations of radical theological scholars including Trevor Huddleston and David Jenkins.) This generation of clergymen was keen to reestablish the clergy as a missionary cadre with radical objectives and democratic methods. Very early they understood the significance of guild socialism and through Neville Figgis developed a theory of the pluralistic state to underpin it. They also took up Orage's promotion of Douglas's theory of social credit with alacrity and later became prominent supporters of Orage's second journal the *New English Weekly*, as of course did T. S. Eliot. An interesting sidelight is the interest of some of them such as Rev. Arthur Lee in theosophy, spiritualism and Buddhism. This in turn led to a renewed concern for Christian mysticism reflected in Lee's editorship of the *Oxford Book of Mystical Verse* (1917). The relative absence of non-conformist clergy and the involvement of several Roman Catholics like Father J. P. O'Connor tends to confirm this view.

Thus the centring of the Club's membership in the newly emergent professions or in older occupations with a newly developed professionalism, indicates the constituency for his journal the *New Age* for which it was in many senses a test run. The *New Age* in turn crystallized its ideology. Orage's transition from Leeds club to London journal, from a local to a national movement, was made possible by the size, composition and geographical location of Leeds. As a place to begin, Orage had to have a town large enough to attract a wide variety of professions, yet small enough for a representative number to be able to meet in one place, to be of a geographically unified nature and to have an identity as a town uncompromised by symbolic references to the national. All of which rules out London, and possibly even Birmingham and Manchester, as a base, though not, for Jackson, his home town of Liverpool.

Leeds too had the geographical advantage of being centrally located at the crossroads of major road, rail and canal communications, in a fiercely independent county proud of its difference but unlike Bradford or Sheffield not dominated by a single industry. Through its textile manufacturing it was also more dependent on women's labour and their early militancy and unionization suggested alternatives to domestic servility.[6] It was a major financial centre dependent on 'mental' labour. It bore an historic burden. Its ageing nineteenth-century Liberal élite's gestures towards civic consciousness seemed like a task in need of completion.

Ideologically, as we have seen, three main strands, or alternatively three overlapping discursive systems seem to have been combined. These are firstly, the strand of nineteenth century 'cultural criticism' articulated in various ways by Ruskin, Carlyle and William Morris, secondly, late nineteenth-century spiritualism, which combined elements of translated eastern mysticism, the theosophy of Blavatsky, Annie Besant and Cyril Leadbetter, Blake and neo-Platonism and thirdly, Nietzsche and high German romanticism. A fourth but subordinated strand was Fabian social democracy.

From the first strand the general critique of capitalist commercialism was taken over wholesale and a general over-valuation of the medieval period as a golden age. Ruskin's architectural critique, especially the 'Nature of the Gothic', his advocacy of medieval guilds were important especially as taken up by William Morris and given a socialist slant. Morris's socialism seems to have been a starting point but there seems to have been a general disillusion with collectivism and democracy. Ruskin and Carlyle's generally aristocratic and hierarchical structure appealed more. Carlyle's hero cult also may have contributed to a latter-day critique of socialist egalitarianism. Morris's arts and crafts emphasis was initially strong but this declined with the onset of post-impressionism currents when industry was, perhaps only temporarily, seen as having its own aesthetic virtues.[7] The Club's tone of political radicalism has its origin in this discourse rather than in democratic socialism. However, the Club's most immanent presence was Edward Carpenter whose socialist mysticism most obviously linked the first discourse, cultural criticism with the second, spiritualism (and had a seminal influence on American anarchist and avant-garde movements).[8]

The spiritualist strand provided an understanding of transcendentalism, the notion of man as permanently becoming and never achieved, and the unconscious, a level of deeper and hardly understood motivation. It was a kind of religion in which the life force substituted for god. Though one can be grateful that it discarded the junk phenomena of seances and astral tripping and so on what was retained was a notion of the force of the unconscious. In pre-Freudian days it was clearly a way of investigating unconscious activity and its forms. Of great significance for the Club's aesthetic development was the belief in 'thought forms' which became integrated into a perhaps crudely symbolist aesthetic. This aesthetic was in turn used as a critique of naturalism, though not realism, from which naturalism was sharply distinguished. Thus the average academy picture and the 'photographic' naturalism of the late nineteenth century were attacked for paying attention only to surface details and neglecting the *underlying* reality. Some were also attacked for superficial prettiness which the artist had mistaken for the deeper quality of beauty. Spiritualism was therefore a mode of entry into the underlying 'reality' of life and furnished a quasi-religious vocabulary of appreciation such as the notion of 'spiritual values'. So when Sadler later introduced the Club to Kandinsky's theory and practice of artistic abstraction, it was immediately assimilable. They saw it, as indeed did Kandinsky, as a kind of symbolism in which colours and shapes all had immanent meanings which could be read if one had the code.[9] That this code was only revealed to the elect or literally the *illuminati* (because of their auras), was silently assumed: the elect would know the meaning and would know each other.

The previous strands were brought together into a new synthesis by the third strand 'Nietzscheism', though this in turn relied on a reading of the other two. In Orage's presentations Nietzsche continued the critique of commercialism in highly dramatic and poetic terms, rubbished conventional 'Christian' morality and insisted on transvaluation. The beyondman or superman advanced a highly developed individualism which reinforced spiritualist notions of reincarnation and transcendence. The superman also had resonances with Carlyle's 'hero' (and as we have seen with the literary heroes of Victorian popular novels).[10] It also fitted well with both the notion of the elect drawn from spiritualism and of non-hereditary aristocracy drawn from cultural criticism, 'aristocracy' and the romanticized vision of the middle ages was current in Nietzsche too.

Nietzsche also offered a tone which was not the muted and 'gentlemanly' discourse of the Victorian ruling class, but the rage of those oppressed by its stupidity and its members unearned status and privilege, the tone of those who would get their desserts through merit rather than birth. The Nietzschean superman constructed by Orage was by turns a rampaging lion and good shepherd. At the most extreme end of this doctrine men had the right, nay the duty, to be tigers and to shoot tigers, to advance their own interest and take no heed of the wishes of others. Paradoxically, they did this for 'humanity' that the race might the sooner evolve to a higher level of being. While the Club members were to be its advance guard, its 'socialist aristocracy', the heroic role for women was not so clear cut; handmaiden to the warrior did not obviously appeal to all. Women were developing their own agenda and Ethel Annakin, Mary Gawthorpe and the Ford sisters were prominent in the struggle for women's rights.

Orage used Nietzsche to construct a critique of Fabian collectivism. One of his first papers to the Fabian Arts Group was called 'Nietzsche contra Socialism', written in Leeds and since lost. Though its justification of individualism found little support amongst the Fabian old guard, it was widely influential on the cultural groups on its fringes. It was central to the political ethos of the *New Age*, found its acme in the shape of Victor Grayson in 1908, was denounced by Keir Hardie and intensified the Webbs' motivation to establish the *New Statesman* to counter the *New Age*'s influence. The new wave writers around the *New Age* or readers of it from Wyndham Lewis, through Edwin Muir to Herbert Read and D. H. Lawrence have all acknowledged Nietzsche's importance to them. Nietzscheism also shaped Edward Carpenter's mystical millenarianism into something resembling a political programme by offering concrete evolutionary goals. Orage's opposition to Lloyd George's National Insurance Act, for example, was on the grounds that it would maintain the working-class in a condition of permanent wage-slavery, by increasing its dependence on the capitalist system, whereas if all supports were taken away it would be forced to pursue its own class destiny of overthrowing capitalism and releasing workers from bondage.

There were aesthetic implications too. Nietzscheism offered an evolutionary aesthetics, which measured the value of artistic works in terms of their ability to advance the evolutionary consciousness – though this gave way before the more complex psychological modifications offered by Bergson. The romanticism associated with Nietzsche's writings had a permanent effect on Herbert Read and many like T. S. Eliot borrowed from Nietzsche apparently without acknowledgement. When Sadler and Rutter brought post-impressionist ideas to the Club in 1912, they already found a well-established and sophisticated aesthetic debate in progress. Though Wassily Kandinsky's approach owed more to theosophical thought than Nietzsche, they owed a common debt to earlier German romanticism and eastern mysticism. For many, like Herbert Read, Kandinsky's kind of abstraction was more digestible than the 'constructivist' or 'structuralist' views of Fry and Hulme precisely because they assayed these romantic debts.

I have argued that ultimately this, for want of a better word, 'romanticized' modernism may have had a greater implantation in modern English culture than the other, 'structuralist', kind. The work of its most celebrated poet, T. S. Eliot, bears its traces as does that of its most respected sculptor, Henry Moore. It may even be possible to talk of a romanticized modernism in politics too, in the shape of guild socialism. The effect of this theory, while only glancing the trade union movement, was all pervasive on the radical intelligentsia (a word first coined in the *New Age* before World War One) from R. H. Tawney, G. D. H. Cole and Archbishop Temple to the founders of the Communist Party, Dutt, Wilkinson and Gallagher. In its advocacy of a modernized version of a medieval political settlement it suggested a functionalist sociology and laid the theoretical groundwork for contemporary state corporatism (Christian versions of which are found in Eliot's *Idea of a Christian Society* and *Notes Towards a Definition of Culture* and less pleasantly in *After Strange Gods*). A version of this corporatism spread even to Franco's Spain and Peron's Argentina through Orage's political columnist Ramiro de Maeztu.[11]

I have tried also to show an almost fated correspondence in the careers of Alfred Orage and Herbert Read: their common rural Yorkshire origins, their emigration to Leeds where each 'found' himself in urban distress, Read's baptism in the Club Orage had founded, apprenticeship on the *New Age*, his rites of passage, and Orage's transmission to him of instruments of power before his 'ascension' and rebirth in the arms of Gurdjieff, is almost biblical narrative. Though Orage's second coming, as founder editor of the *New English Weekly*, lacked the spectacular success of his *New Age* era, it prompted new considerations of 'Englishness' to which Read and, more profoundly, Eliot in his *Four Quartets* contributed. What seems to be common in the career of all three is the *strategic* quality of their writing particularly in the use of the placing essay, the most achieved prose form of each of them. Each of them used the essay form as a causerie in which honed paragraphs delivering decisively authoritative judgements were the core. No justification was offered and no tentativeness allowed: the style was the authority. This style was Nietzsche's and it was introduced to an English audience by Orage in *Nietzsche in Outline and Aphorism*. The strategy of the essays of making the modern acceptable by inserting it into a tradition, and then revaluing that tradition in its light, was brilliant sleight of hand, truly idealist but profoundly conservative. While Orage utilized it in a cultural campaign of 'forward to the past', Eliot used it to prise open a place for his own poetry and, I have argued, Read for the sculpture of Henry Moore.

The implications of such a strategy are perilous. Undoubtedly it rejuvenated and humanized English culture but, instead of overthrowing the 'old corruption' of commercialism the avowed enemy, it allowed a new corruption to take its place. A morally exhausted Victorianism, to which they intended to put the *coup de grace*, merely revived as a modernized medieval corporation complete with feudal apparatus of monarchy and House of Lords. The refusal of a modernism which relied on structural discontinuity rather than expressive essentialism, which embraced plurality rather than hierarchy, may only have assisted the cash-nexus to restore itself for little more than an extension of the franchise to women and an only partially realized welfare state. The national provincial culture which emerged in twentieth-century Britain has found great difficulty in coping with the modernisms of social justice, democracy, and race and gender equality-in-difference. It may be that the 'religious' discourses of art and culture so beloved and sustaining of the Arts Club radicals have ironically only accelerated the metamorphosis of art products into high-priced commodities in which all power to transform and enrich everyday life has been lost. However, the courageous commitment of Orage and his colleagues to a life of creative and emancipated fulfilment for all remains the Club's fitting memorial.

Notes

1. This was also evident in the second phase where, according to Tom Heron, in a letter to Dr David Goodway of Leeds University, the Club was partially financed by Leonard Zossenheim, a shoddy manufacturer from Batley, and a theosophist, who founded the first Jewish Masonic Lodge, the Liberty Lodge, in Leeds. Following his father, who like Conrad's Giorgio in *Nostromo* was a devotee of Garibaldi, he was Italian consul in Leeds and later moved to Harrogate and changed his name to Smith.
2. Alf Mattison, 'Journals', vol. 1, p. 270, Leeds City Reference Library.
3. See Louise Welch, *Orage with Gurdjieff in America*, Routledge, Kegan Paul, London, 1982, *passim* and Gorham Munson, 'Orage in America' in *The Awakening Twenties*, Baton Rouge, 1985.
4. See Harry Braverman, *Labour and Monopoly Capital*, Monthly Review Press, New York, 1974, pp. 403–410.
5. Edgar Jenkins, *A Magnificent Pile*, City of Leeds School, Leeds, 1985, p. 78.
6. Tommy Lamb's *T.N.T. Tales* also portray vigorously independent women working in the munitions factory at Barnbow, noting in the preface, 'Whenever the girls had an adventure they invariably very frankly described their experiences in the train . . . I travelled with the heroine as long as the narrative held out.'
7. I regret not being able to integrate the discussion in S. K. Tillyard, *The Impact of Modernism 1900–1920*, Routledge, Kegan Paul, London, 1988, which covers much of this ground.
8. Linda Dalrymple Henderson, 'Mysticism as the "Tie that Binds": The Case of Edward Carpenter and Modernism', in *Art Journal*, spring 1987, vol. 46, no. 1, pp. 29–37. and 'Mysticism, Romanticism, and the Fourth

Dimension', in the exhibition catalogue *The Spiritual in Art: Abstract Painting 1890–1985*, Los Angeles County Museum of Art, Abbeville Press, New York, 1986, pp. 219–237.

9. See Rose-Carol Washington Long, 'Occultism, Anarchism, and Abstraction: Kandinsky's Art of the Future' in *Art Journal*, spring 1987, vol. 46, no. 1, pp. 38–45.
10. See also Tom Steele 'From Gentleman to Superman, Alfred Orage and Aristocratic Socialism' in C. Shaw and M. Chase (eds) *The Imagined Past*, Manchester University Press, 1989.
11. I am grateful to Maria Moisa of Leeds Polytechnic for this information.

APPENDIX

A. R. Orage – 'What Is the Future of Socialism?'

The recent defeat of the German Social Democrats at the poll has opened the eyes of the English Socialists to the danger of an exclusive alliance with Labour politics. Socialism in England as in Germany, has been so completely identified with the demands of the manual worker that in all probability few people have realised that Socialism in itself is something vastly greater than the attempt to satisfy the working man.

Socialism is in fact nothing less than a new theory of society, a theory which finds place and scope not only for manual labour but for all the crafts, arts and professions, which therefore is no more exclusively designed for the improvement of the condition of the poor than for the improvement of the condition of the rich, a theory in short which in practice is supposed and is certainly intended to create a genuine commonwealth, in which specific provision is made for every type of mind and every shade of temperament.

This scientific sociological theory, as complete in its way as Plato's Republic, has unfortunately been captured by a single class in the community. By a singular stroke of intelligence which does them credit, the working men in England have been the first to realise the advantages offered by such a transformation of society. What of course they could not be expected to realise was the advantages the same theory offered to every other class in the existing state.

In fact, they so far bent the theory to their own wishes as to deny practically that Socialism was intended for everybody. To the best of their ability they perverted the conception of the commonwealth to a repugnant picture of a community dominated by themselves. The class war on which they entered for the so-called emancipation of the wage-slaves was no doubt justifiable in itself; but what they did farther was to proclaim Socialism to be no more than that class-war, and designed for no other end than the abolition of wage-slavery.

Step by step it became more and more materialistic, more and more gross, more and more sordid and narrow. Finally, in the minds of the Socialists themselves there had arisen a feeling of despair not unmixed with dread. Was it for this, they ask, that we have fought? Is our dream of a new society for the redemption of man to end in the creation of a tyranny by a class greater than the world has ever known?

Something like this revulsion has undoubtedly contributed to the defeat of the Social Democrats in Germany. Instinctively men began to feel that there was a splendour and an imagination, a wholeness and a sanity in a national movement even in its chauvinist form of 'Germany over all' which is lacking in the class movement of some millions of wage-slaves seeking salvation. And I do not doubt that this feeling of revulsion will soon be felt by the genuine Socialists of this country.

Already we have had the Fabian Society declaring for Imperialism as against the pettifogging ideals of the grocer turned politician. Already we have seen the line of division grow between the Trade Union Labour party and the Socialist Independent Labour party. Already we have seen the Socialist Keir Hardie threatening to leave the Labour party on account of its narrowness.

The division thus revealed will continue to grow with the growth on the one hand of the Trade Union movement itself and on the other hand of the exodus of disgusted Socialists from the ranks of the Labour party.

There is every sign indeed, that for the first time in the history of English socialism a genuinely political Socialist party might be formed which shall be as free from bias for or against the demands of Trade Unionists as from bias for or against the exclusive dominance of any other class in the state.

Doubtless such political socialists will at first find themselves between two stools. The Labour element with which Socialism has hitherto been associated will naturally resent the divorce and do its best to wreck the chances of Socialist candidates. The middle classes on the other hand, will be long in learning their instinctive dislike of Socialist Labour candidates, and still longer in learning to dissociate Socialism from Labour.

Thus in all probability, while we may certainly expect the gradual disappearance of Socialist doctrines from the platform of the Labour party, and the increasing insistence on purely wage labour proposals, we may also expect to see the slow rise of a Socialist party, to which in course of time representatives of all classes and permanent interests will be drawn. This however, as I have said, will be as slow as the elimination of Socialism from Labour politics will be rapid. For in creating the Labour party Socialism has created an obstacle to its own realisation greater perhaps than any obstacle that had previously existed.

Bibliography

Primary sources

Recorded interviews

Woledge, Geoffrey, 12 December 1983; 20 April 1984; 12 September 1988

Wood, Florence, 19 October 1984

Manuscript and printed materials

Private sources

Colville, Sheila, scrapbook of cuttings about the Eyebrow Club, 385 Otley Road, Leeds 16

Ingle, Marjorie, 'Reminiscences', unpublished typescript, property of Catherine Thackeray, Greenwoods, Reaphurst Road, Birkby, Huddersfield, West Yorkshire

Jones, William Alban, scrapbook of Leeds Arts Club drawings, accounts, receipts and draft letters, the property of Denis Mason Jones, Long Causeway, Adel, Leeds 16

Northern Federation of the Theosophical Society, Minute Books 1893–1908, Harrogate TS Lodge, 6 Alexandra Road, Harrogate

Orage, A. R., notebook 'Leeds School Board, Daily Notes, VI A', Richard Orage, Nuttal's Farm, Russell's Water Common, Henley on Thames, Oxon RG9 6EY

Orage, A. R., and Holbrook Jackson, photocopy of notebook containing correspondence about the impartiality of the critic, 1905, obtained from John Bunting, 17 Northview, Tufnell Park Road, London N7 6QB

Price, Millie, 'This World's Festival', unpublished typescript, property of Agnes Patrick, 16 Bainbrigge Road, Leeds 6

Public sources

Carpenter, Edward, letter to Walt Whitman, 12 July 1874, copy in Alf Mattison Collection, Brotherton Library, University of Leeds

Fabian Archives, Nuffield College, University of Oxford

Ford, Isabella, scrapbook of cuttings, West Yorkshire Archives, Sheepscar, Leeds

Harehills Board School Log Book, Harehills Primary School, Newton Garth, Leeds

Kramer, Jacob, letters and correspondence, Brotherton Collection, University of Leeds

Leeds Arts Club programmes and handbills, Prints Collection, Leeds City Reference Library.

Leeds Arts Theatre programmes, 1922–25, Leeds City Reeference Library

Leeds Civic Playhouse programmes, 1925–26, Leeds City Reference Library

Leeds Civic Society founding document, Thoresby Society archives, No. 22B6, Leeds

Leeds Clubs and Societies (misc. box), Brotherton Collection, University of Leeds

Leeds School Board, Education Committee Minutes, West Yorkshire Archives, Sheepscar, Leeds

Leeds School Board, School Staff Ledgers, 1894, West Yorkshire Archives, Sheepscar, Leeds

Mattison Collection, Brotherton Collection, University of Leeds

Mattison, Alf, Journals 1925–28, Leeds City Reference Library

Moorman, Frederic, Diaries, Special Collections, Brotherton Library, University of Leeds

Orage, A. R., letter to Edward Carpenter, 3 February 1896, Carpenter Collection, Sheffield City Libraries

Roundhay Road Boys School, Log Books 1900–1906, West Yorkshire Archives, Sheepscar, Leeds

Sadler, M. E., Diaries, Accession no.252, Bodleian Library, Oxford

——. 'Premonitions of the War in Modern Art', lecture Leeds, 26 October 1915, Brotherton Library, University of Leeds

Thompson, Herbert, Diaries, Special Collections, Brotherton Library, University of Leeds

Newspapers and journals

Labour Leader, 1895–1898, Keighley Public Libraries

The Lamp of Thoth, vol.3, no.4, Leeds, undated

Leeds Citizen, 1911–1919, Leeds City Reference Library

'Leeds Cuttings', scrapbook volumes of newspaper cuttings, 1902–1923, Leeds City Reference Library

'Leeds People', scrapbook volumes of newspaper cuttings, 1902–1923, Leeds City Reference Library

Leeds Teachers Journal, 1899–1903, Brotherton Library, University of Leeds

Leeds and Yorkshire Mercury, Weekly Supplement, 1902–1906, Leeds City Reference Library

The New Age, 1907–1922, Leeds City Reference Library

New English Weekly, 'A. R. Orage Memorial Number', 15 November 1934

The Times, Obituaries

The Yorkshire Daily Observer, Bradford City Reference Library

The Yorkshire Evening News, 1902–1923, Leeds City Reference Library

The Yorkshire Evening Post, 1902–1923, Leeds City Reference Library

The Yorkshire Post, 1902–1923, Leeds City Reference Library

The Yorkshire Weekly Post, 1902–1923, Leeds City Reference Library

Published works

Besant, Annie, *The Ancient Wisdom*, Theosophical Publishing Society, London, 1897

Carpenter, Edward, *My Days and Dreams*, Allen & Unwin, London, 1914

Chesterton, G. K., *George Bernard Shaw*, John Lane, London, 1914

Ford, Bessie (ed.) *Tom Maguire: A Remembrance*, Labour Press Society, Manchester, 1895

Ford, Isabella, *Women and Socialism*, Independent Labour Party Press, London, 1906

Foster, D. B., *Socialism and the Christ*, published by the author, Leeds, 1921

Gill, Eric, *War Memorial*, Welfare Handbook, no.10, Ditchling Press, Ditchling, 1923

Grant, A. J., *Outlines of European History*, Longmans, London, 1907

Jackson, Holbrook, *The Eighteen Nineties*, Pelican, London, 1939 (first published 1913)

——. *The Rise and Fall of Nineteenth Century Idealism*, Citadel, New York, 1969 (first published as *Dreamers of Dreams*, London)

——. *George Bernard Shaw*, Grant Richards, London, 1907

——. *Southward Ho! and other Essays*, Dent, London, no date

——. 'Personal Recollections', *The Windmill*, (Heinemann house journal), London, 1948, pp.41–50

——. 'The Truth About Nietzsche', *T.P.'S Weekly*, 31 October 1914, pp.475–476

——. *William Morris*, Social Reformers Series, no. 3, London, 1908

'The Holbrook Jackson Library', A Memorial Catalogue with an appreciation by Sir Francis Meynell, Catalogue 119, Elkin Matthews Ltd., Bishops Stortford

Kenworthy, J. C. *The Anatomy of Misery*, 2nd ed., with an Introduction by Count Leo Tolstoy, J. C. Kenworthy, London, 1900

Lamb, T. A., *T.N.T. Tales and a Few Food Fancies*, Blackwells, Oxford, 1919
MacGregor, D. H., *The Evolution of Industry*, Williams and Norgate, London, 1911
Orage, A. R., *Consciousness, Animal, Human and Superman*, Theosophical Publishing Society, London, 1907
——. *Friedrich Nietzsche: The Dionysian Spirit of the Age*, Foulis, London, 1906
——. *Nietzsche in Outline and Aphorism*, Foulis, London, 1906
——. 'The Philosopher', (Orage on Shaw, an unpublished manuscript), *The Shaw Review*, vol.XXII, no.1, Pennsylvania, pp. 3–12
——. 'Politics for Craftsmen', *Contemporary Review*, no. 91, 1907, pp.782–94
——. 'A Study in Mud' and 'Quixotic Energy' in Albert T. Marles (ed.) *Hypnotic Leeds*, Leeds, 1894, pp.17–20 and 43–7
——. 'What is the Future of Socialism?', *Leeds and Yorkshire Mercury*, 6 March 1907, p.4, c.4
——. in J. Clayton (ed.) *Why I Joined the Independent Labour Party, Some Plain Statements*, Leeds, no date
——. 'The First Men' in *The Lotus Journal*, London, August 1907, pp.108–11 and 'The Princess and the Gardener' no date
Roberts, J. D. (ed.) *The Kramer Documents*, Valencia, 1983
Sadler, Michael Ernest, *Modern Art and Revolution*, Hogarth Press, London, 1932
——. 'Premonitions of the War In Modern Art', 26 October 1915, Leeds, report, Brotherton Collection, University of Leeds

Secondary sources

Ackroyd, Peter, *T. S. Eliot*, Abacus, London, 1985
Anderson, Perry, 'Components of the National Culture', *New Left Review*, no.50, July-August 1968, pp. 35–64
——. 'The Figures of Descent', *New Left Review*, no.161, January/February 1987, pp. 20–77
——. 'Origins of the Present Crisis' *New Left Review*, no.23, 1964
Barrow, Logie, *Independent Spirits: Spiritualism and English Plebeians 1850–1890*, Routledge, Kegan Paul, London, 1986
Braverman, Harry, *Labour and Monopoly Capital*, Monthly Review Press, New York, 1974
Bridgwater, Patrick, *Nietzsche in Anglosaxony*, Leicester University Press, Leicester, 1972
Britain, Ian, *Fabianism and Culture. A Study in British Socialism and the Arts c1884–1918*, Cambridge University Press, Cambridge, 1982

Brockway, Fenner, *Socialism over Sixty Years, the Life of Fred Jowett*, Introduction by J. B. Priestley, Allen and Unwin, London, 1946

Buckman, Joseph, *Immigrants and the Class Struggle: The Jewish Immigrant in Leeds, 1880–1914*, Manchester, 1983

Carswell, John, *Lives and Letters*, Faber, London, 1978

Chesterton, Mrs Cecil, *The Chestertons*, Chapman and Hall, London, 1941

Clarke, Tim, 'On the Social History of Art', in Francis Frascina and Charles Harrison (eds) *Modern Art and Modernism: A Critical Anthology*, Harper and Row, London, 1982

Clayton, Joseph, *The Rise and Decline of Socialism in Great Britain 1884–1924*, Faber and Gwyer, London, 1926

Coates, John D. *Chesterton and the Edwardian Cultural Crisis*, Hull University Press, Hull, 1984

Cole, G. D. H., *A Short History of the British Working Class Movement 1789–1947, Allen and Unwin, London, 1925*

Cole, Margaret, *Beatrice Webb*, Longmans, London, 1945

——. *The Life of G. D. H. Cole*, Macmillan, London, 1971

Cork, Richard, *Vorticism and Abstract Art in the First Machine Age*, vol.1, University of California, Berkeley, 1975

Crow, Thomas, 'Modernism and Mass Culture in the Visual Arts' in Francis Frascina (ed.) *Pollock and After*, Harper and Row, London, 1985

Cumberland, Gerald, *Set Down in Malice*, Grant Richards, London, 1918

Dangerfield, George, *The Strange Death of Liberal England*, Paladin, 1970

Delavennay, Emile, *D. H. Lawrence and Edward Carpenter: A Study in Edwardian Transition*, Heinemann, London, 1969

Dictionary of National Biography, Oxford University Press

Dover Wilson, John, *Milestones on the Dover Road*, Faber, London, 1969

Eagleton, Terry, *Exiles and Emigres*, Chatto and Windus, London, 1970

——. 'Recent Poetry reviewed by Terry Eagleton', *Stand*, vol.22, no.2, p.73

Epstein, Jacob, *An Autobiography*, Hulton Press, London, 1955

Fay, Gerard, *The Abbey Theatre*, Clonmore and Reynolds, Dublin, 1958

Fraser, Derek (ed.) *A History of Modern Leeds*, Manchester University Press, Manchester, 1980

Fry, Roger, *Letters* (ed. Denys Sutton), vol.2, Chatto & Windus, London, 1972

Garrould, Ann, 'Henry Moore 1898–1822' in *Henry Moore Early Car-*

vings 1920–1940, a catalogue with three essays, Leeds City Art Gallery, 1982

Gawthorpe, Mary, *Up Hill to Holloway*, Penobscot, Maine, 1947

Gibb, Mildred A., and Frank Beckwith, *The Yorkshire Post: Two Centuries*, Yorkshire Conservative Newspaper Co., Leeds, 1954

Gibbons, Tom, *Rooms in the Darwin Hotel*, Nedlands, Western Australia, 1973

Grady, Kevin, 'Commercial Marketing and Retailing Amenities 1700–1914', in Fraser, op. cit.

Grizzard, Nigel, *Leeds Jewry and the Great War*, Jewish Historical Society of England, Leeds Branch, 1981

Hardman, Malcolm, *Ruskin and Bradford*, Manchester University Press, Manchester, 1986

Hastings, Beatrice, *The 'Old New Age': Orage – and others*, Blue Moon Press, London, 1936

Henderson, Linda Dalrymple, 'Mysticism as the "Tie That Binds": The Case of Edward Carpenter and Modernism', in *Art Journal*, spring 1987, vol.46, no.1, pp.29–37

——. 'Mysticism, Romanticism, and the Fourth Dimension;, in the exhibition catalogue *The Spiritual in Art: Abstract Painting 1890–1985*, Los Angeles County Museum of Art, Abbeville Press, New York, 1986, pp.219–237

Hobsbawm, Eric, *The Age of Empire*, Weidenfeld and Nicolson, London, 1987

Hobson, S. G., *Pilgrim to the Left, Memoirs of a Modern Revolutionist*, Edward Arnold, London, 1938

Holroyd, Michael, *Augustus John*, Heinemann, London, 1974

Hone, Joseph, *W. B. Yeats*, Macmillan, London, 1942

Hough, Graham, *The Mystery Religion of W. B. Yeats*, Harvester Press, Brighton, 1985

Houlton, R., 'Two Aspects of Guild Socialism – Penty, Hobson and the Building Guilds', *Society for the Study of Labour History*, bulletin no.7, autumn 1963, pp.23–28

Howe, Ellic, *The Magicians of the Golden Dawn*, Routledge, Kegan Paul, London, 1972

Hulme, T. E., *Speculations*, Routledge, Kegan Paul, London, 1924

——. in Sam Hynes (ed.) *Further Speculations*, University of Minnesota Press, Minneapolis, 1955

Hynes, S., *Edwardian Occasions*, RKP, London, 1972

Jacob Kramer Reassessed, Introduction by Francis Spalding, Ben Uri Society, exhibition catalogue, London, 1984

Jameson, Storm, *The Pot Boils*, Constable, London, 1919

——. *Journey from the North*, vol.1, Collins Harvill, London, 1969

Jenkins, Edgar, *A Magnificent Pile*, City of Leeds School, Leeds, 1974
Jones, Peter d'A, *The Christian Socialist Revival, 1877–1914*, Princeton University Press, Princeton, 1968
Jones, Philip (ed.) *Henry Moore on Sculpture*, Thames and Hudson, London, 1966
Kandinsky, Wassily, *The Art of Spiritual Harmony*, translated and introduced by M. T. H. Sadler, Constable, London, 1914
Keeling, Frederick, in E. Towshend (ed.) *Letters and Recollections*, intro. by H. G. Wells, Allen and Unwin, London, 1918
Kelly's Leeds Street Directories, 1893–1923, Leeds City Reference Library
Kitson Clark, G., 'The Leeds Elite', *University of Leeds Review*, vol.17, no.2, 1975, pp.232–258
Kramer, Millie (ed.) *Jacob Kramer: A Memorial Volume*, E. J. Arnold, Leeds, 1969
Kunitz and Haycraft, *Twentieth Century Authors*, Wilson, New York, 1969
Lamb, T. A., 'Jacob Kramer – A Leeds Artist', in *Leeds Arts Calendar*, vol.3, no.11, winter 1950, pp.18–25
Lee, Alan J., entry on Orage in J. Saville and J. Bellamy (eds) *Dictionary of Labour History*, vol.7, London, 1984
Linstrum, Derek, *West Yorkshire Architects and Architecture*, Lund Humphries, London, 1978
Long, Rose-Carol Washington, 'Occultism, Anarchism and Abstraction: Kandinsky's Art of the Future' in *Art Journal*, spring 1987, vol.46, no.1, pp.38–45
Mairet, Philip, *A. R. Orage a Memoir*, Dent, London, 1936 (2nd ed. with 'Reintroduction', New York, 1966)
——. 'Orage and Mitrinovic' in *Autobiographical and other Papers*, Carcanet Press, Manchester, 1981
Martin, Kingsley, *Harold Laski (1893–1950) A Biographical Memoir*, Gollancz, London, 1953
Martin, Wallace, *The New Age Under Orage: Chapters in English Cultural History*, Manchester University Press, Manchester, 1967
——. *Orage as Critic*, RKP, London, 1974
Marx, K., and F. Engels, 'Letters to Americans, 1848–1895, International Publishers, New York, 1953
Matthews, Frank, 'The Ladder of Becoming: A. R. Orage, A. J. Penty and the Origins of Guild Socialism in England' in D. E. Martin and D. Rubinstein (eds) *Ideology and the Labour Movement*, Croom Helm, London, 1979
Munson, Gorham, 'Orage in America', in *The Awakening Twenties*, Baton Rouge, 1985

Nairn, Tom, *The Break-Up of Britain*, Kenso, London, 1977

——. 'The British Political Elite', *New Left Review*, no.23, 1964

——. 'The English Literary Intelligentsia' in Emma Tennant (ed.) *Bananas*, Blond & Briggs, London, 1977

New English Weekly, vol.VI, no.5, 15 November 1934

Nietzsche, Friedrich, *The Birth of Tragedy*, Anchor Books, New York, 1956

Nolte, Ernest, *Three Faces of Fascism*, Mentor, New York, 1969

Nott, C. S., *Journey Through This World*, RKP, London, 1969

O'Connor, Fr John, *Father Brown on Chesterton*, Muller, London, 1937

O'Sullivan, V., and Margaret Scott, *Letters of Katherine Mansfield*, vol.1, 1903–1917, Oxford University Press, Oxford, 1984

Orton, Fred, and Griselda Pollock, '*Avant-Gardes* and Partisans Reviewed', *Art History*, vol.4, no.3, September 1981, pp. 305–327

Paintings and Drawings by Bruce Turner, exhibition catalogue intro. by Patrick Heron, Leeds City Galleries, 1964

Pankhurst, E. Sylvia, *The Suffragette*, Source Book Press, London, 1970

Phillips, C. S. (ed.) *Walter Howard Frere, Bishop of Truro*, Faber, London, 1947

Pierson, Stanley, *British Socialists, the journey from fantasy to politics*, Harvard University Press, Harvard, 1979

Pound, Ezra, *Selected Essays*, Faber, London, 1973

Ransome, Arthur, (ed. Rupert Hart-Davis), *Autobiography*, Cape, London, 1976

Read Herbert, *Annals of Innocence and Experience*, Faber, London, 1946

——. *The Philosophy of Modern Art*, Faber, London, 1969

——. *The Contrary Experience*, Secker, London, 1973

——. *Homage to Herbert Read*, a catalogue, Canterbury College of Art, Maidstone, Kent County Council Education Committee, 1984

Herbert Read, A Tribute to, Bradford Art Galleries and Museums, 1975

Reckitt, Maurice, *As it Happened*, Dent, London, 1941

Ringbom, Sixten, *The Sounding Cosmos, A Study in the Spiritualism of Kandinsky and the Genesis of Abstract Painting*, Abo Akademi, Finland, 1970

Robertson, Alexander, 'The Leeds Town Hall Decoration Scheme', *Leeds Arts Calendar*, no.74, 1974, pp.16–22

Rothenstein, John, *Modern English Painters*, vol.1, Eyre and Spottiswoode, London, 1952–56

——. *Summer's Lease*, Hamish Hamilton, London, 1965

Rowbotham, Sheila, and Jeffrey Weeks, *Socialism and the New Life:*

The Personal and Sexual Politics of Edward Carpenter and Havelock Ellis, Pluto Press, London, 1977

Rutter, Frank, *Since I was Twenty-Five*, Constable, London, 1927

——. *Evolution in Modern Art*, Harrap, London, 1926

Sadler, Sir Michael, Commemorative Exhibition, intro. by Bill Oliver, Leeds City Art Galleries, 1963

Sadleir, Michael, *Michael Ernest Sadler*, Constable, London, 1949

Scannell, Vernon, *The Tiger and the Rose*, Hamish Hamilton, London, 1971

Schuchard, Ronald, 'T. S. Eliot as Extension Lecturer, 1916–1919', *Review of English Studies*, New Series, vol.XXV, no.98, Oxford, 1974, pp.163–173

Selver, Paul, *Orage and the New Age Circle*, Allen & Unwin, London, 1959

Shaw, Bernard (ed. Dan H. Laurence), *Bernard Shaw Collected Letters*, Reinhardt, London, 1972

Sheppard, Christopher D. W., 'Jacob Kramer in his Correspondence', *Leeds University Reporter*, vol.30, 1987, pp.205–221

Shewring, Walter (ed.) *The Letters of Eric Gill*, Cape, London, 1947

Shimmin, Norman, *The University of Leeds, the First Fifty Years*, Cambridge University Press, Cambridge, 1954

Spencer, Gillian, Foreword to *Mark Senior Exhibition Catalogue*, Elizabethan Exhibition Gallery, Wakefield, 1983

Steele, Tom, 'From Class Consciousness to Cultural Studies, George Thompson and the W.E.A. in Yorkshire' in *Studies in the Education of Adults*, vol.19, no.2, October 1987

Sullivan, Alvin (ed.) *British Literary Magazines, The Modern Age 1914–1984*, Greenwood Press, Connecticut, 1986

Thatcher, David S., *Nietzsche in England, the Growth of a Reputation*, University of Toronto Press, Toronto, 1970

Thistlewood, David, *Herbert Read, Formlessness and Form, An Introduction to his Aesthetics*, Routledge, Kegan Paul, London, 1984

Thompson, E. P., 'Homage to Tom Maguire' in A. Briggs and J. Saville (eds) *Essays in Labour History*, Macmillan, London, 1960

Tillyard, S. K., *The Impact of Modernism 1900–1920*, Routledge, Kegan Paul, London, 1988

Tomalin, Claire, *Katherine Mansfield, A Secret Life*, Viking, London, 1987

Travis, M. A., 'The Work of the Leeds School Board' in *Researches and Studies*, The School of Education, University of Leeds, no.8, May 1953

Turner, Ben, *About Myself*, Toulmin, London, 1930

Webb, James, *The Harmonious Circle*, Thames and Hudson, London, 1980

——. *The Occult Establishment*, Open Court, La Salle, Illinois, 1976

Welch, Louise, *Orage with Gurdjieff in America*, Routledge, Kegan Paul, 1982

Wiener, Martin, *English Culture and the Decline of the Industrial Spirit 1850–1980*, Cambridge University Press, London, 1981

Williams, Raymond, *Writing in Society*, Verso, London, 1984

——. *Problems in Materialism and Culture*, Verso, London, 1980

Woledge, Geoffrey, 'The Leeds Arts Club and a Successor', Thoresby Society, Annual Report, Leeds, 1980

Wolff, J., and J. Seed, *The Culture of Capital: art, power and the nineteenth-century middle class*, Manchester University Press, Manchester, 1988

Woodhouse, Tom, 'A Political History of the Leeds Labour Movement 1880–1914' unpublished PhD thesis, Brotherton Library, University of Leeds

——. 'The Working Class' in Derek Fraser (ed.) *A History of Modern Leeds*, Manchester University Press, Manchester, 1980

Wyndham Lewis, Percy, 'The Revolutionary Simpleton' in *The Enemy*, vol.1, January 1927, pp.61–62

Yorke, Malcolm, *Eric Gill: Man of Flesh and Spirit*, Constable, London, 1981

Index

Abbey Theatre (Irish National Theatre), 126, 128f
Abercrombie, Lascelles, 247
abstractionism, 162, 233
Allied Artists Association, 181, 206, 227
Anderson-Nairn thesis, 9ff
antisemitism, 242, 254n
Art and Letters, 221, 228
Austin, Alfred, 83
avant-garde, 8, 13ff

Baillie, Sir James, 243
Barton, J. E., 93, 110
Bean, W. H., 37
'Beautiful Warrington', 140
Beecroft, Ada, 163
Belloc, Hillaire, 183, 187
Benson, F. R., 163f
Bergson, Henri, 159, 173n, 185f, 225
Besant, Annie, 34, 36, 55; *Thought Forms*, 162, 193
Bessle, Elizabeth, 164
Bickersteth, Cyril, 211
Blaue Reiter, 180
Bone, Muirhead, 153
Botterill, Denis, 252
Bradford Arts Club, 166, 192, 252

Caldwell Spruce, E. 97f
Calvert, Dr. H. T., 140
Carpenter, Edward, 35ff, 74f, 84n, 137, 164ff, 220, 263
Chesterton, Gilbert Keith, 3, 49, 82f, 160f, 182
Childe, Wilfred, 242, 253, 254n
Christian Socialism, 123
Clapham, Prof. J. H., 125
Clark, E. Kitson, 211
classicism, 154, 186f, 226
Clausen, George, 141f
Clayton, Joseph, 137, 184
Clutton-Brock, A., 228, 238n
Cohen, Prof. J. B., 168
Cole, G. D. H., 7, 123
Colville, Sheila (née Tomey), 251ff
Community of the Resurrection at Mirfield, 123, 262
Craig, Edith, 245ff, 250
Craig, Gordon, 101, 182
Crowley, Aleister, 39f

Dale, Mrs. F. R., 221
Dean, Frank, 221
Dobree, Prof. Bonamy, 253
Dodgson, James ('Kester'), 261
Dolmetsch, Arnold, 127
Dukes, Ashley, 149ff

Eagle and the Serpent, The, 52
Eder, M. D., 48, 185
Eliot, T. S., 8, 163, 216n, 219, 227, 237n, 238n, 266
Engels, Frederick, 29
Epstein, Jacob, 185, 207, 238n
Evans, Frederick, H., 169
experimental theatre, 246ff, 259
expressionism, 184, 189, 224, 226, 240, 256
Eyebrow Club, 250ff

Fabian Arts Group, 137, 148, 265
Fabian Society, 29f, 148, 150
Farr, Florence, 39, 126f, 149
Fearnley, John H., 79, 84, 120
Figgis, Fr. J. N., 7; *Churches in the Modern State*, 123
Forbes, Ernest ('The Hermit'), 221f
Ford, Bessie, 33
Ford, Emily, 222
Ford, Isabella Ormiston, 33, 78f, 95, 140f; *Women and Socialism*, 140
Fordham, Montague, 112f
Foster, D. B., 33
Foster, Gilbert, 84
Foster, Miss S. A., 121
freemasonary, 98f, 135n, 257
Frere, Fr. Walter H., 123, 169

Freud, Sigmund, 47, 185
Fry, Roger, 192, 214f, 220

Gaudier-Brzeska, Henri, 185
Gawthorpe, Mary, 20, 29, 66f, 118; *Freewoman, The*, 20
Gill, Eric, 137, 188; War Memorial, 240ff
Gilman, Harold, 7, 183, 227
Ginner, Charles, 7, 183
Golden Dawn, Hermetic Order of, 39f, 128, 140, 159, 168
Gostick, Alice, 232f
Grant, Prof. A. J., 83f
Grayson, Victor, 137, 146
Greenwood, Arthur, 73, 85, 197, 219, 230
Guild of Saint Michael, 122
Guild Socialism, 69f, 124f, 165, 169, 183f, 229, 266
Guilds Restoration League, 147, 165

Halifax Arts and Crafts Society, 147
Hare, Loftus, 158
Harvey, Martin, 149
Hastings, Beatrice, 39
Headingley Literary Society, 114
Hepworth, Barbara, 236
Heron, Patrick, 2, 8, 223
Heron, Tom, 2, 73, 99, 223, 237n
Hilton, Herman (Hildesheim), 222, 247
Hofmannsthal, Hugo von, 246; *The Great World Theatre*, 246
Horniman, Annie, 130f, 140, 164
Hulme, T. E., 162, 185f, 192, 225, 235
Hutton, Frank B., 120, 138

Ibsen, Henrik, 82, 128, 247
impressionist painting, 181
Independent Labour Party, 29ff, 77, 133, 172
Ingle, Marjorie, 75
Irving, W. P., 79, 142

Jackson, F. P., 75
Jackson, F. W., 153
Jackson, George Holbrook, 45ff, 68, 70ff, 81, 90f, 99f, 103, 106, 109f, 118, 126; meets Orage, 45f, 47; Frances Maynell on, 50; *Bernard Shaw*, 44, 48; *Eighteen Nineties*, 51
Jameson, Storm, 125, 159
John, Augustus, 205
Jones, W. Alban 'Billy', 101, 248

Kandinsky, Wassily, 2, 179, 190f, 202ff, 210, 235, 260, 264; *Uber das Geistige*, 192, 202ff
Kennedy, Miss A. K., 37, 119, 248
Kenworthy, John, 46
Kerr, William, 244
Kramer, Jacob, 103, 186, 193, 199ff, 205ff, 212, 228, 240, 261; Yorkshire Luncheon Club, 244, 252f

Lamb, Tommy A., 190, 206, 248, 267n
Larkin, Jim, 196
Lawrence, D. H., 16, 31, 43n
Lee, Revd., Arthur Hugh E., 7, 37, 76f, 111, 138f, 153
Leeds Art Theatre, 245ff
Leeds Civic Playhouse, 151, 249ff
Leeds Civic Society, 121, 211
Leeds School of Art, 211, 233
Leeds School Board, 28, 31, 47
Lewis, Percy Wyndham, 205, 223, 238n; Cubist and Futurist Exhibition, 223f
Lister, John, 147
Little Theatre, 249
London Stage Society, 149, 248f

Macfail, Haldane, 159
MacGregor, Prof. D. H., 167, 197, 219
Macleod, Fiona (William Sharp), 46
Maguire, Tom, 29
Mann, Tom, 29, 32, 178
Mansfield, Katherine, 39, 184, 190
Mattison, Alf, 36, 165, 258
Moore, Henry, 98, 194n, 231ff
Moorman, Prof. F. W., 93f, 163, 188, 211, 220, 237n, 247f
Morris, William, 32, 100, 112, 263
Moynihan, Berkeley, 205, 251, 255n
Murby, Milicent, 137, 148
Murray's Bitterary Club, 244
Murry, Middleton, 190
Myers, Frederick, 111

Nash Brothers, Paul and John, 212

neo-realism, 188, 224
New Age, The, 137, 143, 159, 161, 183, 225, 230f, 243, 262
Nietzsche, Friedrich, 45ff, 128, 161, 186, 220f, 264, 266, William Blake as precursor of, 138

O'Connor, Fr. J. ('Father Brown'), 160f, 163, 243, 252
Oliver, W. T., 205
Onions, Oliver, 111
Orage, Alfred Richard, *passim*,
and Edward Carpenter, 35f;
Consciousness, Animal, Human and Superhuman, 52, 56, 128;
early life, 25; articles in *Hypnotic Leeds*, 30
and ILP, 30;
and the *Labour Leader*, 32;
and Leeds Arts Club, 1ff, 25, 69, 72, 75, 80, 90f, 97, 99, 107, 113ff, 129, 145f, 184, 230, 243, 253, 257;
on Nietzsche, 72, 88f, 161;
Nietzsche in Outline and Aphorism, 52, 56ff;
Friedrich Nietzsche, the Dionysian Spirit of the Age, 36, 52;
and National Union of Teachers, 41f;
and *New English Weekly*, 253, 262;
and Herbert Read, 230ff;
on socialism, 3, 132, 145, 269f;
as school teacher, 25ff;
and Theosophical Society, 34ff, 48
Orage, Jean (née Watson), 33, 47, 119
Orage, Jessie (née Dwight), 259

Pease, Cyril, Arthington, 27, 119
Penty Arthur J., 38, 113, 164, 229; on Orage, 3; *Restoration of the Gild System*, 2, 113
Perkins, W. H., 138
Picasso, Pablo, 191, 204
Plato Friends, 46
Playgoers Society, 5, 106, 142, 144, 151, 163, 244
Poel, William, 158
post-impressionism, 184, 189ff, 203, 220
Pound, Ezra, 192, 229f
Price, Millie (née Browne), 27, 34, 38, 89, 118f, 130
Priestley, J. B., 166
Prince, Louis le, 259
psychoanalysis, 185

Ramsden, L. B., 245f
Ransome, Arthur, 94
Read, Herbert, 15, 85, 94, 163, 188, 192, 207, 218ff, 243,
and Arthur Greenwood, 85, 230;
and Jacob Kramer, 163, 207, 226;
and Leeds Arts Club, 1, 221ff;
at Leeds University, 219ff;
and Henry Moore, 192, 231ff, 266;
and Orage, 1, 218ff;
and Frank Rutter, 227f
realism, 99, 103, 153, 160f, 162, 188, 207
Renan, Ernest, 41
Robinson, Percy, 98, 260
Rogerson, Revd., James, 46
romanticism, 99, 186, 188, 224, 227, 265
Rothenstein, Albert (Ruthersden), 212
Rothenstein, Charles (Rutherston), 50, 152
Rothenstein, John, 152, 198
Rothenstein, William, 137, 152, 198, 212, 240
Rowntree, Arthur, 84, 211
Ruskin, John, 70f, 200, 212n
Rutter, Frank, 173, 177, 179ff, 189, 196, 205, 227f, 238n

Sadler, Sir Michael, 177ff, 189, 196, 199ff, 210f, 214, 240ff, 264
Sadler, M. T. H. (Michael Sadleir), 179, 190; *The Art of Spiritual Harmony*, 192, 233
Sanderson, T. J. Cobden, 83f, 166
Scannell, Vernon, 253f
Scriven, R. C., 252
Senior, Mark, 121, 213f
Shaw, George Bernard, 48, 95f, 137, 148, 150f, 159, 245, 258
Smith, Charles Frederick, 142, 244ff
Smith, Joe, 197
Smithells, Prof. Arthur, 136
Smythe, Charles, 76, 93, 110, 139, 154
Snowden, Ethel (née Annakin), 141

Sorel, George, 225
Spencer, Stanley, 212
Sutcliffe, Frank, 169
Swarthmore Centre, 159
symbolism, 203f, 208, 222, 234
Synge, John Millington, 126, 130, 244

Theosophical Society, 34ff, 257
Thomas, William, 142
Thompson, George H., 197, 237n
Thompson, Herbert, 101f
Thorndike, Dame Sybil, 250
Thorp, W. H., 77, 95
Tolkein, J. R. R., 242, 245n
Town Hall Panels Scheme, 212ff
Turner, Bruce, 8, 103, 186, 193, 222ff

University of Leeds, 93, 150, 159, 211

Vaughan, Prof. Charles Edwyn, 159
Vorticism, 205, 212f, 223

Waddington, Albert Wheatley, 37f, 69, 77, 80, 85, 90, 113f, 136, 147, 256, 260
Wadsworth, Edward, 192, 205, 212
Webb, Beatrice, 156n
Wells, H. G., 107, 115n, 156n
Whelen, Frederick, 163, 249
Whitehead, Kate, 154
Whitman, Walt, 35, 51; quoted, 73
Whitmell, C. T., 42
Wilkinson, R. E., 158, 168
Wilson, John Dover, 94, 197
Wilson, Sam, 6, 102
Wilson, Thomas Butler, 46
Woledge, Geoffrey, 244
Workers' Educational Association, 85, 94, 197, 200, 219

Yeats, W. B., 39, 126f, 131, 159

Zossenheim, Leonard (Smith), 98, 267n